Don D. Jackson:

Selected Essays at the Dawn of an Era

D1736197

Don D. Jackson:

Selected Essays at the Dawn of an Era

WENDEL A. RAY, EDITOR

Zeig, Tucker, & Theisen, Inc.
Phoenix, Arizona

Library of Congress Cataloging-in-Publication Data
Don D. Jackson : selected essays at the dawn of an era / Wendel A. Ray, editor.
 p. cm.
Includes bibliographical references and index.
ISBN-10: 1-932462-20-1 (alk. paper) / ISBN-13: 978-1-932462-20-X
 1. Jackson, Don D. (Don De Avila), 1920–1968. 2. Psychotherapy. 3. Family therapy. 4. Schizophrenia—Treatment. I. Ray, Wendel A.
RC480.D66 2005
616.89'14—dc22   2005043977

Published by
Zeig, Tucker & Theisen, Inc.
3614 North 24th Street
Phoenix, AZ 85016

Manufactured in the United States of America
10 9 8 7 6 5 4 3 2 1

I wish to express my appreciation to John Weakland and Jay Haley for collaborating with Gregory Bateson, Don D. Jackson, and William Fry in creating the framework of ideas that constitute the Interactional Approach, and for their patient guidance in my journey of learning. A special thanks to Dr. Jackson's daughter Paige and the Jackson family for making access to Dr. Jackson's papers possible. Thanks also to Richard Fisch, Bradford P. Keeney, and Gianfranco Cecchin for many years of mentoring, encouragement, and support.

Table of Contents

JAY HALEY

Foreword

Don D. Jackson, M.D., was a major contributor to Family Therapy in an age of individual therapy. He was a developer of brief therapy when long-term therapy was the fashion. He also specialized in the therapy of schizophrenia when most therapists avoided psychotics as unreachable and incurable. His death came while he was developing these fields and so was even worse than a personal loss for those of us who worked with him.

Jackson influenced many people with his ideas in the short time he was with us. He conducted the earliest training programs in family therapy, doing workshops nationally, and he created the Mental Research Institute, a family and brief therapy center that continues to thrive some 45 years later. He also published over 100 scientific papers and several books. He was a busy fellow.

Jackson died a controversial death just as he lived a controversial life. Apparently, it happened as a result of an overdose of medication, which he took to sleep. My conclusion, having known him well for a number of years and seen him through hard times as well as good, is that the death was accidental. There are others, including his opponents, who said he took his own life.

His death was immediately felt in different fields, especially in family therapy where he was an extremist. He came from a conservative background as a young man. He was properly trained in psychoanalysis, which included a training analysis. When he decided that family therapy was the way to go, he took his couch out of his office and resigned from the psychoanalytical association. This upset therapists who either were avoiding family therapy or trying to do both individual and family therapy without changing their ideas.

They tried to save the individual theories, which had been basic training in therapy for many years. In the 1950s therapy began to change in theory and practice as therapists were expected to initiate what happens and give directives and not just reflect and respond.

An example of Jackson taking extreme positions at times was the way he dealt with Group Therapy. As family therapy developed and became more popular, the group therapists began to argue that family therapy was just a branch of group therapy. One could do both approaches because both brought several people into the room and not just an individual.

The group therapists invited Jackson to a meeting to discuss family therapy as a format of group therapy. There were major group therapists in the room who expected to be reassured that family therapy was not a new field but simply a branch of group therapy. However, when Jackson spoke to the conference, he said that there was no connection between groups; one was made up of separate individuals expressing themselves separately, whereas family members were connected, indeed related, to each other. Family therapists were changing organizations with a history and a future together. The minimum unit to act upon and theorize about was made up of two people, not an individual. Jackson said he thought that group therapists had not added anything new to the field in the way of theory, but had simply borrowed the ideas of individual therapy, such as the theory of repression. He then began to talk about homeostasis and how the problem family required individuals within it to act in systematic ways. Today one can still tell whether or not a therapist is a purist family therapist by whether or not he or she also does group therapy with unrelated individuals.

An early paper by Jackson on family homeostasis, where the symptomatic behavior of family members stabilizes the organization, fit in well with Bateson's ideas about systems theory and Jackson was pleased to be a consultant to the project Bateson was developing. In exchange, Jackson was supervisor of we project members who were seeing families in which a person was diagnosed as schizophrenic. Out of this collaboration, the project managed to have a psychiatric and medical involvement, rather than of only an anthropological bias.

There were a number of ideas introduced by Jackson in those days. One of his views held that if families are systemic, there must be rules followed by the family members. For example, a couple can have the rule that the wife is responsible and the husband is irresponsible. Whatever they do will follow that rule, including going to therapy, which the wife will want to do for responsible reasons and the husband will not. Other ideas developed because of a focus on rules. For example, the past begins to be less important than the present where behavior is happening. Changing the rules of a couple meant changing their current behavior, not their past, except for historical interest.

Jackson was a teacher and spent his time training residents and therapists. He was also interested in training physicians in interview techniques, which is often neglected in medical school.

Apparently, the largest influence on Jackson's own training was the time he spent with Harry Stack Sullivan. He was supervised by Sullivan and in the process had to consider the influence of interpersonal relations. As Jackson described it, when supervised by Sullivan, one was forced to acknowledge that what the patient said was in response to the therapist, not merely to his or her inner thoughts. There were two people in the room. This was in contrast to psychoanalysts who argued that what a patient said was a response to personal ideas. According to Jackson, Sullivan took the therapist influence seriously and considered the patient's messages to be metaphors about the relationship.

Sullivan did not see families, but his interpersonal ideas had a large influence on the ideas of family therapy, which were developing. A survey done for the Group for the Advancement of Psychiatry showed the majority of family therapists had been influenced by Sullivan in some way.

Jackson was trained at Chestnut Lodge and came from there with a major interest in the complexities of schizophrenia. According to Jackson, Sullivan taught certain premises about psychosis. He said that the therapist should treat a schizophrenic with respect, with kindness, and one should assume that what the person says has relevant meaning to the social situation even though it sounds merely bizarre. A primary assumption was that schizophrenics are changeable.

Jackson carried some of these ideas to an extreme. After dealing with a number of schizophrenic individuals and in families, he concluded that nothing was wrong with them. Or, that there were a variety of kinds of schizophrenics, including those with nothing wrong with them that was not in response to the social situation. This was received as controversial. Yet what an effect that premise has on therapy.

Let me give an example of a case I observed intermittently. A young woman was brought in by her parents. She looked as crazy as one might be. She was mute, and she sat pulling at her hair. She had come out of a state hospital in another state. Her parents had brought her home. Left behind was her infant child. Jackson saw the family for a first interview, and the young woman would not participate but sat looking like an idiot. The father said little and the mother talked at length.

The next day, Sunday, the mother called Jackson and said that her daughter was now talking. What is more, she wanted to go get her baby. Jackson invited them in for a Sunday interview, and mother and daughter were quite upset. The daughter said that if she did not get the baby now she never would. The mother said she was not in shape to travel and get a baby. The daughter said she was. The father threw up his hands and didn't know what to do. Mother listed all the reasons she could not get the baby and the daughter responded to each of them. The mother said one reason the daughter could not go was that she could not get airplane ticket because it was Sunday and the travel agent was closed. The daughter said she could use a credit card and telephone for a ticket.

Jackson took the position that if the young woman wanted to get her child, and she thought she could, then she should go. Typically, Jackson allowed patients to decide what they wanted, like if a patient wanted to be taken off medication, Jackson would promptly do so. He was willing to take risks to achieve normality. The young woman went and got her baby, making the arrangements herself, while her mother protested. The family was then interviewed. Jackson greeted them, pleased with the success of the young woman who was still talking and no longer pulling at her hair. The mother and father began to argue, and then talked about divorcing. The young woman began to pull at her hair and stopped talking. The parents got themselves together again and began to share in taking care of the baby. At least three months passed before the young woman began to talk normally again, to go shopping, and start to engage in some social life.

Having watched Jackson with such cases, it seemed apparent that his view was that nothing was wrong with a person diagnosed schizophrenic. Therefore, his therapy was based on normal activity as quickly as possible, not on extensive deep therapy emphasizing psychopathology

Jackson worked with a variety of patients using a variety of techniques. I recall thinking that he had learned about hypnosis from our work with Milton Erickson. Then I found that Jackson had written a paper reviewing hypnotherapy quite early in his career.

One of the controversies in the 1950s was the use of brief therapy techniques and goals. Anyone doing brief therapy was considered shallow. As the

Bateson project, which had emphasized short-term therapy, ended, Jackson created the MRI to carry on some of the ideas. He emphasized brief techniques, some of which he had learned from Erickson. After his death, a competent crew, especially led by John Weakland, carried on the ideas in research and training there. Weakland had an influence on the ideas of the 10-year Bateson Project that was invaluable.

Jackson's writings have never been properly distributed or collected. Now, thanks to Wendel Ray, they are becoming available extensively. Those of us who admire Jackson appreciate the efforts of Dr. Ray in bringing out the biographical material and the collected papers.

WENDEL A. RAY

Introduction

> How did Don Jackson influence the field of family therapy? I'd say in the same way that Watts influenced the steam engine. He made it. Others have refined the steam engine into a better, more efficient machine. Don established the discipline of family therapy. Others have gone on to refine it.
>
> Richard Fisch, M.D.
> Founder and Director, Brief Therapy Center,
> Mental Research Institute

If Don D. Jackson, M.D., were still alive today, he would be a popular, although controversial, innovator in family therapy, just as when he was making his contributions to the field. Jackson was a systems purist, and purists of any kind, especially in the soft science of family studies, are often not in vogue. In this age of compromise, where integration is the buzzword of the family therapy field, and funding from pharmaceutical companies has all but extinguished talk therapies from the curriculum of psychiatric training programs, advocates of a purely relational approach are rare.

But there was a time in the not-too-distant past that many in the behavioral sciences hung on every word Don Jackson wrote or spoke. His tragic, unanticipated death in January 1968 at the age of 48 stunned the emerging field of family therapy, and the effects of this loss continue to reverberate throughout the discipline. It is my conviction that the gradual shift away from the firm grounding of family therapy in systems and communications theory began soon after Jackson's articulate and convincing voice fell silent. The purpose of this volume of Jackson's selected papers is to make available to clinicians, therapists, academicians, and students of family therapy the very best writings of this creative prodigy of family therapy.

Who was Don D. Jackson and why would students of the family find his work interesting today? In essence, Jackson was one of the most prolific of the early family therapy pioneers. He was a therapist of genius, one of those rare professionals who could produce lasting changes in a family, often in only one or a few sessions. Jackson is remembered for the contributions he made to family theory, family homeostasis, family rules, the marital quid pro quo, and with longtime collaborators Gregory Bateson, Jay Haley, and John Weakland, the concept of the double bind. In a career that spanned but 24 years, Jackson's accomplishments are nothing short of astonishing. Author or coauthor of more than 125 professional papers and seven books, Jackson won virtually every prestigious award in the field of psychiatry, among them the Frieda Fromm-Reichmann award for contributions to the understanding of schizophrenia and the first Edward R. Strecker award for contributions to the treatment of hospitalized patients. He was also named the 1967 Salmon Lecturer.

In 1958 Jackson founded the Mental Research Institute (MRI), the first institute in the world designed specifically for studying interactional processes and teaching family therapy and home of the first federally funded family therapy program. In collaboration with Jay Haley and Nathan Ackerman, Jackson founded the first family therapy journal, *Family Process*. To educate the larger medical community about interactional theory, he helped found and was editor of a medical news journal, *Medical Opinion and Review*. In order to create a forum from which researchers in the newly emerging field of family therapy could publish their work, Jackson helped found and was the editor of *Science and Behavior Books*.

What was Jackson's background and how did he develop such an uncommon understanding of interactional processes? After receiving his medical degree from Stanford Medical School in 1944, and completing his residency, Jackson spent two years in the U.S. Army, specializing in neurology. Then, from August 1947 to April 1951, Jackson trained at Chestnut Lodge in Maryland and the Washington School of Psychiatry, two of the most prestigious analytic institutes of the day, under the tutelage of Harry Stack Sullivan. Sullivan offered a radically alternative definition of psychiatry as "the study of processes that involve or go on between people ... the field of interpersonal relations, under any and all circumstances in which these relations exist. It seems a personality can never be isolated from the complex of interpersonal relations in which the person lives and has his being" (Sullivan, 1945, pp. 4–5).

Jackson fully embraced the implications of Sullivan's Interpersonal Theory to the extent that he could legitimately be characterized as being "Sullivanian." But when Jackson returned to Palo Alto, California to enter private practice in April 1951, the differences between the two men soon became evident. The primary difference was that Sullivan worked with mentally ill individuals in isolation from their families, envisioning his brilliant Interpersonal Theory by inferential conception of what past interpersonal relations must have been like. In contrast, Jackson extended Sullivan's theory by focusing on the actual relationship between one individual and other individuals in the present as *Primary Data*.

This fundamental shift in the conception of causality – from looking at past causes of behavior to placing primary emphasis on the relationship between the symptom bearer and significant others in the present — happened partly by accident. Palo Alto is a small, university town, and Jackson could not avoid running into the relatives of some of his patients. In mid-1951 one of Jackson's cases involved a young psychotic woman who was making solid progress. However, she usually came to appointments accompanied by her mother. Jackson asked the mother to stay at home and allow her daughter to come to the next session alone. When the session arrived Jackson saw the mother sitting in the lobby with her daughter. Irritated by the mother's refusal to follow his suggestion, Jackson invited the mother to join her daughter in what was to be one of the first family sessions ever reported. The results were interesting to Jackson and he began experimenting with family therapy.

> I became interested in family therapy ... when I went from Chestnut Lodge to Palo Alto ... which is a small university town. I couldn't avoid the relatives; and this led to a lot of surprising and sometimes not very pleasant results. I became interested in the question of family homeostasis, which seemed most marked in the families where a schizophrenic patient was able to live at home. If he

then went through psychotherapy and benefited from it, any move on his part would usually produce all sorts of disruptions at home ... At any rate, for practical reasons, I started seeing the patient's parents, and then eventually the parent's and patient together.

(From volume 2, p. 84)

Jackson was just beginning to outline a purely here-and-now, Interactional Theory and conjoint family approach to therapy when yet another fortuitous turn of events occurred that would have profound ramifications for the future field of family therapy, Don Jackson met Gregory Bateson. On a bleak day in January 1954, Jackson was giving a lecture on the concept of family homeostasis at the Veteran's Administration Hospital in Menlo Park, California. Gregory Bateson was in the audience and approached Jackson after his talk. Bateson felt that Jackson's work related to research in which he was involved with Jay Haley, John Weakland, and William Fry. As a result of this meeting, Jackson soon became a member of the team. Collaboration with Bateson, Haley, Weakland, and Fry opened new vistas for Jackson. He now had ongoing interaction with a group of thinkers equal to himself in conceptual abilities and daring.

John Weakland (1988) described the rich body of ideas that constitute Interactional Theory as having emerged not so much from any one individual but rather as the product of the interaction between the members of the Palo Alto Group, primarily Gregory Bateson's research team Jackson, Jay Haley, John Weakland, and William Fry. These ideas emerged during the ten-year-long series of research projects on the nature of paradox in communication processes, and later under the leadership of Jackson at the MRI, where Jules Riskin, Virginia Satir, Paul Watzlawick, Richard Fisch, Janet Beavin-Bavelas, and Antonio Ferreira joined the team. Sources of fertile input into the group's work were the many visiting experts, including such eminent scholars as Norbert Wiener, Alan Watts, Weldon Keys, Frieda Fromm-Reichmann, and Ray Birdwhistell, and especially Haley and Weakland's detailed study of Milton H. Erickson. All of these scholars can be considered to have contributed to the creation of Interactional Theory.

Bateson's concept of report and command (1951), and other concepts developed in Jackson's collaboration with the Bateson group influenced his approach to family process. The idea that people are constantly attempting to define the nature of their relationships, the arbitrariness of observer-imposed

punctuation, symmetrical and complementary exchanges of behavior, and focusing on how people qualify their own messages verbally and nonverbally
were concepts Jackson developed that singularly focus on family process:

> With our proclivity for the individual view of things, it runs against
> the grain to see ourselves as participants in a system, the nature of
> which we little understand. Yet I am convinced that we can make
> such dire appraisals (and such undeserved praises) only by translating
> a highly complex composite of people and context into a term,
> which is then inappropriately applied to an individual.
>
> (Jackson, 1963)

The extent to which Jackson's Interactional Theory and its clinical application permeate the field of family and brief therapy is a tribute both to his
willingness to share ideas with others and to his commitment to pointing the
way for psychiatry, psychology, social work, and the other applied human sciences to change direction. Interactional Theory influenced a discontinuous
shift from monadic explanations of human behavior to a contextual perspective, placing primary focus on the relationship between individuals. The "tug
of war" analogy used by Jackson (Jackson, 1967) in describing fear of change
and the illusion of stability cuts through the oversimplifications and reductionistic thinking inherent in theories of human behavior that attempt to explain
the individual in trivializing, artificial isolation from the context in which he
or she exists.

Jackson's most enduring contribution to understanding the nature of humankind was his expansion of the definition of behavior beyond looking at
the individual in vitro to behavior as a manifestation of "relationship in the
widest sense" (Jackson, 1967). This uncompromising appreciation of context
represents an evolutionary step potentially as significant as when "the organism
gradually ceases to respond quite automatically to the mood signs of another
and becomes able to recognize the other individual's and its own signals are
only signals" (Bateson, 1955/1972, p. 178). This discontinuous paradigmatic
shift (in the Kuhnian sense, 1970) profoundly changed the order of data appropriate to understanding behavior (i.e. conceptualization of the relation
between individuals in contrast to a monadic view), context, and causality in
human behavior (cybernetic rather than linear).

Immediately before his death, Jackson collaborated with Paul Watzlawick and Janet Beavin-Bavelas to write one of the most influential books in the fields of family and brief therapy: *Pragmatics of Human Communication* (Watzlawick, Beavin-Bavelas, Jackson, 1967). Watzlawick and Beavin Bavelas describe this groundbreaking book as being the product of their effort to understand and describe Jackson's theoretical and clinical abilities. After months of being observed conducting interviews and asked questions regarding his incredible clinical acumen, Jackson, exasperated, finally drafted an outline and suggested they write the book that was to become one of the cornerstones of an Interactional Theory of human behavior:

> A phenomenon remains unexplainable as long as the range of observation is not wide enough to include the context in which the phenomenon occurs. Failure to realize the relationship between an event and the matrix in which it takes place, between an organism and its environment, either confronts the observer with something "mysterious" or induces him to attribute to his object of study certain properties the object may not possess. Compared with the wide acceptance of this fact in the biological sciences, the behavioral sciences seem still to base themselves to a large extent on the monadic view of the individual and on the time-honored method of isolating variables.
>
> (Watzlawick, Beavin-Bavelas, & Jackson, 1967, p. 21)

Jackson made every effort to expand a relational understanding of human behavior beyond the mental health sciences and to disseminate these ideas to nonprofessional as well as professional audiences. In another such effort Jackson joined with famed author and close friend William Lederer to produce the first systemically oriented marital self-help book, *Mirages of Marriage* (1968) in which they write:

> The systems concept helps explain much of the previously mysterious behavior, which results whenever two or more human beings relate to one another. We know that the family is a unit in which all individuals have an important influence, whether they like it or not and whether they know it or not. The family is an interacting communications network in which every member from the day-old baby to the seventy-year-old grandmother influences the nature of

the entire system and in turn is influenced by it. For example, if someone in the family feels ill, another member may function more effectively than he usually does. The [family as a] system tends, by nature, to keep itself in balance. An unusual action by one member invariably results in a compensating reaction by another member. If mother hates to take Sunday drives but hides this feeling from her husband, the message is nevertheless somehow broadcast throughout the family communication network, and it may be Johnny, the four-year-old, who becomes "carsick" and ruins the Sunday drive.

(p. 14)

This shift of primary focus from the intrapsychic processes of the individual to the relationship between members of the individual's relational system can be seen in the work of many of the eminent clinician-theoreticians of today (Keeney, 1983, 1987; Tomm, 1987, 1988; Penn, 1983, 1986; Palazzoli, Boscolo, Cecchin, & Prata, 1980; Cecchin, Lane, and Ray, 1993, 1994; Papp, 1983; Boscolo, et al., 1987). The durability of Jackson's ideas is evidenced by the fact that two of the books he coauthored, *Mirages of Marriage* (Lederer & Jackson, 1968) and *Pragmatics of Human Communication* (Watzlawick, Beavin-Bavelas, & Jackson, 1967) continue in publication more than 30 years original publication.

The pioneering work done in the 1950s and 1960s by Jackson and his colleagues, first in the Bateson projects and later at MRI, inform most present-day systemically oriented approaches to therapy. The non-pathological, non-normative, interactional focus originated by Jackson forms the most fundamental premises underlying the Brief Therapy Model, developed after Jackson's death, at MRI (Watzlawick, Weakland & Fisch, 1974; Fisch, Weakland, & Segal, 1982). It also underlies the strategic work of Jay Haley and his colleagues (Haley, 1963, 1976, 1980; Madanes, 1981, 1984); the structural model developed by Salvador Minuchin and his colleagues (Minuchin, 1974; Minuchin & Fishman, 1982; Stanton & Todd, 1982); the work of the Milan Associates both before and after their split into two separate groups (Palazzoli et al., 1978, 1980a&b; Boscolo, Cecchin, Hoffman, & Penn, 1987); the Solution Focused brief therapy approach of deShazer and his associates at the Brief Therapy Center of Milwaukee (deShazer, 1982, 1985), the work of Keeney and his colleagues (Keeney & Ross, 1985; Keeney & Silverstein, 1986; Keeney, 1987;

Ray & Keeney, 1993); the work of Andersen (1987); and even the self described "Post-Modern" narrative orientations of Anderson and Goolishian (1990), Hoffman (1993), and Michael White (1989), as well as most other systemically and contextually oriented approaches.

As the founder of the MRI, and clinical supervisor of and having worked closely with the institute's top research associates, Jackson's influence is particularly evident in the Brief Therapy Model developed there. See, for example, the lecture Jackson gave in February 1963 entitled *Brief Psychotherapy*.

Jackson's influence on present-day models of family and brief therapy can be seen in the cybernetic model and systems theory (i.e., if change occurs in one part of the system, the rest will change to accommodate it), social constructionism, ignoring what John Weakland called the received wisdom of the day, attending to pragmatics (i.e., who does what when and to whom in the present), accepting and going with the symptom, speaking the client's language, using circular questioning, and prescribing behavior at one order of abstraction to address the organization of the system at another order of abstraction. Since Jackson's death, the work of his MRI colleagues has continued to inform most of the family-and-brief oriented systemic work being done today.

The theoretical premises and clinical techniques set forth by Jackson continue to provide the solid bedrock for systemically oriented theoreticians and clinicians. Salvador Minuchin's work toward changing family organization by interrupting problematic coalitionary processes across generational lines and strengthening the boundaries of various subsystems has been influenced by Jackson. Minuchin read Jackson (Minuchin, 1987) and for ten years was affiliated with Jay Haley. The original Milan group and the subsequent work by both Palazzoli's and Boscolo and Cecchin's groups have also been strongly influenced by Jackson. Fundamental elements of their work such as circular questioning, hypothesizing, positive connotation, using rituals and tasks, attending to the implications of language (as evidenced in the shift from using "to be" to "to seem") and attending to the importance of the referring person are all ideas originally pioneered by Jackson.

The work of MRI, Haley, Minuchin, the Milan groups, and deShazer and Berg's Solution Focused orientation has, in turn, influenced such notable clinicians and theoreticians as members of the Ackerman group, including Peggy Papp, Peggy Penn, and Joel Bergman, as well as other eminent workers in the field, such as Karl Tomm, Steve deShazer, Goolishian and Anderson,

Tom Andersen, Lynn Hoffman, and Michael White. Behavioral family therapists have explicitly adopted such fundamental concepts as the marital quid pro quo (Stewart, 1974; Jacobson & Margolin, 1979).

This collection of Don Jackson's selected papers demonstrates the penetrating extent to which his work has influenced the development of family therapy. Access to his original papers allows readers to trace for themselves Jackson's contribution. Rather than representing a collection of significant but seemingly unconnected theoretical concepts, Jackson's work constitutes a paradigmatic shift in the conceptualization of human behavior.

In the space of 24 years, Jackson managed to create most of the structure that forms the foundation of today's systemically oriented family and brief therapies. By 1968, the basic tenets of Jackson's Interactional Theory of human behavior and change had been articulated. The MRI had been created to provide a context within which formal research into the interactional nature of human behavior could be conducted. An interdisciplinary training program in how to promote contextually sound change had been established. Vehicles for disseminating interactionally oriented theory and practice ideas, such as *Family Process, Science and Behavior Books*, and *Medical Opinion and Review*, had been launched.

Jackson was ready to lead psychiatry, psychology, social work, and the rest of the human sciences from a view of the individual in isolation to an appreciation of the interconnectedness of humankind when he suddenly died. The unifying factor his presence had provided to the emerging field of family therapy was gone. Meanwhile, the field has yet to achieve the potentialities once imagined by its founders for ushering in a revolutionary shift in how human problems are conceptualized and managed.

Instead of consensus across schools about the systemic nature of the theoretical base, a pervasive lack of appreciation of the fundamental difference between individual theory and interactional theory continues. Efforts to blend the two theories are doomed to confuse both orientations because the two theories focus on different orders of phenomena, with opposite implications for treatment. And so, the field remains theoretically muddled, fragmented into various camps, each claiming to possess a superior understanding of the nature of behavior and change. The field could be likened to a family frozen in grief over the death of a parent, with no unified direction or understanding of its purposes or goals. In the presence of this fragmentation, the field has yet to produce a giant of the stature of a Freud, capable of blazing a path into the future. Had Jackson lived, one cannot help but wonder whether or not he would have attained such stature.

But the shift of focus as set forth by Jackson and his colleagues from the individual to the relationship between and from the "reality" of pathology to the "construction of ecologically respectful realities" carries implications beyond the field of family therapy. These ideas have ramifications of global proportions that influence concerns from ecology to the world political arena.

How today's issues would have been addressed by Jackson is basically unknowable. One can speculate that his utter disdain for reductionistic, non-self-referential thinking would still characterize his thinking. His call for appreciation of the interconnected nature of behavior and context would have endured. He would have continued to protest non-contextual, individual pathology-oriented research and treatment approaches to human problems in living. He would have been aroused by the recent resurgence of individual diagnostics and genetic explanations of "individual pathology." Jackson would have contested the "healthy and for the good of the patient" mentality underlying the recent upsurge of in-patient adolescent "treatment," and substance addiction programs, as thinly disguised, profit-driven, social control measures.

What difference would it make if the fields of brief and family therapy were to reawaken to the implications of Jackson's insights? A glimmer of hope for such a paradigmatic transformation can be evidenced in the on-going work of Haley, Fisch, Schlanger, and colleagues at the MRI, in the work of cybernetic theoreticians, and in the continuing exploration and application of Milton Erickson's work by Zeig, Rossi, and others.

It is equally likely that the opportunity for such a transformation has passed. The effects of humankind's long-standing addiction to the illusion of power and control may have, as Gregory Bateson (1970, 1979) suggests, already corrupted the ecology beyond the point of recovery. It is my hope that making Jackson's work readily available again will have a reinvigorating effect within family and brief therapy, and perhaps ripple beyond the confines of this still young profession.

Divided into three sections, with introductory commentaries for each section, the focus of this book is Interactional Theory. The 23 papers fall into three sections: Early Clinical Observations, Defining an Interactional Theory of Human Relationships, and Research into the Nature of Human Interaction.

In his preface to the two volumes of the papers published to celebrate the tenth anniversary of the founding of MRI, Dr. Jackson stated: "The papers included in these volumes cover a considerable span of time, substantive focus, and levels of generality, yet there is a unity in their manifest diversity" (Jackson, 1968, vii). This statement holds true as well for this volume of Dr. Jackson's selected papers.

References

Andersen, T. (1987). The reflecting team: Dialogue and meta-dialogue in clinical work. *Family Process*, (*26*) 4, 415–428.

Anderson, H., & Goolishian, H. (1988, October). *Systemic practice with domestic violence*. Presented at the American Association for Marriage and Family Therapy, New Orleans, La.

Bateson, G. (1955, December). A theory of play and fantasy: A report on theoretical aspects of the project for study of the role of paradoxes of abstraction in communication. *Psychiatric Research Reports*, (2), 39–51.

Bateson, G. (1970, January). *An anthropologist views the social scene*. [Cassette recording of a talk given at the Mental Research Institute]. Palo Alto, CA: MRI.

Bateson, G. (1972). *Steps to an ecology of mind*. New York: Jason Aronson Inc.

Bergman, J. (1985). *Fishing for barracuda: Pragmatics of brief systemic therapy*. New York: W. W. Norton.

Boscolo, G., Cecchin, G., Hoffman, L., & Penn, P. (1987). *Milan systemic family therapy*. New York: Basic Books.

Cecchin, G., Lane, G., & Ray, W. (1993). From strategizing to non-intervention: Toward irreverence in systemic practice. *Journal of Marital and Family Therapy*, 19 (2); 125–136.

Cecchin, G., Lane, G., & Ray, W. (1992). *Irreverence: A strategy for therapists' survival*. London: Karnac Books.

deShazer, S. (1982). *Patterns of brief family therapy: An ecosystemic approach*. New York: Guilford.

deShazer, S. (1985). *Keys to solution in brief therapy*. New York: Norton.

Fisch, R., Weakland, J., & Segal, L. (1982). *The tactics of change: Doing brief therapy*. San Francisco: Jossey-Bass.

Hoffman, L. (1986). Beyond power and control: Toward a "second order" family systems therapy. *Family Systems Medicine*, 3, 381–396.

Hoffman, L. (1989). A constructuivist position for family therapy. *The Irish Journal of Psychology*, 9 (1), 110–129.

Jackson, D., & Weakland, J. (1961). Conjoint family therapy: Some considerations on theory, technique and results. *Psychiatry*, 24 (2), 30–45.

Jackson, D. (1963). *The sick, the sad, the savage, & the sane*. Presented as the annual academic lecture to the Society of Medical Psychoanalysts & Department of Psychiatry, New York Medical College.

Jackson, D. (1961). Family therapy in the family of the schizophrenic. In Morris I. Stein (Ed.), *Contemporary psychotherapies*, pages 272–287.

Jackson, D. (1967). The fear of change. *Medical Opinion & Review*, 3 (3), 34–41.

Jackson, D. (1968). *Communication, family, and marriage: Human communication volume 1*. Palo Alto: Science and Behavior Books.

Jacobson, N., & Margolin, G. (1979). *Marital therapy*. New York: Brunner/Mazel.

Keeney, B. (1983). *Aesthetics of change*. New York: Guilford.

Keeney, B., & Ross, J. (1983). Learning to learn systemic therapies. *Journal of Strategic and Systemic Therapies*, 2 (2), 22–30.

Keeney, B., & Ross, J. (1985). *Mind in therapy: Constructing systemic family therapies*. New York: Basic Books.

Keeney, B., & Silverstein, O. (1986). *The therapeutic voice of Olga Silverstein*. New York: Guilford.

Kuhn, T. (1970). *The structure of scientific revolution* (2nd edition). Chicago: University of Chicago Press.

Lederer, W., & Jackson, D. (1968). *Mirages of marriage*. New York: Norton.

Mackler, L. (1977). Donald D. Jackson 1920–1968 bibliography. In L. Wolberg & M. Aronson (Eds.), *Group therapy an overview* (pp. v–lx). New York: Grune & Stratton.

Madanes, C. (1981). *Strategic family therapy*. San Francisco: Jossey-Bass.

Minuchin, S. (1974). *Families and family therapy*. Cambridge, MA: Harvard University Press.

Minuchin, S., & Fishman, H. (1982). *Family therapy techniques*. Cambridge, MA: Harvard University Press.

Minuchin, S. (1987). My many voices. In J. Zeig (Ed.), *The Evolution of Psychotherapy*, pp. 5–13. New York: Brunner/Mazel.

Palazzoli, M., Boscolo, L., Cecchin, G., Prata, G. (1980a). The problem of the referring person. *Journal of Marital & Family Therapy*, 6 (1), 3–9.

Palazzoli, M., Boscolo, L., Cecchin, G., & Prata, G. (1980b). Hypothesizing-circularity-neutrality: Three guidelines for the conductor of the session. *Family Process*, 19, (1), 3–12.

Palazzoli, M., Boscolo, L., Cecchin, G., Prata, G. (1978). *Paradox and counter paradox*. New York: Jason Aronson.

Papp, P. (1983). *The process of change*. New York: Guilford.

Penn, P. (1982). Circular questioning. *Family Process*, 21 (1), 267–280.

Penn, P. (1985). Feed-forward: Future questions, future maps. *Family Process*, 24 (3), 299–310.

Ray, W., & Keeney, B. (1993). *Resource focused therapy*. London: Karnac Books.

Reusch, J., & Bateson, G. (1951). *Communication: The social matrix of psychiatry*. New York: W. W. Norton.

Sullivan, H. (1945). *Conceptions of modern psychiatry*. Washington, DC: W. A. White Foundation.

Stanton, M. & Todd, T., & Associates (1982). *Family therapy of drug abuse*. New York: Guilford.

Stewart, R. (1980). *Helping couples change*. New York: Guilford.

Tomm, K. (1987). Interventive interviewing: Part I: Strategizing as a fourth guideline for the therapist. *Family Process*, 26 (1), 3–14.

Tomm, K. (1987). Interventive interviewing: Part II: Reflexive questioning as a means to enable self-healing. *Family Process*, 26 (2), 167–184.

Watzlawick, P., Beavin-Bavelas, J., & Jackson, D. (1967). *Pragmatics of human communication: A study of interactional patterns, pathologies & paradoxes*. New York: W.W. Norton.

Watzlawick, P. (1988, June). [Personal interview with Paul Watzlawick, Ph.D., senior research fellow, MRI and former colleague of Don D. Jackson]. Palo Alto, CA: Mental Research Institute.

White, M. (1989). *Selected papers*. Australia: Dulwich Publications.

About the Editor

Wendel Ray, Ph.D., the Director of MRI, has been a research associate and Director of MRI's Don D. Jackson Archive since the late 1980s. Dr. Ray serves as Professor of Family Therapy at the University of Louisiana at Monroe. He routinely conducts training internationally and nationally on a variety of topics including brief therapy of adolescent substance abuse, brief treatment of ADHD, family violence, as well as lecturing on Gregory Bateson's research projects and Don Jackson's contributions to interactional theory. He is author or co-author of numerous articles and books including *Propagations, Thirty Years of Influence from MRI (Marriage and the Family)* (co-edited with John Weakland); *Resource Focused Therapy* (co-authored with Bradford P. Keeney); *Evolving Brief Therapies: In Honor of John H. Weakland* (co-edited with Steve deShazer); *Irreverence: A Therapists' Guide to Survival*, and *The Cybernetics of Prejudices in the Practice of Psychotherapy* (co-authored with Gianfranco Cecchin & Gerry Lane).

Acknowledgments

Materials in the Don D. Jackson Archive are being placed in a computer database to assure permanent preservation and eventually easier access by scholars, theoreticians, and clinicians interested in studying his work. This work-intensive process has made slow but steady progress, thanks, in large part, to the dedication of graduate assistants at the University of Louisiana at Monroe. I want to particularly acknowledge two doctoral and master-level graduate assistants who helped in the editing and preparation of this volume of Dr. Jackson's papers: David Govener and Craig Moorman.

Don D. Jackson:

Selected Essays at the Dawn of an Era

SECTION I:
EARLY CLINICAL OBSERVATIONS

Introduction and Overview

Jackson's medical and preliminary psychiatric training took place at Stanford Medical School during World War II, when most of the faculty was serving in the military. Subsequently, much of his initial psychiatric education was the product of self-directed reading in the Stanford library, in combination with largely self-directed clinical work with ambulatory and hospitalized patients. Jackson's first article, "The Therapeutic Use of Hypnosis" (1944), was, therefore, a product of this self-study. One of the most interesting aspects of this article, published when Jackson was 24 years old, is that he was already focusing on developing pragmatic skill in influencing patients to make constructive changes in the most efficacious way possible. Jackson's use of hypnosis in his clinical work would continue throughout his career. Many years later, John Weakland, one of Jackson's long-time colleagues, characterized Jackson as having an approach to hypnosis stylistically different from, but in many respects comparable to that of the brilliant Milton H. Erickson (Weakland, 1988).

The second article in this section, "The Psychosomatic Factors in Ulcerative Colitis: A Case Report (1946), was the first of several articles Jackson would publish that focused on the interpersonal aspects of somatic illness. To trace the evolution of Jackson's work in this area, readers are encouraged to also review chapter 23, "Family Research on the Problem of Ulcerated Colitis."

A wealth of seminal ideas, albeit in embryonic form, can be found in chapter 3, "The Relationship of the Referring Physician to the Psychiatrist" (1952). Jackson focuses attention on the importance of attending to the nature of the relationship between the referring person and the therapist. He evidences an early understanding of semantics and what is now labeled social constructivism in his discussion of both the referring physician's and the psychiatrist's "attitudes and preconceived notions" (p. 49) as contributing to the nature of their relationship. He articulates a precursor to the concept of positive connotation, emphasizing the importance of the therapist's use of language:

> ... the individual does the best he can at any given moment. Why should it be otherwise, when we all would rather be comfortable than in distress? The terms "lazy," "stubborn," "no will power" are not merely descriptive but imply moral censure and an unspoken "he could do better if he wanted to." (pp. 51–52)

And important, as well, is circular causality: "certain dynamic interpersonal processes over which the individual has no control are responsible for his character traits." (p. 52).

In chapter 4, "Some Factors Influencing the Oedipus Complex" (1954), Jackson emphasizes the importance of understanding triadic interaction occurring in the present relationship between child, mother, and father, going on briefly to describe the concept of family homeostasis.

In chapter 5, "Office Treatment of Ambulatory Schizophrenics" (1954), Jackson provides one of his first descriptions of the advantages (if the many complexities of such an enterprise can be managed) of working with schizophrenic patients outside a hospital setting, and discusses a number of the technical aspects of doing so successfully. Jackson proceeds in chapter 6, "The Therapist's Personality in the Therapy of Schizophrenics" (1955), to outline in even greater detail the attitudes and preconceptions that can encumber effective therapeutic work with severely mentally ill individuals and in doing so again explicitly articulates what is now called a post-modern and social constructivist position.

Chapter 7, "Further Consideration of Hysterical Symptoms in Women" (1956), is a paper Jackson presented to the American Psychiatric Association but never published. Here Jackson continues to elucidate the nature of the relationship dynamics between parents and daughters who manifest hysterical symptoms in their relations with others.

In chapter 8, "A Note on the Importance of Trauma in the Genesis of Schizophrenia (1957), Jackson sets forth a convincing argument that the concept of trauma as generally understood "does not render justice to the complexity and subtlety of the kinds of human interaction that predispose people to" severe emotional illness (p. 121). He then describes the conjoint family therapy work that he and the other members of Bateson's research group were conducting and during which they had become convinced "that trauma is hardly an appropriate word. Rather, it has constituted a condition operating in the patient's environment, which has been nondiscrete and continuing" (p. 122). In this way, Jackson continued to lay out in skeletal form early descriptions of a new and revolutionary Interactional Theory of human behavior.

The final paper in this section, "Guilt and the Control of Pleasure in the Schizoid Personality (1958), introduces Jackson's idea, developed in collaboration with Jay Haley, that when children assert themselves, they dare to determine the nature of their relationships with their parents. This fundamental concept of control — that is, who determines the nature of a relationship — was to become a cornerstone of Interactional Theory.

Thus, these earliest papers trace the evolution of Jackson's thinking during three distinct periods; the first two were written before he entered training at Chestnut Lodge and the Washington School of Psychiatry under the tutelage of Harry Stack Sullivan. The next four papers, written between 1952 and 1955, reflect the early solidification of Jackson's Interactional Approach to understanding human behavior, and strongly reflect Sullivan's influence. The final three papers make evident yet another advancement and synthesis of Jackson's early thinking after he joined Gregory Bateson's research projects on paradoxes in communication processes.

CHAPTER 1

The Therapeutic Uses of Hypnosis[1]

(1944)

From a perusal of the recent literature on the subject, one gains the impression that hypnosis is slowly rising from the depths of castigation (Erickson, 1944). The history of this interesting subject has been one of misunderstanding and misrepresentation, and from its earliest beginnings it has been a cause of conflict and fierce debate within learned medical societies. Its protagonists have regarded hypnosis as a panacea, while its antagonists have allied it with Svengali and the traveling magician (Mann). However, from its infamous beginnings when Mesmer's claims were entirely discredited by an international committee (of which Benjamin Franklin was a member) to the classical studies of Bernheim, Charcot, Forel, Braid, Vogt, and others, there has been amassed a voluminous amount of careful research.

Oskar Diethelm, professor of psychiatry at Cornell, states: "Modern textbooks neglect to give a clear presentation of the technique [of hypnosis]. I consider it essential for every psychiatrist to master the technique, and for every general practitioner to understand the working factors. There are still many prejudices against the medical use of hypnosis, but it definitely has its place in medicine as a form of therapy."

---

[1] *Stanford Medical Bulletin*, 2 (4), November, pp. 193–196. Reprinted with permission.

THEORY

There are numerous theories as to the mechanism of hypnosis; however, regardless of the finer ramifications, there are two essential points: (1) relaxation and a reduction of sensory input, and (2) the presence of an operator who administers suggestions (White, 1941).

TECHNIQUE

With regard to the actual technique of hypnosis, it must be remembered that this is a very fluid process, and the good hypnotist is one who adapts his technique to the needs of the individual patient. There is no set mode of induction, but one method suggested by Diethelm (1936) is particularly useful. The patient's attention is fixed upon a coin held about a foot from his eyes; the therapist's hand is placed on his forehead. The patient is advised to breathe deeply and quietly, not trying to help but taking a passive attitude, merely listening to the hypnotist's voice. The next suggestion is that he feels relaxed and notices a heaviness in his legs that gradually steals over his body. The coin becomes blurred. His forehead feels warm (due to the warmth of the hand). His eyelids become heavier and heavier as sleep is suggested, and gradually fall.

Spontaneous closing of the eyes generally occurs in one or two minutes; if it does not happen, the patient should be commanded to close them. The subject is gradually carried to deeper levels by monotonous suggestion of rest and sleep. With a little experience, it is not difficult to determine when the patient is in a hypnotic state. The demonstration of catalepsy or the production of anesthesia may be used as a help in determining if a sufficiently deep level has been attained for therapeutic purposes.

The above technique, it must be reiterated, is only a baseline from which the novice with increasing assurance will apply his own modifications. For example, some people would rather sit in a chair than recline; some would rather have their eyes closed during the induction, etc. Another point to be kept in mind is that it is not necessary in every patient to attain profound hypnosis (somnambulism) in order to achieve therapeutic results. However, deep hypnosis is attainable in some 70% of patients in from one to three hypnotic sessions. In general, the best hypnotist is the one who can induce enthusiasm for his subject, and who can be masterful in the gentle art of persuasion.

Each hypnotic session is carefully terminated. The simplest expedient is to tell the patient he will awaken at the count of "three," and that he will feel refreshed without headache or dizziness. The subjective sensations experienced upon awakening will be varied. Some patients will feel elated; others may feel strangely bewildered. The patient may remember the entire experience; but if a sufficiently deep level has been reached, and amnesia has been suggested, the subject will feel as though he had just dropped off to sleep for a few minutes.

THERAPY

Those who claim that hypnosis is of little value in therapy because its effects are not lasting may not have a proper understanding of the process. In the first place, there are numerous reports of symptoms having been removed for years, or permanently, by even one or two hypnotic sessions (Forel, 1906; McCortney, 1937). Second, forceful suggestion is not relied upon, but use is made of a hypnocathartic technique, of dream analysis (Farber & Fisher, 1943), of psychosomatic and psychopathological phenomena (Erickson, 1939, 1943), of age regression back to critical levels (Kubie & Erickson, 1941), and of hypnogogic reverie (Kubie, 1944).

These techniques involve the careful analysis and synthesis that is the basis of any successful psychotherapy. Hypnosis is used as a passport into the patient's unconscious, but once there, the therapist must use all the skill in handling interpersonal relationships that he would exercise in the waking state. However, there are many advantages: the mere submitting to hypnosis not only strengthens rapport, but indicates the patient's willingness for psychotherapy; painful matters that would be accompanied by emotional blocking in the waking state may be discussed; symptoms that might temporarily interfere with ordinary psychotherapy may be removed; the patient's recall is increased; and where psychotherapy extending over months or years is not feasible, hypnosis offers the shortest route to personality resynthesis. It must be remembered that psychoanalysis as a technique arose from Freud's work with hypnosis.

The selection of cases for hypnotic therapy depends in general on the duration of illness, the length of time to be allocated to psychotherapy, the danger of the symptoms to the patient, and the nature of the symptoms. Hypnosis is most efficacious where reversible physiological processes are involved (e.g., constipation or sleep). It is of little or no value (in general) in psychoses, obsessive-compulsive neuroses, or chronic "fixed" neuroses of various kinds. Hysterical conversion symptoms and hysterical amnesia are, of course, the conditions par excellence for suggestive therapy.

Brief mention should be made of some of the other psychogenetically determined diseases in which hypnosis has been of particular benefit (Heyer,

1927; Vogel, 1934; Erickson, 1944; Diethelm, 1936; Forel, 1906; McCortney, 1937; Flatan, 1920; Delirus, 1905; Kraines, 1943) disorders of sleep, headache (Eisenbud, 1937), frigidity, dysmenorrhea, impotence, ejaculatio praecox, diarrhea and constipation, low back pain, intractable vomiting of pregnancy, tics or habit spasms, torticollis, stammering, selected cases of alcoholism, and finally as anesthesia for many kinds of surgical and obstetrical procedures (Forel, 1906; Paramonov, 1937; Heyer, 1927). Naturally, all of the above symptoms can be caused by organic disease; the physician's first responsibility is to exercise judgment in the selection of cases.

HYPNOSIS IN WAR NEUROSES

The value of hypnosis in war neuroses was firmly established in World War I, and in the presence of the much-publicized narcosynthesis of World War II, hypnotic therapy has retained its niche among psychotherapeutic measures. The advantages of techniques that put any patient to sleep and involve only a needle and syringe are readily admitted. However, as most authors have pointed out the disadvantages of barbiturates, and stress that whenever conditions are suitable, or longer-term therapy is advisable, hypnosis should be employed. The reason for this is that a strong transference in a protected situation is conducive to an outpouring of guilt and fears. An interpersonal relationship is built up into which the patient can freely verbalize his anxieties. That the situation is more personal than with the barbiturate techniques, and that the patient is more suggestible, I think, is generally admitted. Anyone interested in this problem should consult especially Fisher's article (1943) or Hadfleld's (1942). Hypnosis has also been employed to advantage in group therapy (Kraines, 1943).

CASE REPORTS

The following are very brief accounts of several cases in which hypnosis was employed.

Case 1

A 23-year-old artist complained of nervousness and fear of jumping out of a window. Her father had died when she was five, and it became evident that her present problems stemmed from psychic trauma previous to his death. She was unable to produce much significant material by conscious recall, so hypnosis was resorted to. She could not be carried to a deep level; however, by suggesting that the blank wall was a screen onto which would be thrown various pictures of her childhood, it was possible to recapture in distressingly vivid detail the sought-for experiences. She continued, however, to remain resistant to suggestion.

Case 2

A 62-year-old man entered the hospital complaining of agonizing pain in the right tibia. The pain had been present for two weeks following a minor blow to that area. Physical examination and X-rays were negative. He was hypnotized following the oral administration of 0.1 g. seconal and passed into the somnambulistic stage. Upon questioning, he disclosed that his wife was forcing him into a business proposition that would mean a great deal of work, and he wished to retire. He was told that he would sleep until 7:00 A.M. and that when he awoke the pain would be gone and would not return. His symptom was explained to him the next day, and he not at all reluctantly accepted its origin, since he had felt that his wife was "pushing him too far."

Case 3

A 33-year-old single switchboard operator had not worked for nine months and had spent the better part of this time in bed for intractable backache. She was seen in the orthopedic clinic and referred to neuropsychiatry. Examination was negative except for extreme rigidity of the lumbar spine. Four one-hour interviews were spent in anamnesis and interpretation without any improvement. She insisted that she would be all right if only her back wouldn't hurt, and meanwhile the family waited on her and virtually carried her to the clinic. She was very suggestible, and within two minutes was put into profound hypnosis. Because she had suggested that she had "shouldered the family's troubles too long," it was suggested that she had been carrying the load of the family's responsibilities on her back for a long time, and that the final straw had occurred to "break" it. She was told that when she awoke she would bend forward and backward without experiencing any pain or stiffness. Actually, although she felt no pain, there was some residual stiffness. However, after three sessions in two weeks, she was able to move her lumbar spine without any complaints. The hypnotic sessions were also utilized in an attempt to track down some of the other complexities in her memories. While under hypnosis she was told she would dream, and to raise her arm when a dream began, and lower it when finished. This technique yielded a large amount of material about which she could be interrogated in the waking state. Dreams to which she could not make associations consciously were easily interpreted while under hypnosis. The following is an example: "My brother was lost. I went out to look for him, but I searched all day and couldn't find him. My sister went out and found him right away." In a hypnotic trance, she stated that her sister had "found her brother's out" and gotten away from the family, while she had continued to let them impose on her.

CONCLUSION

I hope I have not presented hypnosis as a psychotherapeutic cure-all. There are no shortcuts in legitimate psychotherapy, but in some cases it is not advisable or possible to carry out a prolonged analysis. Furthermore, hypnosis is valuable in combination with other methods. Surely psychiatry's most pressing problem is to find methods and means of treating as rapidly as possible the ever increasing horde of psychoneurosis. If the physician would keep his psychiatric armamentarium labile, he will add hypnosis as one of his weapons.

References

Delirus. (1905). *Treatment of disturbances of menstruation by hypnosis*. Wiener Klinische Rundschau.

Diethelm, O. (1936). *Treatment in psychiatry*. New York: Macmillan.

Eisenbud, J. (1937, September). Psychology of headache. *Psychiatric Quarterly, II*; 592.

Erickson, M. (1939, July). Experimental demonstrations of the psychopathology of everyday life. *Psychoanalytic Quarterly 8*; 39.

Erickson, M. (1943). Hypnotic investigation of psychosomatic phenomena. *Psychosomatic Medicine, 5*; 51.

Erickson, M. H. (1944, July). Hypnosis. *Medical Clinics of North America*, p. 647.

Farber, L. H., & Fisher, C. (1943). An experimental approach to dream analysis through the use of hypnosis. *Psychoanalytic Quarterly, 12*; 451.

Fisher, C. (1943, May). Hypnosis in treatment of neuroses due to war. *War Medicine, 4*: 565.

Flatan, C. (1920). *Kursus der psychotherapie und des hypnotismus*. Berlin: Kargen.

Forel, A. (1906). *Hypnotism*. New York: Ribman.

Hadfield, J. A. (1942, August). War neuroses. *British Medical Journal, I*; 320.

Heyer, G. R. (1927). *Hypnose & Hypnotherapie*. Leipzig.

Kardiner, A. (1941). *The traumatic neuroses of war*. New York: Paul Hoeber.

Kraines, S. H. (1943). *The therapy of the neuroses and psychoses.* Lea & Febiger.

Kubie, L. (1943, May). Acute war neuroses. *War Medicine,* 4; 582.

Kubie, L. (1944, January). *American Journal of Psychiatry, 100*; 58.

Kubie, L., & Erickson, M. (1941). The successful treatment of a case of acute hysterical depression by a return under hypnosis to a critical phase of childhood. *Psychoanalytic Quarterly, 10*; 584.

Mann, T. (1931). *Mario and the magician.* New York: Alfred A. Knopf.

McCortney, J. (1937, August). Hypnotism, the rational form of psychotherapy in the treatment of psychoneurosis. *Journal of Nervous & Mental Disorders, 86*; 405.

Miller, E. (1940). *The neuroses of war.* New York: Macmillan.

Paramonov, V. (1937). Hypnosis in surgery. *Khirugiya, 12*; 15.

Vogel, V. (1934). Treatment of stuttering by suggestion under hypnosis. *Hospital News,* USPHS, *1* (6).

White, R. (1941). A preface to the theory of hypnotism. *Journal of Abnormal & Social Psychology,* 36 (4).

CHAPTER 2

The Psychosomatic Factors
in Ulcerative Colitis:
A Case Report
(1946)

Since the studies of Alexander (1934), White, Cobb and Jones (1939), and others, the psychological factors in the production of mucous colitis have been carefully evaluated. However, although most clinicians have appreciated the psychosomatic factors in so-called idiopathic ulcerative colitis, there has been almost no etiological significance attached to this aspect of the disease. There are numerous theories describing etiological factors, most of which have their bases in allergic phenomena, but it is possible that the end result clinically can be produced by heterogeneous etiological factors. Dr. Edward Weiss (personal communication) feels that the initiating factor in some of these cases may be psychogenic, since there are all gradations of severity in ulcerative colitis. Murray (1930) wrote the first paper on the psychological problems of ulcerative colitis, and this was followed by Sullivan's (1932) paper in which he showed at least 60% of his cases to be on a psychosomatic basis. There has not been sufficient attention delegated to these articles.

The following protocol illustrates, more clearly than most, the etiological significance of psychological factors in certain cases of ulcerative colitis.

The patient, Mrs. A., entered the hospital in July 1944. She had had a sudden onset of bloody diarrhea, occurring three to four times a day, in April.

This lasted a week, and recurred in June with six to ten bowel movements daily. She saw her private physician at this time, and was hospitalized a few weeks later. She had recurrent episodes of stiff, swollen, painful joints. In the three months before her transfer to Stanford Hospital, she had lost 22 pounds. On entry she was a thin, very pale, young woman who was obviously tense and anxious. Physical examination revealed that her abdomen was tender and her shoulder and ankle joints were stiff and painful. Her hemoglobin was 50% Sahli, with 3.6 million red cells, and a white count of 9,000 with a normal differential. The urine, blood Wassermann, blood agglutinations and culture were normal. The stool was liquid and grossly bloody, but no pathogenic bacteria were isolated. A Frei test was negative, and an allergic survey revealed no sensitivities. X-ray studies revealed a large, smooth ("lead pipe") atonic colon with no haustrations. Proctoscopic examination to a distance of 24 cm showed friable, bleeding mucosa with many small ulcers. The diagnosis of "idiopathic chronic ulcerative colitis" was made.

The patient was treated supportively with transfusions, iron, vitamins, sedatives, bismuth, and paregoric. She was dismissed after two weeks with instructions to receive further care in the neuropsychiatric clinic. She was interviewed three times a week for the first two months, once weekly for two additional months, and is now being followed every two months.

Mrs. A. was a cooperative, intelligent and attractive woman, but during the early interviews found it very hard to talk about herself. After giving the initial history, it was only by making use of her rather extensive dreams that we were able to bring up new material. Her mother died when she was three, and the patient had no memory of her although the family spoke about their wonderful and beautiful mother; the earliest memories of her father all related to how kind and affectionate he was. When she was four, however, she was entrusted to the care of a fat, motherly housekeeper and saw very little of her father. She had never known how to account for this change, but its effect on her was marked.

When Mrs. A. was ten her father remarried. Despite her father's constant pleas, she was always quarreling with her new, domineering stepmother. She received no affection from this woman. Besides the nagging of her stepmother, there were her sisters to cope with. The oldest was nine years her senior, a quiet, unfriendly person. The twins were seven years older than she, and were noisy and constantly criticizing: "her nose was too long," "she was too quiet," "she ate too fast," etc. The patient thus had no real affection, and no one to be dependent on. She became quiet and spent hours lying on her bed, imagining that she was a princess or some other famous personage. Neither her father nor stepmother ever discussed sex with her. She had several episodes of sex-play with other children when she was small, but never masturbated although she had heard about it. Menstruation was something of a shock.

Her school period was unremarkable. She always did well, was shy but had a few friends, and never went out with boys. At college she became a little more outgoing so that in her senior year she had "dates" and did some petting. Just before graduation, she met a tall, handsome Navy Lieutenant. They went out a few times before he left for sea duty, and she carried on an active correspondence. When he returned in six months they became engaged and were married during his next two-week leave. She felt that she was in love with him, yet envied his being more extroverted. She "enjoyed" intercourse but never had an orgasm; often she would lie awake frustrated for hours afterwards. They had only two weeks of marriage when he left for sea, and her diarrhea began about two weeks after his departure.

She entered treatment willingly because she had realized that her diarrhea was associated with her emotions. The major problem in therapy was to uncover the hostility that lay under the cloak of an "if I am good they will love me" attitude. Her hostility toward her stepmother and sisters was intense, but toward her father she unconsciously maintained an ambivalent attitude. However, an excerpt from a dream late in the treatment indicates the change brought about: "I was a sentry on duty, and a car approached with a man and three women in it. I shot the women, then the man, and put down the gun as I felt I had done enough killing."

The first recurrence of diarrhea was during the second month of therapy. She had spent a night at the home of her sister and was awakened by an attack of diarrhea. This ceased after she spent the next interview ventilating hostility against this sister.

A month later a young man moved into her apartment house, and they met several times through mutual friends. He planned a weekend date with her and during the intervening days an attack began which suddenly ceased when the date was culminated. There had been conflict over wishing to spend the night with him, and it was resolved when she invited him to sleep with her. After this experience she was a different person. She had poise and confidence, spoke more freely, and took an interest in social affairs. The young man left shortly after, and she made no attempt to correspond. He was merely a passing fancy, someone with whom she "acted out."

The patient began to look forward more and more to her husband's return. She had a practical view toward the difficulties that might arise, was no longer idealizing. During the period from August to January she gained 20 pounds. On January 9, 1945, her hemoglobin was 85% and she had been having one or two bowel movements daily for three months. A barium enema at this time was reported as follows: "Haustrations are now pretty good in the transverse colon where the disease appeared fairly extensive in the previous studies, where the mucosal pattern also appeared affected. Conclusion: Remarkable improvement since previous studies."

FURTHER HISTORY

In February, her husband returned and to her astonishment asked for a divorce. He claimed that he had never really loved her and that the war had changed him. Within a day, another attack of diarrhea and bleeding began, which terminated ten days later with her decision to grant him a divorce. She also seemed to gain in self-assurance from this trying situation, and needed almost no help from the therapist in gaining an understanding of how she had placed herself in this situation by overlooking obvious incompatibilities before she married. There have been no further attacks and she has been successfully completing a postgraduate education. Her physical condition is good.

COMMENT

It is not the purpose of this report to make claims for the efficacy of psychotherapy in ulcerative colitis. However, one cannot read this history without being struck by the cause-and- effect relationship of emotion and the attacks of bloody diarrhea. It is also of interest that the rather remarkable (for this disease) improvement of the colon and the patient's general health paralleled the improvement of her psyche. This is in accord with Daniels (1942), but her medical therapists continued to hold out for an "allergic" basis. The psychiatric factors assume greater importance when the nature of the precipitating stress and the patient's personality are compared. Mrs. A. was an emotionally immature woman with a great deal of insecurity and repressed hostility. The attacks of diarrhea occurred when situations arose that threatened her security and aroused her hostility. The initial attack, for example, began when her marriage was threatened by her husband's leaving for sea duty, and when she was unconsciously angry with him.

SUMMARY

A case of ulcerative colitis is presented, and the patient's life history is discussed to show the relationship between her emotions and her disease. It is felt that relegating the emotional factors to merely a secondary role is not justified in this case.

References

Alexander, F. (1934). The influence of psychologic factors upon gastrointestinal disorders; a symposium. *Psychoanalytic Quarterly, 3*; 501.

Daniels, G. (1942). Psychiatric aspects of ulcerative colitis. *New England Journal of Medicine, 226*; 178.

Murray, C. (1930). *American Journal of Medical Science, 180*; 239.

Sullivan, A. (1932). Ulcerative colitis of psychogenic origin. *Yale Journal of Biological Medicine, 4*; 779.

Sullivan, A. (1935). Psychogenic factors in ulcerative colitis. *American Journal of Digest & Nutrition, 2*; 651.

White, B., Cobb, S., & Jones, C. (1939). Mucous colitis. *Psychosomatic Medicine*, 1 (1).

CHAPTER 3

The Relationship
of the Referring Physician
to the Psychiatrist[1]
(1952)

The relationship of the referring physician to the psychiatrist is believed to be of a different order than that of most physicians to one another. Certain facts are postulated as playing a role in this somewhat difficult relationship and examples from actual practice are offered as evidence. Among possible points of discord are mentioned: The length and cost of psychotherapy and relative youth of the specialty, the referring physician's hostile feelings toward it, and the unhelpful attitude of certain psychiatrists.

Oftentimes a physician, in referring a patient to a psychiatrist, seems to have difficulty that he would not have if he were referring to a colleague in another specialty. It seems also that if the psychiatrist is a psychoanalyst or one who does not practice neurology (often a convenient pretense for referral) the difficulty is increased. A psychiatrist may interview a patient, referred because of headache, tremor, fatigue or even "nervousness," who has been directed by the referring physician to see Dr. Smith to have his "nerves checked up." And the patient, becoming indignant when the psychiatrist starts questioning him about his emotional problems, may say: "Dr. Jones sent me here for an exami-

[1] The relationship of the referring physician to the psychiatrist. *California Medicine, 76* (6), June 391–394. Reprinted with permission.

nation." That this situation is in many instances the fault of the referring physician (and not just the patient's delicate feelings) is clear from the fact that a psychiatrist may get consistently well-managed referrals from certain physicians.

Physicians are as a rule well aware that they live perpetually in the shadow of their own ignorance; and, having the welfare of the patient at heart, they welcome special or additional knowledge from a colleague. Why, then, can a specific referral, namely, to a psychiatrist, be difficult? The reply to this question most often obtained from the referring physician is that it is so difficult a matter to broach, that the patient will feel the physician is implying he is crazy. Next most common, in the author's experience, is the answer that when the idea of seeing a psychiatrist was brought up, the patient refused it. Consider some examples:

A woman 29 years of age was referred by an internist because of tremor of the hands. The patient had been examined by a number of physicians during the previous years, had been thought to have disease of the thyroid gland, and had been given many forms of medication. When the psychiatrist started to question her about her symptoms and about the feelings related to them, the patient became actively hostile. She stated that she had seen some wonderful doctors in the last year, that nobody had told her that hers was an emotional problem, and that she was sure the doctors felt it was her "glands." On further questioning, she revealed that she was frightened and discouraged by the symptoms since they had not responded to treatment and had increased to the extent that she could not competently perform her work. She further stated that if hers was an emotional symptom she would handle it herself, and concluded the interview a short time later, rather abruptly, in tears.

A 29-year-old man consulted an internist because of pain in the right lower quadrant of the abdomen. The internist took a careful history and made a thorough physical examination. He noted that the colon was rather tender throughout. He informed the patient that this was probably attributable to emotional tension, but that he felt that radiological examination with barium enema should be carried out in order to rule out other possibilities. No abnormalities were noted in the roentgen studies. The patient was so informed and was referred to a psychiatrist immediately. He came to the psychiatrist with the statement that the internist had ruled out the possibility of physical disease, that he was relieved to know it, and that there were reasons in his life for the emotional disturbance that might be manifest in colonic tenderness. The patient had weekly interviews for eleven weeks and during that time the symptom disappeared. It was necessary to discontinue treatment, as he was leaving for another part of the country. However, the patient expressed interest in getting long-term help for several other things he had noticed about himself, when he could afford it.

Dr. A., the physician who referred the patient in the first of the two cases reported as examples, is an overworked internist who additionally burdens himself by supporting a large number of severely neurotic persons with various drugs and reassurances that chronically tie patients to him. The occasional patient he sends for psychiatric interview is usually a hostile, aggressive person with whom Dr. A. expects the psychiatrist to accomplish miracles in one interview. As a result, Dr. A. earnestly believes that psychiatrist's are of no help to him.

Dr. B. who referred the young man with the spastic colon is an excellently trained internist who himself received psychiatric help for an emotional upset that occurred during the course of his residency. The patients he refers to the psychiatrist are usually less apprehensive and better informed about what they can expect of the consultation.

On the other hand, a physician may refer a patient to a psychiatrist and be disappointed in the outcome for a number of reasons. Consider the following:

A general practitioner referred a man 24 years of age to a psychiatrist because of a diagnostic problem involving headaches. The psychiatrist in an hour-long interview informed the patient that the headaches were owing to "repressed hostility," and that he needed a number of interviews to work out hatred toward his mother. The patient did not return to the referring physician, who next heard of the case when the patient's indignant mother phoned to upbraid him for sending her son to someone who was encouraging him to "wreck their home." In addition, the referring physician learned that the psychiatrist charged $15 for the interview, whereas he himself had charged only for laboratory studies because of the family's financial status.

Dr. C., a psychiatrist, receives referrals from a number of physicians, at least in part because he is one of the few psychiatrists in the area. His fees seem overly large to his colleagues, he rarely discusses his finding with the referring physician, and his letters are replete with psychiatric jargon. After a number of visits to his office, the patients seem to find their way back to the referring physician. Dr. C. earnestly believes that the physicians in his area are not psychiatrically oriented.

It would seem that certain unrealistic attitudes and preconceived notions on the part of the referring physician and the psychiatrist make for difficulties between them. These difficulties are obviously exaggerated when either of them has personality difficulties that make collaboration impossible, or when the referring physician has a negative attitude toward psychiatry and psychoanalysis. In one group of referrals, three physicians referred seven patients ostensibly for neurological examination, and in none of the seven was neurological disease noted. On the other hand, two physicians referred six patients for psychotherapy and four of the six agreed to undergo psychotherapy including one who began psychoanalytic therapy.

The complaints about psychiatric referrals made by referring physicians seem to fall into the following categories: (1) Psychiatrists want to do too much, and therefore psychotherapy takes too long. (2) Psychotherapy is too expensive. (3) The results of treatment are poor. (4) Psychotherapy encourages patients to become too dependent on the therapist and to feel "sorry for themselves." (5) Psychiatrists are crazy or peculiar themselves. (6) Psychoanalytic theory is a lot of jargon — "especially the stuff about sex." It would perhaps be worthwhile to consider each criticism separately.

1. PSYCHOTHERAPY TAKES TOO LONG.

The natural history of medicine has been one of increase in specialization. The more that is discovered, the more arborized become the pathways of discovery. Hence it is not surprising that the 50 or so years of increasing interest in psychiatric treatment has increased realization of the complexity of the human mind and has increased awareness of the kind and extent of required intervention. It is recognized that at present there are no shortcuts to effecting durable relief to someone with severe difficulties in living. No amount of wishful thinking, zealous shoulder-patting, or exhortations to improve will more than scratch the surface of neurotic processes. Physicians do not feel defeated or frustrated because a patient with chronic rheumatic heart disease remains under continuing treatment the rest of his life. Why, then, should there be a double standard with regard to people who are emotionally upset — be they neurotic, psychotic, or otherwise?

Consider the remark of an eminent medical teacher: "I want you to meet Dr. X., our new psychiatrist. He is a very good man; he doesn't go too far with his patients." This is not to say how far he does go, but implies there is a tendency on the part of psychiatrists to go "too far." How far is that? Suppose that, instead of a psychiatrist, it was a surgeon who was being presented and that it was said of him that he was a good man because he judiciously confined himself to matters outside the dark and mysterious realm of the peritoneal cavity.

2. PSYCHOTHERAPY IS TOO EXPENSIVE.

A psychiatric interview on the average must last nearly an hour. This means that the psychiatrist cannot treat more than seven or eight patients a day, especially if he is to remain alert and intuitive. It is apparent he must charge proportionately greater fees per patient in order to compensate for the lack of volume. Statistics released by the sixth economic survey of *Medical Economics* in May 1949 revealed that psychiatrists have less gross income than most other specialists. In addition, it must be remembered that the training of a psychoanalyst takes longer and costs more than does the training of any other specialist. Oddly, the ability to do psychotherapy requires the most extensive training, yet is less remunerative to psychiatrists than shock treatment, consultations, etc.

3. THE RESULTS OF PSYCHOTHERAPY ARE POOR.

A statistical survey of the results of psychiatric treatment cannot be presented simply. This is because results depend to a large measure on the skill of the therapist (hence differing from the treatment of infectious diseases with penicillin, where the therapeutic agent is of prime importance), on the amount of time spent with any one patient (from one interview to interviews over several years), and on the degree of disorganization of the patient's interpersonal processes. A psychiatrist relies on the ego strength of the individual and his drive toward mental health to aid the therapeutic efforts. With some patients the psychic processes could be compared to exhausted bone marrow that can no longer mobilize leukocytes to aid the physician in the fight against infection. It would seem, in general, that individuals become mentally ill as a result of unfortunate experience. There is no theoretical reason to indicate that judicious psychotherapy should not be a fortunate experience. This is in contrast to the "better let well enough alone" attitude so often expressed in reference to emotionally ill people.

4. PSYCHOTHERAPY ENCOURAGES PATIENTS TO FEEL SORRY FOR THEMSELVES.

It seems to be difficult for most persons in our culture to give credence to the idea that the individual does the best he can at any given moment.

Why should it be otherwise, when we all would rather be comfortable than in distress? The terms "lazy," "stubborn," "no will power" are not merely descriptive, but imply moral censure and an unspoken "he could do better if he wanted to." Hence, a psychiatrist is up against social prejudice when he attempts to point out that certain dynamic interpersonal processes over which the individual has no control are responsible for his character traits. When the individual becomes aware of his dealings with others he adopts more healthy patterns. This is not to say that individual psychiatrists may not encourage patients to become dependent upon them (for various reasons — including prestige, power, financial gain or the physician's despair). It is to say, however, that there is nothing in the psychiatric process that makes such dependence necessary.

5.   PSYCHIATRISTS ARE CRAZY OR PECULIAR THEMSELVES.

The abundant jokes about psychiatrists are ample evidence that many people in our culture are afraid of their unconscious feelings and hence resent and fear psychiatry and psychiatrists as though they were mind readers. It is natural for them to attempt to dilute this fear by finding flaws in those of whom they are in awe. In addition, psychiatrists like other physicians have emotional reasons for choosing their particular specialty. As in any young science that is fighting for recognition, there are many radicals and reformers among the early proponents, many whose emotional problems make them zealots. Many psychiatrists also attempt to solve their own problems by treating patients. As the field has gained greater acceptance in recent years, the number of relatively stable young people entering it has increased.

6.   PSYCHOANALYTIC THEORY IS A LOT OF NONSENSE.

The average physician who sits down and reads a treatise on psychoanalysis is generally more incredulous than curious. He does not treat it with the same respect an equally incomprehensible article on neurophysiology would receive. Perhaps a partial reason is that although few of us would claim to be, or expect ourselves to be, experts in many of the various facets of medicine, most of us claim to know a good deal about human motivation and behavior — and especially about ourselves! In addition, we have some carry-over of our childhood days in our feelings of curiosity and disgust toward sexual matters, and in our fear of the unknown, the unfamiliar. It is interesting that the most eloquent and vociferous denunciators of psychoanalytic theory are, in general, those physicians who practice no systematic psychotherapy — who never, therefore, put themselves in the position of discovering whether or not certain of the tenets may be supported. In addition, psychoanalysts may interview a patient several hundred hours; therefore, they reach a depth of psychic material that cannot be judged in terms of meeting with a patient a few times. It is equally true that psychiatrists and psychoanalysts should mend their ways if they would have greater acceptance by other physicians. In the last few years there has been a real attempt on their part to "clean house," especially in regard to their mysterious and incomprehensible language. They also would do well to regard with curiosity and skepticism the universality and absolute veracity of some of their claims.

All the foregoing factors are operating when a physician refers a patient to a psychiatrist. Perhaps another example from actual practice would further this point:

A woman was hospitalized for ulcerative colitis. After life-saving medical treatment she was referred for psychiatric consultation, and it was decided she should undergo psychotherapy after leaving the hospital. After a year of therapy (one-hour interviews twice a week) she was having diarrhea only once or twice a week and an internist examined her occasionally. She was receiving vitamins and ferrous sulfate, no other medications. At this point the patient became pregnant, and this precipitated another acute attack which did not respond to medical therapy including a prolonged course of streptomycin. The psychiatrist felt that the pregnancy brought out strong unconscious fears and resentment in the patient and that this was responsible for the sudden remission. The internist urged colostomy. In alarm, the patient's family turned to the psychiatrist who felt he could not interfere with the medical treatment, but persuaded the internist to call in consultation a leading authority on that disease. The consultant felt that psychotherapy was benefiting the patient and recommended it be continued. He stated that although the patient had slight anemia and was having six to eight bowel movements a day, her state of nutrition was good and there was no need at present for heroic measures such as colostomy. From then on relations between the internist and psychiatrist became increasingly difficult. The patient, although she needed medical supervision, stopped seeing the internist because he would in an oblique manner try to undermine her belief in the efficacy of the psychiatric treatment. He also attempted to persuade the patient and her husband to get her to take a two-week trial of chloramphenicol. The psychiatrist did not take time to talk the situation over with the internist at such length that he could convince the other physician of the rationale for psychotherapy. The situation was finally resolved when the patient returned to the specialist, who had been called in consultation, who in turn referred her to another internist in the area with whom the psychiatrist was able to work out a happier relationship.

It would seem, then, that a situation such as that described, which is not unusual between psychiatrist and referring physician, might be owing to a number of factors that are constantly operating between the two physicians. Psychiatry has only recently come of age, and the referring physician has great doubts as to its value and great expectations as to how quickly results should be forthcoming. His skepticism is only increased by his over-evaluation of the psychiatrist's ability. Psychiatrists have not done enough to explain their science without over-or under-selling it. Some psychiatrists who have not had much experience with psychotherapy over-emphasize the value of organic treatments (such as shock, or lobotomy) and increase the non-psychiatric physician's doubt of the benefits of psychotherapy. The reaction of the physician against psychotherapy may stem also from another source: all persons, and hence physicians too, fear exploration of that part of their mental processes which is out of their own awareness. Therefore, it is possible that the referring physician, despite his reasonable self, unconsciously fears and hence feels hostile toward psychiatry. Despite his conscious wish to help the patient, the physician may unconsciously be putting blocks in the way of referring his patients for emotional help, or may unconsciously be interfering with the psychotherapy once it is under way. If the psychiatrist, on his part, does not take this into account, and instead behaves as if the referring physician were simply being unreasonable, then the situation will become increasingly difficult and unworkable. Experience in psychotherapy leads to at least one outstanding truth — that unreasonable fears and quiet doubts are subject to change once they come into awareness. It is possible that increasing frankness between the psychiatrist and non-psychiatric brethren will result in expediting the welfare of the patient. To make use of an implication in discoveries of recent years of the interdependency of the psyche and the soma: the psychiatrist and the non-psychiatric physician must establish the same sort of homeostasis that they are attempting to establish in the patient.

CHAPTER 4

Some Factors Influencing the Oedipus Complex[1]

(1954)

Quite often in the psychiatric and pedagogical literatures, the term "Oedipus complex" is used as if it alluded to a simple, immutable situation corresponding to the dictionary definition: "the wish of the child to kill the parent of the same sex and possess the parent of the opposite sex." Such oversimplification especially neglects the importance of the preoedipal factors in determining the outcome of the oedipal situation, as Freud himself stressed. It is our purpose here simply to point up one aspect of the oedipal situation, namely, the influence on the outcome of the Oedipus complex that results from the interaction between the two parents; making no claim to originality, the justification lies in the emphasis on the additive effect on the child of the parents' mutual

---

[1] Presented before the San Francisco Psychoanalytic Society, January 11, 1954, and before the American Psychoanalytic Association in St. Louis, Missouri, May 1, 1954.

Since this paper was written, G. L. Bibring has published a paper entitled, On the Passing of the Oedipus Complex in a Matriarchal Family Setting. *Drives, Affects, Behavior.* Edited by Rudolph M. Loewenstein. New York: International Universities Press, Inc., 1953, pp. 278–284. Her interest in the family situation that influences the Oedipus complex is similar to mine, but her paper deals largely with the effect on the male. Another relevant contribution that has recently been published is a paper by Judd Marmor, Orality in the Hysterical Personality (*Journal of the American Psychiatric Association*, I, 1953, pp. 655–659).

adaptation rather than the consideration of the parents as separate objects. I am referring only to personal forces acting at a critical period in the child's development, and such selective emphasis does not ignore intrapsychic or biological forces that obviously form the substratum of the child's development.

The clinical material presented to demonstrate one kind of oedipal triangle is obtained from six female patients who appear to show striking similarity in their manner of integrating with their parents. Two patients were in analysis, and four in long term, analytically oriented psychotherapy. The interaction of the parents seems notably alike in all six families, and in some cases the data were verified by interviews with one or both parents, or by an outside source such as the family physician. The patients ranged in age from nineteen to forty, and the diagnoses from schizophrenia to anxiety hysteria.[2] On the whole, they were attractive, slender, appealing women given to childlike joy and sadness. Superficially they appeared gentle and malleable with a certain apologetic manner. Shortly after therapy commenced, they manifested marked seductive and manipulative behavior, with great vulnerability to being hurt and serious difficulties in becoming aware of, or expressing, anger. During therapy, their apparent passivity and desire for a "strong man" to guide them underwent a transformation that included rebelliousness, envy, feelings of being used, marked acting out, and an open contempt for themselves as women. Not one of them in any way lived up to her potential artistically, professionally, or socially. Their sexual inadequacy was marked, as was their inability to recognize their intellectual capacities. They shared many symptoms in common: anorexia and insomnia, dysmenorrhea and menstrual irregularity, frigidity, headaches, eye symptoms, and migrating aches and pains. They suffered excessively from shame and embarrassment, had fears of pregnancy and of being alone, as well as phobic and counterphobic attitudes, especially street and bus phobias.

The childhood of these women was characterized by a poor relationship with the mother and a marked attachment to the father.[3] In general, their relationship with the mother improved to varying degrees after the menarche

---

[2] These patients have much in common with those described by Noble (1951) and the group discussed by Blitzsten (1936).

[3] There was a significant third person in the homes of all cases but one, the psychotic patient. It appeared in general that the more benevolent was this individual (e.g., grandmother) toward the patient, the less serious were her emotional difficulties.

while that with the father became more strained and distant. One patient's father died when she reached puberty, and in three others there was a well remembered, inexplicable retreat on the father's part especially with regard to any hint of physical intimacy. Kissing became strained and awkward, the father avoided their rooms, and two patients recalled that highly prized automobile trips with their fathers abruptly ceased. One father became rabid on the subject of bobby pins and forbade his daughter to go about with her hair 'put up' because it made her look older, but he continued to rub her chest when she had a cold until she was nearly fifteen and rebelled despite her mother's encouragement. Both parents made "dating" extremely difficult for the girl; the mother with moral innuendoes, the father with jealousy (usually recognized as such by the girl) and domination. Not one of these girls missed the unconscious cues that encouraged behavior in the opposite direction; hence all of them engaged in promiscuous sexual activity during their teens. Poor scholarship, lying and truancy were troublesome problems. As long as the girl was in difficulty, the parents functioned as a team. The father felt important and the mother felt that her dislike of the girl was justified. One father frequently commented: "What would you do without me?" whereas the mother accused her daughter of being tricky. This patient was living at home during her therapy and this afforded current observation of the parental interaction. The parents' behavior toward this girl was outlined in bold relief as their responses to the changes in her during therapy were noted. Both parents became remarkably upset, quarreled openly and violently for the first time, and veered from their previous restrictive behavior to that of ignoring her completely.[4]

Realizing the inadequacies of the method thus far pursued, I would like briefly to outline some of the more important aspects of the parents' personalities, to summarize their interaction, and to indicate the effects on the patients.

THE FATHERS

The fathers as a group were uncommonly successful in social prestige as well as in business, and were considered handsome and attractive to women.

---

[4] The whole question of what I choose to call "family homeostasis" is worthy of further study since during the therapy of one member of the family there is laboratory evidence in the counteractions of the other members for some of our speculations about human behavior. Johnson, Szurek (1952), and others have made significant contributions to our knowledge of this area.

They seemed quite close to their mothers and sisters, and to have taken family responsibilities seriously from an early age. Among the younger brothers of these men there were several psychotics and alcoholics, and two suicides. The patients regarded their fathers as frightening and humorless, but much given to teasing. They tended to be inconsistently moralistic and strict, and with all but one patient there was the distinct impression that this behavior on the father's part was reserved for home consumption. The exception occurred in the only patient who recalled no suspicion of extramarital affairs, but her father had been married previously and her mother worried about the father's attitude toward the former wife. Naturally, as far as the patients were concerned, evidence of the father's interest in other women heightened the possibility of his being interested in them rather than in the mother.

These fathers were invariably drawn toward that aspect of a situation which was flattering or somehow gave prestige. Their daughters responded to this aspect of the father's character and learned to flatter him by mimicking his behavior and interests and, by their helplessness, to make him feel indispensable. One patient described a weekly game during her pre-adolescence. The father would flip a coin to decide whether he would take the patient or her older sister to he movies. Invariably the patient lost, would resort to tears, be teased about being a poor sport, and would end up going to the movies. She used this example to demonstrate her bad luck, and was incredulous when it was pointed out that the father, and not chance, controlled the coin. It became apparent to her that there was mutual gratification in this and similar games.

In one patient's history actual incest had occurred; in another, there had been sex play between father and daughter. The seductive aspect of the relationship to the father seemed apparent in all the patients as demonstrated, for example, by care on the part of the girl to deny or keep quiet about her interest in other men. Being unintelligent, helpless, or in difficulty was calculated to increase the father's godlike propensities. This particular integration was useful when the patients got married in managing their husbands' more superficial needs. In the case of the psychotic patient, the technique was carried to such a fantastic extreme that she constantly traded good for evil with her husband. One night when he was drunk and had intercourse with another woman on their living room floor, she tenderly ministered to his subsequent hangover. Naturally, these matters when brought up during her treatment were so fraught with humiliation that they almost could not be mentioned. To a lesser extent, humiliation was a necessary ingredient in any relationship with a man for the other patients in this series.

Another common difficulty was the fear that something would happen to the father, often commencing at quite an early age and later felt to a less intense degree in relation to the husband. Such fears, usually associated with rituals and phobias, were not only hostile wishes but were in part based on the fear of being alone with mother without father as a buffer and on mother's feelings of weakness, which were tacitly expressed: 'How could we get along without him?' These fears would be abetted by the girl's helplessness through which she attempted to renounce the dangerous relationship with father. This helplessness, sometimes cloaked by ultrafemininity, also furthered the identification with mother and in each case became more marked at puberty. One of the gratifying results of therapy was the discovery of latent interests, hidden talents, and a general increase in activity.

Concisely, then, these were men who had not resolved their attachments to their mothers, which, as is frequently the case, were displaced to a daughter. In several instances the father's selection was made on the basis of a resemblance of the daughter to one of his sisters. Such fathers are exploiters of other people's dependency; they depreciate femininity because they are afraid of it, and substitute success for more human values.

THE MOTHERS

The mothers of these daughters had all of the semblance of motherhood — if none of the feelings. They seemed to have been rather dependent on their own mothers and the maternal grandmother usually was an important figure in the home during the patient's childhood. The mothers married men who gave them material security and from whose success they gained reflected glory. They tended to be zealous housekeepers and to be overly interested in possessions. Four of the mothers discussed their fear and loathing of sex with their daughters while the latter were still preadolescents. In no instance was the mother the father's social equal, and though some of the daughters could appear as adequate socially as their fathers, they did not feel equal.

Harris (1953) has shown that the failure to recognize a resemblance between herself and her daughter by the mother is associated with emotional disturbance in the daughter. It is of probable significance that four patients had brothers (whom the mothers preferred) and their preference was for male children. The fifth patient had a preferred older sister and her desire was for a girl child. The sixth patient was an only child and she also wished for a girl, with the same name as her own. It was rather as if each of these patients served as a repository for unacceptable feelings on the part of both parents. The mother of the psychotic patient was the one in this series who most obviously hated in the child those things she hated about herself. The patient was the third-born, as had been her mother, and she repeated with her third-born girl many features of her mother's behavior toward her. However, even in this situation it was possible to see the protective aspect of the relationship to the father: the patient who had three daughters and no sons gave them boys' names, the eldest daughter's being composed of her father's and her husband's initials.

It was generally true that these patients were not allowed to participate in feminine activities around the house. There is evidence to indicate that the mothers used the daughters, in part, to play a role with the husband in which they did not themselves feel comfortable. One of the choice epithets hurled in anger at the daughter was, "You're just like your father," or "You are a typical Jones," or whatever name was that of the father's family. The fact that the mother had no interests in common with the father aided the girl in believing she would make the father a more suitable wife. The patient who had several incestuous experiences with her father felt pushed by her mother into taking trips with him, and it was on one of these trips that the sexual experiences took place. At one point during treatment she burst out furiously with: "She couldn't satisfy him herself so she had to turn him loose on me."[5] Almost without exception the mothers were pleased only if the daughters had male children, and cautioned them against having more children after the first pregnancy. The typical comment for the patient to make to the therapist about such recollections was: "If I had any doubts about my being unwanted, I knew then it was true."

THE FAMILY INTERACTION

On the surface the parents presented a picture of serenity, orderliness, and religiosity. Despite the lack of intimacy, their mutual dependency decreed that there be no divorces and no separations. The psychotic woman's mother returned to her family's home on her wedding night, but was persuaded to resume the honeymoon three days later. In general, the surface picture of parental harmony was seen through by the little girl although the majority of her perceptions were not within awareness.

---

[5] I feel it would be unwise to regard this comment strictly as a projection.

During the course of therapy the patients were confounded by their own discrepant statements, such as (in two cases) becoming aware that the mother had made suicidal attempts, yet describing her as a contented, self-sufficient person. In these households people did not really communicate. The fiction was prevalent that father was tired, worried, or busy and could not be bothered. The mothers got satisfaction out of abetting this myth, at least in part because it excused their own need for distance. It is no wonder then that the girl's troubles provided a vicarious outlet for the parents, as well as a common emotional meeting ground. Despite the unconscious turmoil, the parents tended to stick together in disciplinary matters The girl was literally unable to talk to one about the other regardless of how unfairly she felt she had been treated, but there were many instances in which the daughter could get something from the father that the mother had refused or had been doubtful about. It does not appear to have been entirely a parental disagreement, but rather a further illustration of the mother encouraging the girl into seductive behavior and the father going along with it. The great discrepancy between surface behavior and unconscious emotion in the parental interaction seems to have been a major factor in the impulse-ridden and acting-out aspects of these patients' personalities. They were warned to be good, yet incited to rebellion; they were shown parental compatibility, yet invited to intervene and alienate. One mother who remarked frequently, "If you don't stop bothering him, he won't have anything to do with you," was covertly encouraging her daughter into activity that led to sexual encounters with her father. The tendency of the parents to appear to be in agreement seems to have encouraged acting out, partly as an attempt to reach them and also to split them.

That this kind of integration was necessary for the parents is verified by two remarriages after the deaths of the spouses. The father of the psychotic patient remarried a year after his wife's death, and the stepmother's traits of character were exaggerations of the major emotional difficulties of the mother; her father's second marriage was one of the chief factors in the patient's own hasty marriage. The mother of another patient remarried some years after the father had died, and at a time when her two oldest daughters would no longer give her bed and board. She frankly told the patient of her feelings of revulsion toward physical intimacy, yet she encouraged the daughter to kiss the stepfather and to "butter him up" so he would buy her things. The fact that these mothers felt like children in their marriages is supported by a number of clinical items: there was an age difference of fifteen years between two sets of parents;

several of the mothers did not have children for some years after marriage; a surprising number of spontaneous and induced abortions occurred; frustration, tears, and helplessness were frequently the response to their children's obstreperous behavior; and neurasthenia pervaded the atmosphere of the mother's bedrooms.

In general, the patients themselves made surprisingly durable marriages. Only one, the psychotic woman, was divorced after 19 years of marriage. She was also the only one of the group who married a man like her father, and the only one in the group whose husband was obviously unfaithful. The others married men who took maternal attitudes toward their wives,[6] and tended to be moderately successful, nonaggressive men who helped about the home and were exceedingly patient with their wives' sexual ineptitudes. The patients were generally fond of their husbands, but with an admixture of contempt. It became apparent that they were experiencing alternating fear of the husband's success and masculinity and a desire to show him up. One patient symbolized the dilemma by the fantasy of a huge penis that attacked and split her in two, and by imagining that she ripped off her husband's penis and beat him over the head. I believe that a factor in not having to marry men similar to their fathers was the fathers' dependence on their wives; though this attachment was denied in the father's surface behavior, it became increasingly apparent as his sexual life declined with age. The daughter's awareness of being used by the father seemed to be another factor in picking someone he did not like.

Toward their children these women showed much conscious effort to provide what they had not had, and male children posed fewer problems. They were partially inclined to take a father's role, that is, to play the kind of games with the children that would more customarily be allotted to the father. Beneath the surface there was resentment against the husband for not doing more, which seemed to be displacement from their dissatisfactions with their mothers. The psychotic patient, for example, decided impulsively to pack up her three children and ship them to their father since she was such a poor mother. When it was pointed out that the real motive in part was to get even with the husband, she had a series of associations about her mother's indiffer-

---

[6] Since this paper was written the young unmarried patient has become engaged. Her fiancé is reported to be: "The only boy I ever brought home that mother had anything good to say about." Her father was unable to veil his jealousy and arranged for a three months' pleasure trip for himself, without his wife.

ence to her children and that she had mothered her younger siblings and, as a result, had had to give up a good deal of social activity.

In summary, the salient features of the tripartite interaction are:

1. None of the mothers was completely rejecting. In all cases but the psychotic patient, the mother permitted a third person to manifest tenderness toward her daughter. As the girl grew older, the mother invariably evinced dependency needs toward her which produced a variety of feelings in the daughter, including superiority, guilt, and contempt. Most of the patients had occupations or activities that brought them into contact with "helpless" women who needed them.

2. The father's closeness to and overt interest in his daughter was the reverse of the mother's in that it tended to decrease as the child grew older and, in some instances, was abruptly terminated at the menarche. The father's narcissism forbade signs of aggressiveness in the girl, and his incestuous fears produced alienation and sporadic hostile, seductive behavior toward his daughter. These elements in the father's personality caused a characteristic response in the girl: "I can overcome father's indifference if I provoke him and make him angry." This, in turn, led to manifest fear about the consequences of the provocation.

3. To say that the daughter clings to the father because the mother rejects her is an oversimplification. As Ferenczi said, "You cannot renounce that which you have not had." These women never really rejected their mothers, though on the surface they appeared remarkably unfriendly toward them. The daughters were scapegoats for both parents. One set of parents quarreled openly before the patient was born, but following her propitious arrival they no longer even disagreed. Another set of parents were not known to quarrel until their daughter had been in therapy approximately a year. One of the obvious kinds of interaction is the mother's encouragement of the girl to do what she cannot; namely, be seductive with the father and get the better of him. One mother laughed delightedly at the sight of her daughter seated on the father's lap and stated, "You are going to be an old man's darling." The father, in turn, may depreciate his wife by demonstrating to her that his daughter in more feminine, or a more satisfactory companion, than she.

4. These patients have been trained symbiotically to feed on triadic involvement. This is most apparent when they are interacting with only one person and must in fantasy involve a third, as though they feel no ego wholeness without a collection of part egos. One of the prices paid for this need to interact in two directions at the same time is a multifaceted inferiority feeling. For example, these women equate head and penis, hence intellect and maleness. Regardless of their actual performance, they question their ability. Associations during therapy reveal a connection between intellectual ability, exhibitionism, humiliation, and castration, and an accompanying sexual excitement and fear when competing intellectually. There is a need to appear stupid, and yet a fierce intellectual competitiveness. These reactions may be accounted for by noting that father's narcissism encourages the little girl to show off for him, but strictly limits any performance that threatens him. On the other hand, he is constantly fostering helplessness. Mother is subtly encouraging in the hope that father will be defeated, but she cannot back up the child if there is a clash. In addition, there is a natural resentment and rivalry if the daughter shows her up and wins the father's praise. Doubtless this kind of description appears unnecessarily awkward, but it is essential to stress the tripartite aspect of the patients' interactions; in effect, father's interest in her makes her miss mother less — especially if she can have his child — but this unconscious solution increases the fear of the mother's retaliation.

In adolescence, five of the six patients acted out their infantile fantasies. There was a "good guy," attentive and reliable, and a "bad guy," fascinating, seductive, and unreliable. With the first they felt secure, but contemptuous and guilty; with the second, hurt and angry, but always hopeful of reform. With the unreliable man, pregnancy fantasies were frequent and accompanied by amenorrhea. The fantasies of pregnancy were not only a wanting to possess the father; they were also related to becoming a mother rather than being a girl who needed a mother. The fantasy is thus in part an attempt to gratify an oral need in the relationship with the father. As these women were disappointed by both parents, the feeling of deprivation was augmented by their own biting and castrative wishes. The oral fantasies of being poisoned by the mother were represented in fears, which equated semen with being soiled, and the like.

Pregnancy fantasies were among those most recurrent and, like memories of playing with dolls, were associated with loneliness and the need for "something" to love. All of these women had had irregular menstruation prior to therapy, and during therapy each had at least one period of amenorrhea associated with the fantasy of being pregnant. Five of the six had at least one sudden, unexpected onset of menstruation. Four recalled similar delayed and premature menstrual periods associated with their adolescent sexual experiences. The father's seductive attitude toward the daughter (and other women) gave a basis in reality for these fantasies. The replacement of loneliness by the fantasy of being a mother, instead of a child needing a mother, is an identification with the baby as well as a fulfillment of the oedipal fantasy.

TECHNICAL IMPLICATION

The first patient in this series was in many ways the most difficult. Mistakes made in her therapy led to disturbing, dangerous acting out. For a time hospitalization was considered. However, the intensity of the expectation of punishment, sexual fears, fear of being trapped (father), and of being abandoned (mother) dissuaded what, in this case, might have been ineradicable intervention. The obvious, intense sexual fears (wishes) were interpreted time and again, and such interpretations were apparently successful during the sessions, but the wispy tie between patient and therapist would dissolve in the aloneness of the world outside the psychiatrist's office. At last it was discovered that the sexual material was intense and threatening because the hatred of mother and need for her created a desperate clinging to father; but father, as a protector, was unsatisfactory because he could not stand the patient's demands and hatefulness nor his feelings toward her. The therapist, naturally, came to occupy a similar role, and similarly was not put to the test. For example, in a dream of one patient she usurped the analyst's chair and he started to tuck a blanket about her (as one would in putting a child to bed) but became greatly uneasy and fled from the room. He returned in a few moments chagrined and angry and ordered the patient out.

In this case and in some subsequent ones, the therapist's rendering it possible to bring out the feelings about mother was most effective in controlling the acting out. Learning to deal with the bad mother inside one means the need for father is less profound and the sexual fears correspondingly less intense. Freud pointed out that a male therapist would be less suitable for understanding the mother transference and predicted we would learn more about the oedipus situation as more women become analysts. To some extent this difficulty can be overcome technically by the male therapist's being alerted to this role of a masculine love object and a mothering one. There are many opportunities for male–female interpretations in dreams, fantasies, etc., such as objects being eaten that are not only father's testicles but are also breasts. Especially in regard to material dealing with pregnancy, the analyst should remain alert for the shadow of mother behind the father transference, in contrast to our usual tendency to deal first with one and then the other.

A further aid in the technical management of these patients was to regard the fear of abandonment not as fear of retaliation alone, but also as the result of the patients' real experiences; hence, questioning about periods when the mother was absent either physically or because of withdrawal did not fail to produce important recollections, especially of depressions and mysterious illnesses on the part of the mothers.

SUMMARY

Clinical material from a group of six female patients is presented to characterize a type of reaction related to emotional difficulties in their oedipal situation as a consequence of the special circumstances of their rearing. This communication attempts to emphasize the specific character of the parental interaction as a decisive factor in the patient's personality. From their behavior, these women appeared to have a strong sexual attachment to the father and they were constantly creating triangular situations in their personal relationships. Beneath this lay an unresolved longing for the mother that kept them from genuinely relating to men or to women. Their lack of identification with the mother and overcompensatory attachment to the father made them feel like boys who despised their femaleness and were afraid of and competitive with men. The main devices for escaping their unbearable dilemma were pregnancy fantasies or actual childbearing. The parental interaction constituted a nidus for the development of the girl's hysterical phobic symptoms, and acting out.

References

Abraham, K. (1941). *Selected papers*. London: Hogarth Press.

Blitzsten, L. (1936). Amphithymia. *Archives of Neurology & Psychiatry, 36.*

Brunswick, R. M. (1940). The preoedipal phase of the libido development. *Psychiatric Quarterly, 9.*

Erikson, E. H. (1950). *Childhood & society.* New York: W. W. Norton.

Fenichel, O. (1945). *The psychoanalytic theory of neurosis.* New York: W. W. Norton.

Freud, S. (1929). *Introductory lectures on psychoanalysis.* London: Allen & Unwin.

Freud, S. (1930). *Three contributions to the theory of sex.* Revised edition. New York: Nervous & Mental Disease Monographs.

Freud, S. (1933). *New introductory lectures on psychoanalysis.* New York: W. W. Norton.

Freud, S. The passing of the Oedipus complex. *Collected Papers,* II.

Freud, S. Some psychological consequences of the anatomical distinction between the sexes. *Collected Papers,* V.

Freud, S. Female sexuality. *Collected Papers,* V.

Fromm, E. (1948). The Oedipus complex and the Oedipus myth. In R. Anshen (Ed.), *Family, its function & destiny.* New York: Harper & Brothers.

Greenacre, P. (1950). General problems of acting out. *Psychiatric Quarterly, 11.*

Harris, I. (1953). On recognition of resemblance. *Psychiatry, 14.*

Hilgard, J. (1951). Sibling rivalry & social heredity. *Psychiatry, 14.*

Hilgard, J. (1953). Anniversary reactions. *Psychiatry, 16.*

Hill, L. B. (1950). The importance of identification with a father figure in the psychology of a woman. In *Feminine psychology: Its implication for psychoanalytic medicine.* New York Medical College-Flower Hospital.

Johnson, A. M., & Szurek, S. A. (1952). The genesis of antisocial acting out in children and adults. *Psychiatric Quarterly, 21.*

Kanzer, M. (1950). The Oedipus trilogy. *Psychiatric Quarterly, 19.*

Kubie, L. S. (1953). Some implication for psychoanalysis of modern concepts of the organization of the brain. *Psychiatric Quarterly, 22.*

Mullahy, P. (1948). *Oedipus myth & complex.* New York: Hermitage.

Noble, D. (1951). Hysterical manifestations in schizophrenic illness. *Psychiatry,* XIV.

Romm, M. E. Unresolved Aggression & Femininity. In *Feminine Psychology. Its implications for psychoanalytic medicine. Loc. cit.*

Silverberg, W. (1938). The personal basis & social significance of passive male homosexuality. *Psychiatry,* I.

CHAPTER 5

Office Treatment of Ambulatory Schizophrenics[1]

(1954)

There are many advantages of treating schizophrenic patients outside a hospital setting, if it can be managed. These advantages include the lesser pecuniary cost to the family and patient and the maintenance of the patient's self-esteem by his continued life in the community, particularly if he can be kept at some sort of gainful occupation. There is also a tendency for schizophrenic persons to increase their loss of contact with reality if, as in a hospital, they are taken care of and not expected to assume any responsibility for themselves.

The office treatment of a schizophrenic person entails special problems not only of therapy but of dealing with relatives and the community. It is felt that attention to these matters results in the successful social restoration of patients who formerly would have been thought too ill to remain outside a hospital setting. Although this is among the most demanding work a psychiatrist can engage in, the rewards are great.

Schizophrenia appears to be one of the major medical problems facing physicians in the United States. Psychotherapy of schizophrenic persons has increased considerably in the past ten to 15 years. Since treatment of this kind

---

[1] *California Medicine*, Vol. 81, No. 4, Oct., pp. 263–267. Presented before the Section on Psychiatry and Neurology, 83rd Annual Session, California Medical Association, Los Angeles, May 9–13, 1954. Reprinted with permission.

has proven valuable in hospital settings, increasing attempts are being made to carry out psychotherapy for schizophrenic patients who are not hospitalized. It has come to be recognized that in many cases severe regressive phenomena can be prevented in psychotic persons if they can be kept out of the hospital. Especially if a patient can work and manifest some semblance of social living, his self-esteem is bolstered. There is a not unimportant financial aspect as well.

Probably no facet of psychiatric practice demands more of a therapist, in terms of ability and patience, than treatment of schizophrenic persons in an office, for he lacks the support of colleagues and staff that he has in a mental hospital: he bears heavy responsibility for a patient who may be, or may become, a danger to himself and to others; and, last but not least, he must withstand the anxious interference of relatives and occasionally of the community. Especially in regard to acting out, hostility, and unutterable demands by the patient, the therapist's inscrutability may undergo severe trial. Small wonder, then, that many psychiatrists regard the whole procedure of psychotherapy with ambulatory schizophrenic patients as an unlikely business, and all too readily become discouraged. Perhaps discouragement can be forfended, however, by consideration and discussion of some important practical matters that, if left unattended, may result in subsequent difficulty.

The first and foremost such matter is the therapist's awareness of whether or not he really wishes to undertake treatment of a given patient. If one has the opportunity to supervise the therapy of schizophrenics by others, he may discover that occasionally the venture is begun with unnoticed reluctance on the part of the therapist. There may be, for instance, evidence of a peculiar rigidity and the need to hold fast to a set schedule that cherishes the psychiatrist's time. Or there may be a coldness during unasked-for phone calls by the patient and a need to make it overly clear to the patient that his "demands will not be met here."

Perhaps under pressure from the patient's family or from colleagues, and with an eye to the prestige value of "handling anything that comes along," the therapist may begin treatment when he is secretly reluctant to do so. The important thing in treatment of schizophrenic patients in the office is that the psychiatrist must be able to enter into an agreement with himself whereby he recognizes there will be unusual and unscheduled demands on his time and patience, and be disposed to pay the price. It is essential that the psychiatrist feel all arrangements, including the financial ones, are to his satisfaction before he undertakes treatment.

The therapist's evaluation of the patient's difficulties will naturally play a part in his decision as to whether to undertake treatment or not. However, evaluation of "how sick the patient is," of "ego strength" and such matters is highly speculative, especially in light of the present-day diagnostic scheme. The estimate is perhaps as much a matter of experience and empathy for the patient as anything else. Sometimes psychological testing may be helpful. An illustrative example occurred in the case of a 40-year-old man who was referred by an internist as having a problem in adjustment. The patient had had a position that required a good deal of foreign travel, and apparently had symptoms as a result of "settling down." He was well dressed, intelligent and prepossessing; and although he answered questions readily, somehow he did not seem to be adequately communicative. After three interviews, there was still a question about the extent of the patient's difficulties and a Rorschach test was done. It revealed a rather well controlled psychogram, but the content seemed to indicate that the patient was psychotic with crumbling control. In the next interview, a more alert and active approach disclosed that the patient felt there was a microphone hidden in the room and had decided on its exact location.

Once it has been decided the patient is psychotic and that psychotherapy should be initiated, a number of practical decisions arise. The frequency of interviews requires careful thought. If the patient is one who is felt to require strong support, it might be decided to see him three or more times a week at the start. Such frequency may also curb harmful "acting out" and lessen suicidal risk. However, it is also an invitation for the patient to become overdependent on the therapist, and such involvement may require years to straighten out. If the therapist is prepared to do intensive long-term psychotherapy, the involvement may do no harm; if not, it may invite a disastrous outcome if the frequency of interviews is cut after an initial supportive period. For example, one patient was greatly concerned about the cost of treatment. Since she was being interviewed three times a week she was asked if she would feel less preoccupied with finances if she cut down to twice a week. This apparently simple, obvious suggestion brought about a week of extremely psychotic behavior. On another occasion she had come in for an extra appointment and it had been agreed that she would skip the next regular meeting. The night before the meeting that she was to miss, she had an extremely frightening dream in which she saw herself among a group of extremely sick patients in a mental hospital and all of them were being treated by the psychiatrist except herself. She felt utterly lost and alone, and was quite depressed for two days.

In general it is desirable for less experienced therapists to see patients once or perhaps twice a week; and if therapy is begun along more ambitious lines, it is necessary that the psychiatrist expect to maintain the pace for some while. Naturally, the patient's financial resources have to be determined before any decision as to frequency can be made.

Another practical matter is: Who else should be concerned in the treatment? Some patients are best dealt with if another physician serves as an administrator. The other physician is not only someone the patient can turn to when the therapist is absent, but can handle medication, deal with questions referable to the patient's job or family, and serve as someone the patient can use to let the therapist know indirectly how things are going.

Then, as to the family: Should they be brought into the treatment, used for history-taking purposes, given instructions as to behavior toward the patient, and kept *au courant* with what goes on in psychotherapy? This again is a matter worthy of thought. If the patient seems able to get along by himself, and especially if he is not financially dependent on his family, it may be expeditious to enforce the idea that this is his treatment and his alone. In these circumstances the patient may feel free to respond to the psychiatrist's confidence in him, and not to involve the therapist in the hatred toward the family. On the other hand, if the success of the treatment will depend on the family's humor, it is simply logical to become an exponent of tact and diplomacy. Should the possibility exist of getting a family member to talk things over with another therapist, it should be seized with alacrity. There is another point here that is often overlooked. The patient's illness has a certain utility as far as the interrelationships within his particular family are concerned. If he starts to get well, all sorts of surprising events may occur in those nearest and dearest to him. If, for example, the therapist has reason to believe that a psychotic husband is integrated in an intense mutually hostile and dependent relationship to his wife, provision must be made for disruptive changes in her as the patient improves. Occasionally, the psychiatrist must insist that the patient cannot undertake treatment unless the other person who is in significant relationship with the patient is also undergoing therapy. Failure to do so may, in extreme cases, lead to suicide, psychosis or severe psychosomatic disorders arising in the spouse or relative.

Another practical consideration concerns how treatment should commence. One might take an exhaustive history, let the patient "free associate," or attempt to discover the precipitating causes of the present difficulty. Here again, the principle of flexibility must apply. There seems little point to questioning the patient about his childhood if the present-day world is falling in ruins about him. A history is useful if it can be obtained with a minimum of inconvenience and anxiety, but perhaps too often a therapist feels a need to get something into the record that will protect him and will serve as a source of data for a letter to the referring physician. Many psychotic persons will state that in retrospect they recognize that they inadvertently stated the central problem of their illness in the first few interviews. In other words it is well to commence by listening and by asking simple questions that clarify the patient's present difficulties in living. If this can be done against a background of knowledge of his past, the listening and questioning may be more meaningful.

A useful frame of reference to guide the therapist's activity is the realization that the patient has missed certain valuable experiences in the growing-up period and has lacked, therefore, the opportunity to consensually validate these experiences. He does not know the relief and joy that can occur in the chum relationship by finding out the chum has had similar experiences. Certain of these "lacks" cannot be mentioned to the psychiatrist either because they are not apparent to the patient as hiatuses in his maturation or because he feels so foolish about them and so unique. Therefore the psychiatrist may have to guess on the basis of his won experience and knowledge of the culture in which we live in order to fill in the blanks for the patient. For example, a patient was walking downtown and was whistled at by a young woman who passed in a car. He had quite a striking reaction to the experience and walked back around the block to see if she was possibly interested in picking him up only to find that she had disappeared. The patient spoke of his frustration and uneasiness in relation to the incident and then there was a rather uncomfortable pause. The psychiatrist mentioned that it would not be unusual for masturbatory ideas to occur following such an exciting but frustrating incident: and the patient, very relieved, expressed agreement and amazement that his feelings were by no means unique. Intervention of this kind is more than simply emotional support because it also aids the patient's maturation. He did not have a chance to discuss masturbation with his peers during his early adolescence.

There is another possible aid for the therapist in understanding experiences the patient is relating; namely, hearing what is said in terms of actual present-day experience and not initially as a projection. This is not to say the past experience is not coloring the present, nor that the patient is not reliving an old story so that he has gotten himself into the present situation because of the past, but it is to say that one's approach can be unacceptable to the patient if the reality of the present-day situation is taken into account. Thus a young schizophrenic man was relating his concern and feeling of responsibility toward a girl he was dating. The therapist, rather than jumping at what he knew to be true — namely, that the patient had a tendency to feel overwhelmingly responsible for women as a way of integrating with them — asked in what way the girl might be making the patient feel responsible. The patient confessed that the girl had a suicidal preoccupation and had pledged him to silence about it, but that bearing the responsibility made him uneasy. He broke into a real grin following the discussion and expressed gratitude that he was not treated as if he were simply putting ideas into a situation in which they did not belong. He described an experience that had happened on several occasions when he was hospitalized: A psychiatrist would urge him to talk, but then point out how unreal what he said was.

It is also useful in therapy if the therapist will make a practice of discussing dependence before hostility. The patient mentioned in the preceding paragraph had a serious problem because of his passive resistance to schoolwork. Rather than taking it up simply as a "spite reaction," the therapist inquired into the patient's earliest school experiences. After some hours of work, it was established that the original reluctance toward school was related to fear that his mother was going to leave when she sent him to school and that she would not be there when he got back. When he was at school there was such a horrible preoccupation with what might be going on at home that it became impossible for him to keep up with his fellows even though he was quite bright. The helplessness was in part controlled by seeing himself as spiteful, that is, powerful in some way.

Many of the difficulties and technical problems mentioned were encountered in a female patient who had been schizophrenic for a year before psychotherapy was undertaken. Just before she was observed by the author, she had fled from another city a great distance away under the impelling delusion that her life was in danger there. She was not hospitalized because she had three children and it was considered of great importance to her that she somehow continue to care for them. She had been a Cinderella all her life, and scullery work and caring for the children were an avocation as well as a culturally prescribed behavior. In addition, she had relatives in the area who would undertake some of the responsibility for looking after her. Psychotherapy was begun at a frequency of three times a week, and it was felt that if a strong rapport were established with her it might be possible to attack rather directly some of the processes responsible for her extreme guilt and suicidal urges, and at the same time to increase, if even slightly, the satisfactions in her daily living. The delusions, hallucinations and other evidences of psychotic thinking were rarely dealt with, since it was felt that a change in her living would result in the minimizing of the need to be psychotic. The exception to the above was that evidence of "craziness" in relation to the person of the therapist was dealt with firmly, often sarcastically and, on occasion, histrionically.

One of the sources of support that was deliberately exploited was the need of the children for her. They were no easy crew, in themselves, but her mastery of even simple practical problems in day to day living aided her Lilliputian self-esteem. When, for example, some months after therapy had begun, she announced that she was shipping the children off to their father, since she was such a terrible mother, it was possible for the therapist to intervene with the fervent comment: "You'd really like to fix the so-and-so, wouldn't you?" Time does not permit further disclosure of events in this case. Suffice to say that the patient was of a type the author once would not have considered treatable outside a hospital setting.

CHAPTER 6

The Therapist's Personality in the Therapy of Schizophrenics[1]

(1955)

As our knowledge of psychotherapy with schizophrenics increases, it becomes more apparent that the attitude and reactions of the therapist are of much greater importance in the treatment situation than is the case with neurotics. It seemed to me important to outline the kinds of difficulties therapists are apt to encounter in doing intensive psychotherapy with psychotics, and, if possible, to determine what attitudes in the therapist are most likely to engender or foster technical problems in therapy. It is important to stress that this is an impressionistic and biased account of the problem.

Most therapists who work with schizophrenics seem to experience intense anxiety at times. If the therapist can accept this and can understand its origin, he may not be too threatened when his uneasiness is apparent to the patient, his colleagues, or other staff members. If it is recognized that one can be an adequate therapist without being uniformly serene, then the therapist may allow himself to get close to the patient without the vertical distance so often necessary for the maintenance of prestige. It seems unlikely that one can treat a disturbed schizophrenic without suffering certain "indignities," such as being ridiculed, scorned, ignored, disarranged, or assaulted. These are not

---

[1] *AMA Archives of Neurology & Psychiatry*, 74, 292–299. Reprinted with permission.

actions one has been led to believe should happen to a physician, and the status hierarchy of the mental hospital does not make the problem any easier.

Early in my work with schizophrenics, it was usual to feel humiliated as I passed the nurses' station after interviews with disturbed patients. Occasionally, my clothing would be somewhat disarrayed and the patient would be screaming curses at me as I walked down the hall. I imagined that the nurses were laughing at the sorry spectacle that I presented, and I often tried to cover up my humiliation by telling wonderfully rich tales about the patient's progress in therapy.

Some of the anxiety which any therapist experiences with psychotics seems to arise from the peculiar problem in communication which such patients pose. The difficulty in understanding what the patient is saying may produce helplessness and resentment in the therapist, and he may be further dismayed by doubt as to the best method of intervention. Should he be silent, make a "direct" interpretation, or concentrate on body language? (Rosen, 1953; Fromm-Reichmann, 1939, 1942) There are the elements of a vicious cycle present, and nowhere is it more apparent than in the problem of handling prolonged silences. The patient's silence becomes more of a personal rebuke as the therapist's helplessness increases, and the therapist is apt to respond with punishing phrases that are draped in a thin veil of, "for your own good," to which the patient responds with a more prolonged silence. On a number of occasions therapy is broken off at this point, perhaps by the therapist thinking in terms of shock therapy or lobotomy or by emphasizing the patient's social participation in the hospital.

Another difficulty peculiar to this kind of therapy is the schizophrenic's ability to pick up nonverbal cues as to what is going on in other people. The patient may notice evidence of anxiety which the therapist unwittingly has tried to hide. This ability of the schizophrenic arises, of course, from his early experience with significant others. Because he feels as though he has been living in a hostile jungle, he has learned to develop certain methods for handling potential danger; one of these methods is to understand that people do not always mean what they say, and he learns to examine carefully any kind of cues that the environment offers. This ability, while quite real, may have exaggerated manifestations, as when a patient distorts a non-harmful situation into a harmful one. The therapist beginning work with a schizophrenic may be inclined to be overtly impressed with the "mind reading" ability of the patient and overlook the mistakes in evaluation of other people that the schizophrenic makes because of the lack of awareness of his own feelings and lack of experience in living.

For example, a beginning therapist was much impressed with the fact that a schizophrenic woman patient detected hostility in a third person, which the therapist had completely missed until the patient called it to his attention. He later discovered that the patient also detected what she believed to be hostility when no confirmation could be found for it and when the patient had no evidence to support her observation. He realized in this situation that she was angry herself, but unaware of it.

While the therapist must be alert to the patient's tendency to confuse his inner feelings with what he finds in the environment, he must at the same time be accepting of the validity of the patient's experiences as they are related. Otherwise, the therapist may fail to pay enough attention to the patient's actual experiences and convey the idea that all feelings and impressions are "projections." Once the therapist evinces skepticism, the patient tends to omit any confirmatory or explanatory data, confirming, in turn, the therapist in his suspicion that this is a distortion of some sort. The reality of the patient's situation must be discussed first before the therapist attempts to find out how much of the patient's past experience is coloring the present, or the patient may cease his attempt to communicate effectively.

A particularly troublesome situation may arise in the treatment of schizophrenics who are partially masking their psychotic difficulties by hysterical symptoms, which include a tendency to dramatize. The therapist may be tempted to intervene by cracking down on the patient and may be unusually alert to the possibility of the patient's exploiting him. The patient's inability to face the tragedy of his illness is furthered by the therapist's attitude, since they both, in effect, focus on the patient's demands or unreasonableness and neglect his difficulty in communicating his underlying loneliness and despair. The therapist who sees the patient in the present and in the past at the same time is not apt to respond only to present symptoms or to over-look the reality of the person who is currently living in an unhappy situation. Similarly, the accepting therapist seems most frequently to interpret dependency before hostility. He realizes that the patient's acceptance of his dependent needs strengthens the therapeutic relationship and allows hostile feelings to emerge with less fearfulness and guilt on the patient's part.

The ability to keep in mind the child but not neglect the adult is of help also as the transference becomes intense. In psychiatric supervisory work one may note at some point in the case being presented that the therapist is responding to a picture the patient has of him, and that the therapist has given the supervisor many cues about this situation, although unaware of it himself. It is as though the patient's transference is perceived unconsciously by the therapist as a *Gestalt*, to which he then reacts before he has consciously assembled the pieces of the puzzle. As the patient describes his picture of the therapist, the therapist may experience uneasiness lest this unflattering picture corresponds too closely to his character; and he may, in effect, then tell the patient to "stop feeling that way."

For example, a schizophrenic woman was able to make her male therapist anxious by her demands and by behaving as if she couldn't live without him, an integration which she had learned early in her childhood. Unfortunately, the therapist had had so much experience with somewhat similar women in his own life that he saw himself as the patient did. He began to confuse the patient, his wife, and his mother in his dreams and tried to be firm toward the patient and to convince her that she was not a weak twig. The treatment situation began to degenerate still further when the patient accused the psychiatrist of hating her, as her husband obviously did; the therapist could confirm her suspicions all too well in his contemplative hours away from the patient. This awkward situation began to be resolved when the therapist, through supervision and his own therapy, began to realize that there was a great deal of difference, in degree at least, between the patient's transference picture of him and his own picture of himself. He saw, more specifically, that the patient's demanding ways arose because of her own extreme inability to tolerate any anxiety whatsoever and that she used involvement with other people as a defense.

Other difficulties in communication may arise from the therapist's need to assure himself and the patient that he is not afraid or anxious. He may develop the habit of staring at the patient as if to demonstrate a lack of uneasiness and may succeed in making the shy patient quite uncomfortable. Another forceful technique is the attempt to "pin the patient down." This consists in asking questions in a district attorney fashion, so that "one gets clear on something," or to demonstrate the patient's lack of contact with reality. The questions are often handled by the patient with a "yes" or "no" answer, and the amount of information garnered starts as a trickle and rapidly diminishes to drops. If an open-ended question can be phrased in a fashion that does not require a humiliating answer, the subject under discussion may be expanded by the patient. The manner of asking questions and clues as to their phrasing

depend to some extent on the realization that the patient may not be just resistant or negativistic but may be protective of hiatuses in his own life experience. The lack of chum relationships and the opportunity to validate consensually his experience in living with another person (Sullivan, 1940) imply that
the schizophrenic has little knowledge of the relief and joy that come through
sharing experiences. He may not be able to mention certain of his feelings to
the therapist because he believes that they are unique, or he may not respond
in the usual fashion to certain questions because he senses something has been
missing in his experience and is humiliated about exposing himself to a stranger — physician or not!

One area in particular where questioning can lead to intense humiliation
is in asking (especially male) patients about their sexual experiences. It is
sometimes obvious in the technique of young psychiatrists that they are hell-
bent on exposing the patient's homosexuality, as a surgeon might excise and
drain a pus pocket. This sometimes leads to outbursts of alleged sexual activity
toward nurses and occupational therapists as the patient attempts to become
the man his psychiatrist does not seem to feel he is. It is helpful if the therapist
is able to note flushing, sweating, bodily movements, respiratory changes, etc.,
as he asks questions, so that he has some information about the effect he is
producing.

A fairly successful way in which to demonstrate observational and questioning techniques is for the supervisor to interview a schizophrenic patient
that is not known by himself or the residents, and to see how much can be
learned about this person's life and difficulties on the basis of a 30 or 40
minute interview. The number of correct guesses (when subsequently checked
against the patient's history) is often a graphic demonstration of the manner in
which cues of all sorts are used in an interview situation; and the blind alleys
are also fruitful topics for discussion. Thus, a therapist noted that a patient's
foot jumped while mentioning a person's name during the course of describing
an episode in an apparently unanxious fashion. Some months later, the therapist was able to get the patient to clarify his homosexual relationship to this
person, and the patient commented with relief that it was the first time he had
ever discussed this with anyone.

Many of the difficulties mentioned thus far are virtually impossible for
young therapists to correct without adequate supervision. It may occur in the
therapy of neurotics that the patient on occasion will set the therapist straight;
but, unfortunately, with very ill psychotics a serious mistake may herald the

beginning of the end for this particular relationship. In addition, adroit super-vision (Szurek, 1949) may render the therapist less anxious and allow him greater freedom to use his resources. A small piece of work done in a supervi-sory session that pays off in a therapy hour may act as a catalyst for a whole chain of helpful interactions.

A young male schizophrenic had particularly strong competitive feelings about his brother and felt hopeless to do anything about them — particularly in the area of his brother's athletic prowess. One day the patient mentioned to his therapist his newly found pleasure in playing volleyball; and although the therapist had actively encouraged the patient to participate in daily activities at the hospital, he did not specifically show his interest when the patient men-tioned this new activity. The supervisor noted the oversight to the therapist and suggested that he mention his interest to the patient at an appropriate time and acknowledge the oversight. Two weeks later the therapist had occasion to mention the incident, and the patient become obviously pleased and excited. He walked over toward the therapist, asked for a light for his cigarette, and spoke rapidly and coherently about his need for help and his recognition of the difficulty he had had in learning to trust the therapist and to rely on him for help.

There are tremendous opportunities for learning for the inexperienced therapist if he works with a disturbed psychotic under adequate supervision. For one thing, young therapists in this situation seem to become remarkably interested in the effect of their own personality on the total treatment situ-ation, and in supervisory sessions will often bring up the subject for discussion without any prompting. Perhaps the lack of fixed techniques in treating schi-zophrenics offers the therapist better opportunity to become acquainted with himself; and the intensity of feeling and sensitivity to the therapist that the patient so commonly manifests acts as an additional aid toward the therapist's self-awareness. Another aspect of the opportunity offered by this kind of thera-py is that the young therapist does not feel that the failure of a therapeutic venture with a schizophrenic carries as much loss of prestige as though it had happened with a neurotic; and he is freer to experiment with various tech-niques without risk to his prestige, and with less chance of feeling that he is running counter to the wishes of his superiors. Because of our relative ignor-ance about the therapy of psychotics, the beginning therapist has fewer sign-posts, rules, and dicta to follow than in treatment with neurotics, where a great many working principles have already been established.

Some tyro therapists, while not planning to devote themselves to therapy with psychotics, seize upon the opportunity to gain experience in this arena of intense emotion as a preparation for their subsequent psychotherapy with neurotics. It is not uncommon to hear a supervisee state that such and such a problem with a neurotic patient has been clarified without help after a more intense experience with a psychotic has been worked through. An example that comes to mind is that of a young therapist who appropriately raised the fee of a private neurotic patient after he had successfully handled his fear of assault from a psychotic in the hospital.

Given a group of inexperienced psychotherapists undertaking work with psychotics, I feel it is often the case that they can be loosely divided into groups that have in common certain prevailing attitudes toward the patient. These attitudes (roles, sets) usually can be seen in every one of the therapists, but certain of them manifest enduring patterns of interaction with the psychotic patients that tend to distinguish them from the other therapists. It may be helpful though potentially misleading, to categorize the therapists on the basis of predominant patterns of interaction, if only to alert the supervisor to the special needs and problems of each group.

One group might be labeled those therapists with an intellectually competitive attitude. A rather large number of psychotherapists who become interested in undertaking intensive psychotherapy with psychotics are overly intellectually curious and competitive. They tend to be tremendously engrossed in the productions of the patient and to ignore, to some extent, what is happening between themselves and the patient.

One therapist who was particularly fascinated by the content of the productions of his very disturbed patient encouraged his patient to free-associate. During one hour with this patient, the therapist made an interpretation involving some guesses about the meaning of the patient's masturbation, which topic the therapist had introduced. The patient greeted him at the beginning of the next hour by stating the he wanted to get out of the hospital and to find a job. The therapist and the patient then got into a long discussion about various job possibilities, with the psychiatrist pointing out the patient should not feel shiftless "because it takes all kinds of people to make a world." The therapist missed the rather obvious connection between the patient's wanting to leave the hospital — and the therapist — and the possibility of the patient's resentment about the interpretation given in the previous session.

It is not unusual for a therapist of this type to be rather fearful of women and unconsciously hostile toward them, an attitude which may result in his developing an erotic attachment to female schizophrenic patients, partly because such a woman is much less threatening than other women that the therapist has known. The patient and therapist may, in effect, relive their adolescence together. Out of this may result a transference jam, with the patient becoming quite disturbed and breaking off treatment. Sometimes the therapist's preoccupation with content is for the purpose of garnering proof of a psychoanalytic doctrine to demonstrate his intellectual capacities and to please his supervisor. This kind of integration with schizophrenic patients is not conducive to adequate communication and may injure the relationship. If the patient reports a pain in his left eye, and the therapist is lost in reflections about sinister and dexter, about one eye seeing evil and the other good, about the eye as an orifice and the proximity of the eye to the brain, he may completely overlook the fact that the patient has made a meaningful gesture which the therapist has missed, being lost in speculation. Such ruminations, while potentially illuminating, may be less important than the interpersonal situation.

A second type of therapist may be one who has an interpretative method for handling all data from the patient. He attempts to resolve the patient's psychosis by "active" interpretations, and perhaps by attempts at camaraderie. Although sometimes the enthusiasm of the therapist may give good results in the initial stages of therapy, this period is typically followed by a lull or actual impasse in the treatment situation. Such a lull or impasse may result in part in the patient's being disappointed in the therapist's failure to live up to his initial promise; or the therapist may be ignoring the primary processes and treating the patient as if he operated at a more integrated level than he is capable of; or the difficulty may stem from strong sexual feelings which develop toward the therapist and are not noticed, or, perhaps most importantly, the interest in symbolization may result in the therapist's overlooking the simple human feelings that the schizophrenic manifests toward someone who is taking an interest in him. It is perhaps a cogent point that the "dynamic" therapist, if inexperienced, will interpret dynamically those facets of the relationship that impinge upon his own awareness and are not necessarily the most currently relevant. A strong statement couched in id terms may be perfectly relevant to the dynamics of the patient's difficulty, but at the moment it is presented may be tangential or obfuscating.

The cautious therapist is one who may not manifest many of the attitudes mentioned in the two previous types. He is apt to make infrequent interpretations and is in a better position to establish communication with a schizophrenic as long as his caution does not arise from his uncertainty and his inability to recognize the patient's or his own anxiety. Thus, the therapist who is by nature rather more characteristically a listener, who is often slow to accept ideas until he has carefully thought them through, and who rarely or infrequently talks at conferences, is often at an advantage when dealing with a schizophrenic. Although the patient may at first seem more active in his symptoms with such a therapist — particularly if the patient has been given to much acting out — he may gradually achieve a kind of communication with the therapist which it would be difficult for him to achieve with a more intellectually competitive therapist. The patient gradually learns to make more open remarks about the cautious therapist, sensing somehow that it is safe to do so. The therapist, in turn, speaks of the patient in terms different from those used by the more dynamic therapist. For instance, he does not seem as sure of ultimate therapeutic success, and he is apparently more perplexed about what is going on. In general, he is not as intrigued by the meaning of symbolic processes and is therefore better able to observe the interpersonal situation. He may be more accepting of the patient's prospective social adjustment and is not as likely to guide the patient along cultural lines, to be a success of some sort, and to conform to the doctor's idea of what a success is. One special problem of this group, however, is that caution and a relaxed manner may actually be masking anxiety and uncertainty. If this is so, the therapist may eventually run into difficulty with the patient and may have to demonstrate that the patient is inaccessible or that another should take over the case. Although this type of therapist may show less defensiveness during supervisory sessions than some of the other groups, he may have a real need for support and encouragement in making decisions. Since forceful intervention is necessary at times in the treatment of schizophrenics, particularly in the case of paranoid ideas, the therapist's caution may represent an actual handicap to the progress of therapy.

The therapist may overlook a golden moment for intervention, and the patient may interpret this caution as fear or as a lack of interest. The increased confidence and good feeling that may follow a properly conducted supervisory session may allow such a therapist to discover certain attitudes in himself that tend to shut the patient up. An overly cautious therapist reported during a supervisory session in a manner that made it obvious he was discouraged with the progress of his patient. The therapist stated that the patient, who in the beginning had been quite accessible, had now become silent and unapproachable. The amount of despair he experienced made him unable to regard this as a temporary block in therapy; rather, it seemed to write a finis to his efforts. He approached the interview following the supervisory session will full awareness of his own dread of the hour, and the patient seemed, surprisingly enough, to be attempting to make the therapist more comfortable. For example, he met the therapist at the entrance to his office rather than in the dayroom, which was their usual rendezvous. This small show on the patient's part seemed to contribute to a quality in the interview that contrasted sharply with the interviews of the previous two weeks. The boost that patient had given him was enough for the therapist to be able to remark spontaneously in the next supervisory session that he suspected that some of the patient's provocative ways had been greeted with a silence that actually reflected anger and disapproval on the part of the therapist.

There is occasionally encountered among a group of young psychotherapists working with schizophrenics one who will stand out among his colleagues by virtue of being a nonconformist. Such a person may be loosely spoken of as manifesting "overidentification" with his patients. He often manifests sizable difficulties in his own interpersonal dealings, and, although socially he may tend to be brusque and to avoid much that can be interpreted as friendly or tender, his patients may experience him as a warm person. The schizophrenic's low self-esteem may not be threatened by such a person, and the therapist in his conversation about the patient reveals a rather strong tendency to side with him against the hospital, ward administrator, or whatever authority seems most relevant. Such persons, because they may be especially gifted, present sizable difficulties for the supervisor. In his attempt to be of help, the supervisor may simply succeed in getting the therapist's back up. Such an encounter will usually be but one of a number of similar encounters with authority figures and a further link in the chain that successfully isolates this person and patient from the rest of the therapeutic community.

A therapist of this type returned home one evening to find that one of his patients, who had privileges outside the hospital at the time, had done irreparable damage to his highly prized garden. After recovering from his initial dismay, he accepted it rather philosophically as a communication from the patient that the therapist was spending too much time in his garden instead of with the patient. The inability of the supervisor to be of aid in this situation was one part in the pattern that succeeded in causing the patient to leave the hospital, and the therapist himself left shortly afterward.

A therapist of this type may say to the patient, in effect; "I know because

I've been there myself." He may, in fact, have been close to psychosis with or without awareness of it, and his adjustment may be primarily obsessional or schizoid. The danger of the development of a paranoid twosome between the patient and the therapist is very real in this kind of integration and they may feel that the rest of the world is responsible for their joint difficulties. The nonconforming therapist may be especially gifted in resolving the acute phase of the patient's psychosis, and his early results may be very encouraging. As treatment progresses and the patient reaches the therapist's level of adjustment, the pace begins to slacken. Perhaps it should be a more standard procedure in the treatment of schizophrenics for this kind of therapist to be used in the early stages of treatment, with a change in therapists as treatment progresses.

Although most people in our culture to some extent adopt a counter-phobic way of life, this attitude can be exaggerated in a therapist to the point that he denies any fear of treating a schizophrenic. Such an attitude, if marked, might be labeled "the counter-phobic attitude in therapy." The therapist who reacts in this way likes to work with schizophrenics partially because he is re-assured by his ability to "stick out the hours." Since this attitude is a cover for intense anxiety, the schizophrenic is apt to react to it in one of two ways; his precarious self-esteem may be further damaged by seeing the therapist as a su-perior, unapproachable person, or he may feel that the therapist is bluffing or lying, in which case he is almost invariably reminded of someone in his past. The patient in such a situation may attempt to humiliate the therapist, or on occasion to attack him physically. The situation can often be resolved if the therapist faces his fears realistically and directly communicates his fear to the patient, for instance, by seeing him in a hot pack.

These categories of therapists are obviously unsatisfactory, arbitrary, and overlapping. They are presented only to emphasize that one of the primary tasks in the successful psychotherapy of a schizophrenic is the understanding of his interaction with the personality of the therapist. Knowledge of dynamics and techniques will increase the therapist's security and effectiveness only if used against the background of knowledge about his own interaction with the patient. In addition, theory can be an encumbering protection for the therapist instead of an aid to understanding the patient.

It will be noted that the phenomena described as being important aspects of the therapist's personality are largely manifestations of anxiety, either as it erupts into the treatment situation or as it is observable in terms of the psy-chiatrist's defenses against it. It would be fatuous to say that the absence of anxiety in the therapist would aid the treatment situation. It is more pertinent to search for fortunate ways of handling anxiety. As present-day observational techniques improve, so will our knowledge of the therapeutic implications of the therapist's personality and so will our ability to make the most of our imperfections.

One therapist's defenses may be found to be most efficacious and least encumbering in the early phases of treatment, while another's will be more suited to the long haul of working through. The use of multiple therapists to support each other, and hence reduce their individual anxieties and increase their individual awareness, seems to offer an avenue for research (Dryud & Rioch, 1953; Dreikurs, 1950; Hayward, Peters, & Taylor, 1952). The presence of more than one significant figure dilutes the untherapeutic aspects of each therapist and the reaction of the patient to any one of the therapists. The schizophrenic's uncompromising tendency to split good from bad seems to have a happier outcome when there is more than one person to divide. Still another possibility should be explored, namely, whether the therapist experiences less anxiety if he is supported in his decisions by another physician who serves as an administrator (Morse & Noble, 1942; Bullard, 1952). This had proved efficacious as well with the psychotic not in the hospital. The therapist is freer to do therapy when the decisions regarding medical matter, privileges, and so forth, are in the hands of an administrator (Jackson, 1954).

It seems reasonable to speculate that increased awareness of the importance of the personality of the therapist in the psychotherapy of schizophrenics will lead to changes in our techniques with the end in view of reducing his anxiety in the treatment situation.

References

Bullard, D. (1952). Problems of clinical administration. *Bulletin of the Menninger Clinic, 16*, 193–201.

Dreikurs, R. (1950). Techniques and dynamics of multiple psychotherapy. *Psychiatric Quarterly, 24*, 788–799.

Dryud, J., & Rioch, M. (1953). Multiple therapy in the treatment program of a mental hospital. *Psychiatry, 16*, 21–26.

Fromm-Reichmann, F. (1939). Transference problems in schizophrenics. *Psychoanalytic Quarterly, 8*, 412–426.

Fromm-Reichmann, F. (1942). A preliminary note on the emotional significance of stereotypes in schizophrenics. *Bulletin of the Forest Sanitarium, 1,* 17–21.

Hayward, M., Peters, J., & Taylor, J. (1952). Some values of use of multiple therapists in treatment of the psychoses. *Psychiatric Quarterly, 26,* 244–249.

Jackson, D. (1954). The office treatment of ambulatory schizophrenic. *California Medicine, 81* (4), 263–267.

Morse, R. T., & Noble, T. D. (1942). Joint endeavors of the administrative physician and psychotherapist. *Psychiatric Quarterly, 14,* 578–585.

Rosen, J. (1953). *Direct analysis.* New York: Grune & Stratton.

Sullivan, H. S. (1940). *Conceptions of modern psychiatry.* Washington, DC: William Alanson White Foundation

Szurek, S. (1949). Remarks on training for psychotherapy. *American Journal of Orthopsychiatry, 19,* 36–51.

CHAPTER 7

Further Consideration of Hysterical Symptoms in Women[1]

(1956)

In 1954, I presented a paper (Jackson, 1954) to this association describing some actions in the family relationships of six female patients and the apparent influence on the outcome of their oedipal situations. These patients shared many personality features in common and all had various hysterical symptoms and a marked interest and concern with pregnancy — both realistically and in fantasy. The essence of the family situation was a tripartite interaction in which the daughter over-evaluated the father and denied her intense ambivalent attachment to the mother. The fathers enjoyed hero worship and were overtly and/or covertly seductive, but became frightened of their sexual interest especially when the daughter reached puberty. In addition, they used the daughter to hide their own fear of women and to express dissatisfaction and contempt toward their wives. Another, often serious problem that arose at puberty was when the daughter's desire for independence, competence, and boyfriends led her into strong conflict with the father who was fearful of being dethroned. The father often reacted by forbidding on the one hand, and by covertly pushing his daughter toward unsuitable, sometimes overtly delinquent boys on the other.

---

[1] Presented at the western regional meeting, American Psychiatric Association, Los Angeles, CA., September 1957.

The mothers were unable to relate in an intimate way to their daughters but did not totally reject them. Instead they used disapproval or desertion as a potent weapon to shape the girl into a counterpart of their relationship with their own mother. It was equally obvious that the girls became not only maternal figures to their own mother, but played a special role in aiding her to cope with her husband. In the more obvious situations, the mother even arranged for the girl to become father's sexual partner and refused to listen to the girl's attempts to confess what was going on.

Pregnancy fantasies or reactions to actual pregnancy played an important part in these patients' unconscious mental activity and appeared to represent to the girl the creation of a new ego. The fantasy of being pregnant condensed into a single symbol, the secret of having father's baby, the desire to be a mother rather than having a need for a mother, and the incorporation of the breast via the penis. Most importantly pregnancy meant a secret union with mother while avoiding the rejecting aspect of her. Obviously, the fantasy of being pregnant was also a Frankenstein since it could result in being rejected or even killed by one or both parents.

Some technical implications of the material were briefly discussed; namely, the importance of the therapist's discerning the shadow of mother behind the material (especially sexual) which would ordinarily be dealt with as relating to father, and the value of treating the fear of abandonment not solely as an intrapsychic reaction to hostile wishes but also as a reaction to realistic fears which stemmed especially from the mother's emotional or physical withdrawal. At that time, I did not emphasize the fear of desertion to the extent I presently would. This is especially true since I now have confirmed that two mothers were clinically depressed during the patient's childhood and a third made a suicide attempt in the patient's presence when the girl was between two and three years of age.

In the present paper I would like to present additional data from these patients and from four more women with hysterical features. I will also refer to several patients whose therapy I supervised. Two of the original patients have become pregnant during therapy (and apparently as a result of therapy), and the teenage girl, from the previous study has gotten married. These events have provided the therapist with an opportunity to study certain reactions at first hand. Two of the husbands have entered therapy since the previous presentation, and their wives' statements about them have been compared with their therapists' impressions. Additional data has been gathered about the parents from outside sources and, in some cases, by psychiatric interviews and psychological testing of the parents.

It is not possible to present all of this data even in summary form. Instead I would like to emphasize the following: (a) some material from the literature relating to this topic that has appeared since the first presentation, (b) a further picture of the family relationship, (c) data relating to the *integrative* aspect of hysterical symptoms, (d) the unique layering of oedipal and pre-oedipal material which is best illustrated by dreams and fantasy involving pregnancy, and (e) further technical considerations in the treatment of this type of patient by psychoanalysis or intensive psychotherapy.

THE LITERATURE

There have been four contributions subsequent to the first presentation of this study that are particularly pertinent. The first and most important, in my opinion, is Fairbairn's paper on "The Nature of Hysterical States." While I do not wish to enter into the debate that centers around his concept of the ego, there are certain of his clinical observations and theoretical concepts that support the kind of family interaction I have previously described. To quote: "So far as the hysteric is concerned, a characteristic feature of the basic endopsychic situation which I have just outlined was that the exciting object is excessively exciting and the rejecting object excessively rejecting; and from this it inevitably follows that the libidinal ego is excessively libidinal and the antilibidinal ego excessively persecutory. These features seem to me to shed considerable light upon the nature of the hysterical state; for they go a long way to explain both (1) the intensity of the hysteric's repressed sexuality, and (2) the extent of the compulsive sacrifice of sexuality which is such a characteristic hysterical phenomenon."

While Fairbairn's paper does not emphasize the family situation, it is obvious from his clinical notes that the fathers he describes are seductive and rejecting, and there is special mentioning of *teasing*. He also states that the fathers tended to intervene between the girls and their mothers. Fairbairn also describes a woman patient who predominantly identified the exciting and rejecting object with the father and states "A fact which incidentally gave rise to an *exceptionally strong*[2] resistance in the transference situation." This is a point

---

[2] Italics mine.

briefly mentioned in my previous paper and will be discussed further under "Therapy."

Fairbairn's views of the exciting and rejecting objects are readily translated into operational description involving family interaction. In essence, the mother is the original "exciting and rejecting" object but because of certain aspects of her nature and the particular family interaction, the father takes on this role. In most of my cases, a third adult (especially maternal grandmothers) also aided the avoidance of mother as *the actual and observable ambivalent object*.[3]

A second paper that is relevant to this study is by Siegman and entitled: "Emotionality, A Hysterical Character Defense." Siegman states: "One aspect, at last, of hysterical emotionality is the dramatic and exhibitionistic demonstration to the superego that the ego is well behaved, proper, and experiences the correct emotions, as if such evidence were demanded in order to avoid the displeasure of guilt or the loss of love." If this statement is translated from intrapsychic into operational terms, emotionality can be viewed as a mechanism whereby the child deals with the mother's guilt in a manner that avoids his being rejected. One of the functions of the characteristic dramatic overstatement of these women is that it allows the mother an opportunity to deny the part statement and thus by implication, the whole. The child denies a feeling by exaggerating it and yet makes his point at the same time. In effect, the child makes a metaphorical statement, which the mother's literalness protects her from responding to.[4] Siegman mentions the "put on" and "shallow" qualities of hysterical affects that seem to irritate the observer because of their hypocritical connotations. The emotionality of these patients is defensive in nature and at the same time integrative. Both the emotionality and the therapist's irritation will be discussed below.

A third contribution of the literature that is especially related to this study is entitled: "The family constellation and overt incestuous relations between father and daughter" by Kaufman, et al. This is a study of eleven girls, ranging in age from ten to seventeen, who were referred for therapy because of various complaints, but all of whom had had incestuous relations with a father or

---

[3] The father, e.g., is the observable object but not the primary one. I shall try to demonstrate that the displacement of the accepting and rejecting aspects of mother to him lends the air of "pretense," "fraud," or "playing a game" to these patients' integrations.

[4] It will be apparent to those familiar with the families of schizophrenics that a similar, though I suspect more intense situation obtains.

stepfather. The parents were also seen in psychiatric interviews. These girls had much in common with the women in my study including marked learning difficulties, promiscuity, loss of appetite, abdominal distress, pregnancy fantasies, running-away behavior, and somatic complaints. The summary of the family relationships in this group rather impressively parallels my material[5] (which has been largely reconstructed from adult patients). Among the important items mentioned are: Despite the long duration of the incestuous relationship, in only two cases did the mother report it to the authorities. The daughters were overtly or covertly encouraged by the mother to assume her role with her husband. The mothers were tied to the maternal grandmothers and often were literally and psychologically unable to move away from them. The daughter was encouraged to assume responsibility beyond her years and gradually developed into a replica of the maternal grandmother. The mother would then displace onto their chosen daughter all the hostility felt for the maternal grandmother. They could not accept independence or hostility from the daughter, and projected onto her their own oedipal guilt.

The authors describe the fathers as being more accepting and warm toward the daughters; however, all the family members appeared to be searching for a mother figure and hence the father offered only pale love. The frustration tolerance to the anxiety of desertion was minimal for the parents and the child, and something in the unconscious of the family members and their affect on each other caused them to handle their anxiety primarily by acting out. The authors further state that although the original sexual experience with the father was at a genital level, the meaning of the sexual act was pre-genital, and for the girl meant receiving parental interest. In addition, like the women in my study, these girls showed a pseudomaturity; but this facade crumbled when they were placed in a dependent position, and some of them experienced psychotic-like states.

This paper by Kaufman et al. is especially relevant because the data were obtained from a study of the whole family and not mainly reconstructed from the therapy of the daughter as with my own data. In addition, these girls had overt incestuous relations whereas none of my patients did, although two had had at least one occasion of some sexual play with their fathers. My subjects constitute a different socioeconomic group than Kaufman's patients, and provide an opportunity for speculation about cultural influence, for example, the

---

[5] "Some Factors Influencing the Oedipal Complex," chapter 4, this volume.

difference between a father who leaves his daughter to go to sea and one who goes behind a newspaper.

Finally, some colleagues and I have published as a part of a larger study the analysis of data obtained via projected tests and the Q-sort on the parents of inhibited and acting out children (Block, Patterson, Block, & Jackson, 1958). Suffice it to mention here that the parents of the acting-out children resembled the family picture described in this paper in that the father overtly encouraged the acting-out behavior and covertly felt guilty for doing so while the mother covertly encouraged the behavior and overtly was disapproving.

FAMILY INTERACTION AND ITS RELATION TO SYMPTOMS AND PREGNANCY FANTASIES

In essence, it is my opinion that the hysterical symptoms and pregnancy fantasies of the women in this study represented, among other things, a response and an attempt at integration[6] to a particular family situation. Obviously, I am stressing only the difference in degree between the situation of these patients and a normogenic group on the one hand, or a schizophrenic group on the other. For example, these mothers had much in common with the mothers of schizophrenics I have encountered. However, they could allow more intervention on the father's part between them and their child, and they presented a vulnerable side to the child, which allowed an amount of exploitation that I feel the mother of a schizophrenic could never permit. In addition, they were more able to manifest concern over helplessness and illness. It may be of significance in the genesis of the importance that pregnancy fantasies had to these women that the mothers could respond to helpless infants more appropriately than to young children. There was further evidence for this in their behavior as grandmothers.

The following factors in the family situation seemed among the more important in the genesis of symptoms and fantasy:

1. The mother had great difficulty in allowing this particular child to identify with her. The most obvious kind of situation was, for example, where the mother was a good homemaker and the girl was discouraged from

---

[6] "Integration" is used in the sense of an attempt to obtain at least partial need fulfillment by adapting to the significant person's anxiety pattern; or more usually, to the anxiety avoidance gestalt of the family.

learning to cook, sex, etc. In the case of a psychotic woman with marked hysterical features, the mother deprecated housework and was a gifted musician. The girl became a kitchen drudge, and at the age of eight years accepted almost complete responsibility for her newborn baby sister. It is relevant that she became acutely psychotic when her husband left her after eighteen years of marriage with the words: "If I had wanted a "housekeeper I could have hired one." One of her delusions during her psychosis was that she had had a child, which was being kept from her. When she was hospitalized she felt she was in the obstetrical ward and that the nursery was directly across the hall from her. The good nurses were taking care of her infant for her, the bad nurses were keeping her from her infant. Interestingly, her "infant" was non-white. After some therapy it became white, but a boy, and only after a long period could it be thought of as a girl.

2. The mother was unable to tolerate strong emotion, and in addition, did not encourage significant verbal communication from the child. The fathers, on the other hand, were apparently more outgoing and more accepting of affection and physical contact. Their hostility had to be expressed mainly through teasing, which provided other gratifications as well.

3. The child's emotional reactions tended to be handled by the mother, and to some extent by the father, in one of two ways:

    a. Open expression of affect was labelled as "bad" and responded to by disapproval and threat of desertion, and the child seemed to develop a confusion between emotion which is "bad" and behavior which is "bad." This confusion helped to create special problems in acting out during therapy.

    b. Emotion was treated tangentially. The angry child was tired, needed an enema, or her "tummy hurt." The child subsequently learned to respond in the manner of: "I didn't do it, my hand did." This technique allowed the mother's affective responses to be disguised by manifesting disapproval or concern (I don't hate you — it is only what you are doing that I don't like or worry about). The ability to express concern was often heightened by physical illness of the child, and it may have been on these occasions that the mother and the child reached the peak of their ability to be intimate. The covert, tangential, and mainly nonverbal handling of the child's emotions aided later displacement onto bodily parts or body functions. It also provided for a secretive or "not-knowing-what-is-going-on" atmosphere that made for difficulties in partial identifications.[7] The "not knowing" aspect was heightened by the overt tranquility between mother and father and the covert hostility, fear, and struggle for power. As will be mentioned below, acting out behavior could often be interpreted as a message that both revealed the parent's unconscious wishes and malignantly exposed their secrets.

One patient as a small child had played such pranks as tying airplane baggage checks on father's luggage after he had lied to his wife and said he had taken the train. In therapy, she had a period where she stole my mail and searched for secrets. In both these instances, she was sharing with father, trying to alienate him and mother (therapist and wife), and secretly siding with mother to win her favors.

c. The mother and father's relation was such that he tended to intervene between mother and child, and she covertly, or occasionally overtly, encouraged it. For the mother, there was the reenactment of her own childhood and oedipal conflicts including vicarious participating in the father/daughter relationship, and the expression of hostility, contempt, and a desire to control her husband by making her daughter a tool, and an attempt to placate him for her own inadequacies, especially in the sexual realm. For the father, there was a masking of his fear of women and especially his dependence. He overtly sided with his wife and covertly used the daughter to replace her and revenge himself. The underlying helplessness that these superficially strong and successful men felt toward their wives was clearly revealed in interviews and by psychological testing.

---

[7] This point has also been made by Minna Emsch in "The Need to Know as Related to Identification & Acting Out," *International Journal of Psychiatry*, 25, 1944.

Some of the items in a psychological report on a typical set of parents were:

Father: Identifies with own mother's helplessness but hides behind a good front. His M.M.P.I. shows clear evidence of defensiveness by high K and a high lie score. There is constant evidence of being unable to fathom other people or to adequately communicate.

Mother: There is a lot of dependence on her own mother and no picture of her father at all. There is no obvious guilt over her own behavior which is in marked contrast to her husband. Evidence of vicarious aggression and concern with material possessions. There is a definite avoidance of sensuality and anxiety about sex with much denial, yet it is done in such a way that the discrepancies would not be obvious to herself.

Symptoms and pregnancy fantasies of the daughter when viewed against the background of the tripartite interaction can be seen to have aggressive and integrative components. There are elements of expiation and manipulation, dividing and conquering through splitting into "good" and "bad," "strong and weak," "acceptable and unacceptable" or in Fairbairn's terms: "exciting" and "rejecting" objects. One patient recalls that as a young child her left hand was "bad and weak" whereas her right was "strong and good." After some months she felt sorry for the way she was scolding her left hand and forgave it. Subsequently, she turned to animals and treated them in much the same ambivalent fashion. Another patient trained her dog to be jealous whenever she was around other dogs or children. He would then be beaten for his bad behavior.

Integrative and assertive aspects of these patients' behavior especially can be seen in relation to the parents' guilt. For example, overstatement on their part would get a response from the parent, yet both the action and reaction were tangential to the main current of feeling. As one patient put it: "Whenever they responded to me it was for the wrong reason." In a sense, overstatement would mean that the mother would be protected from having to feel the true accusation and yet be forced to respond to the child, if only in a defensive way. Bad behavior, lying, or overstatements provided the mother with reason for being angry with the child and provided the child with an opportunity to renounce his bad self and become good and hence lovable. It also allowed her to be hurt, to renounce mother and turn to father or someone else with a justified demand. It was striking how seldom, if ever, these mothers were directly angry at their children with the child's providing them with a good reason. That is, mother herself could not own up to having bad days. Another aspect of the child's apparently provocative or helpless behavior that was integrative was in relation to their mothers' depressive tendencies. Since these mothers tended to withdraw emotionally or to spend a fair amount of time physically away from the child, it is apparent that getting any kind of response was better than desertion.

On one occasion as a child, a patient was extremely envious over a gift given to her sister although the gift she received was far better (for a change). Naturally, she was scolded and shamed for untoward behavior. Upon the repetition of unaccountable envy and complaints in therapy, it was possible to see that the patient feared if things went well, if she got what she wanted — then all debts would be paid and she would be deserted. Helplessness too has a similar meaning — "you will keep me around if I make you feel you need me." Some patients would characteristically develop physical illnesses prior to the therapists leaving on vacation.

The peculiar function that the daughter had as a parental go-between was demonstrated by three additional facts:

1. I was unable to find a single instance of symptomatic behavior occurring in an area in which the parents were in open disagreement.[8]

2. In several cases the mother had had a symptom or a type of behavior that had ceased when the daughter was very young and was later manifested by the girl.

3. The extent of the emotional upset occurring in the parents as the daughter improved as a result of therapy. It was most spectacular in a teenage girl who lived at home during the first year of therapy but later moved into her own apartment and supported herself. Among other things, the mother's physician asked me to stop therapy with the daughter because

---

[8] This is an interesting finding in view of Stanton and Schwartz's observation that blow-ups on a psychotic ward occurred when the therapist and administrator were covertly in disagreement. Stanton, A., & Schwartz, M. (1955). *The Mental Hospital*. New York: Basic Books.

the mother "was becoming a confirmed alcoholic." The parents had virtually forced this girl to get therapy because of their fear she would become an alcoholic, drug addict, and prostitute.

SOME ASPECTS OF THERAPY

Whether those patients were mildly or severely neurotic, or even psychotic, they presented certain similarities of behavior to the therapist. I would like to discuss a few of the problems that commonly arose in therapy and some observations about them. Others have noted, correctly, that it is relatively easy to influence hysterical symptoms but difficult to analyze the underlying personality structure. In all instances reported, the therapy was aimed at the underlying conflicts, and symptoms were analyzed en passant. Probably in the majority of instances, symptoms disappeared without the therapy being specifically focused on them at that moment. A good bit of the understanding of a symptom was therefore retrospective.

A few of the outstanding features of therapy included:

1. Emotionality:

The patients presented, to varying degrees, the characteristic immaturity and emotionality of the hysteric that has received much attention in the literature (Wittels, 1930). This aspect of their personality was usually irritating to others, and often to me. An obvious reaction to their overstatement would be to respond with a reassuring "things can't be that bad" kind of statement, and/or to point up the fraudulent aspects of their exaggeration and histrionic behavior. However, if the therapist is able to keep in mind the picture of the relationship with their parents, he is able to see many of their utterances in the framework of a game. Rather than testing their productions within his own reference terms; namely, "if I were expressing so-and-so, I would feel so-and-so," he learns to think "if this is being acted, it may be because so-and-so is not being felt." The paucity of genuine affects, and their identification by the patient are among the major therapeutic problems. Thus if a patient weeps apparently uncontrollably, the appropriate response might be: "Evidently you don't dare feel as strongly about this inside as you would like to," or "The little girl inside you seems afraid to experience these feelings." It may be necessary to reassure the patient that the therapist can withstand strong feeling. Rather than pointing out that the observable feelings are pretense, and running the risk of making the patient feel "bad" as she originally did, it is more helpful to attempt to state what is missing. Occasionally strong language or a poignant expression may help the patient to see the shallowness of her apparently consuming response. Thus a patient who was expressing grief over her recent estrangement from her mother was told: "I can see how very deeply you wish to care." This remark led her subsequently to discuss her grandmother's death when she was thirteen, and she shed a few seemingly genuine tears.

Usually there is a corollary to the emotionality; namely, a peculiar lack of response to certain apparently hair-raising situations. If the therapist keeps alert to annoying or frustrating situations that were handled with the greatest of blandness, he may be accused of trying to make a mountain out of a molehill, but eventually the patient may see the paradoxical aspects of her emotional reactions. Usually the fear of desertion is strong in those situations which are underplayed, even though superiority, contempt, manipulation, and control are also in the picture.

2.   *Responsibility for feelings and behavior, and "involvement":*
The paradoxical emotional response described above has aspects of a game as if the patient were saying: "This is what I really mean, but by over-stating it, you won't take me seriously." Dreams often take place on a stage, or may contain reassurance to the dreamer that she is only "putting on." Statements that could only be a reflection of being angry may be accompanied by a smile; and genuine expressions of feeling (especially if during an interaction with the therapist) may be followed by a convenient amnesia.

It was characteristic for these women to feel "involved" with the therapist not long after therapy started. They became very concerned about what he thought of them, indicated they "loved" him or had sexual urges toward him, and became very upset about any interruptions of therapy on the therapist's part. The involvement is difficult to analyze because the patients cannot clarify their feelings and tend to use general expressions like "terribly upset," "wonderful feeling," "would die without you" and the like. The therapist may experience irritation if he attempts initially to understand the feelings as an affective response rather than as defensive and integrative behavior. It is imperative to the patient that she not be understood, and she expects anger and rejection. The therapist is in the position of the men in their lives who felt they were being led into sexual intercourse only to have the woman back away at the last moment. As Marmor (1953) has pointed out, "they wish to be cuddled, not seduced." Similarly, in therapy they want loving support but to be understood would be equivalent to inviting desertion. From my own experience, and from questioning colleagues, I would gather that the "involvement" phase is not easily managed by therapists of either sex.

Briefly, I have utilized the following techniques to aid the patient to identify and accept responsibility for her feelings:

a. If the patient described an interaction, I might try and label what the other person probably felt — especially when this was in contrast to their behavior. This approach was a precursor, a sort of trial run, to dealing with the difficult topic of mother (who was often felt not to have any feelings).

b. Dreams were discussed with the frequent statement: "In your own dream" or "since you dreamed this, we must assume you felt, etc.," otherwise the patient tended to dismiss them as "only" dreams.

c. Countertransference reactions that were noted, guessed at, or hinted at by the patient were explicitly agreed with, if correct, and an attempt was made to help the patient note her apprehension and fear of this area. Especially important were the lightly made, smiling comments about the analyst that were not supposed to be taken up. Naturally, if they occurred, as they often seemed to, at the close of a session, the therapist would introduce the topic during the next appointment. I recognize the danger of letting this technique silence the patient's observations or, on the other hand, of its encouraging emotionality toward the therapist.

d. Responses to their children, in those patients who were mothers, often proved a useful topic for aiding the recognition of and responsibility for emotions. The majority of these women treated their children in a more spontaneous fashion than they did adults, but thought of themselves vis-á-vis their children as unrelated to themselves with others.

One patient who was pregnant gave a grunt when the fetus kicked during a session. She was encouraged to associate to her reaction and recognized that she was both afraid and angry, yet pleased. She saw the fetus in two lights: either "it" was retaliating against her and trying to split her open as if it were a brat; or it was having a convulsion, which she identified with her own fear of psychosis. She saw the pregnancy as a terribly aggressive act on her part which the fetus responded to by attempting to destroy them both. On the other hand, she saw procreation as an attempt to create a new ego, which was now asserting itself and was pleasingly different from her own timid manner. She alternated between thinking of the fetus as "her" and as "it." Saying "her" was followed by momentary anxiety. This flood of associations came as a great surprise to her since she was not aware of strong feelings toward anyone else. It was gradually possible for her to see herself in relation to the therapist in much the same light as she pictured the fetus's responding to her.

3. *Helplessness:*

Some aspects of the emotionality and involvement described in the preceding section relate to helplessness. It is my impression that the most important element in helplessness for these patients was its use as a defense against the fear of abandonment. Acting helpless, being incompetent, disorganized, uninformed or physically un-intact (including symptoms, fantasies and pathoneurotic reactions), or experiencing almost panic proportions of helplessness — all arose in situations in which real or imagined abandonment lurked.

Occasionally in therapy, there has come a spectacular moment when the patient's demandingness could be related to helplessness, and this in turn to the fear of recognizing her own adequacy — which recognition they felt would result in being abandoned. The following sequence illustrates such a reaction:

The patient discussed with the therapist her wish for a child and her husband's reluctance to have one. She felt helpless to change his attitude and demanded sympathy and some sort of practical advice from the therapist. Underlying this as revealed by dreams was the request that the therapist give her a child. What the patient did not mention to the therapist at this time was that the husband had had tuberculous epididymitis previously and they both were afraid that he was sterile. His reluctance to have a child was related to her having been cleared gynecologically and his fear (which was later confirmed to be true) that he was sterile. The patient knew this, but was afraid to face her husband's fear and feeling of inadequacy because to do so would mean giving him up as a supporting object. The situation became clear when the patient urged a friend of hers, a woman, to take a direct action and be responsible for it and felt pleased that she had insisted that this friend follow this particular episode through to completion. In the next analytic session, with a good deal of silence and hesitance, she reluctantly mentioned her husband's difficulties and her recognition that she felt she might have to leave him if he was unable to have children since they were so important to her. The episode had particular significance not only in the patient's strong wish for a child, but also because it was the first time in therapy that she had ever seen herself as better off than her husband in any sense. The reasons for such an intense reaction to being the adequate one are numerous and cannot be detailed here.

4. *Acting out:*

There were many technical problems and headaches related to dealing with acting out. Briefly, it seemed to arise in the following situations:

a. When the therapist was dealing with material at the wrong level. The usual situation was interpreting sexual material when the patient was using it as a defense against her intense ambivalence toward her mother.

b. As a response to anxiety over feelings toward the mother that were expressed in a sudden storm at a time when her relation to the therapist, or occasionally husband and therapist, was already in jeopardy. Often the therapist had temporarily neglected the present for the past.

c. As a consequence of unresolved countertransference. It goes without saying that acting out had, as well, the many meanings described by such authorities as Fenichel (1945) and Greenacre (1950). It also occurred, in the healthy sense, as an attempt at mastery — as a substitution of action for previous helplessness.

DREAMS RELATING TO PREGNANCY

Material relating to pregnancy often appears in the dreams of these patients, and the patient may recognize, after a fair amount of therapy, that much of the dream material had been expressed as conscious fantasies sometime during her life and subsequently forgotten.

The earlier dreams in therapy may contain references to pregnancy that are quite disguised. Gradually references in dreams to eating, children, minor aggressions on the patient's part, and maternal figures may lead to an out-and-out dream of being pregnant, having a baby, or in some cases being a baby or fetus.

It has been my impression that the feeling of "having something inside," of being able to contemplate a nidus for the creation of a "new" ego occurs when there is some acceptance, via the transference, of the aggressive and dependent feelings that lie beneath the sexualized demandingness. However, the feeling of daring to create runs counter to the newly experienced dependency, and there is almost always an initial "taking back" period. It has appeared to me important not to bring in incest taboo at this point but to treat the reluctance to have something inside one's self as a fear of giving up the old claims and as actual growth suppression on the part of the parents.

The following material illustrates some of these points:

A patient after several years of therapy has a dream in which the analytic session is to take place in a hospital. There appears to be a mix up as the therapist himself is seeing a doctor when the patient arrives. He breaks off his own appointment to see her and they lie down on a bed together with their arms around each other. She tells him there is something special she wants to say. She has seen her real mother whom she pictures in the dream as an aggressive, fat woman who is not the idealized picture of the mother who died when the patient was two and one-half. The woman in the dream says to the patient with some surprise that she seemed so grown up. The mother then questioned the patient about relatives, her sisters and so on and the patient had the feeling that there was more interest in them than in her. In the dream, the therapist reassures her that the mother hadn't actually felt this way but liked the patient as well as the others. The dream ended with the patient remarking that she is not sure this is true but that she can find out.

This is not only the first dream the patient had in therapy of her real mother, who died when she was quite young, but is as far as she knows the first time she had ever dreamed of her mother. The dream occurred when the patient was far enough along in therapy to be well aware of her desire for a child, and the evening before the dream she had been talking with an older woman who is both maternal and aggressive and who had been urging the younger woman to have a family. She was amazed in the dream to find herself with ambivalent feelings toward her mother whose memory she had cherished and fanned by selected bits of data from maternal relatives.

The patient's additional associations were to various aspects of pregnancy, her fear of the therapist's disapproval at her wish for closeness, and her questioning his willingness and ability to support her especially should she become pregnant.

In a subsequent dream she drives by the house of a childhood boyfriend who is standing on the porch with his two young sons. She is excited and happy to see him but he looks at her coldly and as if there is something wrong with her. Drawing his sons close to him he announces they must go in to dinner.

Here is an illustration of the "taking back" phase — even though the previous dream did not obviously deal with pregnancy. Among the important associations were the fact that her mother had had two sons before the patient was born and that the man in the dream was a childhood friend whom she had assumed she would marry some day. However, during her teens she recognizes that he did not feel as strongly attached to her and they were "too much pals to be lovers."

After this material had been discussed, she had a third dream in which she was taking care of a baby in a girlfriend's house. When the friend came home, she was roundly scolded for neglecting the infant. Upon awakening, the patient suddenly realized the baby in the dream was herself.

I am barely scratching the surface of this material, and am attempting to demonstrate merely the relationship between the patient's ego strivings, her conceptualization of this, in part, as a baby, the connection between the baby, herself and her mother, and all of these presenting "good" and "bad" aspects.

One word regarding theory: "Baby" as an internal psychic object obviously does not fit with our notions of the formation of the psychic apparatus during infancy and childhood. It is a secondary elaboration, built of man-made materials and resembling the procreation fantasies of psychotics. The few patients in this group who stormed through an intense, ambivalent, archaic transference involving "good" and "bad" mother appeared to drop the pregnancy-baby concept. For example, one patient dreamed after a termination date had been set of a Snow White story in which she was brought back to life by her husband's kiss after the doctor had extracted the old witch's poison.

CONCLUSION

A group of women are discussed who have in common hysterical features and a relative emphasis on pregnancy fantasies and dreams, emotionality, pseudo sexuality, helplessness and demandingness. Their symptoms are discussed from the standpoint of the family interaction, the integrative aspects, and the therapeutic problems raised.

References

Block, J., Patterson, V., Block, J. & Jackson, D. (1958). A study of the parents of schizophrenic & neurotic children. *Psychiatry*, 27, 3.

Emsch, M. (1944). The need to know as related to identification and acting out. *International Journal of Psychiatry*, 25.

Fairbairn, W. R. D. (1952). The nature of hysterical states. In W. Fairbairn, *An Object-Relations Theory of the Personality*. New York: Basic Books.

Fenichel, O. (1945). *The psychoanalytic theory of the neuroses*. New York: W. W. Norton.

Greenacre, P. (1950). General problems of acting out. *Psychiatric Quarterly*, *XIX*.

Jackson, D. (1954). Some aspects of the oedipal complex. *Psychiatric Quarterly*, 23 (1). Presented to the American Psychoanalytic Association, St. Louis, Missouri, May 1954.

Kaufman, I., Frank, T., Heims, L., Herrick, S., Reiser, D., & Willer, L. (1960). Treatment implications of a new classification of parents of schizophrenic children. *American Journal of Psychiatry*, *116*, 929–924.

Marmor, Judd. (1953). Orality in the Hysteric. *Journal of the American Psychiatric Association*.

Siegman. Emotionality: A hysterical character defense. I.

Stanton, A., & Schwartz, M. (1955). *The mental hospital*. New York: Basic Books.

Wittels, F. (1930). Notes on the hysterical character. *Medical Review of Reviews*, *36*; pp. 186–90.

CHAPTER 8

A Note on
the Importance of Trauma in the
Genesis of Schizophrenia[1]
(1957)

Adelaide Johnson and her colleagues, in their "Studies in schizophrenia at the Mayo Clinic,"[2] have made an important contribution to the understanding of the psychopathology of schizophrenia. Following the presentation of this paper at the American Psychoanalytic Association meeting in 1955, I heard a good deal of muttering as some of the audience filed into the lobby. One distinguished analyst remarked to a companion: "Good heavens, don't they realize there is such a thing as heredity? Many of my patients have had just the kind of experience she reported and they aren't schizophrenic." Since many psychiatrists and psychoanalysts have great difficulty in considering a theory of psychogenic causation for schizophrenia, this is an almost predictable response to the Mayo Clinic thesis, and one that is not entirely met by postulating a quantitative factor, such as the amount or frequency of the trauma. Thus it is

---

[1] From *Psychiatry 20* (2), 1957. Reprinted with permission.

[2] Peter G. S. Beckett and others (1956). "Studies in schizophrenia at the Mayo Clinic: I. The significance of exogenous traumata in the genesis of schizophrenia," *19*;137–142. Adelaide M. Johnson and others (1956), "Studies in schizophrenia at the Mayo Clinic, *Psychiatry*: II. Observations on Ego Functions in Schizophrenia," *Psychiatry* (1956) *19*; 143–148.

especially important, when such a theory is presented, that it not lend itself to easy dismissal by the skeptical.

It seems to me that the thesis presented in this paper about the relation between "traumatic assaults" and schizophrenia is essentially correct, but that it suffers from the present conceptualization of trauma and punishment. Webster's *New International Dictionary* defines trauma as: "A mental shock; a disturbing experience to which a neurosis may be traced." This is the definition which permeates the paper of Johnson and her colleagues and which, in my opinion, does not render justice to the complexity and subtlety of the kinds of human interaction that predispose people to schizophrenia. The authors say, "Certain types of physical or psychological assault occur too frequently in our series to be fortuitous. Furthermore, in the earliest delusions of the schizophrenic episode, the type of assault is so often specifically reflected as to make a chance relationship seem most unlikely. The types of assault fall into two main groups — first, persistent obstruction to ego differentiation; and, second, discrete physical or psychological assault."[3]

Certainly the first type of "assault" mentioned — namely, "persistent obstruction to ego differentiation" — indicates recognition by the authors that a schizophrenic is not produced only by a series of unholy beatings and an occasional rape. Unfortunately, however, the main focus of the paper seems to be on the second category — "discrete physical or psychological assault" — and this, to me, has a flavor that renders schizophrenia perilously close to a kind of psychological subdural hematoma.

While I have puzzled over the etiology and pathogenesis of schizophrenia since 1943, when the late Jacob Kasanin interested me in the topic, only during the last two years have I felt any real understanding of either. Before that, concepts such as "overwhelming anxiety," "rejection," "flooding of the ego by the id," "breakdown of repression," and so on were conceptual aids, but they had limited meaning, even though I saw schizophrenic patents in collaborative therapy, group therapy, intensive individual therapy, and multiple therapy. But finally, by participating in the interaction of the families of schizophrenics, I have gotten a feel for what the patient has been up against.

The Mayo group has played a large part in the development of collaborative therapy and has documented its usefulness. They have made it clear that the process is only as good as the therapists' ability to communicate with each

---

[3] Reference footnote 1; p. 139.

other. However, apart from the undisputed value of collaborative therapy as a therapeutic method, I am not sure that as a research tool, even under optimal conditions, it can precipitate and crystallize out the patterns of a schizophrenic family interaction in their appropriate subtlety, complexity, and intensity. Even when the parents are seen more often than once a week, their therapy is apt to be oriented toward event-reporting. This is partially appropriate to the situation because, after all, the patient is the patient. Yet although a therapist working in the collaborative setting can get a feel of the parents' personalities, he cannot really appreciate the gestalt when the parent being seen by one therapist, the other parent being seen by a colleague, and the schizophrenic patient in treatment with still a third colleague are blended into a chiaroscuro of blame, hate, dependency, jealousy, and, above all, the terrible, all-pervading "Who am I?" that underlies the family tragedy.

A group of colleagues and I have undertaken conjoint therapy with schizophrenic patients and their parents, tape-recording the psychotherapeutic sessions and later checking with the patient regarding some of the events reported by the parents.[4] Our experience has indicated that often the traumatic assault, to use Johnson's terminology, is of such a nature that trauma is hardly an appropriate word. Rather, it has constituted a condition operating in the patient's environment, which has been nondiscrete and continuing.

A second point of variance with the Mayo group's conclusions concerns their comment that if the child is to survive within the family, the details of the traumatic assault must be dealt with first by denial and then by repression. In our investigations, we have often found that the reporting of the patient is more complicated than can be accounted for by repression or denial, as these terms are ordinarily used. There is truly a perceptual difficulty involved, which is partly a matter of what is paid attention to.

For example, the mother says to the patient, in effect, "Tell me anything; I can take it," whereas the father says explicitly, "Don't be ungrateful and criticize us." The patient turns on the father with angry righteous indignation, but the mother's remark turns out to be the more deadly. The patient, in reporting what went on, doubts that what he told his mother was really his own idea. That is, he feels he was saying something that she put him up to. One

---

[4] This research has been supported in part by the Josiah Macy, Jr. Foundation, USPHS grant #M1673, and the Palo Alto Medical Research Foundation. My colleagues are Gregory Bateson, Jay Haley, John Weakland, and William Fry.

78

might say that there is a psychic trauma involved in this sort of ploy on the mother's part, but it is non-discrete and continuing. The sudden absence of oxygen is a physiological trauma for the human, but a chronically lowered partial pressure of oxygen is a condition that the human can adapt to. To push the analogy further, the person who has adapted to lowered oxygen tension may be unaware that he is "different" until he is confronted with "normal" atmospheric conditions. Then his adaptive measures may cause him difficulty. In a similar way, would there be schizophrenics if the environment were identical to the home situation? Elsewhere, Bateson, Haley, Weakland, and I have tried to demonstrate how schizophrenia can be viewed as appropriate to the patient's particular ecologic niche.[5]

The idea that trauma floods the child's psyche with more affect or instinctual energy than can be mastered might be refined by noting that the effect of a trauma cannot be measured simply by the amount of trauma, or by the chronological age and maturational level of the child. Rather the vital factors are the contextual or operational setting in which it occurs and the relation of the event to the sequence.

The work of Hebb[6] and Lilly[7] might lend support to the idea that not only is the codifying of perceptions essential to the maintenance of "who I am," but vast alterations in classes of percepts and their sequential relationships can be devastating to the maintenance of an intact ego. While the implication by mother that Johnny may become a murderer is undoubtedly traumatic to his future social relations and to his notion of his own personal worth, he may grow up and become a murderer — even of his own mother — without exhibiting notable schizophrenic phenomena. If the implication that he has enough badness, violence, and whatnot in him to become a murderer leads to a perception of himself that is in unresolvable opposition to the percepts that generally keep him in harmony with his family's interactional patterns, then there may be a dissolution of his ego to the extent that he would be called

---

[5] Gregory Bateson, Don Jackson, Jay Haley, and John Weakland, Toward a theory of schizophrenia," *Behavioral Science* (1956) 1:251–264.

[6] O. Hebb, "The mammal and his environment," *American Journal of Psychiatry* (1955) *111*; 826–831.

[7] J. C. Lilly, "Effects of physical restraint and of ordinary levels of physical stimuli on intact, healthy persons," presented at Group for Advancement of Psychiatry, Asbury Park, New Jersey, November 13, 1955.

schizophrenic. For example, the implication that he is dangerous may upset the mother's other signals that she is in control of the definition of their relationship. It may mean the revelation to the child that she sees him as more like his father, when previously he has been dealing with his lack of identification with his father by going along with the mother's control as if he were part of her. To the child who does not see himself as being allowed to blow his own nose because although his hand does it, it was really his mother's idea, being regarded as potentially evil may be a rather different trauma than it is to the child who has known he was nothing but trouble from the start.

Another problem that must be answered in presenting a theory of schizophrenia based on psychogenic trauma concerns those patients who do not present such a history. Kant, for example, studied 56 consecutive cases of schizophrenia and found no precipitating factors involved.[8] The growing literature differentiating between process and reactive schizophrenia would seem to support the belief that in some cases schizophrenia just happens. It may not be enough to say that the lack of a traumatic history is a reflection of the incompleteness of the investigation of the patient, although I am sure that this is often, if not usually, the case. It may be that those patients who have a history and a recollection of trauma, and from whose parents these events can be elicited, are actually the "healthier" schizophrenics, and that those who can offer no clear-cut cause for their illness are in worse shape. This is another way of saying that the reporting of traumatic events may be but a caricature of more enduring events, and that patients who have been reared with subtle malignancy cannot even report trauma, nor can their parents in all honesty, report any horrendous occurrences.

The idea of trauma introduces also, by implication, a corollary, "constitution." Obviously, if a patient falters or falls before a "mild trauma," then he is of a sensitive make-up. While this is possibly a correct notion, it has some pitfalls, for it requires of the psychiatrist value judgments about what constitutes a trauma and how much is too much. An incredible amount of information is required to be able to judge a trauma in reference to context, timing, and sequence — and these matters are crucial. Rats that will put up with electric shocks in order to obtain food, water, and sex will completely forgo these

---

[8] O. Kant, The problem of psychogenic precipitation in schizophrenia, *Psychiatric Quarterly, 1042* (16) 341–350.

basic requirements if the shock is properly timed. Thus if a young male rat just about to mount is shocked, he will renounce his sex life forever.[9]

A final point deals with the concept of "identification with the hostile aggressor." There is no question in my mind that the phenomenon as described by the Mayo group does occur and is important to label. However, it is not clear to me that a sufficiently satisfactory theoretical framework is available to explain why a pre-schizophrenic will assume responsibility for something he did not do. Identification with the hostile aggressor is a description, not an explanation. It might, for example, fit in with the concept of the importance of the definition of control in a relationship.[10] The schizophrenic might have to identify with the aggressor because of habitual experience in relationships in which there is no appropriate definition of who is in control of the control. If one conceives that there are two sets of signals involved, the first acknowledging control and the second, a metacommunicative comment on the first signal, acknowledging who is in control of the one in control, then it is possible to depict mental pathology stemming from confusion and lack of resolution of these signals. Ideally, the mother–child relationship would be one in which the mother increasingly operates with signals of the second sort so that the child has experience in being in control, experience of mastery, and in recognizing who is in control of the control. As the child grows older, the mother relinquishes control of the second kind in an expanding number of areas. Thus the child's playtime may literally be with himself in control, and ideally the mother can allow the child control expressed as "Feed me," "Read me a story," and so on. The mother of a schizophrenic may be seen as having difficulty in distinguishing between the two levels of signals. She can acknowledge neither that she is in control nor that she is not. This situation could theoretically encourage helplessness and withdrawal as ploys on the child's part to force the definition of control. However, such forcing leads to the paradox of power by giving up power, and identification with the aggressor is appropriate to such a context.

These comments are offered in no final way, but only to indicate that various frames of reference can be usefully employed in attempting to expand one's thinking beyond the concept of "psychic trauma." I have attempted to

---

[9] Personal communication from David Mc K. Rioch.

[10] I am indebted to Jay Haley for the idea that the control of the definition of a relationship might be used as a descriptive tool for depicting family interaction.

raise some questions about the relationship of trauma to schizophrenia because I feel that the important contribution of the Mayo group can best be viewed as having limited implications.

Schizophrenia is a response to a perduring situation for which it is, in some sense, appropriate, and the discernible trauma are but labelable situations in an otherwise misty and blurred picture. It may even be that those schizophrenics who have such well-defined situations at their command are more capable of resolving their psychosis. This is not to underestimate the importance in therapy of seeking out and confronting the patient with traumatic events. Since schizophrenics are reputed to be rather unreliable folk who project all over the place, the clinician would do well to take Johnson and her colleagues seriously, and by doing so, they will be taking the patient seriously.

I have raised the trauma question also because it has serious implications for research. Investigators of schizophrenia have for some time been in an anatomical and pathological phase, with emphasis on dissecting individual psychodynamics. Historically, the place of psychogenic trauma in etiology appears to be shifting from Freud's original idea of a single traumatic event to the concept of repetitive trauma. The next step would be not who does what to whom, but *how* who does what. Perhaps the next phase will include a study of schizophrenia (or schizophrenias) as a family-borne disease involving a complicated host-vector-recipient cycle that includes much more than can be connoted by the term "schizophrenogenic mother."[11] One can even speculate whether schizophrenia, as it is known today, would exist if parthenogenesis were the usual mode of propagation of the human species, or if women were impersonally impregnated and gave birth to infants who were reared by state nurses in a communal setting.

---

[11] Jackson, D. (1954). "The question of family homeostasis," presented at the Annual Meeting, American Psychiatric Association, St. Louis, Missouri; see Chap. 10 in this volume.

CHAPTER 9

Guilt and the Control of Pleasure in the Schizoid Personality[1]

(1958)

It is the thesis of this brief presentation that guilt over masturbation, and *mutatis mutandi* other pleasurable activity, stems in part form the fact that the child dares to determine the nature of his relationships. His providing pleasure for himself is autonomous, assertive behavior, which particularly in schizoid personalities may be experienced as dangerous activity. Through the mechanism of guilt feelings the child attempts to reinstate the parental control in reality and within himself that in turn may continue the cycle by creating a further urge toward autonomy.

It is a necessary extension of this thesis that the mother of the schizoid fears the loss of control of her child; and for her, masturbatory activity may exemplify such loss of control. The mother's (or parents') reaction to suspecting or witnessing her child masturbating is anachronistic, because she cannot help but translate the activity into her own adult sexual fantasies. As a result, a complex communication is set up in which the child accepts blame for activity that he cannot comprehend because he has no notion yet of the

---

[1] Presented at the first Frieda Fromm-Reichmann Memorial Lecture, Veteran's Administration Hospital, Palo Alto, California, June 7, 1957. Manuscript received November 5, 1957. Reprinted with permission from the *British Journal of Medical Psychology*, XXXI, Part 2, 1958, pp. 124, 130.

framework for his mother's fantasies. The mother in turn, may feel very possessive toward the child yet reject him because union connotes sexuality to her. Normal adult orgiastic pleasure consists of an explosive autonomy and, at the same time, a feeling of union with another. It is not satisfactory if it is rape, at one extreme, or a nursing situation at the other. The reconciliation of these two poles are impossible for some mothers, and the conflict is communicated to the child over the issue of masturbation. The healthy body, pleasure and ego mastery of the activity gets connected with an unclear notion of doing something wrong.

There is more involved, in my opinion, in the masturbation conflict between parent and child than the acknowledged deep-seated cultural prohibition against sexual activity. The additional factor involves control, that is, who determines the nature of the relationship. Whereas parents may want children to grow up and manage themselves, they may have difficulty in letting the child develop mastery or autonomy. In this situation, it is handy if the child develops guilt feelings, since he may then express himself autonomously and reinstate the parents' control of himself by feeling guilty. Guilt, in this sense, is an integrative phenomenon both in fantasy and in the communication that the adult perceives. Ethologists have described "submissive" behavior in many animal species that communicates, "You have control of me." This behavior in the animal can be life-saving — perhaps the analogy to guilt is not inappropriate. In short, both the parent and the child are reacting to more than the lust component of masturbatory activity.

In order to develop the "control" framework, I will review some historical and etymological aspects of masturbation and compare this theoretical framework with some of Freud's and Fairbairn's concepts.

PLEASURE VERSUS CONTROL

It is trite to note that for the infant it is a life and death matter that his parents assume virtually complete charge of his existence. Those activities that the parents do not control, for example crying, defecation, etc., the parents may define as being "normal" or usual for an infant so that the infant is permitted to be in control of these functions. Obviously, parents vary greatly in the extent to which they have to define who is in control — that is, how much autonomy they can allow the infant just as cultures vary enormously in what kind of activities are considered "normal" for infants. The anxious young mother who is upset because her child cries "too much" may be relieved if an expert defines the activity as normal. If an outsider defines the nature of the mother's relationship to the child for her, the conflict over wanting to be in control and fearing seeing herself as controlling may be avoided.

As the infant grows from an "it" to a "he" or "she," the parents increasingly need their definition of the relationship to be observed and acted upon by the child. An interesting phenomenon occurs in, for example, those mothers who can permit infants to play with their genitals but who are driven to distraction by the same activity occurring in an 18-month or 2 year-old child. Somewhere along in this period comes the imputation of badness to the child, and the mother's need to control this badness or even to stamp it out. My belief is that the difference in the mother's reaction is caused by her suspicion that said child is fantasizing and not merely producing a pleasurable physical sensation. (The mother who cannot permit even the infant to have pleasurable sensation is probably reacting, via identification, as if it were fantasizing.) Why should fantasy (or the suspicion of it) require the mother to strengthen her control? Perhaps because fantasy involves the independent creation of relationships by the child. Masturbatory activity may mean to the mother that the child is defining his relationship to her as one in which he can have pleasure separate from his mother. Even more disturbing, it may mean that he is defining their relationship as one in which he is able to control her as, for example, by obtaining sexual pleasure from her in fantasy. In any case, the mother's suspicion that the child is fantasizing makes his behavior meaningful, a communication rather than a mere wiggling of some fortunately flexible piece of anatomy.

I suspect that the mother of the schizophrenic, in particular, cannot permit the child to have separate relationships, nor permit him to emit those signals that indicate he is having separate relationships, even in fantasy. On the other hand, she cannot permit him to indicate that he is controlling her in reality or in fantasy (Bateson et al., 1956; Jackson, 1957). The mother's dilemma; namely, that she cannot tolerate the thought of being the sexual object of the child's fantasies and cannot tolerate the thought that she is not such an object is avoided as long as she denies those signals from the child which indicate an attempt to define the nature of his relationship to her, and as long as additionally she can deny her wish to control or rationalize it via "God," "sin," and "for your own good."

Some of the secrecy, on a conscious level, surrounding masturbatory activity even in fairly healthy families may be an avoidance of how to handle such an independent act on the part of the child. As long as both parties pretend ignorance, the authority problem is not encountered. It is not uncommon to see this same issue occurring between husband and wife when they are not clear on who is defining the nature of the marital relationship. For example, a young woman came to her therapist quite upset because she had discovered her husband was homosexual. What she actually had discovered was evidence (presumably a communication from him) that he was masturbating and since it was "the same thing as being in love with a man," she assumed he was homosexual. This was a very controlling woman who constantly attempted in all areas, including sex, to define her husband's relationship to her. However, although he went along with her on most issues, she could not control an involuntary activity like his having an erection, and more than once he failed her in the clinches. What is especially pertinent is her denial that he might be having heterosexual fantasies. This fact, in addition to her general alarm about his mental state, provides a rather analogous situation to the parent who fears the child will go insane because he masturbates.

EVIL, INSANITY AND MASTURBATION

The word "masturbation" appears to have arisen in the late eighteenth century. Its etymology may be from a combination of the Latin roots "man," hand; "sutpra," debauchery; and "turbo" or "tupra," motion. Thus we have the connotation of evil doing through manipulation. However, the term "onanism" preceded "masturbation" and was in rather good repute until relatively recently. Tuke, an eighteenth-century English psychiatrist, stated: "Onanism is frequently seen in insanity and often is a cause of it." The term "self-pollution" was a popular synonym at the time and appears to have had a similar origin to "Onanism"; namely, the story in *Genesis*, Ch. 38, of Onan, son of Judah and brother of Er. Er married Tamar and was dispatched by the Lord for reasons unknown. The next son, Onan, was ordered by Judah, his father, to "go into your brother's widow, do your duty to her as a husband's brother and produce a child for your brother." But as the Bible states further, since Onan knew that the child would not belong to him, he used to spill his seed on the ground whenever he went into his brother's widow to avoid producing a child for his brother. For this disobedience, the Lord "cut him off" and interestingly enough, Judah, the father, was then tricked into impregnating Tamar when she disguised herself as a whore and he came upon her outside the city gates. To me, it appears that Onan practiced coitus interruptus, not masturbation, and that the point of the story is not the fact that father cuts off the little boy's penis for playing with it, but that father feels like another son in a matriarchal situation. For example, despite his being head man of the group, Judah is tricked by Tamar into impregnating her and in addition has to pay a fee of some fine young goats for the privilege. Thus the woman has been indirectly responsible for determining the fate of Er, Onan, and the powerful Judah.

Some scholars feel that Onan and Er refer to deceased tribes of the Judahites and, if one dwells for a moment on the facts of that period the biblical passage makes good sense. The Judahites were nomadic tribes and by reason of circumstances were matriarchal. The men roamed the countryside with their flocks while the women maintained a fireside of sorts, presumably an oasis, and raised the children. Evidently, the men returned to camp in a staggered fashion and would cohabit with any available female. The importance of the father was thus lessened since he was not wise enough to know his own child, and since the life or death of the tribe depended upon the woman's getting impregnated and rearing the children. It is obvious that masturbation, zoobestry, and homosexuality would be threats to such a way of life and it may have been to point up such a lesson that the story of Onan originated. Onan was killed for defiance — he refused to accept a communal woman for purposes of furthering the tribe.

There is another story that is perhaps pertinent in a consideration of masturbation myths, the Greek tale of Narcissus. Certainly the term "self-love," "self-abuse," and "Narcissism" are linked in our psychiatric vocabulary, and Freud's choice of this legend for the coining of his term "Narcissism" may have been over-determined. You will recall that this is also essentially a matriarchal story in that Echo, one of the Oreades, the mountain nymphs who were tall women and ardent hunters, falls in love with a youth called Narcissus and wastes away to an echo when he spurns her. Narcissus, in turn, is punished by Aphrodite for refusing the maid and is caused to fall in love with his own reflection, which he sees as a fountain goddess looking up at him from the water. Some accounts have him hearing Echo's voice as he steadfastly gazes at his own image. The fact that he is described as youthful and pale, that he wastes away, and that he changed into a flower which grows from seeds impregnated into the ground are all perhaps relevant to our topic. To overstate the case, when the man refuses to define his relationship to the woman in terms of her having control via the progeny, she becomes the embodiment of emptiness and nothingness, an echo, and he destroys himself in the process. Note that additionally by virtue of the nice touch of having Narcissus hear Echo's voice and seeing his image as a fountain goddess we have analogues to a psychotic state. Narcissus further reveals his schizoid nature by the fact that what really destroys him is his attachment to the woman in himself — the internalized maternal object which he projects as a reflection from the fountain.

Medicine has done its share to perpetuate myths about masturbation. In 1760 Andre D. Simon Tissot published *A Treatise on the Diseases Produced by Onanism*, which many authorities regard as having caused a long-lasting condemnation of masturbation. It was re-published as late as 1832. In 1932 Malamud and Palmer reviewed the literature and a series of their own patients in a very thorough study on the role played by masturbation and the causation of mental disturbances. They concluded that in one group of patients masturbation was responsible for the mental illness since it caused a conflict between the ability to stop the habit and the fear of its consequences. Among other disturbances they felt resulted from such conflict were neurasthenia, depression, hysterical manifestations, and paranoid episodes. They felt psychotherapy was definitely a benefit in such cases.

Freud appears as a somewhat equivocal figure in the masturbation-mental illness question. Although he made lasting original observations regarding masturbation, he does not seem to have taken a clear stand on sanctioning the activity. It is understandable that Freud would not have been free to do so when the culture he lived in is considered. However, Freud's theory itself provides additional reason why the practice might be regarded as harmful. In his paper "On the Passing of the Oedipus Complex" (1924), Freud states that a conflict is established in the little boy over the desire for the love object (mother) and fear of losing the penis, and this conflict is solved by his renouncing the love object in favor of the penis. In the little girl, Freud feels, external intimidation leads to the renouncing of the oedipal desires and the cessation of masturbatory activity during latency. Huschka (1938) has confirmed Freud's idea that the main intimidating threats in both sexes come from women. Dr. Huschka studied information regarding masturbation that was obtained from the parents of 320 problem children. One hundred and twenty-eight of the children's parents stated that the child masturbated and 85% of the children were severely threatened in order to stop the activity, 67% of these threats being physical in character. The majority of threats were made by the mother.

If Freud's theory is altered from regarding the organ (penis) as the crucial element to putting the emphasis on the feeling state (assertiveness, control) there need not be separate theories for male and female. Freud himself (1924) equates masturbation and enuresis. Unfortunately, he did not follow this lead to its natural conclusion, namely, the emphasis on assertion and defiance of the parental prescriptions and the consequent guilt feelings.

PSYCHOANALYTIC THEORY

According to Freud, we have to discriminate between two kinds of feelings of guilt. One makes itself known as social fear, fear of outer authority; the other is a fear of inner authority or pangs of conscience. The feeling of guilt originating from the fear of outer authority coincides with the fear of the loss of love. The fear of the inner authority coincides with the fear of the super ego. Freud's derivation of the feeling of guilt is well known. The incorporation of the aggression, that is, the turning of the destructive instincts against the ego, originates the feeling of guilt and makes its appearance in the ego as an unconscious need for punishment. For this reason he has equated the term "feeling of guilt" with the concept of "the need for punishment."

According to Freud's theory, especially as developed in "Totem and Taboo" (1918) the Oedipus complex is the source of man's sense of guilt and of his morality. Freud supposes that in the primal horde the father was murdered, dismembered and devoured by the sons. Having perpetrated this act they were seized with a longing for the father whom they had thus lost. This longing was converted into dread of the community, which is another term for sense of guilt. As time went on and the longing for the father recurred, being the expression of unsatisfied libido fixated to the father, it became the principal source of the various religions in which the power of the father was re-established by the mechanism of projection. The father was exalted while the son was abased and the primal transgression was redressed. The father's image was revived and in a sublimated form the passive homosexual libido directed toward him attained its goal again. Freud's ideas on the role of the super ego and castration fear can of course apply to any aggressive attempt to achieve gratification — including masturbation.

It is useful to consider Fairbairn's reformulation of the classical psychoanalytic viewpoint (1949) because, to me, it serves as a bridge between the classical view and the concept of control presented here. Taking as his text Freud's statement: "The super ego is, however, not merely a deposit left by the earliest object choices of the id, it also represents an energetic reaction formation against these choices," Fairbairn points out that in describing the super ego as a reaction formation against object choices that Freud is describing it as the instigator of repression, and that if repression involves the reaction against object choices it must be directed against objects and not against guilty impulses. Guilt, or the sense of personal moral badness, thus becomes secondary to a sense of badness in the object. Fairbairn feels that guilt is thus a defense against relationships with bad objects. The guilt over masturbation thus might be regarded as arising from the relationship of this activity to forbidding internal objects rather than over the necessity of controlling libidinal impulses. Guilt, in this sense, is conjunctive and adaptational since it keeps the bad object preserved (and hence the "good" object remains "good") and the conscience pain is offered up as payment for the attempt to control the internalized objects. The sequence described above is perhaps most impressively seen in the repetitious sequence of masturbation, guilt, promise to abstain, and subsequent masturbation that can virtually destroy the rest of life on earth for the schizoid adolescent. The compulsive repetitiousness of such cycles is difficult for me to conceive of as sexual tension, discharge, and rebuilding of charge, but it can be understood in terms of the wish to control the object and the fear of abandonment that such control brings with it. Some wit once remarked about women that "you can't get along with them, and you can't get along without them." Unfortunately some schizoids are in the same position vis-á-vis the maternal object. That the body itself as an object is important in such masturbatory conflict can be noted clinically by the following observations:

1. Rising sexual tension could be handled via nocturnal emissions and then the hand would not be blamed. Obviously this route is not sufficient for such adolescents despite their intense guilt. Perhaps the desire for conscious control of fantasies is an important factor as well as the pleasurable relationship to the body.

2. Hypochondriacal fears are common in such adolescents and again can be understood, in part, as a struggle of the individual for uniqueness, a private totality, a complete managing of the internal objects and the expiation of such unwelcome ideas of independence. The inability to define the nature of his relationships with external objects results in a chaotic state vis-á-vis internal objects and a consequent confusion about who he is and what is him. In this, I am very much in accord with Szasz's ideas (1957).

3.	There may be in such individuals a need to suffer self-inflicted physical or ideational pain. Tics, blushing, excoriations and physical pain and shame are common and have not only an exhibitionistic and self-punitive aspect but may also be unconscious attempts of the individual to define who he is and where he is. In a certain sense, the ability to inflict pain upon oneself, bear it, and feel it subside is much like drawing a line around one's property to declare what is his. That this kind of definition is unacceptable to the mother can be noted clinically in patients who pick their noses, scratch or break out in tics. Such activities may goad the mother to frenzy and she may accuse the child of trying to upset her.

4.	The attempt to use one's own body as a substitute for a lost object is discussed below.

To summarize the application of Freudian, Fairbairnian, and control theories to masturbation, we might say that they agree that: a. It is the fantasies that are important and guilt about the act serves as a displacement and hence a safeguard for repression. b. Problems regularly connected with over-frequent masturbation are conflicts centering about the lacking satisfaction and there is an expectation of punishment for this aggressiveness.

The differences in the theories are that the non-Freudian theories deal with objects, by Fairbairn as intrapsychic occurrences, by the control theory as intrapsychic occurrences directly related to real objects. The latter is thus but a logical extension of Fairbairn's work. For example, the dilemma posed by the child's attempt to define the nature of his relationship to his mother can be understood when one postulates that she is also an object within him. As one schizophrenic patient stated: "In the end we hurt only ourselves." Non-schizophrenics may experience the dilemma as a fear of going crazy because of masturbation. Such fear may develop when the individual is growing closer, socially and physiologically, to making his fantasies become reality of a sort. Going crazy may represent the wild gratification of every whim, and at the same time, it forces "them" to take care of him via the punishment of incarceration in an asylum.

MASTURBATION, AUDITORY HALLUCINATIONS AND ABANDONMENT

There are two clinical observations that have struck me as pertinent to my thesis, but neither has been carefully verified. The first is that although the auditory hallucinations of a schizophrenic may accuse him of all manner of possible and occasionally improbable anatomical combinations with others, they do not accuse him of being, in effect, "a dirty masturbator." If this observation is true, then the following speculation might be pertinent: the voices accuse the schizophrenic of activities in which there is an object other than himself. When his own body is the object, the activity, masturbation, provides a frame which states, "my fantasies are not real" or "this is only masturbation." Though a forbidden activity, masturbation may be a *necessary* activity (apart from the sexual gratification) in order that the transactions that occur as masturbatory fantasies do not become thoughts, which frighten one lest they take over and result in action. According to this explanation then, masturbation does not result merely from the sequence: tension, fantasy, sexual excitement, masturbation, relief of tension. But in schizoid people there is also the cycle: fear of abandonment = attempt to define the nature of the control of one's relationships, fantasy, increased fear of abandonment, the necessity to define the message as "only masturbation" (solitary activity), fear of the autonomy of self, pleasure, guilt and hence reinstatement of the significant other's control, and so on.

The second observation concerns the correspondence between the individuals' feeling abandoned and masturbatory activity. In my experience, it is common for schizoid people when they find no one at home to experience a sudden masturbatory urge. Such urges are common also in stressful situations like final examinations and figuring out their income tax. In understanding such phenomena it is helpful to postulate internal and external objects and the dilemma that controlling them produces. For example, the schizophrenic individual who finds himself alone may experience the phenomena as if he had been abandoned. He immediately turns for gratification to the internal objects which were once external love objects and forces them to gratify him, via fantasy, as well as the taking over of a pleasure, giving function himself, in reality. Often he will experience a momentary return of euphoria only to run headlong into his past and thus to experience guilt and self-abnegation. Now you see, he has behaved in a fashion so that he deserves to be left and is again threatened with abandonment which he now attempts to handle by shame and guilt. The healthy adolescent may also react to abandonment with a masturbatory urge but he finds some comfort in his own body, much as a child stroking his blanket while he chews on a corner of it. Stressful situations may produce a masturbatory urge for additional reasons than mere release of tension. The threat of failure or of success, the urge to defy the authorities by cheating or refusing to comply may light up the old problem about who determines the nature of the relationship. The conflict is acted out in miniature through the masturbatory act and the individual may be freer to take his examination or pay his full pound of flesh.

The concept presented is built around the theme that it becomes increasingly important to the individual from infancy onward to determine the nature of his relationships. The schizoid individual is handicapped in such efforts by his relationship to his mother who is controlling, but who must not be regarded as controlling. The child must therefore develop covert means of handling pleasurable or assertive activity and masturbation becomes an especially meaningful situation because:

1.   Pleasure is obtained from one's own body but guilt feelings make restitution for the assertiveness or defiance involved.

2.   The secretive, bad behavior provides a frame for fantasies that labels them as only fantasies. Disgust cloaks any connections with real wishes and guilt washes over any notions of assertiveness or mastery.

3.   Although masturbation can be an attempt at mastery, at ego growth via a differentiation of one's self from them, it leads to a fear of abandonment and a wish for outside control. Whether there is an appeal to God or one's better nature, a new cycle will be set in motion and a new attempt to determine the nature of one's relationships.

ACKNOWLEDGMENTS

Dr. Frieda Fromm-Reichmann expressed similar ideas to these at a lecture given shortly before her death. She felt that we had conceived the idea independently and urged me to continue to explore it. I am indebted to her, and I would also like to express my appreciation to those who constructively criticized this paper, especially Dr. W. Ronald Fairbairn and Dr. Judd Marmor. This paper is from the Palo Alto Medical Clinic and the Palo Alto Medical Research Foundation. The hypotheses contained in it are shared with Jay Haley and have arisen out of a research project directed by Gregory Bateson and supported in part by a U.S. Public Health Service Grant, M-1673, and the Macy Foundation.

References

Bateson, G., Jackson, D., Haley, J., & Weakland, J. (1956). Toward a theory of schizophrenia. *Behavioral Sciences, 1* (4), 251–264.

Fairbairn, W. R. D. (1949). Steps in the development of an object relations theory of personality. *British Journal of Medical Psychology, 22;* 26.

Freud, S. (1918). *Totem and taboo.* New York: Moffat, Yard & Co.

Freud, S. (1948). The passing of the Oedipus complex. In *Collected Papers,* vol. 11. London: Hogarth Press.

Huschka, M. (1938). The incidence & character of masturbation threats in a group of problem children. *Psychoanalytic Quarterly, 7,* 330.

Jackson, D. (1957). A note on the importance of trauma in the genesis of schizophrenia. *Psychiatry, 20,* 181.

Malamud, W., & Palmer, G. (1932). The role of masturbation in mental disease. *Journal of Nervous and Mental Disorders, 76,* 366.

Szasz, T. (1957). *Pain and pleasure.* New York: Basic Books.

Tissot, S. A. D. (1832). *A treatise on the diseases produced by onanism.* New York: Collins and Hannay.

SECTION II:
DEFINING AN INTERACTIONAL THEORY
OF HUMAN RELATIONSHIPS

Introduction and Overview

The chapters selected for inclusion in this section represent some of the most important and lucid expositions of Interactional Theory ever written. Chapter 10, "The Question of Family Homeostasis" was first presented by Jackson in 1954, although not published until nearly four years later. In it Jackson sets forth the revolutionary concept of family homeostasis, a construct that has come under serious criticism in recent years, but which nonetheless continues to have salience within a broad spectrum of cybernetically-oriented theoreticians and clinicians, including Gregory Bateson, Heinz von Foerster, Paul Watzlawick, Salvador Minuchin, and Bradford P. Keeney.

Chapter 11, "Toward a Theory of Schizophrenia" (1956), is considered by many to be the paper that launched what has evolved into the field of family therapy. Written by Gregory Bateson, Don D. Jackson, Jay Haley, and John H. Weakland, "Toward a Theory" outlined the team's use of Whitehead and Russell's theory of logical types to make plain the (often paradoxical) nature of communication processes occurring between a schizophrenic and other family members. Bateson, Jackson, Haley, Weakland, and Fry were destined to become one of the most influential teams of researchers "in the history of psychotherapy since Freud's inner circle of the earlier part of the century" (Trepper, 1995, p. xvii). Introducing the seminal concept of the double bind, and emphasizing the complex nature of contexts and interpersonal interactions, this article, along with Jackson's "Question of Family Homeostasis," continues to stand as archetypal contributions to the professional literature.

Chapter 12, "The Double Bind, Family Homeostasis, and a Control Theory of Human Relationships" (circa 1963), is another of Jackson's papers that remained tucked away in a file for more that 35 years before its publication in this volume, and which includes a brief but clear articulation of fundamental tenets of Interactional Theory.

In 1963, shortly after the Bateson research projects came to an end, Bateson, Jackson, Haley and Weakland published a final joint statement about their collaboration, "A Note on the Double Bind (1962)," presented here as Chapter 13. At that time the team, individually and collectively, had published more than 70 papers during a ten-year collaboration. Since the projects came to an end, more than 500 books and papers have been published based upon the team's work.

In Chapter 14, "Psychoanalytic Education in the Communication Processes" (1962), Jackson outlines fundamental differences between psychoanalytic theory and communication theory, then challenges basic assumptions underlying psychoanalysis, and posits that the nature of the relationship between analyst and patient adequately accounts for change. While the analytic approach seems to have lost much of its grip on the field of psychotherapy, many of the fundamental distinctions Jackson draws are readily applicable in critiquing the current trend toward self-described post-modern, narrative orientations.

In Chapter 15, "Transference Revisited" (1963), Jackson and Jay Haley take issue with the fundamental analytic concepts of transference, the use of interpretation to promote constructive change, and most importantly, question the heuristic value of promoting insight as a goal of psychotherapeutic treatment.

In Chapter 16, "Social Factors and Disorders of Communication: Some Varieties of Pathogenic Organization" (1964), Bateson and Jackson focus their attention on complementary patterns of interaction, particularly "parent–child relationship as the primary sources from which perhaps all behavior is derived ... [and] assumptions about the role of learning in the development of behavior" (p. 240).

Chapter 17 and 18, "The Study of the Family" (1965), and "Family Rules: Marital Quid Pro Quo" (1965) were originally published as companion pieces, and together represent one of Jackson's most compelling descriptions of Interactional Theory. Report and command, the necessity to define the nature of the relationship, the arbitrariness of observer-imposed punctuation, pattern, constraint, relationship rules (as clearly distinguished from family roles), and the marital quid pro quo as a fundamental example of the rule concept, are among the fundamental tenets Jackson weaves together in this masterful exposition of interactional theory.

CHAPTER 10

The Question of Family Homeostatis[1]
(1954/1957)

A growing tendency is evident in psychiatry to regard the emotionally ill individual as only an instance in a field of force that extends from intrapsychic processes to the broadest aspect of the culture in which he lives. There are those who would see man as a collection of unique individuals strictly limited by their biological propensities; such individuals scorn the "culturists," whose prestige, nevertheless, continues to rise. The contributions of Horney, Sullivan, Fromm and others in the psychiatric field as well as many contributors from psychology, sociology and anthropology require no adumbration.

More recently, Johnson and Szurek, and others have rendered an impressive service by demonstrating, by collaborative therapy, specific instances in which unconscious wishes of the parent influence the behavior of the child. The importance of interaction with others in determining behavioral patterns has resulted in technical changes in therapeutic method. Thus, one hears of child clinics that insist on seeing the mother and father, and of group therapy for the mothers of schizophrenics and wives of alcoholics.

The purpose of this presentation is not to restate the already stated, but to consider certain technical and theoretical aspects of family interactional patterns: the importance of changes in other family members as the result of change in the patient during psychiatric treatment; and the relation of family

---

[1] From *The Psychiatric Quarterly Supplement, 31*, Part 1: 79–90 (1957). Copyright, New York State Department of Mental Hygiene, Utica, NY. Reprinted with permission.

interactional patterns (specifically parental interaction) to psychiatric nosological categories.

The term *family homeostasis* is chosen from the concepts of Claude Ber-
nard and Cannon because it implies the relative constancy of the internal
environment, a constancy, however, which is maintained by a continuous interplay of dynamic forces. Another way of considering the topic of "family
homeostasis" would be in terms of communication theory: that is, depicting
family interaction as a closed information system in which variations in output
or behavior are fed back in order to correct the systems response. For example, a boy won a popularity contest in his grammar school, and, riding home
with his mother afterward, was able to tell that she was not entirely pleased
with his success. This was one event that helped set into motion various adaptive responses, including his not being so popular henceforth. One aspect of
his reaction was the father's indifference toward his mother and the tacit
bargain that the child was to supply her needs. It was apparent to the psychiatrist that an integral part of this boy's treatment would be making provisions
for an upset in the mother.

The topic of family homeostasis in no way concerns itself with a sociological approach to the American family, but rather is aimed at a very practical
problem nearly every psychiatrist must encounter: What effect will the appearance of a patient in his office have upon the patient's family? In particular, if
long-term psychotherapy or psychoanalysis is undertaken, the psychiatrist must
take into account the effect a change in the patient's interpersonal dealings will
have on the most contiguous members of the family. It is true, that in most
cases this problem can be dismissed quickly because there will be a fortunate
outcome for both the patient and his family. In a minority of situations, however, adequate psychiatric planning will require an understanding of the total
family situation. The term "family," as used in this paper, refers to the "significant others" in the patients life, whether mother, father, sister, brother, wife
or others. In addition, "family" refers to the group with which the psychiatrist
becomes acquainted through his distillation and translation of the patient's recollections. The individuals include real people of today, the members of the
family of the patient's childhood (who are similar to, but not necessarily identical with, those of the present-day family) and the family members who are
distortions created out of the special biological conditions of childhood. Thus,
to view the patient's family, the psychiatrist must have a four-dimensional concept, with time serving as the fourth dimension. The view of "how it must

have been" is obscured by the fog of family fictions, the family, as members tell themselves they were, usually contrasts with how they actually were. The family first presented by the patient is usually the version offered for public consumption; and, only after several interviews does the real family emerge for the psychiatrist's scrutiny. If the therapist refuses to bother with understanding complicated family interactions, with knowing who meant what to whom, he will be apt to see the patient in terms of extremes. The patient will be conceptualized either as a hostile individual busily throwing out projections like radar signals, or as a violet dying on the desert of other people's unfriendliness.

In our attempt to understand our patients we deal with matters as yet little understood, such as "psychic energy" and "instinctual forces." The fact is sometimes overlooked that one reason why many of us continue to manifest our neurotic woes is that we manage to find people with whom to integrate at a neurotic level. The tendency to live the present in terms of the past is as constant, consistent, and impressive in the human as the heartbeat. With increasing awareness of interpersonal relations, it appears that the particular dramatis personae with whom each of us plays out his life are as rarely chosen by accident as the cast of a Broadway production. The lonely psychiatrist, working with one individual, may tend to see him as a bundle of interpersonal forces much as the company commander's interest is centered about the disposition of forces within his particular sector. If one overworks the concept of projection, the significant others in the patient's life can so easily be seen as constructs of his mental machinations that they never achieve real form and substance within the therapist's office.

It is usual that the psychiatrist treating adults attempts to alter symptoms in his patient and thus is not apt to think of the family as a homeostatic unit. Child psychiatrists have, with few exceptions, come to treat the child and the "significant others" in so-called collaborative therapy. Even in child clinics, the tendency is to concentrate on the mother and not on the family as a whole — thereby excluding potentially important people such as the father, grandmother and others. Some authorities have called attention to the potential fallacy of this practice. It may be that failure to take a total approach toward the family group creates certain obscurities in our understanding, for example, why severe maternal rejection seems to produce schizophrenia in certain cases and not in others. Before we rush in with the cry of "constitution" or "heredity," it should be important to notice what effect rejection of the child by the mother has on the father, or whether there is a third person somewhere on the periphery who manifests occasional tenderness toward the child, thereby possibly saving him from the psychosis.

It is a fairly recondite matter to attempt to place the patient in a setting and to imagine the interplay of emotional forces. Perhaps the greatest aid is our understanding of the phenomena of transference and countertransference, but even here we are dealing with limited concepts. For example, if the therapist feels the patient is in a "father transference," he may tend to think in terms of the patient's father alone, rather than to think "father as a Gestalt" composed of father as a different person under different conditions; or rather than to think of the parental interaction, the mother's relationship to the patient, the mother's and other individuals' attitudes toward the father, and so on. Is it possible that a child who notices a striking difference between father-in-the-home and father-at-his-club perceives this as father having hateful feelings toward mother — despite the even temperature at home? The presence of relatives and others as continuing members of the household geometrically increases the possibility of the child's picking up cues about who feels what about whom. Thus, implications mother makes about other members of father's family may be sensed by the child as mother's rejection of certain aspects of father and of the child himself. If the despised relative is one from whom the child has also received tenderness, a very conflictual situation arises. Occasionally the covert aspects of such a situation are ineradicably etched into the child's memory by such a relative moving out of the home, whereupon there ensue overt difficulties between father and mother and/or difficulties with that aspect of the child that the relative represented.

The paternal uncle of a woman patient had lived with her parents until she was 10, when he married. Her mother's hatred of him was partially overt; however, his presence seemed to deflect some of the mother's hostility toward her husband away from the husband, and the brother gave moral support to the father. Following this uncle's departure, four events occurred that seemed hardly coincidental: The parents began openly quarreling, the mother made a potentially serious suicide attempt, the father took a traveling job, and the patient quietly broke out in a rash of phobias.

The incredibly complex picture one obtains in studying family interrelations may be compared to the mathematics of the motion of bodies in relation to one another — the simultaneous consideration of more than three such instances is, at present, an insuperable task for the mind of man. Since man is the measure of all things, we accept our conceptual limitations and make the most of certain aids available. One of these aids is collaborative therapy, and it is a beautiful thing if done properly. The unfolding of the psychic drama as two or more therapists relate and correlate their findings embodies the dynamics of chess and topological fascination of a jigsaw puzzle. Unfortunately, collaborative psychotherapy is difficult because the therapists must deal with each other in addition to their patients.

Another aid to conceptualizing is the adding of a temporal concept to our more or less spatial image of the family. Such a temporal concept may be achieved by constructing a picture of the probable family interaction at the period the patient is discussing, or at that period where such-and-such a symptom seems most likely to have been engendered. We can make use of our information about the patients' siblings, about the age of one or other of the parents when significant events occurred, about the differential handling of the children by the parents, and so forth to help obtain the proper setting for understanding what might have been momentous to the patient at that period of his life.

Considering the difficulties in forming a concept of the emotional interactions of a family group, the obvious rejoinder might be: "What is the value of such brain-wracking exercise on the part of the psychiatrist?" It is felt that two main benefits may ensue: facility in understanding the patient and in helping those who will undergo change as the result of the patient's change; and theoretical and research implications brought to light by this kind of orientation.

There are two rather well-known situations in which one automatically takes into account the "significant others" of the patient. The best-known instance is that already mentioned where the treatment of a child would be futile or even dangerous without mother and/or father consenting to therapy as well. Another more spectacular situation is that of folie a deux, or as Gralnick aptly labels it, "psychosis by association." Actually, folie a deux is merely a caricature of the underlying principles of any family interaction. Acquaintance with this fact may mean that a psychiatrist will not — in certain situations — undertake treatment of a patient, especially long-term psychotherapy, unless the other significant family member, or members, enter treatment, or unless provision is made for therapy if the need in another family member becomes evident. Most of us are acquainted with situations where one person has started treatment, and soon the entire family has been parceled out among the circumambient psychiatric brotherhood. Such on-the-spot instigation of treatment may work out well if money and psychiatric facilities are available, but they are not always available; and in any event, it would seem helpful to have some data with which to predict the potential need of other family members for treatment. Furthermore, it seems likely that alert inquisitiveness into the entire family interrelationship will aid in understanding of the member who is in therapy. This applies as well to the family of the patient's childhood, where it is not only a question of what mother was like or what father was like but how they related to each other and what their relationship meant to the patient. The meanings of the patient's position in the family, of the patient's sex and of other matters constitute subtle but important dynamic factors in shaping emotional patterns. It is possible that our present largely descriptive classification of mental disorders might be made more meaningful by understanding diagnosis phenomenologically — in terms of parental interaction. For example, it may be possible to say that where there is a rejecting mother and a narcissistic father who can accept his daughter more fully than he can his wife, the daughter will tend to develop hysterical symptoms which include expressions of sexual difficulties and over-evaluation of men, regardless of what other emotional difficulties she may manifest.

There seem to be few tools at present to measure or even delineate such a factor as parental interaction and its effect in shaping the child's emotional patterns. Epistemologically, we are not well acquainted with the variables here and the quantitative aspects of these variables. The clinician has a ringside seat to study such forces, however, if he carefully notes changes in other family members as the patient in psychotherapy alters his reactions. The writer would like to give a few oversimplified examples of how one may conceptualize diagnostic categories in terms of family interactional patterns. These are offered only to illustrate a way of thinking; there is a good deal of research to be done before such patterns could be considered in etiological terms, and in every instance the patterns could be considered as differing only in degree. Thus the hysterical situation blends into the schizophrenic one, and in fact, might become the schizophrenic one if unusual life stresses should occur, such as the death of one of the parents or severe physical illness in the child, who, for a variety of reasons such as ordinal position, sex, appearance and so on, is the most important child in the particular interaction described.

1. The development of hysterical symptoms is favored by a situation in which a daughter serves as the main repository for unacceptable sexual

and aggressive wishes on the part of both parents, especially if certain other factors are also present. These are (a) An ambivalent mother who lends herself to being split into "good" and "bad," the splitting being further aided by the father's attraction to his daughter and the mother's tendency to push the girl in his direction. A third figure who serves as a "good" mother (such as a grandmother or older sibling) may minimize the tendency toward a psychotic situation but aid the development of the hysterical integration. (b) The mother must be able to manifest concern (especially in relation to illness) although she cannot manifest tenderness.

2.   In a family where the parents' hostility toward each other is handled in part by covertly disagreeing over the child, but overtly appearing firm and united, special ways of integrating will be developed by the child. For example, if the mother is markedly fearful of any aggression, including her own; and the father, despite a stern front, allows her to exploit him with phobic symptoms (masking his hostility by assuming a protective role toward his wife and child), then the child caught in the middle of such a situation may manifest phobias, and particularly if a girl, may have a marked fear of "losing control" — a fear pertaining to sexual and aggressive expressions.

3.   If the mother is a cold individual who veils rejection of the child by a martyr role and by maintaining that the father is "no good," and if the father is dead, divorced or accepts a considerable maligning of himself there may be overwhelming pathogenic elements present for the boy. For example, if this boy is a marked disappointment because of his mother's wish for a daughter, there exists a nidus for various degrees of homosexual difficulties, and if the mother is markedly helpless and has the need to deny her own feelings — especially through the mechanism of saying one thing and meaning another — then the possibility exists for producing a pre-schizophrenic personality in the son.[2] Certain psycho-

---

[2] The present writer considers the designation "schizophrenogenic mother" a rather useless or possibly misleading one. He has never studied an instance of schizophrenic psychosis where the individual's environment, in general, had not let him down. In addition to "acts of God," physical illness, unusual stress and so on, an important aspect of the schizophrenic situation is the inability or unwillingness of other family members to rescue the child from the unbelievable sadomasochistic tie to the mother. The father may be an

somatic disorders may occur in a somewhat similar situation, when, although the mother is strongly rejecting, the father is able to manifest spotty, but real tenderness: or these disorders may come at that point in intensive therapy when the therapist is invested with strong dependent and hostile feelings by the schizoid patient from the parental set-up just described.

4.   Some severely obsessional individuals may arise out of a less pathogenic but similar family constellation to that just described (paragraph 3), with the addition that hypocrisy, intellectualization and religiosity may be an important aspect of the parents' techniques.

5.   The manic-depressive integration may be associated with a somewhat special parental interaction in which the mother is an unhappy individual who emphasizes the child's obligation to make up to her for what the father and others have denied her. She is ambitious for her child, yet his striving, ambition, and success are threatening to her and may be handled by disparagement and pessimism. The father may be an apparently successful individual who also emphasizes his ambitions for his offspring but who is more aggressively and overtly threatened by his child than the mother is. Neither parent, however intelligent, is able to be of much aid in teaching the child about people. Somewhat in contrast to schizophrenic parents, these people stress performance and "appearance" in such a way that their superficial behavior may look like a relatively good adjustment.

It is hoped that these hypotheses will be seen as only a possible way of thinking about psychiatric nosology. All are sketchily presented. As has been previously indicated, the development of psychiatric thinking along such interactional lines help in discovering, for example, situations where serious conse-

---

apparently successful and aggressive individual, though more often a weak and passive character, but in either case, he cannot or will not intervene to give the child the so necessary "other one." The child's tie to the mother prevents further growth, in part because other experiences have a diluted meaning, in the sense that every problem is the original problem.

quences will occur in a parent or spouse because the parent or spouse has been "buying" mental health from the illness of the person who is in treatment. Such a situation occurred in the following case.

A young male schizophrenic is brought to the psychiatrist's office by his fiancée and his older brother. He has been more or less abducted by these two from his parents, who feel he is incurably ill, and wish to devote themselves to taking care of him. The psychiatrist judges that intense hostility between the fiancée and the brother is veiled by their mutual concern over the patient; and he guesses that the same situation obtains between the parents and the patient. He advises intense psychotherapy for the patient and recommends that the brother and fiancée do not rent a house and care for the patient as they had planned. He is especially interested in discouraging the arrangement, since he is puzzled about why the young woman should be so attracted to this patient as to leave her home, her job, and friends in order to care for him, and as to why the brother has taken a leave of absence from an important position when he was away from home so much during the patient's growing-up period that it was hard to account for his strong affection for the patient.

Needless to say, the advice was disregarded by the two, and the psychiatrist felt forced to deal with the situation by strongly supporting the patient and bringing the conflict between the brother and the fiancée out into the open as soon as feasible. The young man made rapid progress in treatment; and a few months after its inception, the brother left in a rage, after a quarrel with the fiancée during which the patient sided with her. As an interesting aside, the brother did not want to return to his job, but became financially involved in psycho-religious matters that more or less pointed out that psychotherapy was crude, old-fashioned, and perhaps crooked. The patient meanwhile continued to improve so much that he took a job. His dissatisfaction with his fiancée became more obvious; and following what was more or less a declaration of independence by him, she immediately responded with a psychotic episode. Parenthetically, she had been seen in a psychiatric interview initially — that is while the patient was still very psychotic — and had not been judged to be more than mildly neurotic by the examining psychiatrist.

The emphasis on homeostatic mechanisms within the family group carries implications for therapy. It would be a boon to the practice of psychiatry if we could increase our ability to predict with reasonable probability what would be the outcome for patient and family if, say, a psychotic lives at home during his therapy — or if it could be predicted, if a woman is pregnant, whether childbirth could result in a postpartum psychosis, or in a schizophrenic episode in a husband. The following brief clinical examples depict some situations involving homeostatic mechanisms:

1. A young woman undergoing psychotherapy for recurrent depression began to manifest increased self-assurance. Her husband, who initially was eager that she become less a burden to him, called the psychiatrist rather frequently and generally alluded to her "worsening" condition. The therapist had not made an appraisal of the husband; and when the extent of the husband's alarm became clear, he had become too antagonistic to enter therapy. He became more and more uneasy, finally calling the therapist one evening, fearful that his wife would commit suicide. The next morning he shot himself to death.

2. A husband urged his wife into psychotherapy because of her frigidity. After several months of therapy she felt less sexually inhibited, whereupon the husband became impotent.

3. A young woman with anorexia nervosa was persuaded to enter psychotherapy by her husband. Following a period of intense, rather dangerous, acting out, she began to relate more intimately to her husband. The husband's initial pleasure at her response was marred by his developing a duodenal ulcer.

4. A young woman requested psychotherapy for a variety of reasons, none of which included dissatisfaction with her marriage. Her mother had died when she was two years old, as had the mother of her husband. The couple married in their late teens and, after a stormy beginning, apparently had made a pleasant, if markedly symbiotic, adjustment. The wife was fearful of having a child, but both she and her husband wanted one, and hoped therapy would make it possible to have one. With a good deal more information than there is time to present, the psychiatrist felt that therapy for her alone would endanger the marriage, and that if she became pregnant, the husband, unsupported, might become seriously disturbed. The husband agreed to start psychotherapy with another psychiatrist; and a somewhat stormy, but eventually fruitful, time was had by all.

CONCLUSION

The writer would like to suggest that emphasis on family interaction is but a logical development in the natural history of psychiatry. As the steps are logical from the single symptom to the patient's character, from his instinctual forces to emphasis on his interpersonal dealings and environmental possibilities, so it is but a logical step from the savant isolated from the community and scarcely seen abroad, to the role of "family" psychiatrist. In America, it has been the physician more than the family solicitor or the minister who has played the counseling role. This long tradition is undergoing change, as the family doctor dies out and the psychiatrist gains importance.

But with the help of the sociologist, social psychologist, and anthropologist, psychiatrists are amassing a body of data on the family that has possibilities for use in devising therapeutic interventions. The importance of studying complex interactions within the family group is stressed the more because of the value of data from such a study in treating patients psychotherapeutically, because of the possibility of being helpful to a family member other than the patient and of avoiding unpleasant counteractions in such other members, because of the possible economy and expeditiousness of collaborative therapy, and, finally, because of possible research implications for understanding psychiatric nosological genetically. It becomes a matter of some practical importance for the psychiatrist to employ every conceivable aid for predicting behavior. The postulated outcome of the patient's responses to therapy, as well as the responses of those persons significantly interacting with the patient, become matters upon which the outcome of therapy may hinge. Aids to predicting behavior are not a firm aspect of our psychodynamic formulations or teaching.

A prediction that has been successful in the writer's own experience is one in regard to the mate of the overtly-dependent person who enters psychotherapy. If therapy is at all successful, the patient will feel more competent and the mate will become more upset for several reasons: (a) He cannot disguise his own fear of dependency by his complaints about his spouse; (b) his spouse's greater freedom and competency increase his own wish to be dependent; and (c) both of these circumstances weaken his "controls."

Psychiatrists should be increasingly able to predict such situations before, for example, the husband develops an ulcer. The psychiatrist who is oriented to "this-patient-in-my-office" may, in some cases, be misapplying his ability. Unless one sees the patient as a dynamic social force interacting with other people, the finger of psychiatric knowledge may truly muddy the waters of inquiry.

Author's note:

It is nearly four years since this paper was written. Although some of the ideas expressed here have been subsequently modified, the author feels it important to publish this paper without changes, so that future modifications will be obvious.

CHAPTER 11

Toward a Theory of Schizophrenia[1]

Gregory Bateson, Don D. Jackson,

Jay Haley, and John Weakland

(1956)

Schizophrenia — its nature, etiology and the kind of therapy to use for it — remains one of the most puzzling of the mental illnesses. The theory of schizophrenia presented here is based on communications analysis, and specifically on the Theory of Logical Types. From this theory and from observations of schizophrenic patients is derived a description, and the necessary conditions for, a situation called the "double bind" — a situation in which no matter what a person does, he "can't win." It is hypothesized that a person caught in the double bind may develop schizophrenic symptoms. How and why the double bind may arise in a family situation is discussed, together with illustrations from clinical and experimental data.

This is a report[2] on a research project which has been formulating and

[1] Reprinted with permission from *Behavioral Science*, 1 (4), 251–264.

[2] This paper derives from hypotheses first developed in a research project financed by the Rockefeller Foundation from 1952–1954, administered by the Department of Sociology and Anthropology at Stanford University and directed by Gregory Bateson. Since 1954 the project has continued, financed by the Josiah Macy, Jr. Foundation. To Jay Haley is due credit for recognizing that the symptoms of schizophrenia are suggestive of an inability to discriminate the Logical Types, and this was amplified by Bateson who added the notion that the symptoms and etiology could be formally described in terms of a double bind hy-

testing a broad, systematic view of the nature, etiology, and therapy of schizophrenia. Our research in this field has proceeded by discussion of a varied body of data and ideas, with all of us contributing according to our varied experience in anthropology, communications analysis, psychotherapy, psychiatry, and psychoanalysis. We have now reached common agreement on the broad outlines of a communicational theory of the origin and nature of schizophrenia; this paper is a preliminary report on our continuing research.

THE BASE IN COMMUNICATIONS THEORY

Our approach is based on that part of communications theory which Russell has called the Theory of Logical Types (Whitehead & Russell, 1910). The central thesis of this theory is that there is a discontinuity between a class and its members. The class cannot be a member of itself nor can one of the members *be* the class, since the term used for the class is of a different level of abstraction, a different Logical Type, from terms used for members. Although in formal logic there is an attempt to maintain this discontinuity between a class and its members, we argue that in the psychology of real communications this discontinuity is continually and inevitably breached (Bateson, 1955), and that a-priori we must expect a pathology to occur in the human organism when certain formal patterns of the breaching occur in the communication between mother and child. We shall argue that this pathology at its extreme will have symptoms whose formal characteristics would lead the pathology to be classified as a schizophrenia.

Illustrations of how human beings handle communication involving multiple Logical Types can be derived from the following fields:

1. *The use of various communicational modes in human communication.* Examples are play, non-play, fantasy, sacrament, metaphor, etc. Even among the lower mammals there appears to be an exchange of signals which identify certain meaningful behavior as "play," etc.[3] These signals are evidently

---

pothesis. The hypothesis was communicated to Don Jackson and found to fit closely with his ideas of family homeostasis. Since then, Dr. Jackson has worked closely with the project. The study of the formal analogies between hypnosis and schizophrenia has been the work of John H. Weakland and Jay Haley.

[3] A film prepared by this project, "The Nature of Play; Part I, River Otters," is available.

of higher Logical Type than the messages they classify. Among human beings this framing and labeling of messages and meaningful actions reaches considerable complexity, with the peculiarity that our vocabulary for such discrimination is still very poorly developed, and we rely preponderantly upon nonverbal media of posture, gesture, facial expression, intonation, and the context for the communication of these highly abstract, but vitally important, labels.

2. *Humor.* This seems to be a method of exploring the implicit themes in thought or in a relationship. The method of exploration involves the use of messages which are characterized by a condensation of Logical Types or communicational modes. A discovery, for example, occurs when it suddenly becomes plain that a message was not only metaphoric but also more literal, or vice versa. That is to say, the explosive moment in humor is the moment when the labeling of the mode undergoes a dissolution and resynthesis. Commonly, the punch line compels a re-evaluation of earlier signals which ascribed to certain messages a particular mode (e.g., literalness or fantasy). This has the peculiar effect of attributing *mode* to those signals which had previously the status of that higher Logical Type which classifies the modes.

3. *The falsification of mode-identifying signals.* Among human beings mode identifiers can be falsified, and we have the artificial laugh, the manipulative simulation of friendliness, the confidence trick, kidding, and the like. Similar falsifications have been recorded among mammals (Carpenter, 1934; Lorenz, 1952). Among human beings we meet with a strange phenomenon — the unconscious falsification of these signals. This may occur within the self — the subject may conceal from himself his own real hostility under the guise of metaphoric play — or it may occur as an unconscious falsification of the subject's understanding of the other person's mode-identifying signals. He may mistake shyness for contempt, etc. Indeed most of the errors of self-reference fall under this head.

4. *Learning.* The simplest level of this phenomenon is exemplified by a situation in which a subject receives a message and acts appropriately on it: "I heard the clock strike and knew it was time for lunch. So I went to the table." In learning experiments, the analogue of this sequence of

events is observed by the experimenter and commonly treated as a single message of a higher type. When the dog salivates between buzzer and meat powder, this sequence is accepted by the experimenter as a message indicating that "the dog has *learned* that buzzer means meat powder." But this is not the end of the hierarchy of types involved. The experimental subject may become more skilled in learning. He may *learn to learn* (Bateson, 1942; Harlow, 1949; Hull, et al., 1940), and it is not inconceivable that still higher orders of learning may occur in human beings.

5.   *Multiple levels of learning and the Logical Typing of signals.* These are two inseparable sets of phenomena — inseparable because the ability to handle the multiple types of signals is itself a *learned* skill and therefore a function of the multiple levels of learning.

According to our hypothesis, the term "ego function" (as this term is used when a schizophrenic is described as having "weak ego function" is precisely *the process of discriminating communicational modes either within the self or between the self and others.* The schizophrenic exhibits weakness in three areas of such function: (a) He has difficulty in assigning the correct communicational mode to the messages he receives from other persons. (b) He has difficulty in assigning the correct communicational mode to those messages which he himself utters or emits nonverbally. (c) He has difficulty in assigning the correct communicational mode to his own thoughts, sensations, and percepts.

At this point, it is appropriate to compare what was said in the previous paragraph with von Domarus' (1944) approach to the systematic description of schizophrenic utterance. He suggests that the messages (and thought) of the schizophrenic are deviant in syllogistic structure. In place of structures which derive from syllogism, Barbara, the schizophrenic, according to this theory, uses structures which identify predicates. An example of such a distorted syllogism is: Men die.

Grass dies.

Men are grass.

But as we see it, von Domarus' formulation is only a more precise — and therefore valuable — way of saying that schizophrenic utterance is rich in metaphor. With that generalization we agree. But metaphor is an indispensable tool of thought and expression — a characteristic of all human communication, even of that of the scientist. The conceptual models of cybernetics and the energy theories of psychoanalysis are, after all, only labeled metaphors. The peculiarity of the schizophrenic is not that he uses metaphors, but that he uses *unlabeled* metaphors. He has special difficulty in handling signals of that class whose members assign Logical Types to other signals.

If our formal summary of the symptomatology is correct and if the schizophrenia of our hypothesis is essentially a result of family interaction, it should be possible to arrive a priori at a formal description of these sequences of experience which would induce such a symptomatology. What is known of learning theory combines with the evident fact that human beings use *context* as a guide for mode discrimination. Therefore, we must look not for some specific traumatic experience in the infantile etiology but rather for characteristic sequential patterns. The specificity for which we search is to be at an abstract or formal level. The sequences must have this characteristic: that from them the patient will acquire the mental habits which are exemplified in schizophrenic communication. That is to say, he must live in a universe where the sequences of events are such that his unconventional communicational habits will be in some sense appropriate. The hypothesis which we offer is that sequences of this kind in the external experience of the patient are responsible for the inner conflicts of Logical Typing. For such unresolvable sequences of experiences, we use the term "double bind."

THE DOUBLE BIND

The necessary ingredients for a double bind situation, as we see it, are:

1. *Two or more persons.* Of these, we designate one, for purposes of our definition, as the "victim." We do not assume that the double bind is inflicted by the mother alone, but that it may be done either by mother alone or by some combination of mother, father, and/or siblings.

2. *Repeated experience.* We assume that the double bind is a recurrent theme in the experience of the victim. Our hypothesis does not invoke a single traumatic experience, but such repeated experience that the double bind structure comes to be an habitual expectation.

3. *A primary negative injunction.* This may have either of two forms: (a) Do not do so and so, or I will punish you," or (b) "If you do not do so and so, I will punish you." Here we select a context of learning based on

115

avoidance of punishment rather than a context of reward seeking. There is perhaps no formal reason for this selection. We assume that the punishment may be either the withdrawal of love or the expression of hate or anger — or most devastating — the kind of abandonment that results from the parent's expression of extreme helplessness.[4]

4. *A secondary injunction conflicting with the first at a more abstract level, and like the first enforced by punishments or signals which threaten survival.* This secondary injunction is more difficult to describe than the primary for two reasons. First, the secondary injunction is commonly communicated to the child by nonverbal means. Posture, gesture, tone of voice, meaningful action, and the implications concealed in verbal comment may all be used to convey this more abstract message. Second, the secondary injunction may impinge upon any element of the primary prohibition. Verbalization of the secondary injunction may, therefore, include a wide variety of forms; for example, "Do not see this as punishment"; "Do not see me as the punishing agent"; "Do not submit to my prohibitions"; "Do not question my love of which the primary prohibition is (or is not) an example"; and so on. Other examples become possible when the double bind is inflicted not by one individual but by two. For example, one parent may negate at a more abstract level the injunctions of the other.

5. *A tertiary negative injunction prohibiting the victim from escaping from the field.* In a formal sense it is perhaps unnecessary to list this injunction as a separate item since the reinforcement at the other two levels involves a threat to survival, and if the double binds are imposed during infancy, escape is naturally impossible. However, it seems that in some cases, the escape from the field is made impossible by certain devices which are not purely negative, e.g., capricious promises of love, and the like.

6. Finally, the complete set of ingredients is no longer necessary when the victim has learned to perceive his universe in double bind patterns. Almost any part of a double bind sequence may then be sufficient to pre-

---

[4] Our concept of punishment is being refined at present. It appears to us to involve perceptual experience in a way that cannot be encompassed by the notion of "trauma."

cipitate panic or rage. The pattern of conflicting injunctions may even be taken over by hallucinatory voices (Perceval, 1836, 1840).

THE EFFECT OF THE DOUBLE BIND

In the Eastern religion, Zen Buddhism, the goal is to achieve enlightenment. The Zen master attempts to bring about enlightenment in his pupil in various ways. One of the things he does is to hold a stick over the pupil's head and say fiercely, "If you say this stick is real, I will strike you with it. If you say this stick is not real, I will strike you with it. If you don't say anything, I will strike you with it." We feel that the schizophrenic finds himself continually in the same situation as the pupil, but he achieves something like disorientation rather than enlightenment. The Zen pupil might reach up and take the stick away from the Master, who might accept this response, but the schizophrenic has no such choice since with him, there is no not caring about the relationship, and his mother's aims and awareness are not like the master's.

We hypothesize that there will be a breakdown in any individual's ability to discriminate between Logical Types whenever a double bind situation occurs. The general characteristics of this situation are the following:

1. When the individual is involved in an intense relationship; that is, a relationship in which he feels it is vitally important that he discriminate accurately what sort of message is being communicated so that he may respond appropriately.

2. And the individual is caught in a situation in which the other person in the relationship is expressing two orders of message and one of these denies the other.

3. And the individual is unable to comment on the messages being expressed to correct his discrimination of what order of message to respond to, i.e., he cannot make a metacommunicative statement.

We have suggested that this is the sort of situation which occurs between the pre-schizophrenic and his mother, but it also occurs in normal relationships. When a person is caught in a double bind situation, he will respond defensively in a manner similar to the schizophrenic. An individual will take a metaphorical statement literally when he is in a situation where he must respond, where he is faced with contradictory messages, and when he is unable to comment on the contradictions. For example, one day an employee went home during office hours. A fellow employee called him at his home, and said lightly, "Well, how did you get *there*?" The employee replied, "By automobile." He responded literally because he was faced with a message which asked him what he was doing at home when he should have been at the office, but which denied that this question was being asked by the way it was phrased. (Since the speaker felt it wasn't really his business, he spoke metaphorically.) The relationship was intense enough so that the victim was in doubt how the information would be used, and he therefore responded literally. This is characteristic of anyone who feels "on the spot," as demonstrated by the careful literal replies of a witness on the stand in a court trial. The schizophrenic feels so terribly on the spot at all times that he habitually responds with a defensive insistence on the literal level when it is quite inappropriate, e.g., when someone is joking.

Schizophrenics also confuse the literal and metaphoric in their own utterance when they feel themselves caught in a double bind. For example, a patient may wish to criticize his therapist for being late for an appointment, but he may be unsure what sort of a message that act of being late was — particularly if the therapist has anticipated the patient's reaction and apologized for the event. The patient cannot say, "Why are you late? Is it because you don't want to see me today?" This would be an accusation, and so he shifts to a metaphorical statement. He may then say, "I knew a fellow once who missed a boat, his name was Sam and the boat almost sank, etc." Thus he develops a metaphorical story and the therapist may or may not discover in it a comment on his being late. The convenient thing about a metaphor is that it leaves it up to the therapist (or mother) to see an accusation in the statement if he chooses, or to ignore it if he chooses. Should the therapist accept the accusation in the metaphor, then the patient can accept the statement he has made about Sam as metaphorical. If the therapist points out that this doesn't sound like a true statement about Sam, as a way of avoiding the accusation in the story, the patient can argue that there really was a man named Sam. As an answer to the double bind situation, a shift to a metaphorical statement brings safety. However, it also prevents the patient from making the accusation he wants to make. But instead of getting over his accusation by indicating that this is a metaphor, the schizophrenic patient seems to try to get over the fact that it is a metaphor by making it more fantastic. If the therapist should ignore the accusation in the story about Sam, the schizophrenic may then tell a story about going to Mars in a rocket ship as a way of putting over his accusation. The indication that it is a metaphorical statement lies in the fantastic aspect of the metaphor, not in the signals which usually accompany metaphors to tell the listener that a metaphor is being used.

It is not only safer for the victim of a double bind to shift to a metaphorical order of message, but in an impossible situation it is better to shift and become somebody else, or shift and insist that he is somewhere else. Then the double bind cannot work on the victim, because it isn't he and besides he is in a different place. In other words, the statements which show that a patient is disoriented can be interpreted as ways of defending himself against the situation he is in. The pathology enters when the victim himself either does not know that his responses are metaphorical or cannot say so. To recognize that he was speaking metaphorically, he would need to be aware that he was defending himself and therefore was afraid of the other person. To him, such an awareness would be an indictment of the other person and therefore provoke disaster.

If an individual has spent his life in the kind of double bind relationship described here, his way of relating to people after a psychotic break would have a systematic pattern. First, he would not share with normal people those signals which accompany messages to indicate what a person means. His metacommunicative system — the communications about communication — would have broken down, and he would not know what kind of message a message was. If a person said to him, "what would you like to do today?" he would be unable to judge accurately by the context or by the tone of voice or gesture whether he was being condemned for what he did yesterday, or being offered a sexual invitation, or just what was meant. Given this inability to judge accurately what a person really means and an excessive concern with what is really meant, an individual might defend himself by choosing one or more of several alternatives. He might, for example, assume that behind every statement there is a concealed meaning which is detrimental to his welfare. He would then be excessively concerned with hidden meanings and determined to demonstrate that he could not be deceived — as he had been all his life. If he chooses this alternative, he will be continually searching for meanings behind what people say and behind chance occurrences in the environment, and he will be characteristically suspicious and defiant.

He might choose another alternative, and tend to accept literally everything people say to him; when their tone or gesture or context contradicted what they said, he might establish a pattern of laughing off these metacommunicative signals. He would give up trying to discriminate between levels of message and treat all messages as unimportant or to be laughed at. If he didn't become suspicious of metacommunicative messages or attempt to laugh them off, he might choose to try to ignore them. Then he would find it necessary to see and hear less and less of what went on around him, and do his utmost to avoid provoking a response in his environment. He would try to detach his interest from the external world and concentrate on his own internal processes and, therefore, give the appearance of being a withdrawn, perhaps mute, individual.

This is another way of saying that if an individual doesn't know what sort of message a message is, he may defend himself in ways which have been described as paranoid, hebephrenic, or catatonic. These three alternatives are not the only ones. The point is that he cannot choose the one alternative which would help him to discover what people mean; he cannot, without considerable help, discuss the messages of others. Without being able to do that, the human being is like any self-correcting system which has lost its governor; it spirals into never-ending, but always systematic, distortions.

A DESCRIPTION OF THE FAMILY SITUATION

The theoretical possibility of double bind situations stimulated us to look for such communication sequences in the schizophrenic patient and in his family situation. Toward this end we have studied the written and verbal reports of psychotherapists who have treated such patients intensively; we have studied tape recordings of psychotherapeutic interviews, both of our own patients and others; we have interviewed and taped parents of schizophrenics; we have had two mothers and one father participate in intensive psychotherapy; and we have interviewed and taped parents and patients seen conjointly.

On the basis of these data we have developed a hypothesis about the family situation which ultimately leads to an individual suffering from schizophrenia. This hypothesis has not been statistically tested; it selects and emphasizes a rather simple set of interactional phenomena and does not attempt to describe comprehensively the extraordinary complexity of a family relationship.

We hypothesize that the family situation of the schizophrenic has the following general characteristics:

1. A child whose mother becomes anxious and withdraws if the child responds to her as a loving mother. That is, the child's very existence has

a special meaning to the mother which arouses her anxiety and hostility when she is in danger of intimate contact with the child.

2.   A mother to whom feelings of anxiety and hostility toward the child are not acceptable, and whose way of denying them is to express overt loving behavior to persuade the child to respond to her as a loving mother and to withdraw from him if he does not. "Loving behavior" does not necessarily imply "affection"; it can, for example, be set in a framework of doing the proper thing, instilling "goodness," and the like.

3.   The absence of anyone in the family, such as a strong and insightful father, who can intervene in the relationship between the mother and child and support the child in the face of the contradictions involved. Since this is a formal description we are not specifically concerned with why the mother feels this way about the child, but we suggest that she could feel this way for various reasons. It may be that merely having a child arouses anxiety about herself and her relationships to her own family; or it may be important to her that the child is a boy or a girl, or that the child was born on the anniversary of one of her own siblings (Hilgard, 1953), or the child may be in the same sibling position in the family that she was, or the child may be special to her for other reasons related to her own emotional problems.

Given a situation with these characteristics, we hypothesize that the mother of a schizophrenic will be simultaneously expressing at least two orders of message. (For simplicity in this presentation we shall confine ourselves to two orders.) These orders of message can be roughly characterized as (a) hostile or withdrawing behavior which is aroused whenever the child approaches her, and (b) simulated loving or approaching behavior which is aroused when the child responds to her hostile and withdrawing behavior, as a way of denying that she is withdrawing. Her problem is to control her anxiety by controlling the closeness and distance between herself and her child. To put this another way, if the mother begins to feel affectionate and close to her child, she begins to feel endangered and must withdraw from him; but she cannot accept this hostile act and to deny it must simulate affection and closeness with her child. The important point is that her loving behavior is then a comment on (since it is compensatory for) her hostile behavior and consequently it is of a

121

different *order* of message than the hostile behavior — it is a message about a sequence of messages. Yet by its nature it denies the existence of those messages which it is about, i.e., the hostile withdrawal.

The mother uses the child's responses to affirm that her behavior is loving, and since the loving behavior is simulated, the child is placed in a position where he must not accurately interpret her communication if he is to maintain his relationship with her. In other words, he must not discriminate accurately between orders of message, in this case, the difference between the expression of simulated feelings (one Logical Type) and real feelings (another Logical Type). As a result the child must systematically distort his perception of meta-communicative signals. For example, if mother begins to feel hostile (or affectionate) toward her child and also feels compelled to withdraw from him, she might say, "Go to bed, you're very tired and I want you to get your sleep." This overtly loving statement is intended to deny a feeling which could be verbalized as "Get out of my sight because I'm sick of you." If the child correctly discriminates her metacommunicative signals, he would have to face the fact that she both doesn't want him and is deceiving him by her loving behavior. He would be "punished" for learning to discriminate orders of messages accurately. He therefore would tend to accept the idea that he is tired rather than recognize his mother's deception. This means that he must deceive himself about his own internal state in order to support mother in her deception. To survive with her he must falsely discriminate his own internal messages as well as falsely discriminate the messages of others.

The problem is compounded for the child because the mother is "benevolently" defining for him how he feels; she is expressing overt maternal concern over the fact that he is tired. To put it another way, the mother is controlling the child's definitions of his own messages, as well as the definition of his responses to her (e.g., by saying "You don't really mean to say that," if he should criticize her) by insisting that she is not concerned about herself but only about him. Consequently, the easiest path for the child is to accept mother's simulated loving behavior as real, and his desires to interpret what is going on are undermined. Yet the result is that the mother is withdrawing from him and defining this withdrawal as the way a loving relationship should be.

However, accepting mother's simulated loving behavior as real also is no solution for the child. Should he make this false discrimination, he would approach her; this move toward closeness would provoke in her feelings of fear and helplessness, and she would be compelled to withdraw. But if he then withdrew from her, she would take his withdrawal as a statement that she was not a loving mother and would either punish him for withdrawing or approach him to bring him closer. If he then approached, she would respond by putting him at a distance. The child is punished for discriminating accurately what she is expressing, and he is punished for discriminating inaccurately — he is caught in a double bind.

The child might try various means of escaping from this situation. He might, for example, try to lean on his father or some other member of the family. However, from our preliminary observations we think it is likely that the fathers of schizophrenics are not substantial enough to lean on. They are also in the awkward position where if they agreed with the child about the nature of mother's deceptions, they would need to recognize the nature of their own relationships to the mother, which they could not do and remain attached to her in the modus operandi they have worked out.

The need of the mother to be wanted and loved also prevents the child from gaining support from some other person in the environment, a teacher, for example. A mother with these characteristics would feel threatened by any other attachment of the child and would break it up and bring the child back closer to her with consequent anxiety when the child became dependent on her.

The only way the child can really escape from the situation is to comment on the contradictory position his mother has put him in. However, if he did so, the mother would take this as an accusation that she is unloving and both punish him and insist that his perception of the situation is distorted. By preventing the child from talking about the situation, the mother forbids him using the metacommunicative level, the level we use to correct our perception of communicative behavior. The ability to communicate about communication, to comment upon the meaningful actions of oneself and others, is essential for successful social intercourse. In any normal relationship there is a constant interchange of metacommunicative messages, such as "What do you mean?" or "Why did you do that?" or "Are you kidding me?" and so on. To discriminate accurately what people are really expressing we must be able to comment directly or indirectly on that expression. This metacommunicative level the schizophrenic seems unable to use successfully (Bateson, 1955). Given these characteristics of the mother, it is apparent why. If she is denying one order of message, then any statement about her statements endangers her and she must forbid it. Therefore, the child grows up unskilled in his ability to communicate about communication and, as a result, unskilled in determining what people really mean and unskilled in expressing what he really means, which is essential for normal relationships.

In summary, then, we suggest that the double bind nature of the family situation of a schizophrenic results in placing the child in a position where if he responds to his mother's simulated affection her anxiety will be aroused and she will punish him (or insist, to protect herself, that his overtures are simulated, thus confusing him about the nature of his own messages) to defend herself from closeness with him. Thus the child is blocked off from intimate and secure associations with his mother. However, if he does not make overtures of affection, she will feel that this means she is not a loving mother and her anxiety will be aroused. Therefore, she will either punish him for withdrawing or make overtures toward the child to insist that he demonstrate that he loves her. If he then responds and shows her affection, she will not only feel endangered again, but she may resent the fact that she had to force him to respond. In either case in a relationship, the most important in his life and the model for all others, he is punished if he indicates love and affection and punished if he does not; and his escape routes from the situation, such as gaining support from others, are cut off. This is the basic nature of the double bind relationship between mother and child. This description has not depicted, of course, the more complicated interlocking gestalt that is the "family" of which the "mother" is one important part (Jackson, 1954b, 1954c).

ILLUSTRATIONS FROM CLINICAL DATA

An analysis of an incident occurring between a schizophrenic patient and his mother illustrates the "double bind" situation. A young man who had fairly well recovered from an acute schizophrenic episode was visited in the hospital by his mother. He was glad to see her and impulsively put his arm around her shoulders, whereupon she stiffened. He withdrew his arm and she asked, "Don't you love me any more? He then blushed, and she said, "Dear, you must not be so easily embarrassed and afraid of your feelings." The patient was able to stay with her only a few minutes more and following her departure he assaulted an aide and was put in the tubs.

Obviously, this result could have been avoided if the young man had been able to say, "Mother it is obvious that you become uncomfortable when I put my arm around you, and that you have difficulty accepting a gesture of affection from me." However, the schizophrenic patient doesn't have this possibility open to him. His intense dependency and training prevents him from commenting upon his mother's communicative behavior, though she comments on his and forces him to accept and to attempt to deal with the complicated sequence. The complications for the patient include the following:

1. The mother's reaction of not accepting her son's affectionate gesture is masterfully covered up by her condemnation of him for withdrawing, and the patient denies his perception of the situation by accepting her condemnation.

2. The statement "don't you love me any more" in this context seems to imply:

    (a) "I am lovable."

    (b) "You should love me and if you don't you are bad or at fault."

    (c) "Whereas you did love me previously you don't any longer," and thus focus is shifted from his expressing affection to his inability to be affectionate. Since the patient has also hated her, she is on good ground here, and he responds appropriately with guilt, which she then attacks.

    (d) "What you just expressed was not affection," and in order to accept this statement the patient must deny what she and the culture have taught him about how one expresses affection. He must also question the times with her, and with others, when he thought he was experiencing affection and when they seemed to treat the situation as if he had. He experiences here loss-of-support phenomena and is put in doubt about the reliability of past experience.

3. The statement, "You must not be so easily embarrassed and afraid of your feelings," seems to imply:

    (a) "You are not like me and are different from other nice or normal people because we express our feelings."

    (b) "The feelings you express are all right, it's only that *you* can't accept them." However, if the stiffening on her part had indicated "these are unacceptable feelings," then the boy is told that he should not be embarrassed by unacceptable feelings. Since he has had a long training in what is and is not acceptable to both her and society, he again comes into conflict with the past. If he is unafraid of his own feelings (which mother implies is good), he should be unafraid of his affection and would then notice it was she who was afraid, but he must not notice that because her whole approach is aimed at covering up this shortcoming in herself.

The impossible dilemma thus becomes: "If I am to keep my tie to mother, I must not show her that I love her, but if I do not show her that I love her, then I will lose her."

The importance to the mother of her special method of control is strikingly illustrated by the interfamily situation of a young woman schizophrenic who greeted the therapist on her first meeting with the remark, "Mother had to get married and now I'm here." This statement meant to the therapist that:

1.   The patient was the result of an illegitimate pregnancy.

2.   This fact was related to her present psychosis (in her opinion).

3.   "Here" referred to the psychiatrist's office and to the patient's presence on earth for which she had to be eternally indebted to her mother, especially since her mother had sinned and suffered in order to bring her into the world.

4.   "Had to get married" referred to the shot-gun nature of mother's wedding and to the mother's response to pressure that she must marry, and the reciprocal, that she resented the forced nature of the situation and blamed the patient for it.

Actually, all these suppositions subsequently proved to be factually correct and were corroborated by the mother during an abortive attempt at psychotherapy. The flavor of the mother's communications to the patient seemed essentially this: "I am lovable, loving, and satisfied with myself. You are lovable when you are like me and when you do what I say." At the same time, the mother indicated to the daughter both by words and behavior: "You are physically delicate, unintelligent, and different from me ("not normal"). You need me and me alone because of these handicaps, and I will take care of you and love you." Thus the patient's life was a series of beginnings, of attempts at experience, which would result in failure and withdrawal back to the maternal hearth and bosom because of the collusion between her and her mother.

It was noted in collaborative therapy that certain areas important to the mother's self-esteem were especially conflictual situations for the patient. For example, the mother needed the fiction that she was close to her family and that a deep love existed between her and her own mother. By analogy the relationship to the grandmother served as the prototype for the mother's relationship to her own daughter. On one occasion when the daughter was seven or eight years old, the grandmother, in a rage, threw a knife which barely missed the little girl. The mother said nothing to the grandmother but hurried the little girl from the room with the words, "Grandmommy really loves you." It is significant that the grandmother took the attitude toward the patient that she was not well enough controlled, and she used to chide her daughter for being too easy on the child. The grandmother was living in the house during one of the patient's psychotic episodes, and the girl took great delight in throwing various objects at the mother and grandmother while they cowered in fear.

Mother felt herself very attractive as a girl, and she felt that her daughter resembled her rather closely, although by damning with faint praise it was obvious that she felt the daughter definitely ran second. One of the daughter's first acts during a psychotic period was to announce to her mother that she was going to cut off all her hair. She proceeded to do this while the mother pleaded with her to stop. Subsequently the mother would show a picture of herself as a girl and explain to people how the patient would look if she only had her beautiful hair.

The mother, apparently without awareness of the significance of what she was doing, would equate the daughter's illness with not being very bright and with some sort of organic brain difficulty. She would invariably contrast this with her own intelligence as demonstrated by her *own* scholastic record. She treated her daughter with a completely patronizing and placating manner which was insincere. For example, in the psychiatrist's presence she promised her daughter that she would not allow her to have further shock treatments, and as soon as the girl was out of the room she asked the doctor if he didn't feel she should be hospitalized and given electric shock treatments. One clue to this deceptive behavior arose during the mother's therapy. Although the daughter had had three previous hospitalizations, the mother had never mentioned to the doctors that she herself had had a psychotic episode when she discovered that she was pregnant. The family whisked her away to a small sanitarium in a nearby town, and she was, according to her own statement, strapped to a bed for six weeks. Her family did not visit her during this time, and no one except her parents and her sister knew that she was hospitalized.

There were two times during therapy when the mother showed intense emotion. One was in relating her own psychotic experience; the other was on the occasion of her last visit when she accused the therapist of trying to drive her crazy by forcing her to choose between her daughter and her husband. Against medical advice, she took her daughter out of therapy.

The father was as involved in the homeostatic aspects of the intrafamily situation as the mother. For example, he stated that he had to quit his position as an important attorney in order to bring his daughter to an area where competent psychiatric help was available. Subsequently, acting on cues from the patient (e.g., she frequently referred to a character named "Nervous Ned") the therapist was able to elicit from him that he had hated his job and for years had been trying to "get out from under." However, the daughter was made to feel that the move was initiated for her.

On the basis of our examination of the clinical data, we have been impressed by a number of observations including:

1.   The helplessness, fear, exasperation, and rage which a double bind situation provokes in the patient, but which the mother may serenely and un-understandingly pass over. We have noted reactions in the father that both create double bind situations, or extend and amplify those created by the mother, and we have seen the father, passive and outraged but helpless, become ensnared in a similar manner to the patient.

2.   The psychosis seems, in part, a way of dealing with double bind situations to overcome their inhibiting and controlling effect. The psychotic patient may make astute, pithy, often metaphorical remarks that reveal an insight into the forces binding him. Contrariwise, he may become rather expert in setting double bind situations himself.

3.   According to our theory, the communication situation described is essential to the mother's security, and by inference to the family homeostasis.

If this be so, then when psychotherapy of the patient helps him become less vulnerable to mother's attempts at control, anxiety will be produced in the mother. Similarly, if the therapist interprets to the mother the dynamics of the situation she is setting up with the patient, this should produce an anxiety response in her. Our impression is that when there is a perduring contact between patient and family (especially when the patient lives at home during psychotherapy), this leads to a disturbance (often severe) in the mother and sometimes in both mother and father and other siblings (Jackson, 1954a, 1954b).

CURRENT POSITION AND FUTURE PROSPECTS

Many writers have treated schizophrenia in terms of the most extreme contrast with any other form of human thinking and behavior. While it is an isolatable phenomenon, so much emphasis on the differences from the normal — rather like the fearful physical segregation of psychotics — does not help in understanding the problems. In our approach, we assume that schizophrenia involves general principles which are important in all communication and therefore many informative similarities can be found in "normal" communication situations.

We have been particularly interested in various sorts of communication which involve both emotional significance and the necessity of discriminating between orders of message. Such situations include play, humor, ritual, poetry, and fiction. Play, especially among animals, we have studied at some length (Carpenter, 1934). It is a situation which strikingly illustrates the occurrence of meta-messages whose correct discrimination is vital to the cooperation of the individuals involved; for example, false discrimination could easily lead to combat. Rather closely related to play is humor, a continuing subject of our research. It involves sudden shifts in Logical Types as well as discrimination of those shifts. Ritual is a field in which unusually real or literal ascriptions of Logical Type are made and defended as vigorously as the schizophrenic defends the "reality" of his delusions. Poetry exemplifies the communicative power of metaphor — even very unusual metaphor — when labeled as such by various signs, as contrasted to the obscurity of unlabeled schizophrenic metaphor. The entire field of fictional communication, defined as the narration or depiction of a series of events with more or less of a label of actuality, is most relevant to the investigation of schizophrenia. We are not so much concerned with the content interpretation of fiction — although analysis of oral and destructive themes is illuminating to the student of schizophrenia — as with the formal problems involved in simultaneous existence of multiple levels of message in the fictional presentation of "reality." The drama is especially interesting in this respect, with both performers and spectators responding to messages about both the actual and the theatrical reality.

We are giving extensive attention to hypnosis. A great array of phenomena that occur as schizophrenic symptoms — hallucinations, delusions, alterations of personality, amnesias, and so on — can be produced temporarily in normal subjects with hypnosis. These need not be directly suggested as specific phenomena, but can be the "spontaneous" result of an arranged communication sequence. For example, Erickson (1955) will produce a hallucination by first inducing catalepsy in a subject's hand and then saying, "There is no conceivable way in which your hand can move, yet when I give the signal, it must move." That is, he tells the subject his hand will remain in place, yet it will move, and in no way the subject can consciously conceive. When Erickson gives the signal, the subject hallucinates the hand moved, or hallucinates himself in a different place and therefore the hand was moved. This use of hallucination to resolve a problem posed by contradictory commands which cannot be discussed seems to us to illustrate the solution of a double-bind situation via a shift in Logical Types. Hypnotic responses to direct suggestions or statements also commonly involve shifts in type, as in accepting the words, "Here's a glass of water" or "You feel tired" as external or internal reality, or in literal response to metaphorical statements, much like schizophrenics. We hope that further study of hypnotic induction, phenomena, and waking will, in this controllable situation, help sharpen our view of the essential communicational sequences which produce phenomena like those of schizophrenia.

Another Erickson experiment (Jackson, 1954c) seems to isolate a double bind communicational sequence without the specific use of hypnosis. Erickson arranged a seminar so as to have a young chain smoker sit next to him and to be without cigarettes; other participants were briefed on what to do. All was ordered so that Erickson repeatedly turned to offer the young man a cigarette, but was always interrupted by a question from someone so that he turned away, "inadvertently" withdrawing the cigarettes from the young man's reach. Later another participant asked this young man if he had received the cigarette from Dr. Erickson. He replied, "What cigarette?" showed clearly that he had forgotten the whole sequence, and even refused a cigarette offered by another member, saying that he was too interested in the seminar discussion to smoke.

This young man seems to us to be in an experimental situation paralleling the schizophrenic's double bind situation with mother: An important relationship, contradictory messages (here of giving and taking away), and comment blocked — because there was a seminar going on, and anyway it was all "inadvertent." And note the similar outcome: Amnesia for the double bind sequence and reversal from "He doesn't give" to "I don't want."

Although we have been led into these collateral areas, our main field of observation has been schizophrenia itself. All of us have worked directly with schizophrenic patients and much of this case material has been recorded on tape for detailed study. In addition, we are recording interviews held jointly with patients and their families, and we are taking sound motion pictures of mothers and disturbed, presumably preschizophrenic, children. Our hope is that these operations will provide a clearly evident record of the continuing, repetitive double binding which we hypothesize goes on steadily from infantile beginnings in the family situation of individuals who become schizophrenic. This basic family situation, and the overtly communicational characteristics of schizophrenia, have been the major focus of this paper. However, we expect our concepts and some of these data will also be useful in future work on other problems of schizophrenia, such as the variety of other symptoms, the character of the "adjusted state" before schizophrenia becomes manifest, and the nature and circumstances of the psychotic break.

THERAPEUTIC IMPLICATIONS OF THIS HYPOTHESIS

Psychotherapy itself is a context of multi-level communication, with exploration of the ambiguous lines between the literal and metaphoric, or reality and fantasy, and indeed, various forms of play, drama, and hypnosis have been used extensively in therapy. We have been interested in therapy, and in addition to our own data we have been collecting and examining recordings, verbatim transcripts, and personal accounts of therapy from other therapists. In this we prefer exact records since we believe that how a schizophrenic talks depends greatly, though often subtly, on how another person talks to him; it is most difficult to estimate what was really occurring in a therapeutic interview if one has only a description of it, especially if the description is already in theoretical terms.

Except for a few general remarks and some speculation, however, we are not yet prepared to comment on the relation of the double bind to psychotherapy. At present we can only note:

1. Double bind situations are created by and within the psychotherapeutic setting and the hospital milieu. From the point of view of this hypothesis we wonder about the effect of medical "benevolence" on the schizophrenic patient. Since hospitals exist for the benefit of personnel as well as — as much as — more than — for the patients' benefit, there will be contradictions at times in sequences where actions are taken "benevolently" for the patient when actually they are intended to keep the staff more comfortable. We would assume that whenever the system is organized for hospital purposes and it is announced to the patient that the actions are for *his* benefit, then the schizophrenogenic situation is being perpetuated. This kind of deception will provoke the patient to respond to it as a double bind situation, and his response will be "schizophrenic" in the sense that it will be indirect and the patient will be unable to comment on the fact that he feels that he is being deceived. One vignette, fortunately amusing, illustrates such a response. On a ward with a dedicated and "benevolent" physician in charge, there was a sign on the physician's door which said "Doctor's Office. Please Knock." The doctor was driven to distraction and finally capitulation by the obedient patient who carefully knocked every time he passed the door.

2. The understanding of the double bind and its communicative aspects may lead to innovations in therapeutic technique. Just what these innovations may be is difficult to say, but on the basis of our investigation, we are assuming that double bind situations occur consistently in psychotherapy. At times, these are inadvertent in the sense that the therapist is imposing a double bind situation similar to that in the patient's history, or the patient is imposing a double bind situation on the therapist. At other times, therapists seem to impose double binds, either deliberately or intuitively, which force the patient to respond differently than he has in the past.

An incident from the experience of a gifted psychotherapist illustrates the intuitive understanding of a double bind communicational sequence. Dr. Frieda Fromm-Reichmann (1956) was treating a young woman who from the age of seven had built a highly complex religion of her own, replete with powerful gods. She was very schizophrenic and quite hesitant about entering into a therapeutic situation. At the beginning of the treatment she said, "God R says I shouldn't talk with you." Dr. Fromm-Reichmann replied, "Look, let's get something into the record. To me, God R doesn't exist, and that whole world of yours doesn't exist. To you it does, and far be it from me to think that I can take that away from you, I have no idea what it means. So I'm willing to talk with you in terms of that world, if only you know I do it so that we have an understanding that it doesn't exist for me. Now go to God R and tell him that we have to talk and he should give you permission. Also you must tell him that I am a doctor and that you have lived with him in his kingdom now from seven to sixteen — that's nine years — and he hasn't helped you. So now, he must permit me to try and see whether you and I can do that job. Tell him that I am a doctor and this is what I want to try."

The therapist has her patient in a "therapeutic double bind." If the patient is rendered doubtful about her belief in her god then she is agreeing with Dr. Fromm-Reichmann, and is admitting her attachment to therapy. If she insists that God R is real, then she must tell him that Dr. Fromm-Reichmann is "more powerful" than he — again admitting her involvement with the therapist.

The difference between the therapeutic bind and the original double bind situation is, in part, the fact that the therapist is not involved in a life and death struggle himself. He can therefore set up relatively benevolent binds and gradually aid the patient in his emancipation from them. Many of the uniquely appropriate therapeutic gambits arranged by therapists seem to be intuitive. We share the goal of most psychotherapists who strive toward the day when such strokes of genius will be well enough understood to be systematic and commonplace.

References

Bateson, G. (1942). Social planning & the concept of "Deutero-learning." *Conference on Science, Philosophy, & Religion, Second Symposium*. New York: Harper.

Bateson, G. (1955). A theory of play & fantasy. *Psychiatric Research Reports, 2*, 39–51.

Carpenter, C. R. (1934). A field study of the behavior and social relations of howling monkeys. *Comp. Psychological Monographs, 10*, 1–168.

Erickson, M. H. (1955). Personal communication.

Fromm-Reichmann, F. (1956). Personal communication.

Haley, J. (1955). Paradoxes in play, fantasy, & psychotherapy. *Psychiatric Research Reports, 2*, 52–58.

Harlow, H. (1949). The formation of learning sets. *Psychol. Rev., 56*, 51–65.

Hilgard, J. (1953). Anniversary reactions in parents precipitated by children. *Psychiatry, 16,* 73–80.

Hull, C., et al. (1940). *Mathematico-deductive theory of rote learning.* New Haven: Yale.

Jackson, D. (1954a). An episode of sleepwalking. *Journal of the American Psychoanalytic Association, 2,* 503–508.

Jackson, D. (1954b). Some factors influencing the Oedipus complex. *Psychoanalytic Quarterly, 23,* 566–581.

Jackson, D. (1954c). The question of family homeostasis. Presented at the A.P.A., St. Louis, May 7.

Lorenz, K. Z. (1952). *King Solomon's ring.* New York: Crowell.

Perceval, J. (1836 & 1840). *A narrative of the treatment experienced by a gentleman during a state of mental derangement, designed to explain the causes & nature of insanity, etc.* London: Effingham Wilson.

Ruesch, J., & Bateson, G. (1951). *Communication: The social matrix of psychiatry.* New York: W. W. Norton.

von Domarus, E. (1944). The specific laws of logic in schizophrenia. In J. S. Kasanin (Ed.), *Language & thought in schizophrenia.* Berkeley: University of California Press.

Whitehead, A., & Russell, B. (1910). *Principia mathematica.* Cambridge: Cambridge University Press.

CHAPTER 12

The Double Bind,
Family Homeostasis, and a
Control Theory of Human Relationships[1]
(1963)

A number of authorities have indicated that the Palo Alto Group has a more complete personality theory than has been spelled out to date (Bateson, Jackson, Haley, & Weakland, 1956, 1963; Jackson, 1959; Jackson & Weakland, 1961). I feel this to be true, although I would doubt if the group is anywhere near complete agreement within itself. However, I feel it is important to attempt to set down the basic findings of the group and what appears to me at least to be our theoretical position.

The concept of the double bind, coupled with the concept of family homeostasis, has been well received as an important adjunct to our thinking about the relationship of family interaction to individual psychopathology. One obvious reason is that these concepts focus on multilevel communication between humans rather than on the individual's intrapsychic state or on more

---

[1] Jackson's personal and professional papers contain numerous rough and working drafts that were never published. This is one such paper. Found in a folder marked "Double Bind," the draft is dated 11–2–63. The reader will note the ideas contained in this chapter predate by nearly five years the book *Pragmatics of Human Communication*, Watzlawick, Beavin-Bavelas & Jackson, 1967. It is being published here because of the early date of the paper and the clarity of thought contained within.

reductionistic concepts, such as "hostility," "masochism," and so forth. Such concepts have the unfortunate implication that the individual is shot by emotional arrows and wounded in his psyche, that is, too many of our pathological terms lack any implication of process. Certain other attempts at explaining etiology have equally strong drawbacks. Thus, papers on the etiology of numerous nosological classes refer to passive fathers and castrating or dominating mothers, without sufficient specificity as to how this combination affects the individual or without considering that this combination may be a normogenic factor, especially in upper-middle-class samples.[2]

However, while the concept of the double bind has important ramifications as a way of thinking about psychopathology, it has justly been criticized on the grounds:

1. It does not explain the shift from functioning to the psychotic episode.

2. It does not account for normal siblings who presumably have also been exposed to the parents' double binding.

3. It does not explain the absence of schizophrenia in families where double binds occur.

4. It does not account for the nature of psychotic thinking. The reader is referred to the paper, "A review of the double bind theory," by Dr. Paul Watzlawick (1963).

I think it is possible to add further data to fill in some of the blanks and to extend the double bind theory into a somewhat more complete clinical concept.

THE PSYCHOTIC EXPERIENCE

Clinicians all too often talk as if the schizophrenic were adjusting one day and crazy the next. In doing so, they are focusing on a probably small group of patients who have acute psychotic episodes, rather than on the larger group of patients who have been marginal or decompensating for years, or who have

---

[2] This statement is based on the work of Epstein and Wesley (1960), as well as on the sample of "normal" families seen at the Mental Research Institute.

been actively psychotic for a long time, but have not been picked up by the social sieve (physicians, police, army, etc.), or who are brought to the attention of the psychiatrist because of a change in the family, not a change in the condition of the identified patient.

The point, I think, is to describe how exposure to a chronic double bind situation[3] cripples the individual so that he gradually is unable to interact socially at a peer level.

THE NATURE OF THE DOUBLE BIND SEQUENCE

1.   The postulation of a "double bind" sequence assumes certain formal aspects of communication and relates these aspects to examples from living human communication. It should be noted that the double bind concept describes only one aspect of the problem of multiple levels in communication.

2.   The formal elements assumed are:

   a.   A *relationship* between the communicator and the communicant that provides an intensity to the communication or mutual "involvement." The relationship may be personal, as between family members, or may be produced by the participants' roles, as in the situation between a cop and a robber. The relationship provides a field within which the communication operates.

   b.   A *context* in which the exchange of messages goes on. Actually, there are several contexts for any message, depending on how the situation is viewed. The most important aspect of the context is whether it is similarly labeled by the communicator and communicant and whether there is a shift in context (or a switch in contexts) during the communication sequence or in a particular exchange, compared to the participant's shared view of previous similar exchanges. (For example, when individuals frequently indulge in

---

[3] A double bind situation is one where the individual is exposed to double bind statements, rendered intense because of his relationship to the other, and where he is prohibited from either leaving the field or keeping within awareness the contradictory nature of the messages he receives.

spoofing and, without apparent warning, on one occasion it is taken seriously.)

c.   A *message* and a *meta-message* — a message can be considered a signal or cue sent by one individual indicating the kind of transaction he desires with a second individual or individuals. What he wants is always modified by a meta-message indicating his right to the indicated transaction or his right to initiate the desired transaction. A meta-message thus may be a signal of power, a request, a plea, a bargain, etc. The simplest example of message and meta-message (used in the sense defined here) is verbal behavior as the message and nonverbal behavior or vocalization as the meta-message. It is recognized that this is an arbitrary view since every message has a message "meta" to it, and one becomes swamped in an infinite regression series unless he arbitrarily picks a starting point. However, since there are always messages "meta" to another message, levels of messages always exist and give rise to communication complexities.

Given these formal elements, a double bind sequence can be defined as an incongruence between levels of messages (or between a message and a shared context) that occurs in a relationship where the communicator may punish or imply punishment for the communicant if he acknowledges or makes an issue of the incongruence between the messages or between the message and the context.

"Incongruence" in this sense refers to messages that are fundamentally incompatible because they define a relationship in a contradictory way. Thus, in hypnosis, the question of who is in charge of the relationship is kept in question by asking the subject what trance phenomenon he would like to experience. There is a conflict between what is to happen and who has the right to cause it to happen or whether the relationship is a voluntary or an involuntary one.

Formerly the idea of the double bind arose from a consideration of messages of different logical types. However, since we find the double bind in clinical work occurring between two people engaged in some sort of relationship, it is only necessary to postulate that the messages define the relationships in a contradictory manner.

Example:

Mother says to son: "Come here and kiss me," in a tone that indicates "Do what I say" and "drop dead."

1. Context:

    a. Mother and son should have a loving relationship or it is a reflection on the mother, since she reared the son.

    b. In our culture, a loving son spontaneously shows his affection toward his mother.

    c. A son who is unloving is an ingrate and people feel sorry for mistreated mothers.

2. Verbal message: "Demonstrate your affection for me — make me feel like a good mother."

3. Meta-messages:

    a. I hate you for not loving me spontaneously.

    b. I have the right, as your mother, to tell you what conflicts with "spontaneous."

If the son responds he:

    a. Pretends to ignore the noteful aspects of the situation, which action labels him as a faker.

    b. Demonstrates that he is doing what he is told and not being spontaneous.

    c. Labels his mother's statement as congruent when it is incongruent and thus perpetuates her blindness.

If he does not respond, he:

a. Does not clarify the mixed message but opens himself to criticism that is a red herring.

b. Indicates that he doesn't love his mother by the refusal to kiss her when, in fact, he can have positive (affiliative) ties to her that cannot be equated to kissing or not. That is, the refusal tends to define the situation at a literal level.

c. His action does not define the nature of the relationship, but binds his mother to him by calling for an attempt at redefinition on her part.

In this example it is clear that, whereas the term "double bind" originally referred to the victim being caught in a bind that was multiple, this term can also appropriately refer to the fact that a double bind also binds the binder. There is no longer a logical question of "who the captain, who the keeper, pray?" Since the two individuals do not clarify the nature of their relationships by agreement, disagreement, compromise, or whatever.

It is useful to distinguish between a double bind sequence and a double bind statement. The latter exists when the communicator makes a statement, which, if the communicant responds in the terms described above, would create a double bind sequence. If instead, because of the intervention of another party, the communicant is free to leave the field, or to respond in a different way, the double bind statement does not result in a double bind response on the part of the communicant.

DOUBLE BIND AND CONTROL THEORY

The double bind concept represents in capsule form a theory of personality, although this is far from obvious (even to its originators). For example, to nominate the double bind as a severely pathogenic human interaction is to state implicitly a great deal about our group's view of human interaction, since this seed (the double bind) would not flourish in just any soil. The double bind theory states implicitly several categories and levels of assumptions about human behavior:

1. It implies that communication is behavior and vice versa, and that the concept of affect need not be brought into a description of human interaction, even into a very devastating piece of interaction. That is, the idea of psychological trauma often carries with it a kind of violence scale where the most suicidal person has the most affect turned inward, and the most homicidal carries the most outward hate (cf. Jackson, A note on the importance of trauma in the genesis of schizophrenia, 1957). The double bind, on the other hand, postulates almost mechanistically a communication pattern that will shatter the bindee's ordinary communication processes, even if the binder administers his remarks with the aplomb of a surgeon.

2. However, it is also stated that the double bind situation involves a field, and escape is prohibited. Thus, the idea of relationship or involvement is crucial and, as far as I know, relationships are emotionally charged. Thus, the group does not deny the intrapsychic situation — it merely does not make use of it. This choice of direction has sometimes resulted in criticism from psychoanalysts. I think this is caused by our not starting off with developmental history and thus seeming to eschew it. The linking of the intrapsychic to the developmental to the current interactional state of the individual is simply too much for us at present. We leave such data aside as we do neurophysiological observations — all data are important but not all are relevant to the immediate theory we are trying to refine and burnish.

3. As stated earlier, the double bind theory implicitly implies that the bindee is vulnerable to the binder, not only because of a dependent tie (this is stated explicitly), but because human communication has trained him to respond and signal according to rules, and the manipulation of these rules creates the double bind situation.

The rules of communication that are involved have appeared in scattered fashion in the papers of the group and are demonstrated vocally and lexically in Watzlawick's anthology (1964). Some of the more important premises include:

1. **Control Theory:**

Each individual attempts to influence the nature of his relationships. This is not just an inborn "instinct toward mastery" nor is it "competitiveness" nor "aggression." This premise rises from the simple fact that one cannot not communicate. No response is a response just as surely as the interruptions in Morse code are as vital as the dots and dashes. It is convenient to picture the newborn letting out a howl and receiving milk as the initial stage for attempting to influence the nature of his relationships. Even if he were born with a built-in food supply, it would seem that this tactic would still develop. Thus "control theory" is a description and not a postulation of motivations or instincts.

Let us assume that a man from Mars arrives on earth and is a totally compliant creature. Whatever is asked of him, he does cheerfully. Whatever response is called for, he gladly gives. However, being intelligent, he quickly discovers several things about human interaction:

a. His compliance is positively rewarded whereas some others in the environment are negatively rewarded; or, if his timing is off or if he makes a mistake, he experiences negative sanctions in the form of hurt feelings, withdrawal, anger, and so forth, from the one with whom he is interacting. Thus he is taught to influence his relationships even if he were born without such a tendency. All communication occurs within a context and this context as well as the messages sent shape and define how to communicate in addition to exchanging information. When A utters x he narrows the range of B's reply; and once B has stated zy he has limited the randomness of A's next message. Severe limitation of the kinds of messages exchanged is linked to the exhibition of pathological or symptomatic behavior in families.

b. His behavior arouses suspicion and mistrust because those others feel he does not really want to do so and so, he is just pretending. Our man from Mars discovers that the *punctuation* of communication must contain an occasional negative, or how is one to know what is positive? Once the naturally compliant Martian discovers that his ability to get along is positively rewarded, he must now attempt to influence the nature of his relationships toward compliance on his part. Human communication is of such a nature that the kind of interaction described is inevitable. If the

Martian did not attempt to influence the nature of his relationships he would be *not* doing and this, too, is taking action.

2. **Rules:**

Once it is acknowledged that control exists in relationships, then it is a logical step to [establishing] rules in relationships since "how who is influencing who when" would become a dreadful bore if *A* and *B* had to work out this problem for every exchange or every situation they engage in.

Two individuals who are perfect on the Alfonse and Gaston routine[4] can get along fine until they attempt passage through a doorway. There are constant doorways to negotiate in human interaction, and these require that Gaston determine that he goes first, or Alfonse signals that it is all right if Gaston goes first and so forth. In the mother and child picture, which all too often pervades our thinking and behavior, it is possible to imagine a healthy, happy child, who receives from the mother, like a kind of psychological maw into which she drops "instinctual need" filling material. In this idyllic picture it would appear the child had no need to determine the nature of his relationships. However, after he has given his first giggle to her "coochie-coochie-coo," then can he ever again not regard a smile on his part as a tactic?

References

Bateson, G., Jackson, D., Haley, J., & Weakland, J. (1956). Toward a theory of schizophrenia. *Behavioral Science, 1* (4), 251–264.

Bateson, G., Jackson, D., Haley, J., & Weakland, J. (1963). A note on the double bind — 1962. *Family Process, 2,* (1), 154–161.

Epstein, N., & Westley, W. (1960). Parental interaction as related to the emotional health of children. *Social Problems, 8,* 87–92.

Jackson, D. (1957). A note on the importance of trauma in the genesis of schizophrenia. *Psychiatry, 20* (2) 181–184.

Jackson, D. (1959). Family interaction, family homeostasis and some implications for conjoint family psychotherapy. In J. Masserman (Ed.), *Individual and familial dynamics* (pp. 122–141). New York: Grune & Stratton.

---

[4] A vaudeville comedy act in which actors portray two waiters who caricature elaborately exaggerated politeness.

Jackson, D., & Weakland, J. (1961). Conjoint family therapy: Some considerations on theory, technique, and results. *Psychiatry*, *24* (suppl. 2), 30–45.

Watzlawick, P. (1963). A review of the double bind theory. *Family Process*, *2* (1), 132–153.

Watzlawick, P. (1964) *Anthology of human communication* (tape and text). Palo Alto, CA: Science & Behavior Books.

CHAPTER 13

A Note on the Double Bind

Gregory Bateson, Don D. Jackson,
Jay Haley, and John H. Weakland
(1962)

Because of the reaction in the literature to the concept of the double bind as presented in our joint article "Toward a Theory of Schizophrenia," it seems appropriate to state briefly the research context of that article, to clarify what we consider most significant about our work generally, and to describe the further developments in our research since 1956.

Prior to the 1956 paper the research project had investigated a variety of phenomena from the communication point of view — the nature of metaphor, humor, popular films, ventriloquism, training of guide dogs for the blind, the nature of play, animal behavior, the formal nature of psychotherapy and the communicative behavior of individual schizophrenics (Bateson, 1955, 1956; Haley, 1955). All communication involves the use of categories and classes, and our focus of interest was on the occurrence in classification systems of combinations which generate paradox; a particular interest was in the ways two or more messages — meta-messages in relation to each other — may qualify each other to produce paradoxes of Russellian type.

Originally the idea of the double bind was arrived at largely deductively: given the characteristics of schizophrenic communication — a confusion of message and meta-message in the patient's discourse — the patient must have been reared in a learning context which included formal sequences where he was forced to respond to messages which generated paradox of this type. In this sense the double bind hypothesis was initially a conjecture about what must have happened granted the premises of the theoretical approach and the observations of the schizophrenic individual's way of communicating. By 1956 this conjecture was beginning to be supported by empirical observation of mothers and their disturbed children.

However, although our investigations thus involved various fields of phenomena, and the particular concept of the double bind was a striking one — as attested to by the specific attention that both we and others have given it — neither these specific subject matters nor this specific concept has been the real core of our work as we see it. This point needs special attention, as it seems that a number of existing criticisms or misunderstandings of our statements rest on a lack of clarity at just this level.

A COMMUNICATIONAL APPROACH TO THE STUDY OF BEHAVIOR

What is more important in our work, and may not have been sufficiently emphasized or clear in our 1956 paper, is a general communicational approach to the study of a wide range of human (and some animal) behavior, including schizophrenia as one major case. The present and future status of the more specific double bind concept can appropriately be considered only within this, its more general and inclusive framework. This communicational approach might be described or characterized in various ways, as it has been in other of our publications. It will suffice here to note that we are always concerned when examining the activity of people (or other organisms) to consider how this behavior may be in response to observable communications from others, and how it in turn itself is communicative. Especially, we have been concerned with the importance of attending adequately to the complexity of communication. That is, there is never "a message" singly, but in actual communication always two or more related messages, of different levels often conveyed by different channels — voice, tone, movement, context, and so on. These messages may be widely incongruent and thus exert very different and conflicting influences. This approach seems to us to be helpful when we try to examine and conceptualize many sorts of social or psychological problems, and we have continued to pursue and extend its application.

Since 1956 when "Toward a Theory of Schizophrenia" appeared, the project members have published papers on a variety of areas of investigation.

These papers are listed here with reference numbers referring to items in the bibliography at the end of this article. The publications are arranged roughly by subject matter although many of them included overlapping subjects.

1. *Schizophrenic Communication and the Nature of Schizophrenia*
The distortions of schizophrenic communication were discussed (6), a subjective account of a psychosis was presented (16), and schizophrenic behavior was described in terms of levels of communication (32).

2. *The Family Context as an Etiologic Factor and a subject of Study in Itself*
The etiology of schizophrenia was discussed in terms of the mother as a factor (27), and trauma vs. patterns (45). There was a description of the immediate circumstances of a schizophrenic episode (65).
The families of schizophrenics were described in terms of feedback and calibration patterns (15), the family was described as a cybernetic system (35, 36), guilt and its relation to maternal control was discussed (50), and letters of mothers to their schizophrenic children were described (70).
Family organization and dynamics were discussed with reference to incest (9), patterns (15), family homeostasis (66), the relationship between an anxiety syndrome and a marital relationship (28), experimentation with families (41) and family therapy as an arena of research (69).

3. *Therapy*
A report on investigating was given (15), the detailed study of a therapeutic interview was provided (22), psychoanalysis was described in communications terms (31, 33), transference was discussed in terms of paradox (63), brief psychotherapy was described (38) as well as psychotherapy with schizophrenics (39), and family therapy (40, 52, 56, 58, 59, 64).

4. *Hypnosis in Communication Terms*
A description of the interaction of hypnotist and subject was made (32), an analysis was done of a verbatim trance induction (23), the relief of fear with hypnosis was discussed (37), and hypnosis was discussed as a model for describing psychotherapy (38).

5. *Wider Studies of Communication and Organization*
Various general areas of investigation included studies of hospital wards

(7, 15), wider social spheres (5, 10, 20), a detailed analysis of an interview segment (22), and levels of learning (17, 18). The Theory of Games was discussed (11, 13, 15), and evolution was described in terms of communication and double bind patterns (12).

The research project terminated in 1962 after ten years of association. A summary statement of the group agreement about the double bind at the time of termination would include the following: (1). The double bind is a class of sequences that appear when phenomena are examined with a concept of levels of communication. (2). In schizophrenia the double bind is a necessary but not sufficient condition in explaining etiology and, conversely, as an inevitable by-product of schizophrenic communication. (3). Empirical study and theoretical description of individuals and families should for this type of analysis emphasize observable communication, behavior, and relationship contexts rather than focusing upon the perception of affective states of individuals. (4). The most useful way to phrase double bind description is not in terms of a binder and a victim but in terms of people caught up in an ongoing system which produces conflicting definitions of the relationship and consequent subjective distress. In its attempts to deal with the complexities of multilevel patterns in human communications systems, the research group prefers an emphasis upon circular systems of interpersonal relations to a more conventional emphasis upon the behavior of individuals alone or single sequences in the interaction.

References

1. Bateson, G. (1955). A theory of play and fantasy. *Psychiatric Research Reports,* 2, 39–51.
2. Bateson, G. (1956). The message "This is play." In *Second conference on group processes.* New York: Josiah Macy Jr. Foundation.
3. Bateson, G., Jackson, D., Haley, J., & Weakland, J. (1956). Toward a theory of schizophrenia. *Behavioral Science, 1* (4), 251–264.
4. Bateson, G. (1958). Language & psychotherapy, Frieda Fromm-Reichmann's last project. *Psychiatry, 21,* 96–100.
5. Bateson, G. (1958). *Naven,* 2nd edition with a new chapter. Stanford, CA: Stanford University Press.
6. Bateson, G. (1958). Schizophrenic distortion of communication. In C. Whitaker (Ed.), *Social psychiatry in action.* Springfield, IL: Thomas.
7. Bateson, G. (1958). Analysis of group therapy in an admission ward. In H. A. Wilmer (Ed.), *Social psychiatry in action.* Springfield, IL: Thomas.

8. Bateson, G. (1959). Anthropological theories. *Science, 129,* 334–349.

9. Bateson, G. (1959). Panel review. In J. H. Masserman (Ed.), *Individual & familial dynamics.* New York: Grune & Stratton.

10. Bateson, G. (1959). Cultural problems posed by a study of schizophrenic process. In A. Auerback (Ed.), *Schizophrenia, an Integrated Approach,* APA Symposium 1958. New York: Ronald Press.

11. Bateson, G. (1958). The new conceptual frames for behavioral research. *Proceedings of the Sixth Annual Psychiatric Institute,* Princeton, NJ.

12. Bateson, G. (1960). Minimal requirements for a theory of schizophrenia. *Archives of General Psychiatry, 2,* 477–491.

13. Bateson, G. (1960). The group dynamics of schizophrenia. In L. Appleby, J. M. Scher, & J. Cumming (Eds.), *Chronic schizophrenia: Explorations in theory & treatment.* Glencoe, IL: Free Press.

14. Bateson, G. (1960). Discussion of "Families of schizophrenic & of well children: Method, concepts & some results," by Samuel J. Beck. *American Journal of Psychiatry, 30,* 263–266.

15. Bateson, G. (1961). The biosocial integration of behavior in the schizophrenic family, & The challenge of research in family diagnosis & therapy, Summary of panel discussion: I. Formal research in family structure." In N. W. Ackerman, F. L. Beatman, & S. Sanford (Eds.), *Exploring the base for family therapy.* New York: Family Service America.

16. Bateson, G. (Ed.) (1961). *Perceval's narrative, A patient's account of his psychosis, 1830–1832.* Stanford, CA: Stanford University Press.

17. Bateson, G. (In press). Structure and the genesis of relationship. Frieda Fromm-Reichmann Memorial Lecture. *Psychiatry.*

18. Bateson, G. (In press). Exchange of information about patterns of human behavior. *Symposium on information storage and neural control.* Houston, Texas, 1962.

19. Bateson, G. (In press). Communication theories in relation to the etiology of the neuroses. *Symposium on the etiology of the neuroses.* Society of Medical Psychoanalysis, New York, 1962.

20. Bateson, G. (1962). *Problems of credibility & congruence in applying computational methods to problems of peace.* Delivered at the Spring Joint Computer Conference, American Federation of Information Processing Societies, San Francisco.

21. Bateson, G. (To be published). *The prisoner's dilemma & the schizophrenic family.*

22. Bateson, G., Brosin, H. W., Birdwhistell, R. & McQuown, N. (Mimeograph). *The natural history of an interview.*

23. Erickson, M. H., Haley, J. & Weakland, J. (1959). A transcript of a trance induction with commentary. *American Journal of Clinical Hypnosis, 2,* 49–84.

24. Fry, W. (1958). The use of ataractic agents. *California Medicine, 98*, 309–313.

25. Fry, W. (1959). The destructive behavior on hospital wards. *Psychiatric Quarterly Supplement, 33*, Part 2, 197–231.

26. Fry, W. F., & Heersema, P. (1963). Conjoint family therapy: A new dimension in psychotherapy. In *Topic. Prob. Psychotherapy*, V. 4, 147–153. New York: Basel & Karger.

27. Fry, W. (1963). The schizophrenogenic who? *Psychoanalysis & Psychoanalytic Review, 49*, 68–73.

28. Fry, W. (1962). The marital context of an anxiety syndrome. *Family Process*, 1, 245–252.

29. Fry, W. (In press). *Sweet madness: A study of humo*, Palo Alto, CA: Pacific Books.

30. Haley, J. (1955). Paradoxes in play, fantasy, psychotherapy. *Psychiatric Research Reports, 2*, 52–58.

31. Haley, J. (1958). The art of psychoanalysis. *Etc.*, 15, 190–200.

32. Haley, J. (1958). An interactional explanation of hypnosis. *American Journal of Clinical Hypnosis, 1*, 41–57.

33. Haley, J. (1959). Control in psychoanalytic psychotherapy. *Progress in Psychotherapy, 4*, 48–65. New York: Grune & Stratton.

34. Haley, J. (1959). An interactional description of schizophrenia. *Psychiatry, 22*, 321–332.

35. Haley, J. (1959). The family of the schizophrenic: A model system. *American Journal of Nervous & Mental Disorders, 129*, 357–374.

36. Haley, J. (1960). Observation of the family of the schizophrenic. *American Journal of Orthopsychiatry, 30*, 460–467.

37. Haley, J. (1960). Control of fear with hypnosis. *American Journal of Clinical Hypnosis, 2*, 109–115.

38. Haley, J. (1961). Control in brief psychotherapy. *Archives of General Psychiatry, 4*, 139–153.

39. Haley, J. (1961). Control in the psychotherapy of schizophrenics. *Archives of General Psychiatry, 5*, 340–353.

40. Haley, J. (1962). Whither family therapy? *Family Process, 1*, 69–100.

41. Haley, J. (1962). Family experiments: A new type of experimentation. *Family Process, 1* (1); 265–293.

42. Haley, J. (1963). Marriage therapy. *Archives of General Psychiatry*.

43. Haley, J. (1963). *Strategies of psychotherapy*. New York: Grune & Stratton.

44. Jackson, D. (1956). Countertransference & psychotherapy. In F. Fromm-Reichman & J. L. Moreno (Eds.), *Progress in Psychotherapy, 1*, 234–238. New York: Grune & Stratton.

45. Jackson, D. (1957). A note on the importance of trauma in the genesis of schizophrenia. *Psychiatry, 20*, 181–184.

46. Jackson, D. (1957). The psychiatrist in the medical clinic. *Bulletin American Association of Medical Clinics, 6*, 94–98.

47. Jackson, D. (1957). The question of family homeostasis. *Psychiatric Quarterly Supplement, 31,* 79–90.

48. Jackson, D. (1957). Theories of suicide. In E. Shneidman and N. Farberow (Eds.), *Clues to Suicide.* New York: McGraw Hill.

49. Jackson, D. (1958). The family & sexuality. In C. Whitaker (Ed.), *The psychotherapy of chronic schizophrenia patients.* Boston: Little Brown.

50. Jackson, D. (1958). Guilt & the control of pleasure in schizoid personalities. *British Journal of Medical Psychology, 31,* part 2, 124–130.

51. Jackson, D., Block, J., Block, J., & Pattern, V. (1958). Psychiatrists' conceptions of the schizophrenogenic parent. *Archives of Neurology and Psychiatry, 79,* 448–459.

52. Jackson, D. (1959). Family interaction, family homeostasis & some implications for conjoint family psychotherapy. In J. Masserman (Ed.), *Individual & familial dynamics.* New York: Grune & Stratton.

53. Jackson, D. (1959). The managing of acting cut in a borderline personality. In A. Burton (Ed.), *Case Studies in Counseling & Psychotherapy.* New York: Prentice Hall.

54. Jackson, D., & Weakland, J. (1959). Schizophrenic symptoms and family interaction. *Archives of General Psychiatry, 1,* 618–621.

55. Jackson, D. (1960). (Ed.). *The etiology of schizophrenia.* New York: Basic Books.

56. Jackson, D. (1961). The monad, the dyad, & the family therapy of schizophrenics. In A. Burton (Ed.), *Psychotherapy of the Psychoses.* New York: Basic Books.

57. Jackson, D., Satir, V., & Riskin, J. (1961). A method of analysis of a family interview. *Archives of General Psychiatry, 5,* 321–339.

58. Jackson, D., & Satir, V. (1961). Family diagnosis & family therapy. In N. Ackerman, F. Beatman, & S. Sherman (Eds.), *Exploring the base for family therapy.* New York: Family Service America.

59. Jackson, D., & Weakland, J. (1961). Conjoint family therapy, some considerations on theory, technique, & results. *Psychiatry, 24,* Suppl. to No. 2, 30–45.

60. Jackson, D. (1962). Action for mental illness but what kind? *Stanford Medical Bulletin, 20,* 77–80.

61. Jackson, D. (1962). Interactional psychotherapy. In M. E. Stein (Ed.), *Contemporary psychotherapies.* Glencoe, IL: Free Press.

62. Jackson, D. (1962). Family therapy in the family of the schizophrenic. In M. E. Stein (Ed.), *Contemporary psychotherapies.* Glencoe, IL: Free Press.

63. Jackson, D., & Haley, J. (1963). Transference revisited. *The Journal of Nervous & Mental Disease, 137* (4), 363–371.

64. Jackson, D., & Watzlawick, P. (1963, May). The acute psychosis as a manifestation of growth experience. *Psychiatric Research Reports, 16:* 83–94.

65. Weakland, J., & Jackson, D. (1958). Patient and therapist observations on the circumstances of schizophrenic episode. *Archives of Neur. Psychiatry, 79,* 554–574.

66. Weakland, J. (1960). The double-bind hypothesis of schizophrenia and three-party interaction. In D. Jackson. (Ed.), *The etiology of schizophrenia*. New York: Basic Books.

67. Weakland, J. (1961). The essence of anthropological education. *American Anthropology*, *63*, 1094–1097.

68. Weakland, J. (1961). Review of E. H. Schein, I. Schnier, & C. H. Barker, *Coercive persuasion*. New York: W. W. Norton. *Journal of Asian Studies, 21*, 84–86.

69. Weakland, J. (1962). Family therapy as a research arena. *Family Process, 1*, 63–68.70.

70. Weakland, J., & Fry, W. (1962). Letters of mothers of schizophrenics. *American Journal of Orthopsychiatry, 32*, 604–623.

CHAPTER 14

Psychoanalytic Education in the Communication Processes
(1962)

Why should a term like "communication processes" even be juxtaposed with a broad term like "psychoanalytic training," since communication between analyst and patient is essential to the analytic process? As a matter of fact, one could claim that our understanding of neurotic and psychotic communication came into being when Freud explained the nature of the beast and taught us to look for meaning within meaning. But two general assumptions are implied in my topic:

1. The rubric "communication processes" must differ in quantity or quality from the usual psychoanalytic view of the communication between patient and analyst.

2. That behavior subsumed under the term "communication processes" is not part of the usual curricula of psychoanalytic institutes.

Let me list some of the areas and assumptions involving communication processes that might be different in degree or kind from the usual emphasis given in psychoanalytic training and might be, some time in the future, a more usual part of such training:

1. Communication processes imply an interaction within at least a two-person system.

2. Communication terminology is more suitable for the description of a wide range of human behavior than analytic terminology, which is strictly oriented to the individual and his implied intrapsychic processes.

I use terms like "communication processes" rather than "communication theory" because the latter does not yet exist. There is gradually being built up a body of knowledge about human communication and at present these data occupy a spectrum from mathematics to purely clinical observation. However, this embryo collection of ideas and data has enough cohesiveness to have been attacked in certain analytic quarters and thus has been bestowed with a respectability that it perhaps does not deserve. Such articles contend that:

1. "Communication processes" represent a point of view already covered by psychoanalytic concepts.

2. These two points of view, i.e., the communication and the psychoanalytic, are necessarily antithetical.

Mortimer Ostow, in discussing a paper of Arieti's on various theories of schizophrenia, states:

> Let me now turn to the double bind theory, a non-psychologic approach to schizophrenia. During the past decade and a half, mathematical theories of some eloquence have been devised to deal with problems of measuring and communicating information, extending logical thinking beyond the capacity of the human mind, predicting the probable outcome of dreams. These theories have proved themselves in application to the specific area to which they were directed. Together they constitute a general systems theory. In the journal, *Behavior*, [I think Dr. Ostow must be referring to *Behavioral Science*] one can find many attempts to apply this general systems theory to psychologic and psychiatric problems. I have yet to see such an attempt, which has made a real contribution to our understanding. The reason for this failure is not that the theory is incorrect, or even that it is essentially inapplicable to human behavior. In my opinion, the reason is that those who try to apply the theory, in general, refuse to deal with the ultimate variables of human behav-

ior as expressed in psychoanalytic metapsychology and postulate their own variables based solely on naive, a priori, and invalid assumptions. Such assumptions, no matter how elegant the theory applied to them, can yield only naive and invalid conclusions. The double bind theory is an example of this mathematical-logical-pseudopsychologizing. It is no novelty to any psychoanalyst that signals are communicated from one person to another by routes other than verbal. In psychoanalytic clinical reports of half a century ago, one will find reference to facial expressions, posture, vocal intonation, and even silence as modes of communication more faithful than speech. It is also no novelty to the psychoanalyst that a single situation may trigger more than one, often conflicting, response in the observer. It was a discovery of unverbalized and indeed unconscious intrapsychic conflict that marked the beginning of Freud's study of the neuroses.[1]

It can hardly be made more clear, short of pistols and bloodshed, how strongly this opinion would differ from my own. For clarifying this difference, I am grateful to Dr. Ostow. His statements serve as a model of the need to clarify the relationship between psychoanalysis and communication processes. For example, there is the statement that the double bind theory which is based on a communications framework is a "non-psychologic approach." The psychiatric dictionary of Hinsie and Campbell defines psychology as, "The science that deals with the mind and mental processes — consciousness, sensation, ideation, memory, etc." According to this definition, much communication work is non-psychologic. But it is a simple fact that in our field there is no other way to measure the patient than by using oneself as a measuring stick. As to Ostow's comment that our observations are based on naive, a priori, and invalid assumptions, I can only say that the patient is the source of our data, just as he is in psychoanalysis proper. I will refrain from telling the story of the blind men and the elephant.

Perhaps the most troublesome comment in his discussion, and the most important for this paper, is the statement that it is no novelty to analysts that signals are communicated from one person to another by routes other than

---

[1] Arieti, S. Recent conceptions and misconceptions of schizophrenia. *Am. J. Psychotherapy, 14*:320, 1960.

verbal. In any simple sense, to agree with this statement is like equating love of country with ability and diligence at saluting the flag. I am quite aware that psychoanalysts believe in nonverbal behavior, but the fact is that to date this belief has not become an important part of psychoanalytic theory. David Rappaport stated three years ago that the most serious weakness in psychoanalysis was its lack of a learning theory.[2] Researchers in communication are particularly interested in learning contexts, but formal psychoanalysis, to date, has not been. There is not only the problem of the "dynamics" of our patients but the learning situation in which these dynamics developed.

In the usual psychoanalytic view, movement goes from inside the patient's head to the outside. Whether this concept is expressed by neurophysiological and energic models or by terms like "free association," "transference," "topographic," "economic," and "structural," the primary focus is on how output reflects the intrapsychic situation rather than on what has been fed into the machine. The psychoanalytic situation itself is created in order to minimize input. This situation has many desirable features, as its long history will attest, but it would be fatuous to assume that the purest form of human communication — beamed direct from the "mind" — is occurring because the analyst and patient are obeying a very specific set of rules. On the contrary, a recognition that communication is at least dyadic implies that one could never hope to have really "free" associations, but rather a flow of words appropriate to the psychoanalytic situation which is labeled "free associations." If the analyst and the patient had never met and the therapy was conducted through a one-way glass window, and the analyst's voice was mechanically modulated to remove its distinctive characteristics, even then there would be a dyadic system, since the patient cannot help having expectations of "analysts" and in particular his analyst, and would be reacting to that kind of individual who would study him in such a situation.

It is usual in my experience to encounter enthusiastic residents who speak of the "id" as if they were observing from a seat on the fifty-yard line. Conversely, patients' expectations about psychoanalysts and the manner in which the analyst interacts with these expectations becomes a communication problem the moment the two participants meet. Occasionally, one has the opportunity to watch such an encounter and it can be rather disquieting. For exam-

---

[2] In a speech at the Center for Advanced Study in the Behavioral Sciences, Stanford, CA.

ple, a young man I was examining for the psychiatric boards tested a patient on the Benjamin proverbs. Unfortunately, he was not aware that his manner toward the patient was patronizing and that he was covertly rewarding every literal statement she made. Although this patient was a recovered psychoneurotic who had come back to the clinic for the examinations in order to pay a debt of gratitude, the young man diagnosed her as schizophrenic. Later in the same day, I witnessed another candidate examine this same patient with totally different results. The first young man was not stupid. Indeed, he was in his third year of candidacy at a psychoanalytic institute where competition for selection is very keen. Under the pressure of the examination, he oversold himself on the possibilities of the pure pipeline to the mind just as some analysts will oversell themselves on the meaning of a slip of the tongue even at a cocktail party (as long as they are not the ones to make it). When the first rule of communication theory is ignored and the analyst behaves as if the patient could carry on a private conversation in his presence, then blind bias dilutes the utility of the data collected.

A second assumption I would like to make about communication concepts in comparison to analytic theory is that the former is more suitable for handling a wide range of human interaction and endeavor. Analytic terminology, when correctly used, has specific meaning within a well-delineated context, but even Freud himself ran into difficulty in restricting his terminology to the original meaning he gave it. For example, Freud in "Analysis, Terminable and Interminable," describes his treatment of a young Russian (The Wolf Man) with whom he felt he had made good progress and then had come to an impasse. He told the patient that the coming year would be the last of his analysis, regardless of progress, and reports in this paper that in the last months of treatment, the patient produced all the memories and connecting links which were necessary for understanding his childhood neurosis. Freud then reports that following the war, the patient returned to Vienna in a severely neurotic state and required further psychoanalysis. Freud says, "There can be only one verdict about the value of this blackmailing device. The measure is effective provided that one hits the right time in which to employ it. But it cannot be held to guarantee perfect accomplishment of the task of psychoanalysis. On the contrary, we may be quite sure that while the force of the threat will have the effect of bringing part of the material to light, another part will be held back, become buried as it were, and will be lost to our therapeutic efforts." He further states that the analyst must not extend the time once the date for discontinuing treatment has been fixed, or the patient will lose all his faith in the analyst. I mention this particular case because, in discussing the patient's subsequent breakdown, Freud mentions, and I quote, "Some of these relapses were caused by still unresolved residues of the transference; short-lived though the attacks were, they were distinctly paranoiac in character." In other places in this article, Freud uses the term "transference" in a similar fashion, even when he is describing a real-life interaction between himself and the patient.

You may remember that later in this same paper, Freud discusses whether it is advisable to stir up for purposes of prophylaxis a conflict, which is not at the moment manifest. He rejects this idea from several angles especially because "we have not the plenary powers which such intervention would demand and most certainly the object of this therapeutic experiment would refuse to cooperate with it." Freud further states that any deliberate procedure of the kind mentioned would necessitate "unkind behavior on the part of the analyst toward the patient. This would have an injurious effect upon his affectionate attitude toward the analyst, i.e., upon the positive transference which is the patient's strongest motive for cooperating in the work of analysis." If one refers back to the examples Freud gave of his intervention with the young Russian, he states that the analysis came to an impasse before his setting a deadline because the patient was enjoying the luxurious, undemanding, Viennese life that he was leading. There is the implication that the patient was something of a spoiled child. Surely Freud's setting a time limit must have seemed unkind to the patient, and yet he attempted to keep the analysis going by providing Freud with the material for which he was seeking. It is misleading to assume that the patient's transference and the nature of his verbal productions were not markedly influenced by his special situation with Freud, and Freud almost, but not quite, grapples with this point.

These observations of Freud's can now be matched against the "Memoirs of the Wolf Man," translated by Felix Augenfeld and Muriel Gardiner. In describing the period of 1914 to 1919, the Wolf Man describes his leaving Vienna and states:

> During my treatment by Professor Freud, I had had the opportunity of hearing from the very mouth of the founder of psychoanalysis, from the original spring, the fundamental principles of this completely new science of the deeper layers of the human psyche. Since

we often discussed all manner of things, *I became familiar also with Freud's views on literature, art, and various other matters.*[3] Shortly before the end of my treatment, Therese, my future wife, came to Vienna and together we visited Professor Freud. I had not expected that Therese would make such a favorable impression upon him. Not only was he obviously impressed by her appearance (he had evidently doubted whether Therese was really such a beautiful woman as I had described), but he was also pleased by her reserved and serious nature. So my intention to marry Therese met with his full approval. (In *Bulletin of the Philadelphia Association of Psychoanalysis,* 1961.)

These examples from Freud's paper and from the Wolf Man's memoirs illustrate that if one focuses on the intrapsychic mechanisms of the patient, he is very apt to overlook what is occurring in the two-party interaction and he may be further aided in this overlooking by the very language of psychoanalysis. In this sense, the inadequacy of the word "transference" is obvious since it is used unwittingly by Freud to cover both the reactions of the patient to Freud himself and manifestations of the patient's childhood neurosis. This can be noted by the Wolf Man's observations of his attitude toward Freud, which certainly consist of more than what is ordinarily meant by the word "transference;" and by Freud's willingness to participate with him in "real interaction." This view is strongly supported by the final section of Freud's paper in which he states: "It is too much to expect that the patient should have a firm conviction of the curative power of analysis, but he may have come to the analyst with a certain amount of confidence and this, reinforced by the various factors in the positive transference *which it is our business to evoke*[4] makes him capable of doing his share." Here we have a double use of the word transference. In one sense, it is used to mean the laying over of the patient's past onto the present, and in another sense, it is meant to describe a reaction to the analyst's attempts to gain the patient's confidence. When Freud put the pressure on, results were forthcoming.[5]

---

[3] Italics mine.

[4] Italics mine.

[5] Some years ago I suggested the term "palintropy" or "palintropic process" to describe the back-and-forth interaction in therapy which is more than implied by the concept of

Others have also questioned the concept of transference as it is defined in psychoanalysis. For example, in an important paper, Ackerman asks, among other things the question: "Why do we prize the irrationality of transference neurosis?" He goes on to state: "The weakest aspect of the Freudian conceptual model seems to be in the crucial question of reality testing and new social learning."[6] Destructive and hostile critics of psychoanalysis have raised questions about the therapeutic value of transference neurosis but usually with the almost moral implication that it is better to let sleeping dogs lie. Ackerman seems to be raising the question in order to ask: "Are we too busy digging the mine to process the ore?" If psychoanalysts were more interested in the actual nature of the exchange of messages between themselves and their patients, they might be more cautious about equating the irrationality of the transference neurosis with "depth" (and thus potential insight), and would look at the elements in the psychoanalytic situation that are then labeled as evidence of transference neurosis. For example, I would hypothesize that, within certain limits, the more passive the analyst, the more irrational the transference neurosis. The "certain limits" refers to the kind of patient and to the fact that a completely passive analyst would probably lose the patient before treatment progressed far enough for a transference neurosis to occur.

I do differ with Ackerman slightly in regard to his stress on the fact that the analyst's anonymity does not provide the architecture for a true social experience. Even though I have just stated that the more passive the analyst, the more irrational the transference neurosis, I am using "irrational" not in an absolute sense but in terms of how the material would be labeled by analysts. In communication terms, the analytic situation, no matter how passive or anonymous the analyst, is as real a situation for two-person communication as any other. The analyst's anonymity does not create an unreal situation; it simply provides a different kind of context from the one the patient usually experiences, and hence the kind of communication differs from that in ordinary social intercourse.

For example, analysts have labeled one type of communication, "Primary

---

transference. See Jackson, D.: Counter-transference and psychotherapy. In F. Fromm-Reichmann & J. Moreno (Eds.), *Progress In Psychotherapy Volume I* (234–238). New York: Grune & Stratton, Inc.

[6] Ackerman, N: Transference and countertransference. *Psychoanalysis & Psychoanalytic Review* 46:3, 1959.

process material." This kind of communication can be thought of as the language of the unconscious, or it can be thought of as a partial outgrowth of the psychoanalytic situation. By utilizing this kind of communication, the patient can do several things at the same time:

1. He is obeying the rules of the game, and therefore furthering his own wish to get something out of the analysis and to please the analyst.

2. He is making the analyst work, and thus proves to himself that he is indeed complicated and requires the services of an expert for whom he is giving up time, money, and energy.

3. By being somewhat obscure, he can indicate many things about his feelings toward the analyst without shouldering the responsibility for having said them. That is, he can deny that his symbolism has any meaning or that it has the meaning the analyst attaches to it, or he can deny that he said it even though his "unconscious" did. He can state "it was only a dream" just as in a social situation, a person might claim: "I was only kidding."

4. He can frame his comments to the analyst in terms of the past and hence implicitly deny that they have any reference for the present situation between him and the psychoanalyst.

To those acquainted with the work of our research group on communication processes in schizophrenia, much of the above has a familiar ring. This is not surprising because schizophrenics have been described as utilizing more primary process material in their comments than ordinary individuals, and the analytic situation has many of the covert contextual messages that exist in the schizophrenic's family. As one example: If the analyst is silent, the patient usually assumes that he is withholding for specific reasons, not that the analyst hasn't anything to say. On the other hand, the patient is in the process of saying more and more about himself, which implies a relative ignorance on the analyst's part. Further, to the extent the patient uses symbolic communication, including dreams, to that extent he is vulnerable to having the meaning of his utterances explained to him. The schizophrenic gets himself exactly in the same spot, and then feels suspicious and victimized by other people. Let me hasten to make it clear that I am not accusing formal psychoanalysis of the propagation of schizophrenia. I am simply illustrating how one may look at the context in which communication is occurring and hypothesize the relationship between the communication and the implicit messages that arise in such a context.

Ackerman concludes the paper mentioned above by stating that when we know more about family interactions, we will learn more about the nature of transference and countertransference. You will not be surprised to know that I am in complete accord with this statement. However, I have very little to offer at this moment as to the language needed to make these relationships clear, observable, and measurable. Let me give you an example of an approach I can imagine being useful but one that barely scratches the surface at the present time. I have mentioned that context is an important tool in judging the analytic situation. Context can be thought of as a spatial temporal envelope which serves as a frame within which messages are uttered. The context in which a message occurs can carry very broad implications, including cultural and sub-group definitions and expectations, private rules of the family, and even what currently is being "done" or is "chic" or "gauche." Context, on the other hand, can impose as specific limitations as one's behavior in the process of being given a traffic ticket. In our family work, we have felt that a frequent way in which one family member attempts to define the nature of his relationship to another member is to change the context from that assumed by one of the other persons involved in the communication. The extent to which contexts are switched can be related to the extent of social pathology in the children, that is, there are more and less harmful ways of switching contexts. Some of the methods utilized include:

1.   Implying that this message was all right at one time but is not now appropriate — a method I have labeled "past-present switches." The mother might say to the child, "I want you to be frank, but you shouldn't have chosen this moment because I have a headache."

2.   Implying that the individual has misinterpreted the context in which the message was uttered. This is a mechanism frequently used by parents to put a halt to certain behavior. For example, if they and the child are teasing each other, the teasing can be broken off by the parents' suddenly taking the situation seriously.

3. Implying that only this individual would send such a message, and that he differs from others in his family, his group, and so on, in his selection of messages.

4. Implying that when other individuals utter similar messages, they don't mean them in the same way as this individual does. That is, the parents might say to the child, "Yes, but when I said that to you, I was only kidding."

It is possible to characterize certain methods of changing contexts as being more typical for a particular family than other possible choices. For example, some families regularly use tangentialization. This refers to the selection of one element of the sender's statement or message that is not necessarily the most relevant for understanding at that moment. The new element that is connected with, but not identical to, the most meaningful aspect of the sender's message is thus developed until the focus becomes more and more removed from the starting point. A husband might ask his wife to please use stretchers whenever she washes his socks. Instead of replying, "Yes, I will," or "No, I won't," the wife who uses tangentialization would reply that the husband must be buying a different brand of socks lately or else his feet were getting bigger. Further, she can't understand why a manufacturer cannot guarantee against shrinking when he charges $5.95 for a pair of socks. This method differs from and, in our opinion, is less pathological than, the complete change of context that would occur if the wife replied: "Incidentally, if I am going to have time to do all that is expected of me lately, I'm going to have some help from the doctor. I'm just tired out all the time." Such a statement does not merely say to the husband, "You have no right to criticize me," it states: "You have no right to ask anything of me at all." Further, if the husband were to challenge the statement on the ground that she was refusing to use stretchers on his socks, she could deny this and ask him if he wasn't interested in her state of health.

The relevance for the analytic situation of having an intimate knowledge of contextual matters in communication is obvious. An individual from a family that uses a particular method of handling contexts will obviously try to adapt the analytic situation to his previously learned technique and vice versa, both because he will tend to repeat his experience and because he expects to be communicated to in the old-fashioned way, and the best defense is a good offense. The analyst who can imagine the kind of family situation that would produce the patient's way of switching contexts may be more able to help this patient for two reasons:

1. His emphatic understanding will increase and he will be alert to the material which the patient hasn't mentioned but which has to be there.

2. He not only can try to avoid putting the patient in his old spot, but may devise techniques which will point out to the patient has limited patterns of communication, or actually teach him new ways of communicating. Education can occur only if the learning contexts are different from the patient's previous experience.

Much of the above is now done implicitly in a psychoanalytic situation by skilled analysts. I am merely pointing out that terms like "transference" make it difficult to define explicitly the interaction between patient and analyst and to select those techniques, which might be most useful in maximizing the leverage in this relationship.

I have made two points about the communication versus the analytic framework. One, that the communication viewpoint assumes at least a two-person system and thus introduces a different way of viewing or describing analytic situations; and two, the language of communication covers a broader descriptive range of human behavior and can implement classic terminology. Given these two assumptions, what about their immediate relevance to analytic training?

COMMUNICATION AND TRAINING

Obviously, the kind of training a psychoanalyst should have depends on how his task is defined and the qualifications needed to carry it out. Thomas Szasz has stated[7]:

> There is no widely accepted definition of the psychoanalyst's exact task. Unfortunately, this problem itself is somewhat controversial,

---

[7] Szasz, T. S.: *The Myth of Mental Illness.* New York: Paul B. Hoeber, Inc., 1961.

reflecting disagreements concerning the nature of psychoanalytic therapy. In general, the qualifications demanded of an expert will depend upon, and will reflect, the observer's conceptions of the expert's tasks and the mode of operation. We may consider the example of medical practice as an illustrative analogy. Our model of a qualified medical practitioner depends upon and reflects our image of the nature of medical illness and cure. If we think along scientific physico-chemical lines, we shall require qualifications such as are asked of physicians. If, however, our image of illness and cure happens to be essentially hystico-religious, for instance along the lines of Christian Science, then we shall demand qualifications that in fact are asked of Christian Science practitioners. So much for the dependence of the therapist's qualifications on our conceptions of his task.

The task of the psychoanalyst could be defined as that of understanding his patient and the nature of the psychoanalytic process within the framework of classical psychoanalysis. However, it appears that candidates and members of psychoanalytic institutes are increasingly being called upon to exhibit a wide range of psychiatric competency. As medical school professors, consultants, researchers, advisers to social agencies, they often have first call because analytic training has high status with the public and with the majority of psychiatrists. It would appear that institutes will have to take such development into account as they devise new curricula, and indeed, a glance at some of the electives in various institute curricula convinces me that such changes are already under way.

The training of the psychoanalyst depends not only on how his task is defined, but what range of professional function is open to him. "Good" psychoanalytic patients are getting harder to find and most of the younger analysts conduct a grab bag sort of practice with a wide variety of patients, techniques, and results. Frequency of visits must be varied, some patients do and some do not use the couch, and it appears that relatives are getting harder to avoid and that the psychotherapy of married couples is definitely on the rise. Further, there is widespread interest in conjoint family psychotherapy and a number of analysts are in the vanguard of this movement.

Interest in communication processes can augment the dynamic formulations that the psychoanalyst uses in his psychotherapeutic work. For example, each spouse of a married couple can be understood by a psychodynamic formulation. However, an interest in the communication patterns between the two individuals will supplement the impression that the analyst has of each.

For example, if we label the wife a castrative female and the husband a passive masochist, we will be describing an apparent dominance-submission pattern. If we watch these two individuals interact, it becomes clear that neither is truly dominant or submissive, but that both are frustrated and unhappy. We might further learn that these individuals engage in a series of interlocking ploys to keep each other involved in a hopeless impasse. This impasse can be blamed on sadism or masochism or it can be regarded as the outcome of how each member is defining the nature of the relationship. The rigidity of the system can be attributed to the need of each member to systematize change and their inability to foresee what kind of change might take place. As you can see this is a very different way of describing couple interaction than if one were to use psychoanalytic terminology. Such conceptualization may influence the nature of the therapeutic interventions as I can illustrate with the following example:

I have been treating a young executive who was referred because of recurring panic states. We came to know something of these attacks, their relation to his past and so on and yet it seemed to me, but not to the patient, that a weekend at home was a frequent prerequisite for a panic on Monday — although it could be claimed, as the patient did, that Monday signaled his return to the pressures of work. One day this gentleman called me from a distant city with the news that he was falling apart to the extent he doubted he could return to Palo Alto. I suggested a few ounces of man's best friend and a quick return. He called the next day for an immediate appointment and I suggested he bring his wife with him. He was obviously disgruntled but agreed. When they were seated opposite me, the patient immediately began an account of the horrors of this trip almost as if he were in one of his usual sessions with me alone, and I interrupted him to suggest to his wife that she must have had a pretty good week. There was some struggle in getting them to accept the relevance of this remark, but fortunately the wife was able to confirm my suspicion and the patient began to learn a new view of his difficulties. Among other things, we were able to nail down that both members used rather stereotyped messages that they would not desert one another. As a consequence, they were constantly arousing fear of desertion in each other. Neither was consciously aware of these messages and yet there were many standardized interactional patterns, that is, ways of communicating with each other that could be elucidated in a few hours of seeing them together.

Obviously this gentleman's symptoms could have improved during the course of analysis. He would have changed with the analyst's even knowing the kind of data described above. The patient would have changed the nature of his communication with his wife because of the analytic experience, and since it takes two to tango, she would be affected by receiving a different kind of feedback from him and could not engage in their characteristic transactions. This kind of example also raises questions of economy, efficiency, and whether couple therapy effects changes as deep seated as psychoanalysis, but these matters are all apart from the purpose of the paper.

What place, then, has training in communication in the psychoanalytic curriculum? I think it can be simply stated that no formal courses need be offered to introduce the communication point of view, for it is just that, a point of view — a matter of emphasis. Candidates could be encouraged to examine psychoanalytic concepts in different frames of reference and some candidates might then become curious and add to our meager knowledge.

Along with this "point of view" approach, I think an exposure to certain materials would be appropriate. Here I would think of the book, *Communication — The Social Matrix of Psychiatry*, by Bateson and Ruesch (1951), the recent book by Scheflen analyzing Rosen's technique; a very brief exposure to slow motion or frame-by-frame movies with reference to Birdwhistell's "microkinesics"; a smatter of information theory, perhaps via a paper by James G. Miller; and some notice of linguistics, especially micro-linguistic analysis. These materials would occupy only a few hours, but would help to alert the student to one of the scientific dangers in the study of psychoanalysis; namely, that the very attractiveness of psychoanalytic theory can render one a convert rather than a seeker after light. Freud was an excellent clinician and a beautiful writer. Only careful attention to his writings reveals his cautionary statements about buying the whole package, and his occasional forgetting to take his own advice.

Education in communication theory would impel the student to examine constantly the arena in which he works because then he could never ignore the influence of himself as an observer. Even the most convincing consistency in his experience with certain patients would not be taken as the scientific proof of psychoanalytic concepts but would be examined at least from the standpoint of shared labels between him and his patient. Similarity in experience, interests, and even in psychopathology between analyst and patient can create an illusion of "getting somewhere." Communication that is indicative of ego, superego, or id can create the illusion of neuroanatomic structures and Freud's statement *"our psychoanalytic mythology"*[8] is all too easily forgotten.

Currently, the majority of critics of psychoanalytic theories are those hostile to the whole system rather than those devoted to the movement yet discontented with the nature of the proof of its validity. The enormous popularity of psychoanalysis puts a great burden on those who would wear the critic's mantle. Indoctrination of the student begins early and is apt to last a lifetime. Typically the experience of the tyro therapist is to glean from psychoanalytic teachings a language that enables him to interpret to himself the actions, words, or dreams of the patient, and this becomes an exciting and convincing experience that sends him back to the books to learn more, and eventually produces yearnings for the nearest psychoanalytic institute.

The delight one experiences in learning a foreign language and conversing with the natives should not be mistaken for "understanding them." The student who foresees great victories in the consultation room because of his grasp of psychoanalytic principles will either suffer severe disappointment or decide he just doesn't see the right kind of patients. To attempt another kind of analogy, it is quite possible for anthropologists to learn and understand the symbols, rituals, and social structure of a community and to make shrewd speculations as to their probable origin and function. However, this knowledge in no way guarantees that the anthropologist could become a well-adjusted efficient member of this community, or even that his suggestions as to how this community might improve itself would be any better than chance. Furthermore, the "understanding" of a patient or, if one is an anthropologist, of a culture, belongs to the natural history or descriptive phase of scientific endeavor and does not imply action information any more than the ability to classify rocks helps one to build a bridge. While it is true that it is necessary to distinguish granite from clay in order to build a sound bridge, the geological information will not overcome the engineering problems.

Our use in psychoanalysis of "interpretation" does not include the pressure on the patient from his environment to stay the same. The student needs

---

[8] Italics mine.

help in understanding that interpretations are not Dr. Ehrlich's Magic Bullet; otherwise he is apt to find resistant patients wherever he goes.

I think it would be useful for candidates to be taught that all interpretations are, in some sense, inexact. If we assume that event A inside the patient's head produces behavior B, we must assume the analyst experiences this behavior as B^1 since he is not identical to the patient. The analyst then comments on this behavior in terms of B^2 since his own psychic apparatus has selective functions, time lags, and so on. This situation would not be too bad, but unfortunately, the patient doesn't even hear B^2 as the interpretation because he also reacts to the analyst's having said B^2. Hence when textbooks on psychoanalytic technique refer to the timing of interpretations solely in terms of the relation of the interpretation to the equilibrium between the patient's id, ego, and superego, it may mislead the student into thinking of an interpretation as a scalpel rather than as a fairly blunt instrument (occasionally, the blunter, the better!).

The difference between psychoanalytic terminology and a communication framework can be vividly seen in relation to this question of interpretations. In the psychoanalytic sense, the interpretation, or intervention: "Every time you mention your father, I notice you close your fist," is not a deep interpretation and may be accepted by the patient and even repeated by him through carrying out the gesture again for his own verification. On the other hand, the statement that the patient's voyeurism relates to his futile attempt to confirm his wish that women have a penis is a deep interpretation not only in the sense that the patient is unconscious of this linkage, but also because the material referred to has an origin in the patient's very early years. The patient's inability or unwillingness to benefit from this interpretation can be ascribed to resistance and/or incorrect timing on the part of the analyst. However, from the standpoint of communication theory, one could not use the term "deep interpretation" in the same sense as in psychoanalysis. Rather, one would view these two statements on the analyst's part from the standpoint of a transaction between two individuals occurring in a particular context. When the analyst mentions the closed fist, he is instructing the patient in a fashion that is appropriate to the analytic context and which is appropriate also to the patient's prior knowledge. That is, the patient has previously learned from his culture that closing one's fist can connote anger; thus, the analyst's observation may form a bridge to the patient's awareness and his own repetition of the act will be further convincing to the patient as to the correctness of the analyst's labeling. However, connecting voyeurism with the fact that male and female anatomy is different and becomes a perplexing problem to some children is the kind of information that is usually out of the patient's prior conscious experience. In this sense, the analyst is not merely lancing a psychodynamic pus pocket; he is imparting a new system of labeling to the patient. To the extent that patient repeats this system back to the analyst, he can be considered to have been instructed. Furthermore, in the interpretation, there are actually at least two instructions: One, the imparting of a new method of symbolizing or labeling or teaching; and two, the implicit instruction, "As a psychoanalyst, this is the sort of data I am interested in relabeling for you in this way." The patient is learning a new way to communicate and hence to regard his own communications, and he is also learning to learn this new system; or if you will, he programs himself under the analyst's direction and learning to program himself in this fashion facilitates further programming of the same sort. Note again that the essential difference between these two ways of describing the function of an interpretation is that the communication view assumes at least a two party interaction that is specific for these individuals in this particular context. This is a very different view from a classical analytic one, which would regard the analyst as having caused an energy shift in the analysand that allowed a piece of data that he had already known but repressed become conscious once again. The analytic view would assume that if the interpretation produces a useful change in the patient, it is because it was exact and properly timed. However, the peculiar problem of those patients who don't improve despite insight and self-understanding tells us that our present conceptual tools are not enough. A communication view of this problem might add something: For example, the kind of learning context that the patient experiences in psychoanalysis may influence his response to interpretations, however correct. This latter point is the subject of a paper in itself, but for the slightly far-out in the audience, I offer a bit of Zen that states it clearly:

> To think that I am not going
> To think of you any more
> Is still thinking of you.
> Let me then try not to think
> That I am not going to think of you.

CHAPTER 15

Transference Revisited[1]

Don D. Jackson and Jay Haley

(1963)

Among the key concepts in psychoanalytic theory are the assumptions that therapeutic change is caused by an increase in the patient's self-understanding and the assumption that transference is necessary if that self-understanding is to be sufficiently effective or "deep." Intimately related, these two assumptions are the bedrock of the theory of psychoanalytic therapy. In this paper we will attempt to review the concept of transference from a somewhat different point of view. We will suggest a partially different way of looking at transference and the phenomena associated with it; a view that does not refute previous conceptions but simply adds a possible new dimension.

The concept of "transference" is generally used to explain peculiar behavioral responses by the patient in psychoanalysis and as an explanation of the cause of therapeutic change. Transference responses are associated with the concept of "regression," with the implication that the patient becomes more infantile as he projects upon the analyst unconscious ideas rooted in his infantile needs and strivings. We suggest that this description is perfectly valid if one focuses only upon the patient. If, however, the analyst is also included in

[1] Paper presented at the Orthopsychiatric Association Annual Meeting, Los Angeles, California, March 1962. We wish to thank the Max Fleischman Foundation of Reno, Nevada, and the Ampex Foundation, Palo Alto, for support of this research. *Journal of Nervous & Mental Disease*, *137* (4), 363–371. Reprinted by permission.

the description, it is possible to see the transference in a different light. (Note that "transference" in this paper refers to the restricted use of this concept in the psychoanalytic situation. It does not refer to the general use of the term as synonymous with Sullivan's "parataxic distortion.")

When the analyst is included in the description, psychoanalysis appears to be a rather peculiar communication situation. This peculiarity is a result of the paradoxical nature of the relationship between analyst and patient. As the patient attempts to deal with this paradoxical situation, he will exhibit a variety of behavioral tactics, many of them part of his past repertoire learned at an early age. However, the use of these tactics does not necessarily mean that he has regressed to that early age. Since psychoanalysis moves from the present backward, an anachronistic bias is introduced which influences both patient and analyst. As a result, there is a tendency to overlook the current interaction between analyst and patient and to consider only the patient's past.

Therapeutic change resulting from psychoanalysis may reside not only in the greater self understanding which comes about as the result of analyzing the transference, but in the forced change in the patient's behavior which is required if he is to deal with the psychoanalytic situation. In emphasizing something other than transference interpretations as a cause of change, we join others who have sought other explanation. For example, Hans Sachs, Freud's first training analyst, is credited with saying that analysis terminates when the patient realizes it could go on forever. He thereby implies that the resolution which occurs in analysis is dependent upon something in addition to the patient's understanding the influence of his past on the present.

In Hinsie and Campbell's *Psychiatric Dictionary* (1960), transference is defined as follows:

> In psychoanalytic therapy the phenomenon of projection of feelings, thoughts and wishes onto the analyst who has come to represent an object from the patient's past. The analyst is reacted to as though he were someone from the patient's past: such reactions, while they may have been appropriate to the conditions that prevailed in the patient's previous life *are inappropriate and anachronistic when applied to an object (the analyst) in the present.*[2]

---

[2] Italics added by author.

The definition goes on:

During psychoanalytic treatment, the repressed unconscious material is revived, and since this material contains many infantile elements, the infantile strivings are reactivated and seek gratification in the transference. As the most important relationship of the child is that with his parents, the relationship between patient and analyst established in the transference becomes analogous to, or, at times, similar to the patient's relationship with his parents in childhood. The patient endows the analyst with the same magic powers and omniscience, which in childhood he attributed to his parents. The traits of submissiveness and rebellion in transference likewise reflect the attitude of the child to his parents. The patient behaves irrationally in the psychoanalytic situation: it often takes a long time to make him see the irrationality of his behavior, which is deeply rooted in his unconscious infantile life.

In this standard definition, the only object of observation is the patient. The larger social field within which transference occurs is not included since transference is something, which emanates from the patient and invests the analyst — a unilateral transaction. Yet in recent years, the focus on countertransference has indicated that the personality of the psychoanalyst can be a distorter of "pure" transference and the patient may react to these new elements. With the inclusion of the analyst in the description, the point of view about transference must inevitably change. As Ackerman has pointed out, when counter-transference was introduced as a concept, the psychoanalytic situation became a dyadic one even though the terminology remained monadic (1959; cf. also Jackson, 1956).

While there is little doubt that the patient's past experience affects his behavioral tactics within the psychoanalytic situation, it is only by ignoring the psychoanalyst that the responses of the patient appear irrational and inappropriate. In fact, the question whether the patient's responses are appropriate or not must depend upon a description of what he is responding to and a value judgment by the analyst as to what is "appropriate" in this very complex treatment situation involving two people.

When the possibility is raised that a patient may be responding to the immediate psychoanalytic relationship rather than merely to his unconscious infantile life, then a definition of the analytic situation is important. A standard definition is provided by Stone (1951), who lists eight conditions for psychoanalytic treatment:

1. Exclusive reliance during the hour on free association.

2. Regularity of time, frequency, and duration of visits in a clearly defined financial agreement.

3. Three to five appointments per week.

4. Recumbent position.

5. Confinement of activity of the therapist to interpretation, purely informative intervention, or occasional questions.

6. Emotional passivity and neutrality with abstention from gratification of the patient's transference wishes.

7. Abstention from advice, direct intervention, or participation in the patient's day to day life.

8. No immediate emphasis on curing symptoms.

Granting these conditions, and leaving aside whether they can be completely carried out, the question could be raised whether transference responses by the patient to this situation are irrational, inappropriate and regressive, or whether any other type of behavior is possible given these conditions.

What would be appropriate behavior in this unique situation? Ordinarily when two adults meet, they share information about each other either deliberately or unwittingly. In the psychoanalytic situation, such sharing is kept to a minimum. Similarly, adults attempt to phrase what they say in a reasonably logical and consistent manner so that the other individual can follow the meaning they are attempting to convey. In the analytic situation, the patient is asked to follow the fundamental rule and say what comes into his head, no matter how silly and no matter how lacking in context; that is, he must learn to omit those verbal cues which would acquaint himself and his hearer with the setting in time and in context of his remarks. In ordinary adult conversation, either member may comment on the manner and behavior of the other and his comments are accepted if they are not considered rude. In the analytic situation, only comments about the patient are permitted; comments on the analyst are turned aside or subjected to interpretation and so are not accepted at face value in the usual adult fashion. In addition, the analytic patient must respond to a regularity of time and duration of visits more reminiscent of his school days than adult social intercourse. Further, he must pay a fee for the company of the analyst and carry on his conversation while he is recumbent and the analyst is not, hardly a situation where adult behavior is possible, far less appropriate. Finally, the patient is expected to express himself freely and spontaneously to a man who shows the utmost reserve and inscrutability.

In this situation, the patient cannot possibly manifest the easy exchange of adult conversation and is forced to attempt an interchange more reminiscent of earlier learned tactics when he was small and others were large. In fact, to respond in a rational and mature way, the patient would have to refuse to follow the analyst's directions to lie down and free associate. Indeed, should the patient behave in an "adult" way, it would be said that the treatment was going badly; for example, the concept of resistance is employed when the patient does not follow the analyst's directives.

Viewing psychoanalysis as an interchange between two people provides an opportunity for explanation of the patient's behavior, which is rather different from a point of view that is only patient-oriented. If one focuses only upon the patient, it is perfectly satisfactory to describe the analytic situation as one where primary mental processes are permitted to flourish and the skillful analyst offers progressively deeper interpretations until the infantile neurosis is resolved. With a patient orientation, unconscious factors are the subject of interest and the source of all explanations of behavior. Focusing only upon the patient, it is also reasonable to argue that to ignore unconscious processes is to view the psychoanalytic situation superficially.

Yet if one shifts one's frame of reference to include both patient and analyst in the description, unconscious factors assume a different position in the theoretical framework and other factors in the situation come to the fore. Let us take an example to demonstrate how a viewpoint can shift within the space of only a few years. When experiments on perceptual isolation were first reported, experimental subjects demonstrated hallucinations and disorganization of thinking. This appeared to be a situation where the forces of the id were given free play because of the restrictions on outside stimuli. More recent work, especially by Levy, demonstrates that the effects of isolation appear to depend upon the relationship with the experimenter. Levy (1962) reports that in a group of subjects who were unusually well prepared for their experience and had a good relationship with the experimenters, only two subjects out of one hundred had hallucination-like experiences and these were clearly hypnogogic. If one takes into account both subject and experimenter rather than just subject, the situation appears as different as psychoanalysis does when both patient and analyst are included in the description.

The current direction of psychiatry would seem to be toward including two people, at least, in a description of therapy or a description of a psychiatric malady. (For a further consideration of this viewpoint (*cf.* Haley, 1963). For example, prior to Freud it was assumed that an individual could change if he understood that his fears were irrational and groundless, and if he could not he must be suffering from an organic brain disturbance. If a man with a healthy heart handicapped his life because of fear of dying of a heart attack, it was thought that when he was reassured that nothing was wrong with his heart, this self-understanding would dissipate his fear. This rarely happened. Freud accepted the idea of change through self-understanding but added the concept of the unconscious. Thus, a patient who irrationally feared a heart attack had to understand that his fear represented, among other things, repressed hostile wishes and threatened self-punishment for having such wishes. At first, Freud assumed that if the repressed idea was merely explained to the patient, this self-understanding would cause him to change. This did not occur. Instead of discarding the idea that self-understanding causes change, it occurred to Freud that self-awareness alone was not enough and that the self understanding must take place in a particular type of therapeutic relationship, which involved the transference phenomena as we describe them today.

Instead of emphasizing the interpretation of the transference with consequent insight to the patient, it is possible to regard the analytic situation itself as largely responsible for a change in the patient, with self-understanding an accompanying but not necessarily crucial factor. This notion arises because when both analyst and patient are included in the description of the analytic situation, one discovers that they have a very unusual communication context. This viewpoint goes along with the current tendency to see the patient in terms of his interpersonal and social relationship and not merely in terms of his intrapsychic dynamics.

For example, if we include the wife in our description of the above-mentioned heart phobia patient, we get a different point of view about his symptoms. We may find that husband and wife have a particular sort of relationship, for example, one that is both controlling of and protective of each other through the use of certain behavioral tactics. Since the patient fears a heart attack, he protests that he cannot be left alone, thereby constantly supervising his wife. His wife finds that her life becomes organized around his state of health, since all family activities depend upon his reports about feeling better or worse. When the husband feels better, she struggles to be amiable so that he will not collapse again and lose his job, and when he is worse, she struggles to be amiable so that he will continue working. At times she will threaten to leave him to stir him into activity. In this struggle, she settles for a man who will manage her in a helpless way but who still will not make the demands on her that a healthy man would make. This is to say that it is becoming generally known that when a patient has severe symptoms, the spouse has interlocking problems. Often the man who fears a heart attack has a depressed wife. If she has suicidal thoughts, her husband's expressions of fears about his heart occur at those times she is withdrawn and he is anxious about what is on her mind and what she will do. When he takes his pulse or expresses his fear about his heart, she becomes angry at his irrational behavior and thereby comes out of her withdrawal and depression temporarily. Yet her depressions are responsive to his helpless managing and irrational fears, just as his fears are responsive to her depressions and threats of leaving as the two of them work out a vicious circle of psychopathology.

When such a patient enters psychoanalysis to overcome his fear of a heart attack, he is experienced at manipulating relationships by his phobia. Meeting the psychoanalyst, he finds that he cannot deal with this relationship in the ways he has dealt with others. He is forced to change his behavior and with that change comes a change in his fears and subjective sensations. Essentially what he meets when he enters analysis is a situation that is impossible if he continues with his distress because it is a thoroughly paradoxical one. We will list a few of the obvious paradoxes faced by the patient. By paradox, we mean those messages which the patient receives at one level which are in conflict with other messages he receives at another level. For example, if one person says to another, "Disobey me," the other person is faced with a paradox: he cannot disobey without obeying, nor can be obey without disobeying because a message at one level is in conflict with the message it classifies at another.

Problems posed by such multilevel communication have been discussed previously (Bateson, Jackson, Haley, & Weakland, 1956; Haley, 1955; Jackson, 1956).

When we list these paradoxes, we do not mean to imply that they are imposed in a Machiavellian way by the analyst. We suggest that they are implicit in a therapeutic setting which was designed without the deliberate intention of imposing paradox.

1.   First, the patient faces a relationship that is defined in one way at the beginning and then undergoes an abrupt transition to quite a different sort. When the patient first talks with the analyst, the analyst spends a session or two diagnosing the problem. In these early sessions, the analyst wishes to encourage the patient to open up as much as possible and express what is on his mind. Therefore the analyst tends to be warm, encouraging, and responsive. He defines the relationship as a benevolently helping one for a person in distress. When treatment begins, the analyst suddenly becomes a silent, unresponsive man, and the patient may see him as cold and distant. Although the patient will inevitably feel deprived of the warm responsiveness he first experienced, he cannot easily get angry at the analyst for his unresponsiveness because he knows it is part of the method to help him; it would be like being angry at the surgeon's scalpel. The patient can only feel helplessly frustrated.

2.   When the patient comes to the analyst, he expects an expert who will help him by taking charge and telling him what to do — as experts are supposed to. The analyst responds by putting the patient in charge: He indicates that he will not tell the patient what to do or how to do it. He is a kind of psychological midwife merely assisting natural forces, and the success of the treatment is the patient's responsibility. He emphasizes that he will not direct the patient.

3.   While indicating that he will not tell the patient what to do and putting the patient in charge, the analyst takes charge by directing the patient to lie down, to free associate (which is a direction about how to talk) and what sort of material is acceptable (which the patient learns from the response of the analyst even if it is only uh-huh or silence). The analyst will also not let the patient direct him what to say, and may be silent

even if the patient demands that he talk. Therefore, in a non-directive setting at one level, the analyst at another level directs the crucial behavior in the situation: Who is to speak, what is to be said, and how it is to be said. (The rule that the patient must make no important changes in his life during the analysis is also an interesting communication. Although the analyst does not tell the patient what to do, he is taking charge of the patient's life by telling him what not to do and framing the message in terms of the patient's not knowing what is best for himself.)

4. The patient comes to the analyst for help in getting over his symptomatic behavior, and the analyst indicates that they will not deal with the symptomatic behavior, thereby indicating that he will change the patient but not by dealing with what he came to change. Yet typically when the patient free-associates and deals with other matters, the analyst will use an interpretation to relate these other matters to the symptomatic behavior.

5. Not only is the patient unable to use his symptomatic behavior to manipulate the analyst because the analyst directs him to other matters, but the patient also cannot use improvement or getting worse in a manipulative way. The analyst does not respond to threats open or implied. In fact, the patient is faced with a paradoxical response no matter what he says in this direction. If he states he is getting worse, he is advised that this is a necessary part of treatment and affords the opportunity to better study his problem. If he improves and says he is feeling fine, the analyst indicates that he is resisting treatment by escaping into health. Thereby the patient becomes incapacitated if he attempts to control this relationship in the ways he has controlled other intimate relationships in his life.

6. The general framework of analysis is one of benevolent help. Within that framework, the patient is put through a rather distressing ordeal. The patient is required to talk with as little censorship as possible about all his problems and all the unsavory aspects of his life. If he does not wish to discuss something that reflects too badly upon him, this is defined as resistance. It is not a pleasant experience to undergo psychoanalysis either emotionally or financially, and insofar as it is a punishing experience the patient faces a paradox: he is undergoing a punishing experience within a framework of benevolent help. If he refuses to accept the punishing ex-

perience, perhaps by resisting, he is further punished by being labeled as the kind of person who eschews help.

7. Another paradox resides in the question of whether the analytic relationship is compulsory or voluntary. Typically the patient is excessively concerned in his personal life with the question whether his intimates associate with him because they want to or because they must, just as he is uncertain whether he is with them because he is ill or because he wishes to be. In psychoanalysis, the patient is told that his relationship is voluntary and his improvement depends upon his willingness to cooperate and attend sessions. Yet if the patient is late or misses a session, the analyst objects and so indicates that the relationship is compulsory. Similarly, the patient faces a man who talks to him only because he is hired to, while within that framework the analyst indicates that analysis offers an opportunity for a deep relationship and this concept is reinforced by transference interpretations, which imply that the patient is being markedly influenced and controlled by the analysis. For example, if he is late he is resisting and if he complains about finances he is actually resenting what he pays the analyst.

8. Finally, the patient is in a situation where he cannot behave in an adult way, and when he does not the analyst points out to him that his childlike behavior is evidence of a point of view carried over from childhood. Although the analyst has other purposes in interpreting the transference, from the point of view of the formal structure of the psychoanalytic situation, the patient is responding appropriately only to find that his response is labeled as inappropriate and irrational.

Typically, patients have managed to control the responses of other people by symptomatic behavior, but they become incapacitated if they attempt to deal with a psychoanalyst in these ways. They are forced to develop new techniques to gain a response from an unresponsive man. In his attempt, the patient will go through his whole repertoire of past ways of gaining responses from people. This repertoire will include tactics that he has not used since childhood. When the patient uses these rather desperate tactics, the analyst will assume that the transference relationship has been established. After that, a change by the patient tends to be accepted. However, the patient's behavior is only accepted if he is agreeing with the analyst that his tactics are irrational and based upon childhood experiences. When the patient begins to say, "It isn't you, it's my father I'm really angry with," the last stages of therapy are reached, since the patient and the analyst are now using the same labels.

§

From the point of view we are presenting, the patient is forced to change his ways because the analytic relationship is one he cannot deal with by using the ways he has dealt with others in the past. The more desperate his attempt to deal with the impossible and paradoxical relationship he faces, the more an observer would say that a transference phenomenon is taking place. To restate: the essential paradox in the psychoanalytic situation and, indeed, in most forms of psychotherapy (including some which do not focus upon self understanding) consists of the following conflicting levels of messages: First, the situation is defined as one in which the patient will be benevolently helped to change. Second, the patient is encouraged to continue his usual behavior (and symptoms) because of the permissiveness of the analyst and in order that he will demonstrate his problems so they can be studied. Third, the patient is required to undergo a punishing ordeal as long as he continues his usual behavior. The patient is caught in an impossible paradox: To change, he must continue unchanged, while being benevolently helped to go through an ordeal until he changes. A patient must behave differently if he is to resolve the situation, but his different behavior will only be accepted if it occurs on the analyst's terms — otherwise, it is mere resistance. It does not seem surprising that a patient caught in this situation will exhibit "irrational" behavior quite independent of his early infantile life and anachronistic forces that are also affecting his behavior.

The development and resolution of the transference (infantile) neurosis is the key therapeutic agent in most theories of psychoanalytic treatment. Authorities such as Edward Glover (1955) recommend five to six sessions a week in order to establish a sufficiently deep transference neurosis. Changes brought about by less intensive psychotherapy are regarded by such authorities as superficial and probably not lasting. It does not seem that the frequency of sessions alone can account for the intensity of the transference. Rather, we are suggesting that the analyst's behavior and how the patient views that behavior may be a factor in producing transference phenomena. If this is so, then it may be possible to expedite psychoanalytic therapy by sharpening the paradoxes posed by the treatment situation. The paradoxes are sharpened when the analyst poses the opposite extremes of the paradox quite sharply. For example, when the analyst clearly defines the relationship as voluntary and entirely up to the patient and then reacts quite sharply and firmly when the patient misses an appointment or is late.

From the point of view we are presenting, the analyst induces a kind of behavior in a patient, which he then treats. However, this behavior need not necessarily mirror the infantile neurosis experienced by the patient in his early years. The patient's responses to the analytic situation are not necessarily a duplicate of moments in his early life history. He may respond idiosyncratically, but still his responses might be similar to those anyone would make who sought out this situation and cooperated within it. Under certain stressful situations the individual will exhibit unusual behavior that is related to his human biological possibilities as well as his experiential history. But his response is not necessarily *repetitive* of his life history. The adult patient who "regresses" in psychoanalysis does not behave as he did when he was a child, he behaves like an adult being childlike. The notion of "deep" when it is applied to phenomena occurring in psychoanalysis requires a good deal of further study. One area of study is the family situation where someone may exhibit inappropriate and irrational behavior quite similar to transference responses when he is caught in a particular kind of paradoxical relationship. These responses are not infrequently seen in family therapy.

The question of insight also appears in a somewhat different light when the frame of reference is the dyadic analytic relationship — although patients benefit from understanding their present behavior in terms of the past, a question can be raised whether this understanding is "causal" to a basic change in their behavior and their perceptions. Some patients manifest considerable insight and continue in their distress. Other patients improve in types of psychotherapy where insight of the psychoanalytic sort is not utilized. Yet the argument that insight causes change is essentially irrefutable if one wishes to make it so; one can always say that a patient who manifests insight but does not change has not yet sufficient insight, and if patients change with non-insight therapeutic methods, it can be said they have not *really* changed. There is, of course, no answer to such arguments. But the question of what causes therapeutic change is of such profound importance that the relation between change and insight requires thorough scrutiny.

One important argument for the necessity of insight is the point of view that change can only persist if understanding has taken place. Yet if a broader description of a patient is made, other reasons for the persistence of change appear. For example, if a patient changes he is going to behave differently with his intimate family members, and if he does so they are going to behave differently with him. As the patient establishes different sorts of relationships within his family, a change can continue because a different living context has been established. Although the patient might say that his life is different because he understands himself better and so is behaving differently, it can also be argued that his life with his intimates is different because he has been behaving differently and cannot go back to the old ways without disruption of a whole network of relationships.

Sometimes it appears that a fascination with Freud's brilliant contribution to the understanding of unconscious symbolism has contributed to a confusion over what causes therapeutic change. Some psychoanalysts appear to believe that if they can understand the patient's symbolic processes, and certainly if they can help the patient understand them, inevitably change will occur. But what we are discussing here is the context within which that understanding takes place with the suggestion that it is the context rather than the self-understanding, which leads to improvement in a patient.

The idea that people undergo therapeutic change when they understand themselves better is as deeply rooted in psychiatry as the notion, once widely held, that the earth was the center of the universe. If only the individual is studied, one can only say that he has changed because he has learned to understand himself better. What other explanation is there? However, if both patient and the person attempting to change him are described, other possible causes of change appear. We suggest that an important causal factor is the paradoxical situation imposed upon the patient in psychoanalysis which forces him to change his ways. From this point of view, the notion of self-understanding has two purposes: It provides a subject for patient and analyst to talk about; a *modus operandi* for dealing with each other. It also provides the two people with an explanation of why change has occurred after it happens. In other words, the emphasis upon insight and self-understanding can be seen both as tactic and a rationalization. The fact that psychoanalysis could not be conducted without an emphasis upon understanding does not mean that self understanding is causal to change: Paradoxical factors in this peculiar relationship appear equally important as a cause of change.

When one shifts from a focus on the individual to an interpersonal orientation, many problems in psychotherapy appear in a different light. This does not mean that one point of view is more true than the other; each is equally valid from the point where the observer stands. Individual psychology has built a solid foundation; interpersonal psychology is just beginning to be structured. The ultimate choice will reside in which approach is most consistent theoretically and most practical in application.

References

Ackerman, N. (1959). Transference & countertransference. *Psychoanalysis, 46*: 17–28.

Bateson, G., Jackson, D., Haley, J., & Weakland, J. (1956). Toward a theory of schizophrenia. *Behavioral Science, 1* (4); 251 264, 1956.

Glover, E. (1955). *The Technique of psycho-analysis.* (p. 20). New York: International Universities Press.

Haley, J. (1955). Paradoxes in play, fantasy & psychotherapy. *Psychiatric Research Reports*, 2: 52–58.

Haley, J. (1963). *Strategies of psychotherapy.* New York: Grune & Stratton.

Hinsie, L., & Campbell, R. (1960). *Psychiatric Dictionary.* (Pp. 751–752). Oxford: Oxford University Press.

Jackson. D. (1956). Countertransference & psychotherapy. *Progress in Psychotherapy, 1*; 234–238.

Jackson D. (1958). Guilt & the control of pleasure in schizoid personalities. *British Journal of Medical Psychology, 31*: 124–130.

Levy, E. Z. (1962). The subject's approach: Important factor in experimental isolation? *Bulletin of the Menninger Clinic, 26*: 30–42.

Stone, L. (1951). Psychoanalysis & brief psychotherapy. *Psychoanalytic Quarterly, 20*: 215–236.

CHAPTER 16

Social Factors and Disorders of Communication: Some Varieties of Pathogenic Organization[1]

Gregory Bateson and Don D. Jackson

(1964)

It is necessary to delimit the subject of the present paper. First, the paper will not deal with that whole genus of interaction patterns which has been classified (Bateson, 1936) as "symmetrical," *i.e.*, the behavior in rivalries and other relationships, where *A* is stimulated to do something because *B* has done this same thing; and where *B* does more of this because *A* did some of it; and *A* does more of it because *B* did some, and so on. This is the sort of symmetry characteristic of keeping up with the Joneses, some armaments races, and so forth.

This leaves the complementary side of interactive behavior, in which

[1] Reprinted with permission from *Disorders of Communication* Vol. XLII: Research Publications, A.R.N.M.D., 1964, Association for Research in Nervous and Mental Disease. This paper is indebted to research conducted under Grant OM-324 from the National Institute of Mental Health sponsored by the Palo Alto Medical Research Foundation at the Veterans Administration Hospital, Palo Alto, Calif.

what *A* does fits, in some sense, with what *B* does but is essentially different from it. This category of complementary interaction includes, for example, dominance and submission, exhibitionism and spectatorship, succoring and dependence, and so forth — a series of patterns where there is a mutual fitting between *A*'s behavior and that of *B*.

Within this category of complementary patterns of interaction, a number of subcategories may usefully be discriminated:

a. A very important subgroup is that which has been schematically organized by Erikson (1950) in his analysis of behavioral modes and their relationship to the erogenous zones of the body. Characteristically, all the themes related to the erogenous zones — intrusion, invasion, exclusion, ejection, retention, and so forth — are complementary.

b. To these we may add the themes related to locomotion and bodily mechanics — support, balance, rise and fall, control, reach, grasp, and the like.

c. A third category of complementary themes includes those related to sense organs and perception — understanding, ignoring, attending, and the like. Note in this connection that, probably for all animals, there is a strong tendency for organs of sense to become transmitting agents for outgoing messages. When the dog pricks up his ears, he is not simply improving his sensory reception, he is transmitting a statement about the direction of his attention, and in relationships between dogs to prick the ears becomes also a statement of self-confidence vis-à-vis the other individual.

d. Lastly, two important themes of complementary interaction are so closely interrelated that it is appropriate to mention them together. These are the themes of parent–child relationship and of territory. Neither can perhaps be separated clearly from a, b, and c above. The themes of parenthood are clearly closely related to the themes derived from the erogenous zones, and the themes of territory could perhaps be conveniently understood by regarding territory as an extension of body. It appears, however that, at least for mammals, the first learning associated with territory occurs in regard to territory defined by the mother (or possibly both parents) (Blauvelt, 1956). The archetypal definition of territory might perhaps be areas "that are defined by mother's presence within which the infant has an autistic or absolute right to safety." Such a view of the relationship between parenthood and territory would explain not only such metaphors as *motherland* and *patria* but also the differential degree of confidence, which an animal shows according to whether he is on or off his own territory.

In sum, restricting this paper to complementary patterns will focus attention close to the body and to parent–child relationship as the primary sources from which perhaps all behavior is derived. Further, any such classification as is attempted above makes certain assumptions about the role of learning in the development of behavior. The morphology of the erogenous zones and, in large measure, their erogenous character, are no doubt genotypically determined, but to assume transference of patterns derived from them to other spheres of life is to invoke learning. (If this sort of coherence should be demonstrated to occur in those invertebrates whose behavior is much more completely determined by the genotype and uninfluenced by relationship with a parent, this discovery would present serious problems for evolutionary theory.)

Second, another limitation is necessary. The paper will not deal with digital systems of message-making. Language, insofar as there is such a thing as pure language, is a digital business in the sense that the units of which it is made resemble numbers, 1, 2, 3, 4, 5, from which of course the word "digital" comes. There is nothing particularly five-like in the number 5; there is nothing particularly table-like in the word "table." These words are arbitrary signs which can be manipulated according to various sorts of rules, called algorithms, and it is a characteristic peculiar to the human species that we have developed a very massive apparatus for communicating digitally. This linguistic system, as such, will fall outside the area of relevance of this paper, except insofar as the *sequence* of linguistic events may constitute analogue communication about complementary relationship, or insofar as the differences between analog and digital communication must be explored.

The other side of human and mammalian communication, namely that which one can refer to by the technical term, analog communication, this will be our subject matter. Here, the message material is much more directly recognizable for what it means. If you observe two natives of some unknown culture engaged in interaction, you will notice that you have no understanding of the words which they use but that you have at least a guesswork understanding of their gestures, postures, facial expressions, voices, and silences. You may be seriously wrong in how you interpret these signals, but at least you are not faced with totally opaque material. When the natives raise their voices, you will guess (probably correctly) that the quantitative change, measurable in decibels, is simply analogous to some quantitative change in the intensity of relationship either between the persons or between them and the (unknown) subject of their discourse.

The primary definition of analog communication turns upon this notion of analogous magnitudes. The digital computing machine manipulates ciphers that have no magnitude, whereas the analog machine reproduces within the black box some physical process involving real magnitudes, which have direct relation to magnitudes existing within the subject matter about which the machine is being asked to compute. The digital machine is fed with *bits* of information and gives back its answer in a similar currency. The analog machine is fed with quantitative settings of dials and the like and gives back its answer in a similar quantitative form.

In addition, however, to this quantitative characteristic of analog communication, there is also the fact that in such systems patterns of relationship are likely to be formally analogous, a pattern in the subject of discourse being represented in the discourse by patterns or *gestalten* which are rather direct representations of these. In many cases, it is actually impossible to separate the subject matter of complementary analog communication from the message material in which some proposition about the subject matter is encoded. The actual events of the interchange may contain both: a) an element of signaling, for example, if *A* clenches his fist he is mentioning or proposing the possibility of violence and the gesture has communicational function in that the clenched fist serves as a *name* for a species of action and b) another, more direct element in that the act of clenching the fist is a real change in *A's* readiness for violent action. The statement of readiness is not separated from the pragmatic reality of readiness by a step of coding. The clenched fist is not just a name for a type of action, it is also a part or sample of such action. It is therefore dangerous to use in our thinking the very notion of coding which has been so fruitful in the analysis of digital communication. The relationship of analog communication to the problems of logical typing is evidently quite different from that which holds for digital systems.

One result of this direct relation between message and subject matter will be that you, observing two individuals from some strange culture, will be able to guess at complementary themes in their relationship. Watching their linguistic sequences but understanding none of the words, you will still see who initiates segments of interchange and may well be able to detect patterns of respect, intimacy or distance, if these are expressed in styles or overtones of language.

Moreover, as we proceed to the next higher level of abstraction, it will probably be still easier for the observer to guess at what is going on. He may have difficulty in evaluating the patterns of interchange so long as these are constant, but a *change* in expressions of respect, intimacy or distance may be unambiguous.

Indeed, it would seem that precisely because the patterns of interchange are discussed by an exchange of samples of this interchange, the participants themselves are likely to be in some doubt about what is going on. They too may have to rely more upon changes in the pattern than upon ongoing constancy. The implications of a handshake or a kiss become blurred when these idioms of interchange become constant. The relationship only becomes clear as a result of changes in the kiss or the handshake. Lovers' quarrels are perhaps necessary for validation of the underlying patterns.

However, even if we disregard these higher levels of patterning, in discussing complementarity we are already concerned with an order of phenomena outside the field of behavioral psychology. There is, strictly speaking, no such thing as a complementary piece of "behavior." To drop a brick may be either complementary or symmetrical; and which it is depends upon how this piece of behavior is related to preceding and subsequent behaviors of the vis-à-vis.

It is, of course, as legitimate for the behaviorists to limit their discussion to those levels of abstraction in which they are interested as it is for us in this paper to limit discussion to the next higher level. What is important is to keep these levels clearly defined and to understand the difference between them.

The stimulus-response (S.R.) psychologist typically confines his attention to sequences of interchange so short that it is possible to label one item of input as "stimulus" and another item as "reinforcement" while labeling what the subject does between these two events as "response." Within the short sequence so excise, it is possible to talk about the "psychology" of the subject. In contrast, the sequences of interchange which we are here discussing are very much longer and therefore have the characteristic that every time in the sequence is simultaneously stimulus, response and reinforcement. A given item of *x's* behavior is a stimulus insofar as it is followed by an item contributed by *y* and that by another item contributed by *x*. But insofar as *x's* item is sandwiched between two items contributed by *y*, it is a response. Similarly *x's* item is a reinforcement insofar as it follows an item contributed by *y*. The ongoing interchanges, then, which we are here discussing, constitute a chain of overlapping triadic links, each of which is comparable to a stimulus-response-reinforcement sequence. We can take any triad of our interchange and see it as a single trial in an S.R. learning experiment.

If we look at the conventional learning experiments from this point of view, we observe at once that repeated trials amount to a differentiation of relationship between the two organisms concerned, the experimenter and his subject. The sequence of trials is so punctuated that it is always the experimenter who seems to provide the "responses." These words are here deliberately put in quotation marks because the role definitions are in fact only created by the willingness of the organisms to accept the system of punctuation. The "reality" of the role definitions is only of the same order as the reality of a bat on a Rorschach card — a more or less over-determined creation of the perceptive process. The rat who said "I have got my experimenter trained. Each time I press the lever he gives me food" was declining to accept the punctuation of the sequence, which the experimenter was seeking to impose.

It is still true, however, that in a long sequence of interchange, the organisms concerned, especially if these be people, will in fact punctuate the sequence so that it will appear that one or the other has initiative, dominance, dependency, or the like. That is, they will set up between them patterns of interchange (about which they may or may not be in agreement) and these patterns will in fact be rules of contingency regarding the exchange of reinforcement. Although rats are too nice to relabel, some psychiatric patients are not and they provide psychological trauma for the therapist!

It is appropriate now to ask what is gained by the shift in our attention from asking about the response system of an individual to looking for contingency patterns within a relationship. The answer would seem to be that limitation to the S.R. level would limit us to the discussion of the nonverbal communication of invertebrates with possibly some analysis of human *verbal* behavior, and would exclude from our analysis almost the whole of mammalian non-verbal communication. When you open the refrigerator door and the cat comes and rubs against your legs making certain sounds, she is not touching off a reflex response in you — which might be the case if both you and she were members of some invertebrate species. Neither is she saying "Milk!" because she does not have denotative language. It would seem, rather, that the primary referent of her discourse is what we might call "dependency." She is asserting the contingency pattern of her relationship with you, or, in the language of the anthropologists, we might say that she is using something like a kinship term. In reply to this highly abstract message, you are expected to achieve a deductive step and guess that you should give her milk.

It is not possible to conduct any meaningful analysis of this order of communication in simple S.R. terms. It is absolutely necessary to conduct the analysis in terms of those units, which are the contingency patterns of the interchange.

If this argument be sound, it follows that mammals, including human beings, should be subject to pathologies of communication at this level, that is, that errors regarding the contingency patterns of relationship between individuals will be pathogenic. At the beginning of this paper, it was asserted that the complementary patterns of mammalian relationship have their roots in the body and in primary interchanges between offspring and parent and in such essential matters as physical balance and support. It is in these areas that we must look for pathology when the premises of complementary relationship are disrupted.

In this connection, it seems that the experimental psychologists have contributed crucial data. The classical experiments on breakdown of discrimination among dogs and other animals fall neatly into place as exemplifications of what happens when a mammal is placed in a situation where he cannot be right about the contingency patterns of his relationship to the outside world or to the experimenter. It is worthwhile to summarize the course of such an experiment. In the opening phase, the animal subject is trained to discriminate between two stimulus objects, e.g., ellipse and circle, one of which shall mean x, while the other is to mean y. When this preliminary training is complete, the stimulus objects are modified in the direction of greater resemblance. The ellipse is fattened and the circle is flattened. In this stage the animal is forced to make greater efforts at discriminating between them, and if he is successful, he receives an even stronger impression that the context in which he finds himself is one which demands discrimination. The same message also comes to be carried by the ancillary objects, the experimental harness, smell of the laboratory, and so forth.

The experimenter, of course, will probably be guided by pencil marks on the backs of the stimulus objects so that he may remember which is the "ellipse" and which the "circle"; and he will use a tossed coin, or perhaps a table of random numbers, to decide which object he should administer next. It would never do to have some patterning of this order, which the animal might detect.

Finally, the stimulus objects become, from the animal's point of view, indiscriminable, and at this point the animal is likely to show nonadaptive or pathological behaviors. He may refuse food, go comatose, bite his keeper, or do something similar.

If we now ask about the contingency patterns of the contexts in which the animal successively is placed, we observe that in the initial phase of the experiment the contingency patterns called for discrimination. In the middle phase of the experiment this demand was underlined, but in the final phase of the experiment, the most appropriate course for the animal would have been to stop trying to discriminate and to use a coin to decide which response he should give. In this phase the context has become one for guessing or for gambling, and indeed, the experimenter was guilty of some redundancy if, in this final phase of the experiment, he continued to use two stimulus objects instead of one; he might just as well have used one stimulus object, consulting his random number table between each presentation of the object to decide what it would mean. From where the animal sits, there is in this final phase, only one stimulus object seen in the trance of a strong expectation that the contingencies of the context demand that he discriminate.

That some such reading of these experiments is correct is supported by other experimental data. Liddell has shown that without the ancillary stimuli provided by the harness and the laboratory, the pathological behavior does not develop, and it is also known that the initial phase of the experiment in which the animal is trained to discriminate is necessary. A naive animal faced with a stimulus object which sometimes means x and sometimes y will in fact guess, without any development of pathological symptoms.

It is not that the dog's discrimination broke down; it is that the psychologist failed to discriminate between a context for guessing and a context for discrimination while giving the animal the impression that there has been no change in context.

These classical experiments have been discussed here in order to illustrate the difference between theory based upon S.R. behaviorism and theory, which takes into account the contingency patterns of interpersonal relationship. If the reading here offered of the cat's mew and of the classical discrimination experiments is correct, it follows that mammals must be deeply and vitally concerned with correctness at this level.

The same considerations apply to human beings, who are similarly prone to exhibit psychotic symptomatology when placed in the wrong regarding the contextual structure of their relationship. This argument is, in fact, the core thesis of the so-called "double bind" theory of schizophrenia (Bateson, Jackson, Haley, & Weakland, 1956; Bateson, 1960; Weakland, & Jackson, 1958), that schizophrenic behavior arises in sequences of experience in which one or more individuals are continually put in the wrong regarding the contingency patterns of relationship.

A very little parlor experimentation along these lines will evoke "schizoid behavior," that is, the emitting of messages whose logical type is obscured by their metaphoric form. One of us (GB), teaching a class of affiliate nurses at the hospital, talked to them about "Tiny," the 5-foot sow at Cornell, who learned that she ought to recognize whether a given signal meant food or an electric shock in the food box. When the indiscriminable signal was given, Tiny would stand trembling for hours and finally make a great rush, smashing the food box and even forgetting to look for the food. The nurses wanted this translated into more human terms. The lecturer then picked one of the girls and started a conversation with her. Lecturer: "How are you enjoying your three months' psychiatric experience?' She: "Very much." Lecturer: "You had to say that, didn't you?" She: "But I really am." Lecturer: "Really? Really is one of those words we use when we want to overcompensate a little. Now *honestly*, how do you feel about your psychiatric experience?" She: "Oh, go play pig with somebody else!'"

In this instance the hurt of both the nurse and the lecturer was relieved by the balm of laughter in which all joined, but this overt recognition of what has happened is not available in more malign settings.

A schizophrenic person is one who has learned to be abnormally cautious about committing himself to any particular view of the relationship between himself and important others. We may think of his messages as constructed according to the following recipe:

Imagine a Western Union telegram blank. It has on it a series of slots, one of which is for the text of the message. Others are marked "To whom"; "From whom"; "Time"; "Date"; "Code used"; "Priority"; and so on. All of these subsidiary slots are for messages about the message. In conversation we similarly accompany our messages with messages about the message, and it is these that the schizophrenic patient will selectively distort. These are the messages that would otherwise disclose his view of the contingencies of relationship between himself and the other. To use a first person pronoun is to refer to himself as in a relationship to you. To indicate that he cares about the content of his message is to imply that his relationship to you is such that an expression of caring would be appropriate. He will therefore distort the "priority" of his message. He may even change the address, making a message "from me to you" into a message "from Christ to the world."

A schizophrenic patient was told by the therapist that the latter would be away for 2 weeks attending American Psychiatric Association meetings in Honolulu. The patient turned his back to the therapist and gazed out the window and said "That plane is flying awfully slowly." The original form of this message before schizophrenic coding was perhaps "I shall miss you," but to have left the text in this form would have been to presume upon the relationship to the therapist. It was therefore safer to change the text to a more impersonal and metaphoric form.

It is, however, not sufficient to assert (a) that mammals preponderantly communicate about the contingency patterns of the relationship and (b) that traumatization at this level leads to schizoid manifestations. Over and above all this is the fact that while mammals, including man, primarily use analogic methods (intention movements and the like) in their discourse about the contingencies of relationship, man is unique in his attempt to combine digital language with this discourse.

Obviously an organism which uses two methods of discourse and which attempts to discuss the same subject matter with both of these methods will need to be able to translate from one method into the other. Any systematic errors in the machinery or rules of this translation will inevitably bring about pathologic behavior. It is therefore appropriate to consider the difficulties inherent in such translation and the probable forms of error.

We may note first that a combination of analogic with digital communication systems already has been achieved in mammals at the physiological level. Although the central nervous system at least in its microscopic functioning, is digital, depending upon the discontinuities provided by the "all or nothing" law (or some modification of this law), the hormonal system undoubtedly depends upon the use of real magnitudes and is to this extent strictly analogic.

It also appears that the whole evolutionary process turns upon a combination of digital with analogic communication. The corpus of genotypic messages is in the main digital, whereas the soma appears to be in every instance an analogic exemplification or trial model that tests the genotypic recipe. The analogic proof of the egg is the hen into which it develops.

These evolutionary problems have been discussed elsewhere (Bateson, in press) where it was argued that, while it is essential to embryology that there be a method for creating analogic transform of the genotypic recipe, it is equally essential that the characteristics of the analogic model shall not be communicated back to the genotype but shall be tested and filtered through the processes of natural selection. Lamarckian inheritance would make evolution non-viable.

However, when we come to consider the weaving of analogic with digital process in the phenomena of interpersonal relations, that is, in phenomena external to the body, it is clearly essential that the organism have means of maintaining some degree of consistency between its digital and analogic behavior.

What is needed is a digital transform of the analogic message material such that: a) all important information be retained in the transform, and b) that no new information of an unreliable or unsupported kind be added. We shall see that in fact there is a very strong tendency towards such inappropriate addition.

Three characteristics of the analogic material contribute to the difficulty of transformation into words; these characteristics must be considered together, because the difficulties of translation arise from a combination of the characteristics. First, the analogic material contains real (and therefore always *positive*) magnitudes; second, the analog material contains no simple negative, *that is*, no word for "not"; and third, the analog material contains no morphemic signs. There is no analogue of "as if" or "perhaps," no differentiation between "and" and "or" and, in sum, no sign in analog communication which shall classify a message as to its logical type.

These characteristics of analog communication may be illustrated by considering the problem of translating the sentence "The man did not plant the tree" into a purely pictographic script. We can readily imagine the series of pictures available: "man," "spade," "hole in ground," "tree," "tree in hole," and others, but what about the word "not"? We might perhaps be tempted to express this word by superimposing a deletion mark upon that word in the sentence to which the "not" most specifically applies. If it was not the man who planted the tree, we shall delete the picture of "man." Or if it was that he did not plant it, we shall delete "spade" or "tree in hole," and so on.

But now a serious difficulty arises. The receiver of the message will want to know whether we deleted one of these pictures because we made an error when we wrote the message. Or did we intend both the picture and its deletion to stand as part of the message? At this point the absence of logical typing signals has the effect that our negative cannot be understood by the receiver. What is precisely needed to discriminate between a correction and a negation is a logical type marker, and here no pictorial representation is available.

In fact, if the receiver of the message is sufficiently sophisticated to know that the sender could not, in the nature of the case, have inserted a negative if he wanted to, he will be able to deduce that the message can contain no simple indicative affirmative. Any sequence in the message which might appear to be an affirmative statement may owe this appearance only to the fact that the sender of the message had no meaningful negatives at his disposal. The analogic message can mention or propose; it cannot affirm or deny its own truth.

Similar difficulties will apply to a number of other elements in the sentence. We shall lack pictorial representation for the definite article and for the past tense, and more especially we shall lack that more fundamental logical type marker that would tell the receiver that we are not in this context talking about a man and a tree but only talking about a diagrammatic sentence created to illustrate a theoretical point.

In a word, the analogic communication about which we are talking suffers from the same limitations as those which characterize "primary process" and indeed, this finding is scarcely surprising inasmuch as these modes are evidently in an evolutionary sense much more archaic than the specifically human babble of language.

The limitations, however, can serve as a warning to the would-be translator who can be sure that if his verbal transform of the analog material contains simple negatives (or indeed, affirmative indicative statements) or logical type markers these must all have been added in the process of translation. The translation in fact will contain information that is unsupported by the analogic source and is therefore unreliable.

It is, of course, true that a major effort of psychoanalysis is to insert such markers and indicatives into dream material, a procedure that can hardly fail to induce change in the patient. The scientific problem remains: How much is the change caused by an accurate decoding of the patient's dream material, how much by the insertion of erroneous markers, and how much by the fact that, right or wrong, acceptance has been extended to this material?

What has been said above has stressed the paucity of analogic communication, and it is necessary to insist that this paucity is systematic and arises out of the very nature of the analogic mode. In considering the case of an organism using both analog and digital modes for the same subject matter, there is, therefore, no question of this organism's achieving consistency by means of a translation process, which would reduce digital material to the analog mode where then comparison might be achieved. Translation in this direction, from the digital to the analog, must always be accompanied by gross loss of information, unless the original digital material was so composed as to contain none of the elements that cannot be expressed in analog form. Presumably the genotypic corpus of instructions to the developing organism is limited in this way.[2]

However, when we consider the plight of man, we observe at once that he has great paucity on the digital side. There is probably no systematic reason why language should be so poor, but the fact remains that, for the discussion of contingencies of relationship, human language has yet evolved only a small vocabulary of words, which even the experts in human relations are unwilling to define in any critical manner. We refer here to such words as dependency, hostility, aggression, dominance, responsibility, spectatorship, prestige, respect, impertinence, rudeness, familiarity, intimacy, love, hate, and the like. For almost all these words it is unclear whether they are descriptive of an individual, of the actions of an individual or of a pattern of relationship; and almost every one of them contains that peculiar ambiguity (amphibole) which is characteristic of the word "tender." We say that a bruise is "tender" but also that the nurse who handles the bruise is "tender." We may suspect that these words still carry with them some of the ambiguity with which we endow them in our attempts to translate from analogic representations of contingencies of relationship into digital language. There is, however, no evident limiting factor in the nature of language that would preclude the evolution of a more critical vocabulary.

Be all that as it may, the creature who must translate from analogue to digital is continually liable to project upon his analog sources the characteristics of the digital mode into which he is translating. The clenched fists of the vis-à-vis may be a signal that the latter is aggressive or that he is exerting self-restraint, or it may mean both of these, but the recipient is likely to translate

---

[2] Experts in computing machines assert that any computation of an analog machine can be simulated on a digital machine, but that the converse does not hold. It is not possible to simulate all that digital machines can do on analogue machines.

it as a positive assertion of one or the other. The dream of a horrendous maternal figure may be a direct expression of the dreamer's fear, or it may be an ironic caricature either of mother or of the dreamer. The dreamer, with or without psychiatric aid, will tend to push this dream in one direction or another, adding logical type markers where there were none in the dream itself.

Finally, one other aspect of analogic communication about relationship must be mentioned, namely, that the message material is commonly empirical in nature rather than time-binding. The juxtaposition of these two terms, "empirical" and "time-binding" as contrasted opposites, may appear novel, but what we want to suggest is derivable from the traditional notion of empiricism. An "empiric" used to be a term of abuse for a medical practitioner who treated without theory, being guided only by trial and error. This is no longer considered to be discreditable and indeed, the "empiric" has certain advantages of flexibility as compared with his colleague who is theory-bound. It is this order of contrast that we invoke in saying that analogic communication tends to be empirical while the digital tends to be time-binding. (A rather similar contrast between calibration and feedback methods of adaptation has been discussed elsewhere (Bateson, 1961)

Precisely because no indicative, negative or affirmative statement can be issued in analog terms, this mode is appropriate for the trying out of styles of relationship, and in many fields of life, human beings have ritualized this fact. Courtship is noncommittal up to a certain point and consists very largely of analogic interchange. Finally the persons are ready for the contractual and digital statements of marriage and the shift from one stage to the other is marked in the analogic mode by ritual. The problem for the young people concerned may be stated in the language of the present paper: At what stage in the experimental and empirical interchange of analog signals does it become wise to translate these messages into affirmative digital statements with logical type markers?

A similar problem surrounds the matter of interpersonal anger. We live in a culture in which a very large number of people are afraid that to act in an angry manner will "tear" their relationships, and one of the recurrent problems of the psychiatrist is how to have the patient discover that it is all right to express his anger by analogic modes. It has for some reason become difficult for us to believe that we can get, by the empirical use of anger, a new insight into important relationships without destroying the relationship. Indeed, it is almost impossible for many of us to believe that sometimes only by this empirical use of anger can the relationship be saved. Our pathology derives from perceiving any expression of anger as an indicative negative and time-binding statement about the relationship.

And then there is the more complex problem of the relationship in which one spouse expresses anger freely and even compulsively, only to be met with a digital reply, "I was angry with my friend. I told my wrath, my wrath did end." But perhaps this relief could only be achieved if the friend was equally ready to express his wrath!

A converse, but much more complex, problem arises in regard to hysteria. No doubt this word covers a wide range of formal patterns, but it would appear that at least some cases involve errors of translation from the digital to the analogic. Stripping the digital material of its logical type markers leads to erroneous symptom formation. The verbal "headache" which was invented as a conventional excuse for not performing some task may become subjectively real and be endowed with real magnitudes in the pain dimension.

The essence of the matter is that an element of secrecy regarding the nature of the communication is conferred by the very fact of translation from the digital to the analogic.

In this connection it is interesting to consider the waxing and waning of conversion hysteria as a form of expression and interchange between humans, which has been the subject of numerous scientific papers. Viewed from the perspectives we are presenting, it could be predicted that advances in medicine and the current enormous consumption of placebos and analgesics (and the placebo effect of physiological analgesics) would go far to render hysteria untenable. In addition, there is perhaps an increasing popular awareness of the functions of such symptoms in malingering and as protests in the field of relatedness. The hysteric thus finds himself in a dilemma — either his symptoms are spoiled by modern pharmacology, which he must nominally accept, insofar as he claims that the symptoms have organic origin, or his secrecy is threatened by the suspicions of his friends.

In many cases, of course, the hysterically sick member of a family finds himself surrounded by other family members who are in a tacit coalition to regard the sickness as organic. This view frees them from responsibility and from the covert accusations that the symptom partly expresses and partly conceals. But it is becoming a little more difficult for such family systems to maintain their status quo. Medicine and health are becoming increasingly a duty, so that to maintain a sick member without recurrent appeal to the medical profession is becoming both difficult and guilt-provoking. On the other hand, the doctor, when they appeal to him, is more and more likely to expose the communicational aspects of the symptom.

References

Bateson, B. (1936). *Naven*. London: Cambridge University Press.

Bateson, G. (1960). Minimal requirements for a theory of schizophrenia. *AMA Archives of General Psychiatry, 2*; 477–491.

Bateson, G. (1961). The biosocial integration of behavior in the schizophrenic family. In Ackerman, Beatman, & Sherman (Eds.), *Exploring the base for family therapy* (pp. 116–122). New York: Family Service America.

Bateson, G. (in press). The role of somatic change in evolution. *Evolution*.

Bateson, G., Jackson, D., Haley, J., & Weakland, J. (1956). Toward a theory of schizophrenia. *Behavioral Science, 1*; 251–264.

Blauvelt, H. (1956). Neonate-mother relationship in goat and man. In *Group Processes* (Transactions of Second Conference), pp. 94–140. New York: Josiah Macy Jr. Foundation.

Erikson, E. H. (1950). *Childhood and society*. New York: W. W. Norton.

Weakland, J., & Jackson, D. (1958). Patient and therapist observations on the circumstances of a schizophrenic episode. *AMA Archives of Neurology & Psychiatry, 79*; 554–575.

CHAPTER 17

The Study of the Family[1,2]
(1965)

For the past six years, we at the Mental Research Institute in Palo Alto have been studying family interaction to see whether and how such interaction relates to psychopathology or deviant behavior in one or more family members. The "normal" as well as the "disturbed" family is studied in order to infer conditions conducive to mental health. Our approach has been interaction oriented because we believe that individual personality, character, and deviance are shaped by the individual's relations with his fellows. As the sociologist Shibuntani has stated:

> Many of the things men do take a certain form not so much from instincts as from necessity of adjusting to their fellows ... What characterizes the interactionist approach is the contention that human nature and the social order are products of communication ... The direction taken by a person's conduct is seen as something that is constructed in the reciprocal give-and-take of interdependent men who are adjusting to one another. Further, a man's personality

[1] Reprinted with permission from *Family Process, March 1965, 4* (1), 1–20.
[2] Don D. Jackson founded and was first Director, the Mental Research Institute, Palo Alto, California. Indebtedness is here expressed to the members of the Mental Research Institute for their numerous contributions to this paper. This work has been supported by National Institute of Mental Health Grant MH-04916, by the Robert Wheeler Foundation, and the Ampex Foundation. This paper was written with the assistance of Janet Beavin.

— those distinctive behavioral patterns that characterize a given individual — is regarded as developing and being reaffirmed from day to day in his interaction with his associates (Thibaut & Kelley, 1959).

Thus, symptoms, defenses, character structure, and personality can be seen as terms describing the individual's typical interactions, which occur in response to a particular interpersonal context. Since the family is the most influential learning context, surely a more detailed study of family process would yield valuable clues to the etiology of such typical modes of interaction.

PROBLEMS OF FAMILY STUDY

Operating from this interactionist view, we began (as did many other family study centers) by studying families, which had a schizophrenic member, to see whether or not these families had processes in common.[3] Various projects have since gone on to study families with delinquent, neurotic, or psychosomatically ill members.

Although our original approach, assessment of the family's influence on the individual patient, yielded many useful concepts, hunches, and observations, it also had inherent difficulties and potential fallacies. To study family process per se is difficult enough; to try to uncover the origins of pathology inevitably becomes part science and part crystal ball.

PROBLEMS OF THEORY

When searching for one-to-one relationships between an identifiable family process and a characteristic individual response, it must be kept in mind that:

1. The same behavior in two people can spring from quite different interactional causes. Thus, according to the principle of equifinality, different causes may produce similar results; for example, two different sets of family reactions may each produce a child who steals.

---

[3] Before the formation of the Mental Research Institute in November 1958, I had worked five years with Gregory Bateson on his "Communication in Schizophrenia" project. Jack and Jeanne Bloch, Virginia Patterson, and I studied the families of neurotic and autistic children at the Langley Porter Neuropsychiatric Institute from 1953–1956.

2. Behavior is multi-determined. A child is exposed to a vast number of learning contexts, all of which help to mold behavior.

3. Stress resulting from outside pressures on the family can exacerbate family processes destructive to a child's development. As a matter of fact, stress may so alter family processes that even after the circumstances producing it have ceased, there may be a "snowball" effect.

4. Certain variables might be present that help to soften the effect of a destructive family process. A child might, by happy circumstance, escape the family often enough to form a protective relationship with a schoolteacher, for example. Another child might not come upon such an opportunity.

5. There is a possible importance of so-called constitutional factors, even though such factors are not independently assessable by present methods except in cases of severe mental deficiency.

Most important of all, however, is to remain alert to the fundamental precariousness of using the symptom as a starting point from which to investigate family interaction. Families of schizophrenics, delinquents, and neurotics may be more alike than different, both in their formal structure and in their response to society's discovery that they contain a deviant member. (The Bateson group, when first studying families of schizophrenics, recognized all these problems. We labeled each index case *schizophrenia p* in order to signify: "This is a way of describing the people we are observing, and not of describing all schizophrenics.")

When the symptom is used as the starting point, the problem is further compounded by the fact that the psychiatric nosology, or system, for labeling deviance is not only individual-oriented but often idiosyncratic and not clearly related to observed behavior. Psychiatrists are often more interested in pinning the patient with a label than in studying how he got into the spot of being pinned. Psychiatric terms frequently include labels for different kinds of individual behavior, in widely varying interpersonal contexts; for example, the word "delinquent" covers children who steal, rape, beat up others, are truant, and so forth. When labels that are used for individuals are extended to describe a dyad, they are unhelpful because they are undifferentiating. For example, the label "sadomasochistic," when applied to a couple, describes little; from our observations, almost all troubled marital pairs can be described this way.

All these impediments to family theory and research can be seen to be variations of two related conceptual issues:[4] individual versus interactional process, and linear versus circular causality. From our resolution of these issues will emerge general criteria of family theory by which the rest of this presentation will be guided.

INDIVIDUAL VERSUS INTERACTIONAL PROCESS

We have just noted that to focus on a family because of the psychiatric symptom[5] of a family member introduces an inappropriate individual bias, making the analysis of interactional processes more difficult. But even if the object of study is ostensibly the family unit, any examination of the characteristics of the various individual family members remains in the domain of individual theory. When we say that the patient is disturbed but one or both of his parents cause this, or that various family members manifest perceptual, emotional, or cognitive disturbances, or that a family member other than the identified patient is "really" sick — in all these ways we may quantitatively increase the number of individuals under study, but the theory remains individual in orientation. It is only when we attend to transactions between individuals as primary data that a qualitative shift in conceptual framework can be achieved. Yet our grasp of such data seems ephemeral; despite our best intentions, clear observations of interactional process fade into the old, individual vocabulary, there to be lost, indistinguishable and heuristically useless. To put the problem another way, we need measures that do not simply sum up individuals into a family unit; we need to measure the characteristics of the supraindividual family unit, characteristics for which we presently have almost no terminology. We can only use this rule of thumb: the whole is more than the sum of its parts, and it is that whole in which we are interested.

---

[4] To the proponents of a new theory falls the sometimes pedantic and arid, but more often illuminating, task of boring down to basic premises, to conceptual models and metatheoretical considerations, which those who have a broad framework of agreement, theoretically, need not constantly remind each other of. When alternative premises, methodologies, and data are proposed, the old and the new must be laid out side by side for comparison, and the newcomer has the duty to state with maximum possible clarity just what he does and does not assume.

[5] Or absence thereof, which amounts to the same thing.

LINEAR VERSUS CIRCULAR CAUSALITY

Much of the work done in the behavioral (and many other) sciences can be said, essentially, to be devoted to finding causes for given observed effects. These cases are supposed to be lineally related to their effects, that is, event B happens (or happened) because event A is happening (or previously happened). Since longitudinal studies are, unfortunately, the exception, and cross-sectional or time-sample studies predominate research studies, this assumption has never been adequately tested. Still, despite an embarrassing simultaneity of observation, the "cause" and "effect" are treated as if they occurred in linear series and in the appropriate order. One important concept ignored by this theory is that of feedback, which proposes that information about event B impinges on event A, which then affects B, etc., in a circle of events which modify each other. Since psychological "events" seldom occur only once, but rather persist and overlap with maddening complexity, this circular model is often more appropriate than one which artificially abstracts such events from the intricate time sequence in which they occur.

When applied to the family, the notion of linear causality is particularly inappropriate and leads directly to several of the problems outlined earlier (especially equifinality, multi-determination of behavior, and even the process whereby the patient is labeled). Faced with the undeniable fact that family members act constantly on each other, modifying each other's behavior in the most complex ways, a conceptual model that would have us delineate event A from event B, much less put them in causal order, is of little help. Furthermore, such goals are sterile because they must ultimately lead to unanswerable questions, such as whether the parents of the schizophrenic are the way they are because they have an organically ill child, or the patient is schizophrenic because of his parents' behavior. The study of present process in the family, then, seems both more accurate and more fruitful.

The "double-bind" theory (Bateson, Jackson, Haley, & Weakland, 1956) has been subject to considerable misunderstanding on this issue and provides us with a good example. It was not immediately clear in the original paper that there was no "binder" and no "victim" in the relationship described as a double bind but rather two binder-victims. This is obvious when one realizes that there is no possible response to a double bind except an equally or more paradoxical message, so if neither can escape the relationship, it can be expected to go on and on until it matters little how it all got started. Thus, both for theory and for therapy, we do much better to study the present operation of this pathological interaction than to seek the ultimate villain.

It follows that the first step must be to study family interaction per se; to study interaction patterns in families of all kinds, whether or not the family has a labeled symptom-bearer. The goal is to classify families in terms of how they characteristically interact, in other words, to try to build a typology of families. While this is being done, it might also be possible to note any one-to-one relationships between certain kinds of family interaction and certain types of individual behavior. Such a task is, of course, Herculean, since one can look at family interaction in a variety of ways and draw from many different theoretical formulations. Our approach has been exploratory and crude. But while polyadic systems are unquestionably more complex than our present research strategies can assess, there is the curious fact that attention to such systems — because of their lawfulness — simplifies the observation of human behavior.

FAMILY RULES

Briefly stated, the major assertion of the theory to be outlined here is that *the family is a rule-governed system*: that its members behave among themselves in an organized, repetitive manner and that this patterning of behaviors can be abstracted as a governing principle of family life.

THEORETICAL BACKGROUND

Both common sense and clinical observations argue for the organized nature of family interaction. If there were not some circumscription of the infinity of possible behaviors in which its members might conceivably engage, not only the daily chores but the very survival of the family unit would be in question. And, indeed, we can observe more or less strict divisions of labor and of power that comprise the cultural and the idiosyncratic "styles" of family life. (The latter may, for instance, bewilder the small child when he begins visiting friends' families and discovers they have a way of doing things, which is alien to his privately held definition of family operations.)

We need not rely only on the practical argument that family life must be organized (and therefore, have "rules" of organization), nor on the commonly shared observation that family behavior is organized and that we can and do infer the "rules" governing this organization. The theory of communication and interpersonal relations, even in its present infancy, permits logical deduction of the hypothesis of family rules. To accomplish this derivation, it is necessary to review a few pertinent aspects of communications theory.

In 1951, Bateson (1951, see also Jackson, 1957) noted that communications[6] can be said to have two distinct aspects or functions, *report* and *command*. Most obviously, every communication bit conveys information of a factual nature which, presumably, can be evaluated in terms of truth and falsity, and can be dealt with logically as the "object" of communication; this is the communication report; for example, "the streets are icy," "Darwinian evolution does not necessarily invalidate the concept of a Supreme Being," or a shake of the head.

But, in addition to this report, and of immeasurably more interest to our theory of interpersonal relations, the same communication bit also conveys a command, which indicates how this information is to be taken. Although this theory holds for a wider variety of communicational phenomena, we will limit ourselves to human communication where we will see that the command aspect can be paraphrased "this is how I define the relationship in which this report takes place, that is, this is how you are to see me in relation to you." None of the examples above was in the imperative mood grammatically, yet each effectively defines the nature of the relationship in which it occurs. Even the (superficially) impersonal statement about Darwinian evolution is not the sort of opinion one renders to the barber or even to one's wife without defining the relationship in a highly specific manner.[7]

This definition may not be accepted; it may be rejected, countered, modified, or ignored. It may also be redundant — confirming a longstanding or stereotyped relationship agreement such as teacher–student. But the offering of a "command" and the response by the other are distinguishable issues. Their interaction will be taken up shortly. Here, we can summarize the general report-command theory of communication into terms suitable for the specific aspects of human communication: Every message (communication bit) has both a content (report) and a relationship (command) aspect; the former conveys information about facts, opinions, feelings, experiences, etc., and the latter defines the nature of the relationship between the communicants. It is

---

[6] By communication is meant behavior in the widest sense: words and their nonverbal accompaniments, posture, facial expressions, even silence. All convey messages to another person, and all are subsumed in our term "communication."

[7] The relationship of the report to the command aspect of communication can be seen to be one of logical levels. One classifies the other, but is also classified by the other. For the sake of exposition, we will leave this reciprocity implicit and speak of commands as a "higher" level than report.

the relationship level of communication which will be our primary focus in this paper.

In every communication, then, the participants offer to each other definitions of their relationship, or, more forcefully stated, each seeks to determine the nature of the relationship. Each, in turn, responds with his definition of the relationship — which may affirm, deny, or modify that of the vis-à-vis. This process, at the relationship level of interaction (communication), warrants close attention.[8]

One of the simplest examples is the behavior of strangers in public places (in an airplane, in a bar, waiting in line). They may exchange trivial comments which lead to, say, a "small talk" relationship being agreed upon; or one may seek such a relationship and the other may quell it; or they may mutually define theirs as a "stranger" relationship — a special relationship with its unique rules, rights, and expectations. Note especially that the context exchange in these circumstances (offering a cigarette, comments about the weather, chuckling "to oneself") is of little consequence; it may be false or virtually nonexistent (feigned deafness, pretended concentration, simple ignoring). But the relationship struggle and resolution are definitive even in the unlikely case where they simultaneously decide to ignore each other.

If we now narrow our focus even more, from human communication in general to ongoing (perdurable) relationships only, we see that what is relatively simple and unimportant between strangers is both vital and complex in an ongoing relationship. An ongoing relationship may be said to exist when, for some reason, the relationship is (a) "important" to both parties and (b) assumed to be of long term duration, as is true of some business relationships, between friends and lovers, and especially in marital and familial relationships. When these conditions impinge on a relationship, the determination of the nature of that relationship cannot *not* be accomplished, nor can it be a haphazard process. The give and take of relationship definitions must stabilize or lead to a so-called runaway that would endanger the maintenance of this ongoing

---

[8] In our view, the definition of the self, the relationship, and the other are an indivisible whole. We especially do not isolate or abstract the individual from the individual-in-this-relationship-with-this-other. This bias is implicit throughout the present work, and any tendency to read otherwise in the following will only lead to confusion.

relationship, that is, divorce, desertion, or disaster would ensue, and there would be not relationship to study.[9]

Thus, the population of families which is ours to study — those which remain family units — have stabilized the process of determining the nature of their relationship, "agreeing" on a mutually acceptable definition or at least on the limits for dispute. These relationship agreements, which are here called rules, prescribe and limit the individuals' behaviors over a wide variety of content areas, organizing their interaction into a reasonably stable system.

By way of illustration, we might speculate how rules must develop and operate in a new relationship: Boy meets girl on their first date. Take any aspect of the many behaviors involved; say, he arrives a little late. Suppose further that she delays her entrance (consciously or not) by exactly the amount of time he kept her waiting. He gets the message that she will not tolerate his keeping her waiting. At the same time, though, he cannot be sure whether this is just her mood tonight, or coincidence, or characteristic of her. If they are exceptional persons, they might discuss this "interchange," which would be a step toward resolution or change. But, whether they verbalize it or not, real change would require several repetitions of the corrected behavior. That is, if he were really unavoidably detained the first time, he would have to be on time the next several times to "prove" this. So suppose they still have this question, undiscussed, and unresolved. In the course of the evening, he decides they should go to a movie, and while she agrees, she picks the movie. He could decide he must treat her as an equal, and start practicing equality; she responds by treating him equally, that is, she does not overdo it and push him around. Within a few dates, they would have something which could last a lifetime — although of course we cannot prove this. Mate selection must be in large part the matching of certain expected behaviors (and self-definitions) in certain crucial areas.

At this point we must, proleptically, digress to lay to rest questions of "consciousness," "intention," "purposefulness," or any of a variety of other terms implying that extremely troublesome issue: Is the behavior motivated or not? (And if so, how?) To propose that every individual moves to determine the nature of his relationship with another would seem to imply a theory of

---

[9] However, relationships do not necessarily terminate in actuality when they terminate in legality. Many divorced persons, for instance, remain intensely involved with each other and have even been known to participate in "marital" therapy.

the individual which is based upon an Adlerian motivation to power. This is emphatically not so. No theoretical assumptions about the individual have been or need be invoked, only assumptions on the nature of communication qua communication. Only the premise of a report–command duality of communication is necessary to our theoretical model. Similarly, although we find it convenient to say family members "agree" on relationship rules, we do not intend or need to assume that this is a conscious process. Most relationship rules are probably out of our awareness, but the issue is moot and irrelevant in this context.

THE RULE AS REDUNDANCY IN RELATIONSHIPS

If a man from Mars were to hover outside some living room window any given night, he might discover four people sitting around a small table, passing pasteboard rectangles to one another and muttering such phrases as "one no-trump." After watching for a while and noting redundancies in the players' behavior, our intelligent Martian could discern that what these people were doing was highly rule–governed. He might discover, for example, that spades are higher than clubs, that play goes from left to right, and so forth. He might or might not immediately discover certain other rules of bridge, depending on whether special circumstances arose while he happened to be watching. For instance, it is assumed that no one will cheat. If one partner gives the other a significant glance, his opponents scowl angrily as a warning that this behavior is on the road to out-and-out cheating. Or, a really clever extraterrestrial observer might realize that the players could gain advantage by cheating, and that since they consistently refrained from this behavior, it must be against the rules. However, groups who have played together for sometime will follow rules that are not overtly evident and which could only be inferred by an outsider after long, patient observation and recording of redundancies. Even if he spoke English and queried the players, it might not occur to them to mention certain rules that they abide by but are not consciously aware of observing. For example, A may "know" that when B says "one no-trump," he usually has minimal points and therefore A needs a strong hand to raise B.

When the game is family relationships, behavioral scientists are alien observers. The rules of play are not known completely even to the participants. What confronts the observer is a plethora of behaviors (communication) from which rules can be inferred which "explain" the patterning of the behavior. Just as a relatively few rules permit games as complex as chess or bridge, so a few family rules can cover the major aspects of ongoing interpersonal relationships. (The comparative difficulties of deducing many possible behaviors from a few given rules and of inducing the rules from a wide variety of behaviors should, however, be obvious.)

In other words, a redundancy principal operates in family life. The family will interact in repetitious sequences in all areas of its life, though some areas may highlight these repetitions (or pattern) more quickly and systematically than do other areas.

The rule approach to the study of family interaction is similar to that of the biologist studying genes and to Bateson's approach to the study of the learning process. As Maruyama (1962) describes the former, biologists were long puzzled by the fact that the amount of information stored in genes is much smaller than the amount of information needed to account for the structure of the adult individual. However, the puzzle is solved if one assumes that the genes carry a set of rules to generate information for the whole system. Similarly, Bateson (1962) described "deutero-learning" or "learning to learn," which concisely governs the wider range of what is learned. Although the family-as-a-unit indulges in uncountable numbers of different specific behaviors, the whole system can be run by a relatively small set of rules governing relationships. If one can reliably infer the general rules from which a family operates, then all its complex behavior may turn out to be not only patterned, but also understandable — and, as a result, perhaps predictable.

Again, we must emphasize the rule is an inference, an abstraction more precisely, a metaphor coined by the observer to cover the redundancy he observes. We say a rule is a "format of regularity imposed upon a complicated process by the investigator" (Jackson, 1965), thereby preserving the distinction between theoretical term and object of Nature, which is maintained by many of our more sophisticated colleagues in the natural sciences. A rule is, but for our paucity of expression, a formula for a relationship, no one shall control anyone else, father shall overtly run the show but mother's covert authority shall be respected, husband shall be the wooer and wife the helpless female. Such formulations are inference, just as is the concept of gravity; they explain the data in the sense that they incorporate the relevant visible evidence and relate it to a larger heuristic framework.

A LEXICON OF RULES

I have come to refer to family relationship rules in general as *norms*. This usage not only corresponds roughly with similar (non-family) explanations in the literature (Garfinkel, 1964; Leary, 1957; Thibaut & Kelley, 1959), but it also connotes some of the important characteristics of the concept:

1. That the norms are usually phenomenologically unique for each family observed. We thus keep our focus firmly centered on the family unit, with individual and broader social or cultural considerations remaining secondary, even though we assume that a given set of norms or relationship rules is more common in one culture than another.

2. That the norm is a setting or baseline on which family behavior is measured and around which it varies to a greater or lesser degree.

Norm thus implies both the focus and the mechanics of our theory. This might be represented schematically as in Figure 1, which can be seen to resemble a graph for a mechanical regulating device such as the household furnace thermostat, in which case the "range of behavior" would be the temperature scale and the "norm" the desired temperature setting.

One type of norm, described elsewhere (Jackson, 1958, Chap. 9 in this volume), is the marital quid pro quo. This term (literally "something for something") is a metaphorical statement of the marital relationship bargain; that is, how the couple has agreed to define themselves within this relationship.

Inseparable from our definition of norm would have to be a definition of *homeostatic mechanisms*, the means by which norms are delimited and enforced. The scowl the Martian observed on a bridge player when his competitor might have cheated indicated that the rules of the game had been or were about to be violated, or to put it another way, indicated that the class of behaviors in which the offending player has just indulged is to be excluded in their future dealing.[10]

Homeostatic mechanisms are therefore an extension, in an ongoing relationship, of the give-and-take of relationship definitions by which the original rules were worked out. It can be safely assumed, however, that the homeo-

---

[10] Most of us, as bridge players, would readily perceive that our opponents meant to exclude not only the specific cheating tactic just attempted but any cheating behavior at all. Further, few of us would interpret the specific behavior (e.g., the exchange of significant glances) to be excluded in subsequent non-bridge situations. But the classification of behavior is not always so self-evident. The problems of mutually understood generalizations from specific behavior will be dealt with in detail in a later article.

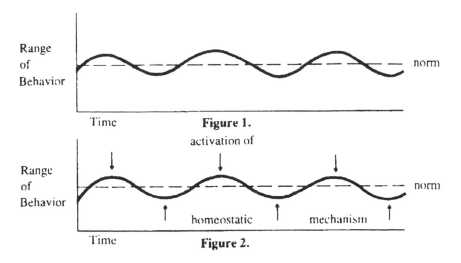

Figure 1.

Figure 2.

static mechanisms probably operate to restrict behavior to a much original narrower range when the interactional system has stabilized into a family system than when the relationship was being worked out. Couples, such as described earlier, who may engage in wondrously varied behavioral ploys during courtship, undoubtedly achieve considerable economy after a while in terms of what is open to dispute, and how it is to be disputed. Consequently they seem both to have mutually excluded wide areas of behavior from their interactional repertoire (and never quibble further about them), and to have learned to cue each other homeostatically with a privately understood "code," so that little gestures may mean a lot. Such economy, of course, is inversely related to the effort required of the researching observer.

In terms of the schema just presented for norms (Figure 1, above), homeostatic mechanisms can be seen as behaviors that delimit the fluctuations of other behaviors along the particular range where the norm is relevant.[11] Again, the analogy with the household thermostat is useful: When the temperature deviates from a pre-set norm, this deviation is registered and counteracted by the homeostatic mechanism of the thermostat system (Figure 2, p. 213). Thus, if the norm of the family is that there be no disagreement, when trouble begins to brew, we might observe general uneasiness, a sudden tangentialization or change of topic, or even symptomatic behavior on the part of an identified patient, who may act out, talk crazy, or even become physically ill when family members begin to argue. The family is distracted and brought into coalition (frequently against the patient) and the norm holds until the next time.

It is significant in the development of family theory that it was the observation of homeostatic mechanisms in the families of psychiatric patients (Jackson, 1957) that led to the hypothesis of the family as a homeostatic, and eventually specifically as a rule-governed, system. For norms become quickly apparent if one can observe the reaction to their abrogation and infer there from the rule that was broken. Tiresome long-term observation of the beaten path, with careful noting of possible routes which were not taken, can eventually yield a fair guess about the rules of the game. But the observable counteraction of a single deviation is like a marker to our goal. Therefore, though it is still difficult to assess exactly the norms of the system the schizophrenic patient and his family maintain when the patient is "ill," one need only witness the immediate and frequently violent reaction to his recovery to be convinced that there are powerful family mechanisms for maintaining these norms.

NORMS AND VALUES

Norms as herein defined and discussed are not to be confused with the important sociological concept of values. Certainly both constructs represent guideposts, which organize behavior, and both are enforced by observable sanctions. So one might be tempted to put the two in the same class and distinguish them on some minor ground, for example, values are generally presumed to exist a priori and to result in ("cause") certain behavior patterns,

---

[11] Again, homeostatic behaviors obviously belong to a higher level, logically, than the behavior to which they refer. We might speculate that this higher range of behaviors also has norms and if so, that paradoxes might arise.

while norms are inferred from behavior and are not seen to be causative; or, one might propose that values are overt and acknowledgeable while norms are covert, the two being analogous perhaps to laws and customs, respectively.

These apparent comparabilities are, however, superficial and misleading. A norm describes interpersonal relations; that is, they are interpersonal both in unit and subject matter. Values, on the other hand, are non-personal in subject matter and individual in unit. One person can value something or "have" a certain value, and several family members (individually) can value something, but a family as a whole cannot. Even if all family members concur in a certain value, the result is a summation of individuals — and therefore remains in the domain of individual theory.

Where, then, do values fit into our scheme of family rules? Certainly not in terms of specific injunctions for or against certain individual behaviors, or in the meaning of these behaviors for the individual (in terms of dissonance, guilt, etc.). Behavior that may be guided by a presumed value is not distinguishable from any other kind of behavior in our interactional framework. But values, or more precisely, the invocation of values, can have interpersonal ramifications: Values can be cited to demand, enforce, or justify a particular kind of behavior in a relationship. If the family norm proscribes disagreement, when a family discussion begins to get out of order, almost any member can invoke the shared value of democratic functioning (taking turns, etc.), and thus re-establish family order. In short, values in this theory of the family are one kind of homeostatic mechanism. Because values represent an extra-familial coalition (with religion, society, culture, etc.), they exert leverage on relationships within the family. Thus, from our perspective, inside the family looking out, so to speak, values are used as interpersonal tactics that affirm or enforce a norm.[12]

Mother and infant, for example, have a strictly complementary relationship (that is, one based on differences which fit together), in which the norm is that the infant is totally dependent on the mother for all gratification. As the child grows older, he may engage in behaviors that abrogate this norm, especially masturbation. Whatever else masturbation may mean to either individual,

---

[12] This is not, of course, the same as saying that this is all a value is, the student of value orientations cuts the pie quite another way and validly so, but this is all a value can be within the theory here outlined if consistency is to be maintained.

in this ongoing relationship, it is an indication of self-sufficient pleasure on the part of the child (Jackson, 1958) and as such, threatens the norm of their relationship, that is, that the mother controls all the child's needs and pleasures. If the mother is unwilling to accept this change in the norm, she may punish the child, and/or she may invoke strong moral injunctions against the "deviant" behavior. In this case, her value judgment against his masturbation represents a forceful coalition of mother and society, a coalition that may in fact succeed and perpetuate the complementary norm to absurdity.

As is readily apparent, values usually have recognizable origins in the culture, subculture, ethnic background, or social group, but there are idiosyncratic values as well. Some may be ignored, and some espoused with special fervor, as these values tend to fit into the enforcement of the family norms. Thus, while the psychoanalyst often sees values as rationalizations of intrapsychic phenomena, and the sociologist and anthropologist discuss them as idealized constructs somehow "possessed" by the individual, or on which many individuals concur, this family theory focuses on the communicative function of value-guided behavior and concludes that such behavior is tactical, within the family, where it serves as a homeostatic mechanism.

This use of the term "value" corresponds with that of others who have previously used "norm" as it is defined here. Thibaut and Kelley, in *The Social Psychology of Groups* (1959), describe a norm as a behavioral rule that is accepted, at least to some degree, by both members of a (non-family) dyad. They state that the observer, after noting a regularity in behavior or regular routine shifts in the activities of the pair, can help explain this regularity by inferring that the behavior is organized around norms. They also note that if the regularity is disrupted, the "injured" person will often attempt to restore it by exercising his personal power to enforce the norm, or by appealing to a supporting value.

Garfinkel (1964) discusses what he calls "constitutive rules" — rules that one is not aware of until they are broken or abrogated. "Constitutive rules" correspond, in some ways, to my use of the word "norm." For example, supermarket shoppers were disconcerted to observe a graduate student buy a package of cigarettes and then proceed to open the pack and count the cigarettes. This deliberately staged behavior called into question the norms of the relationship between shopper and producer, which might be paraphrased as: "If I (shopper) buy a pack of cigarettes, I can count on you (producer) to put 20 cigarettes in the pack." Thus the shopper is spared the impossible task of verifying the size, weight, and number of everything he purchases; in other words, a certain level of trust is established. If some shopper discovered only 10 cigarettes in a package, he might or might not realize the exact nature of his trust in the producer, but he would probably write him a letter invoking values, even laws. (The effect on other shoppers produced by the psychology student's behavior is an indication that people react against discovering their own norms. It is similar to becoming aware of one's breathing — what once worked silently and smoothly is now a problem.)

RULES VERSUS ROLES

Probably the most generally accepted notion in family study is that of roles, which has wide currency among an unusually varied group of investigators — psychoanalysts, sociologists, learning theorists, to name a few. A family role is a model abstracted from the legal, chronological, or sexual status of a family member (mother, husband, son, sister, etc.); this model describes certain expected, permitted, and forbidden behaviors for the person in that role. Several kinds of analysis follow from the family role concept: Study of the process of learning the role behaviors, of the inevitable multiplicity of roles with which any given individual is labeled (spouse and parent, child and sibling, and so on), and, of course, of the integration of roles into a family structure.

This last field of study would seem, perhaps, to be very similar to our proposed theory of family rules, focusing as both do on the interlocking behaviors of family members. This is not true, for a number of reasons. Most important, in the role concept we again face a term that is basically individual in origin and orientation and which, therefore, is ill-suited for the discussion of family process. A role encases the individual as a separate unit of study so that the relations between two or more individuals must necessarily be secondary phenomena. If we would study relationship first, then we cannot, as will be illustrated shortly, base this study on individual constructs.

A second point of difference is the inseparability of the role concept from a culture-limited view of family structure. There is no clear line between the role as descriptive or as idealistic; that is, people are classified by conformity or nonconformity to predetermined categories which are products either of cultural stereotype or of theoretical bias. The implication is that a healthy family has Father in the father role, Mother in the mother role, Son in the male child role, etc. This neglects and even obscures the aspects of interactional process that may be significant, which may in fact be the more general phenomena of which role-taking is only a by-product.[13]

This leads to a more basic difference between rules and roles — the reliance on observation as opposed to a priori definitions. A role, with its theoretically concomitant behaviors, exists independently of behavioral data. That is, not only the general notion of role but the specifics of the various sorts of family roles are theoretical, not phenomenological. When observational data is involved, it is in relation to the theoretical role as a model ("inadequate performance of a role," "role breakdown," "role reversal"). It seems apparent that analysis of such discrepancies between model and reality only emphasizes further the gap between category and data.

To illustrate that rules and roles are two fundamentally different ways of looking at family data, let us consider a specific role theory — the sex-role view of marriage — and an alternative view that has been proposed in terms of family rules (Jackson, 1965, Chap. 18 in this volume). The incontrovertible and inevitable fact that marriages are composed of one man and one woman only has led to the belief that sex differences between spouses are highly significant in the nature of marriage. Men and women have certain fundamental differences at birth, which are presumed to be amplified by social learning of a wide variety of sex-linked behaviors and attitudes; in short, each adult should have achieved a male or female role. The convergence of the two roles, as the only immediately obvious similarity between all marriages, is commonly assumed to be the key to marriage as an institution. Thus sexual compatibility is greatly stressed as vital to the success of a marriage (though this may be only a special case of the more general necessity for collaboration in marriage). Conformation by each spouse to the proper role stereotype is presumed to be basic, not only to sexual compatibility, but to the mental health of the spouses and their children and the permanence of the marriage.

There are, however, other characteristics true of marriage (and of almost no other relationships), which might therefore be just as reasonably considered

---

[13] There is a growing body of theory on idiosyncratic family roles especially in relation to psychopathology, e.g., the notion of the identified patient as the family scapegoat (Bell & Vogel, 1960), as well as Berne's (1961) pungent descriptions of the many roles for many persons that comprise the interactional setting of various forms of symptomatic behavior. These certainly bring us much closer to interactional data, but there is a tendency to inject such formulations with individual motivational schemes (such as masochism), which detract from the originality of the descriptive approaches.

basic to the nature of marriage as is its sexual composition. These are seldom considered, I feel, because they refer, not to individual spouses, but to the relationship of marriage and thus do not fit our usual language. Consider that the marriage (not the persons involved) is (a) a voluntary relationship, (b) a permanent or at least open-ended, non-time-bound relationship, (c) an exclusive relationship, which is supposed to suffice for the partners in a great many areas of human functioning, and (d) a broadly and complexly goal-oriented relationship, with vital tasks covering not only a wide cross-section of human affairs, but extending indefinitely through time. This is a unique and by no means spurious, inconsequential combination of characteristics and must certainly be considered at least as important to the nature of marital relationships as individual sexual factors.

Thus, the marital quid pro quo (as defined earlier) has been proposed. The quid pro quo theory of marriage is used as an illustration here because it represents a full reversal of the role theory of marriage: the individual differences that are unquestionably present in a marriage are seen as results of the active process of working out this unique and difficult relationship, not as the primary cause of the relationship phenomena.

Let us review the distinction we have made between rules and roles, in terms of these two specific theories of marriage. First, sex-role constructs are inevitably individual in orientation; any deductions about relationship consequences must be greatly limited by the premises to which these individual notions are limited. Second, there are theoretical and cultural preconceptions about "proper" sex roles, such that men are supposed to work, be strong and not openly emotional, defend the home, and so forth, while women are to keep house, stay inside it, be soft, loving, and maternal. No allowance is made for the relationship that underlies this arrangement, or for the possibility that this is a good way of working out rules for a relationship but not the only way.

This brings us to point three, which is that real marriages may deviate widely from these cultural stereotypes and be highly successful, because an equally workable relationship agreement (quid pro quo) has been maintained. There seems to be little question that difference per se is necessary in marriage: The specifics of such differences are much less important than the circularity of their evolution and maintenance. Therefore, a priori categories of differences will only lead us astray.

Some of the problems of family theory and research have been considered, and general criteria have been suggested by which these problems might be avoided. A theory of the family has been proposed, based on the model of the family as a rule-governed, homeostatic system. A companion paper to follow will discuss clinical and experimental applications of this theory, with special emphasis on pathological family systems.

References

Bateson, G. (1942). Social planning and the concept of 'deutero-learning'. *Science, Philosophy, & Religion*, Second Symposium, New York.

Bateson, G. (1951). Information and codification: A philosophical approach. In Ruesch, J., & Bateson, G., *Communication: The social matrix of psychiatry* (Pp. 168–211). New York: W. W. Norton.

Bateson, G., Jackson, D., Haley, J., & Weakland, J. (1956). Toward a theory of schizophrenia. *Behavioral Science, 1*, 251–264.

Bell, N., & Vogel, E. (1960). The emotionally disturbed child as the family scapegoat. In N., Bell & E. Vogel (Eds.), *The Family*. Glencoe, IL: Free Press.

Berne, E. (1961). *Transactional analysis*. New York: Grove Press.

von Bertalanffy, L. (1950). An outline of general systems theory. *British Journal of the Philosophy of Science, 1*, 134–165.

Garfinkel, H. (1964). The routine grounds of everyday activities. *Social Problems, 11*, 225–249.

Haley, J. (1962). Family experiments: A new type of experimentation. *Family Process, 1*, 265–293.

Jackson, D. (1965). Family rules: The marital quid pro quo. *Archives of General Psychiatry, 1*, 589–594.

Jackson, D. (1957). The question of family homeostasis. *Psychiatric Quarterly Supplement, 31*, 79–90.

Jackson, D. (1958). Guilt and the control of pleasure in schizoid personality. *British Journal of Medical Psychology, 31*, part 2, 124–130.

Leary, T. (1957). *Interpersonal diagnosis of personality*. New York: Ronald Press.

Maruyama, M. (1962, September). The second cybernetics: Deviation-amplifying mutual causal processes. Unpublished manuscript.

Shibuntani, T. (1961). *Society and personality* (Pp. 20–23). Englewood Cliffs, NJ: Prentice-Hall.

Thibaut, J., & Kelley, H. (1959). *The social psychology of groups*. New York: Wiley.

CHAPTER 18

Family Rules: Marital Quid Pro Quo[1]

(1965)

Because they are so obviously and invariably composed of only one man and one woman each, marriages in our society are usually described in terms of sexual differences, which are of course considered innate or at least fixed characteristics of the individuals involved. All manner of behaviors quite removed from primary sexual differences can be brought into the framework of male–female differences, which framework then becomes an explanatory model of marriage. This view pervades our popular mythology of sexual stereotypes, it influences marriage manuals and similar advisory accoutrements, and it certainly guides our scientific study of the marital relationship, no matter how inconsistent or unspecific this theory proves to be. The rich variety of forms which anthropologists have shown us "masculinity" and "femininity" take in marriage across the world should indicate something is amiss with the assumption that absolute, specific sexual differences in marriage are of heuristic value. The function of such differences in organizing a special relationship is seldom considered; it may be that a shared belief in any difference at all would serve the same purpose. It is proposed here that the individual differences which are so evident in marital relationships may just as reasonably be a result of the nature

---

[1] Reprinted with permission from the *Archives of General Psychiatry*, June 1965, Vol. 12, pp. 589–594.

of that relationship as of the nature of the individuals who compose the relationship.

Heterosexuality is not the only unique feature of marriage; there is another characteristic which, strangely enough, often goes unnoticed, but may be the most important aspect of marriage: it is the only well-known, long-term collaborative relationship. Thus there are several nonsexual aspects, which must be considered in any analysis of marriage and marriage problems.

1. It is a voluntary relationship, even though undertaken in a culture that views marriage as almost compulsory.

2. It is a permanent relationship; that is, it is supposed to be a lifetime contract. ("Till death do us part.")

3. Marriage in the Western world is an exclusive relationship, in which the parties are supposed to be virtually sufficient each unto the other, with a marked exclusion of third parties and outside relationships.

4. It is a broadly goal-oriented relationship with many vital mutual tasks to be carried out on a long-term basis and marked by time-bound eras — each with its special problems.

To describe these premises of marriage is not to imply that they are necessarily realized nor that the parties enter into marriage with such concepts in mind. These are shared beliefs about the nature of marriage as an institutionalized relationship, and the assets and liabilities of marriage as a legal arrangement stem, in large part, from the workability of these norms.

Unused as we are to thinking in terms of different kinds of relationships (rather than different kinds of individuals), still we can see that there are probably no other dyadic relationships which, regardless of the sex of the partners, can be similarly characterized. For instance, the assumption (not to say the reality) of permanency excludes most other volitional relationships that are not troubled by the curious paradox of "having to want to stay together." The homosexual "marriage" comes to mind immediately as a possible example of a relationship in which primary sexual differences are absent but the relationship problems as outlined above are more or less relevant. We might question whether being against the social grain — two against the world — has something to do with the durability of some such relationships. Yet, even in homosexual "marriages" there is the evolution of sex-role differences. Homosexuals may choose for their relatively permanent partners their opposites in terms of "masculinity" and "femininity," (and they often use a sex-role language for their relationship even when parent–child or sibling terms would seem more appropriate). While it can always be asserted that sex-role identification preceded the relationship (i.e., one partner is "really" female), this cannot be proven; so, just as in heterosexual marriage, the differentiation of the individuals along sex lines can be seen as primary or as a means of working out the problems posed by the rules of the marital relationship, that is, as effect, not cause.

Other instances in which the same relationship problems seem to be posed are fairly easily distinguished. In the roommate arrangement, for instance, volition, relative permanence, and mutual tasks do frequently apply; but there is no expectation that the two will not engage in highly important, independent, third-party relationships. In fact, it would be unusual for each roommate not to maintain independence or external coalitions with regard to financial, sexual, intellectual, and even companionship needs. Lacking a premise of virtual self-sufficiency of the dyad, the roommate arrangement also avoids many of the problems that arise in marriage. Business relationships are oriented to an explicit and specific central goal, as opposed to marriage, which cannot be said to have any single goal. In fact, for marriages we have to make up goals such as "the rearing of children" or "companionship" even when such functions can successfully be carried on without legal or secular blessings. Business relationships are also necessarily diluted by a wide variety of intrinsic factors, not the least of which are the time-defined working day and, again, the vital role of third parties such as customers, staff, even the stock market. There must be enduring, nonhomosexual relationships between, perhaps, unmarried, possibly related women; here one thinks of the maiden aunts or old-maid schoolteachers of our American mythology, and one begins to wonder how such relationships are worked out. Unfortunately for our research interests, these relationships seldom come to the attention of professionals. So it seems we are unable by means of counterexample to prove immediately whether marriage is the way it is because a man and a woman are involved, or because it is a unique kind of a relationship for any two people at all. Thus, it is possible that one could outline marriage as a totally non-sexual affair, nearly excluding all sexual differences, or at least minimizing the causal role usually assigned such differences.

The sex-role view of marriage is so widely accepted that the position just taken seems nearly impudent. It nevertheless seems important to reconsider some of our beliefs about marriage since our present knowledge of individual theory is quite exhaustive when contrasted with the paucity of systematic knowledge of relationship per se. In our traditional conceptual framework, the individual is held by the boundaries of his skin, and whatever transpires between two such captives — that which is neither clearly "I" nor clearly "thou" — is a mystery for which we have no language or understanding. Our thoughts, research efforts, and even what Benjamin Whorf called "our view of the cosmos" are limited or facilitated by the language which we use. Therefore, we must first have a language that enables, even forces, us to think interactionally. The necessity for a language with which to study interaction may lead to the abandonment of terms that belong to the study of the individual in favor of terms which focus on the relationship. The concept of "family rules" (Jackson, 1965) represents one such tool. The observation of family interaction makes obvious certain redundancies, typical and repetitive patterns of interaction that characterize the family as a supraindividual entity. One of the simplest such rules is proposed in this paper: the marital quid pro quo, an alternative to the theory of individual differences in marriage.

To suggest that the individual, sex-aligned differences that we witness in marriages may not be due to individual sexual differences, or indeed have anything to do with biological sexual requirements, is not to say these differences do not exist. To the contrary, just such differences can be the basis of working out a relationship. The stresses and successes of marriage still need not be attributed to sexual or even individual personality differences, but could conceivably be expected to be true of any hypothetical relationship which is also voluntary, permanent, exclusive, and task-oriented. The actual differences between marriage partners are probably not nearly so important as the difficulty in collaborating; furthermore, any two people in these conditions have to work out rules based on differences or similarities. Sexual differences are readily available, but if there were no real differences to help define the relationship, differences would probably be made up. In this light, our present language of marriage imposes many encumbering myths about maleness and femaleness, for it seems that differences are inevitable in a relationship, especially in an ongoing, goal-oriented relationship such as marriage.

Imagine two perfectly identical persons, not real-life identical twins who have long since become distinguishable to themselves and others, but a carbon-copy pair who are in fact the same person in two bodies. If such a pair were to live together, it is obvious they would have to evolve differences, which did not exist before. The first time they approached a door that must be entered in single file, the die would be cast. Who is to go first? On what basis is this decision to be made? After it is made and effected, can things ever be the same again? If they fight, someone must win. If one precedes and the other forbears, it cannot then be said they are identical, since one would be aggressive, thoughtless, or "the one who takes the initiative," while the other would be passive, patient, or sluggish. In short, a relationship problem that has nothing to do with individual differences — for there were none in our hypothetical pair — has been solved by evolving differences which may be considered shorthand expressions of the definition of the relationship which was achieved. Later, these differences are available to handle other, similar circumstances wherein identical simultaneous actions are neither possible nor desirable. There is an old European tale of a detective posing as a lodger in a boarding house where a number of mysterious suicides have occurred. He notices across the courtyard from his window an old woman who is weaving. As he becomes entranced by her elaborate movements he begins to mimic them. Then with slow horror it become apparent to him that it is she who is following his movements, not he who is following hers. As the cause and effect become inextricably tangled, he throws himself out of the window at the spinner.

When we consider the work to be done by marital partners, moneymaking, housekeeping, social life, lovemaking, and parenting, the tasks that must be attempted and to greater or lesser degree accomplished, then we are overwhelmed by the impossibility of sameness and the efficiency of differences. In the marital relationship, at least, two individuals are faced with the challenge of collaboration on a wide variety of tasks over an indefinite, but presumably long, period of time. In most of these areas — sexual, financial, occupational — no simple or nonpersonal division of labor is obvious. Cultural stereotypes are of some help, but even these appear to be fluid in middle-class America.

From research done on the parents of white, middle-class families observed at the Mental Research Institute, it seems that the way couples handle this crucial relationship problem is by a marital quid pro quo. When two people get together, they immediately exchange clues as to how they are defining the nature of the relationship; this set of behavioral tactics is modified by the other person by the manner in which he responds. The definition that is agreed to (and if the marriage is to work some sort of agreement must be reached), this definition of who each is in relation to the other can best be expressed as a quid pro quo. Quid pro quo (literally "something for something") is an expression of the legal nature of a bargain or contract, in which each party must receive something for what he gives and which; consequently, defines the rights and duties of the parties in the bargain. Marriage, too, can be likened to a bargain that defines the different rights and duties of the spouses, each of which can be said to do X if and because the other does Y. Quid pro quo then is a descriptive metaphor for a relationship based on differences, and expression of the redundancies that one observes in marital interaction. One of the most common quid pro quos observed in white, middle-class, suburban families is the following arrangement: the husband is, broadly, an instrumental type who deals with matters logically and intellectually, and is considered the practical, realistic one; his wife is the more sensitive, affective or "feeling" sort of person who understands people better than things. This sort of quid pro quo is extremely utilitarian for the sort of life such a couple is likely to lead, since the exchange implies a fairly clear division of labor that defines the contribution made by each. Carried to the extreme, this quid pro quo could result in rigidity and misunderstanding, though it is probably not as prone to pathology as some other relationship agreements. That this arrangement has little to do with fixed "sex roles" as we ordinarily think of them has been confirmed by Robert Leik (1963) who recently measured this mode of differentiation in actual families as well as "mock family" stranger groups (i.e., stranger groups with the same sex and age composition as the real families tested). He found that:

> The traditional male role (instrumental, non-emotional behavior) as well as the traditional female role (emotional, non-task behavior) appear when interaction takes place among strangers. *These emphases tend to disappear when subjects interact with their own families* (italics mine).

And he concluded that:

> In general, *the relevance of instrumentality and emotionality is quite different for family interaction than for interaction among strangers* (italics mine). This major finding poses new problems for the theoretical integration of family research with that based on ad hoc experimental groups. Such integration is possible only through recognition of

the fact that the context of the interaction with strangers places a meaning on particular acts, which is different from the meaning of those acts within the family group.

Thus, though this quid pro quo is a common and culturally convenient arrangement, it is not intrinsic to sex roles in marriage. Quite the opposite — the ongoing family relationship apparently custom-tailors the marital bargain to its own particular situation.

Another type of quid pro quo is a "time-bound" relationship, that is, one in which the marital agreement is seriate. If A says to B, let us do X, spouse B assents because they have established a time-bound relationship in which the next move would be B's. The husband may suggest to his wife that they go to a movie; she says yes, and then she has the right to say, we can have a beer afterwards. Similarly, the wife may take certain rights, which the husband will grant because he knows he will have a turn in the near future. This time-binding is finite, and while it may not always be a matter of minutes (as it is in sexual intercourse) or of days, it is probably not months or years. Flexibility in time-binding is probably another word for "trust" in a relationship, and this may be the most workable of quid pro quos.[2]

The phenomenon of time in relationships — especially marriage — needs study. Relationships that are not rigidly time-bound have great flexibility, while some of the crises of various periods of family life may relate to time. That is, the unspoken promise never kept may, with the passing of time, become more obviously unlikely to be kept, for example, that the husband will spend more time with the family as soon as his business gets on its feet becomes less believable as time goes by and the children grow up; at some point the "promise is broken" simply by the passage of time.[3]

---

[2] Trust is obviously a key concept in marital and even national relationships. It is a belief that the other will do for you what you just did for him, and since you do not know when this will occur, trust appears not to be time-bound. But these are probably intervening signals that declare A's intent to repay B even though no specific date is ever set. I hope not to have my life insurance cashed, but that ad of the great Rock of Gibraltar constantly refurbishes my trust.

[3] So-called menopausal depression is often related by clinicians to the onset of women's inability to have children. My own observations led me to seriously question this. Among other considerations is the fact that the wish for a child may help deny an unsatisfactory marriage.

There is then a peculiar relationship, which can be observed in both marital and exploitative political situations, when the quid pro quo is not in fact time-bound but is treated as if it is. If A says to B, let us do X, B says yes because A indicates that eventually B will get his reward. B's day is allegedly coming, and though it never does, A keeps acting as if it is going to and B keeps acting as if he accepts this. These are often pathological relationships that in marriage are frequently characterized by depression and even suicide. The vicious cycle aspect of this relationship is apparent, the more B lets himself be conned, the more he has coming eventually and the less free he is to try another game, since he has so much already invested.

If the gist of these examples has been clear, it should not be necessary to point out that the quid pro quo is not overt, conscious, or the tangible result of real bargaining. Rather, this formulation is the pattern imposed by the observer on the significant redundancies of marital interaction, and should always be understood metaphorically, with the tacit preface, "It seems as if." The specifics of marital bargaining are not of interest to us. It is at the level of exchange of definitions of the relationship (and, therefore, of self-definition with the relationship) that we can usefully analyze in terms of quid pro quo. If we were to focus only on the content level of marital interaction, we might miss the probability that the so-called masochist does not like or need to suffer; he gets something out of the relationship by using the one-down position as a tactic.

Note, for instance, the following example[4]:

H: I wish you would fix yourself up. Take $50 and get a permanent, a facial
    — the works!
W: I'm sorry dear, but I don't think we ought to spend the money on me.
H: *%(@)! I want to spend it on you!
W: I know, dear, but there's all the bills and things.

Here the apparently one-down behavior of the wife is actually quite controlling. If we look beyond the particular $50 about which they are disputing, we can see the relationship they have worked out: the husband is allowed to complain about the wife and act in charge, but the wife indicates she does not intend to follow his orders, that in fact his orders are stupid, and, since she sets no time conditions, we do not know if she will ever get a permanent or not.

---

[4] These are not transcribed examples but were reported in couple therapy.

This is one clue to the quid pro quo. Rather than executing a piece of action, this couple is going through a repetitive exchange, which defines and redefines the nature of their relationship. Thus on another occasion:

H: Hey, I can't find any white shirts!
W: I'm sorry, dear; they're not ironed yet.
H: Send them to the laundry! I don't care what it costs!
W: We spend so much on groceries and liquor; I felt I should try to save a few pennies here and there.
H: Listen for @#$%!, I need shirts!
W: Yes, dear, we'll see about it.

Note that just as the wife does not specify when, nor whether she is really saying yes or no, the husband does not insist on clear, definite information. It would be misleading to ascribe motivation to this couple. To say he likes to bluster or she likes to frustrate him is senseless and yet irrefutable. What is important is their interactional system: once having established such a pattern of interaction, they are victims of blindness and reinforcement.[5] Further, their roles are defined not by "male aggressiveness" and "female passivity," but by the simple fact that wives are supposed to be pretty and to take charge of the laundry and husbands are affected by whether or not wives fulfill these expectations.

This is so obvious, yet we as researchers are victims of the sex-role propaganda, too. Most psychiatrists would probably doubt that a family in which the husband runs the house and the wife brings home the money could rear apparently healthy children. Yet in two such examples brought to our attention, this appears to be the case. To understand why these couples function well, we would do much better to analyze their present relationship and seek to identify their particular quid pro quo than to seek the answer in their individual backgrounds and calculate the probabilities that such individuals would meet and marry.

It is becoming more accepted among clinicians that there are no marital

---

[5] B. F. Skinner has stated that a periodic negative reinforcement is the most potent conditioner. Because couples are apart a good deal and engage in a variety of contingencies some of their negative interactions take on a periodic aspect. This may make it difficult for *A* to label *B* in black and white and yet enhance *B*'s vulnerability.

relationships that are unbalanced or impoverished for one spouse. Observation of the interaction reveals the "bargain" struck between alcoholic and spouse, or between wife-beater and wife. The quid pro quo reasoning, then, is still tautological and, within its own sphere of proof, just as irrefutable as notions of human instincts and sex roles. If one believes that marriage is a relationship bargain and is the judge of the terms of this bargain in any particular case, then he can prove his own hypothesis. Again it is important to restate that the concept of family rules in general and of the quid pro quo in particular is only a descriptive metaphor imposed by the observer on the redundancies he observes in interaction. This is not only true in the many important areas of the social sciences where the researcher must be both judge and jury, but it is also highly desirable as long as we avoid the pitfalls of reification and acknowledge the fictitious nature of all our constructs. This is a necessary first step if we are to devise a language which will elucidate and convey the process, not the property. Our goal is to do verbal justice to the phenomena in which we are avowedly interested. In our early attempts at interpersonal research, we are constantly limited by the only terminology we have — an ill-fitting bequest from theories of the individual. The notions of family rules and the marital quid pro quo are levers to force us away from the characteristics of individuals onto the nature of their interaction, and are at least somewhat more appropriate to describe the phenomena we will observe in interaction.

It is possible that the formulation of "rules" such as the quid pro quo has enormous predictive potential. If we are reasonably accurate in our formulation of a metaphor for a couple's relationship, we can forecast the likelihood of success or failure and even the fate of children in the family system. For instance:

The "Big Daddy Baby Doll" arrangement is not likely to be a workable quid pro quo. While Baby Doll may be able to continue her half of the bargain for some time, the material offerings with which Big Daddy must be constantly forthcoming are, after all, finite in number. There are only so many countries to tour and so many jewels that can be bought and worn. No matter what his wealth, her satiation will probably eventually endanger the quid pro quo so that the marriage must terminate or find a new level of operation.

Other arrangements may survive the early period of marriage but cannot be expected to accommodate children. For instance:

A couple had a quid pro quo of total independence; each pursued his own career and was succeeding. They scorned the usual financial and housekeeping arrangements, basing all decisions on the maximization of the independence of both. Though one might wonder how it happened in an atmosphere of total independence, the wife became pregnant; her career and way of life were drastically limited. The marriage foundered because the original quid pro quo could not possibly be made to include maternity and motherhood. A new relationship had to be established.

Some parental relationships can survive the onslaught of a little stranger, but cannot accommodate his emotional health: The family maxim seemed to be "People who live in glass houses shouldn't throw stones. Husband and wife scrupulously avoided even the mildest — and to us — criticism of each other, and in turn were not criticized by the spouse. This ban on information, however, provides a poor teaching context for children and is not likely to encourage healthy, spontaneous curiosity. The marriage lasts, but the brighter-than-average son was referred to therapy for marked academic underachievement.

These examples are, of course, retrospective. But our success in post-diction of psychopathology in children from blind analysis of examples of marital interaction in terms of the quid pro quo leads us to hope that, with refinement, prediction and prophylaxis of pathological systems are possible.

SUMMARY

A theory of marriage is proposed which is based on the relationship rather than the individuals. Specifically, the quid pro quo formulation holds that the similarities and differences between spouses comprise the metaphorical "bargain" on which the marital relationship is based. The advantages of this scheme are that (1) we have a language to aid our observation of truly interactional phenomena, and (2) there is the promise of improved predictive power when the "rules" of the relationship are grasped.

References

Jackson, D. (1965). Study of the family. *Family Process, 4* (1), 1–20.

Leik, R. (1963). Instrumentality & emotionality in family interaction. *Sociometry, 26*; 131–145.

Introduction and Overview

Webster's *New World Dictionary* (1970) defines research as "careful, systematic, patient study and investigation in some field of knowledge, undertaken to discover or establish facts or principles." Segmenting the following five chapters into a section on "research" distinct from the preceding ten papers on theory is misleading, in the sense that most of the papers presented thus far have been reports of research findings based on many years of careful, systematic, patient study of how people influence one another interactionally in the present moment. This has established a radically alternative theory of human behavior and a fresh approach to treatment consonant with this new ecologically oriented, contextual, and relational epistemology. On the other hand, as Jackson stated:

> To the proponents of a new theory falls the sometimes pedantic and arid, but more often illuminating, task of boring down to basic premises, to conceptual models and meta-theoretical considerations, which those who have a broad framework of agreement, theoretically, need not constantly remind each other of. When alternative premises, methodologies and data are proposed, the old and the new must be laid out side-by-side for comparison, and the newcomer has the duty to state with maximum possible clarity just what he does and does not assume (Chapter 17).

While Jackson was referring to theory here, the same can be said of research — especially when one is attempting to research behavioral phenomena based upon an alternative set of assumptions and data. The old and the new must be laid out side-by-side for comparison. In Chapter 19, "Patient and therapist observations on the circumstances of a schizophrenic episode," John Weakland and Jackson apply cultural anthropological research methodology, coupled with strict reliance on interactional theory, in the analysis of the therapy of a hospitalized schizophrenic patient.

Jackson's first book, entitled *The Etiology of Schizophrenia*, provided an overview of the existing research and treatment of this complex problem. In the introduction, included here as Chapter 20, Jackson reviewed the existing literature on schizophrenia from 1940 to 1960, setting forth a critique of the assumptions and (often erroneous) conclusions on which much of this research was based. Since this review was conducted more than 40 years ago, obviously prior to the recent advances in genetic, DNA, and pharmacological research, many will be tempted to dismiss as irrelevant Jackson's thorough review. Such off-handed dismissal would be naïve and unfortunate, in that many of the questions Jackson raised are as relevant (perhaps even more so) today as therapists attempt to make a case that Jackson articulated so well:

> Before we rush in with the cry of "constitution" or "heredity," it should be important to notice what effect rejection of the child by the mother has on the father, or whether there is a third person somewhere on the periphery who manifests occasional tenderness toward the child, thereby possibly saving him from the psychosis [and by implication any other symptom] (Chapter 10).

Jackson also clearly articulates the fundamental necessity of realizing the influence of the therapist as an observer who imposes his assumptions on that which is being observed:

> Over and over again it has been necessary to learn the lesson that the observer influences the observed ... In the field of mental health, we have not only to reckon with the natural effect of the observers' own bias but we also have to deal with a second variable: the effect of this bias on the patient (Chapter 20).

In Chapter 21, "Some Assumptions in the Recent Research on Schizophrenia" (1962), Robert Kantor and Jackson continue to review the primary assumptions upon which much of the research into schizophrenia then taking place was based. First outlining the assumptions implicit in Harry Stack Sullivan's Interpersonal Theory of human behavior, the chapter categorizes the then current research and provides a comprehensive review in light of Sullivan's conception. In reading this chapter, the readers might find impressive the balance that existed during the 1960s between the number of genetic and pharmacologically based studies on the one hand, and interpersonally and psychologically oriented studies on the other. Compare this with the overwhelming dominance of genetic and drug based research and the almost nonexistence of interactionally focused studies being funded today.

In Chapter 22, "A Method of Analysis of a Family Interview" (1961), Jackson, Jules Riskin, and Virginia Satir present the basic conceptual tools necessary to comprehend interactional process: symmetical and complementary behavioral exchanges, and the concept that people are constantly exchanging messages that can be understood metaphorically to be proposals about the definition of the relationship. An analysis is then made of a five-minute "blind" audio recoding of a couple's interaction. In "Family Research on the Problem of Ulcerated Colitis" (1966), Chapter 23, Jackson and Irving Yalom describe a research investigation they were conducting with eight families, each with a child experiencing the problem of ulcerated colitis. In this original study, the family dynamics unique to the development of this particular psychosomatic illness are conceptualized and discussed, and in so doing "restrictiveness," "restricted family," and "recursive arborization" are introduced as concepts useful in the study of family interactional patterns.

CHAPTER 19

Patient and Therapist Observations on the Circumstances of a Schizophrenic Episode[1]

John H. Weakland and Don D. Jackson

(1958)

"Now see that noble and most sovereign reason,
Like sweet bells jangled, out of tune and harsh."
— "Hamlet"

Bateson, Jackson, Haley, and Weakland[2] have recently outlined a theory of schizophrenia in rather general terms. This paper consists of the verbatim transcript of the major portion of a psychotherapeutic interview with a schizophrenic patient, with accompanying analytic comments based on the concepts presented in the earlier article (Bateson, Jackson, Haley, & Weakland, 1956).

---

[1] From the *AMA Archives of Neurology & Psychiatry*, May 1958, 79, pp. 554–574. Reprinted with permission.

[2] From the Palo Alto Medical Clinic, Palo Alto, Calif. This investigation has been aided by a grant from the Josiah Macy, Jr. Foundation. From the Communication in Research Project directed by Gregory Bateson, administered by the Department of Anthropology, Stanford University, and carried out at the VA Hospital, Palo Alto, Calif.

Thus their theory is here shown in relation to basic psychiatric data, the actual interpersonal communication of a patient, including the messages of the other party, which heretofore have too often been neglected.

This particular interview is focused on the circumstances of the patient's psychotic break (his second). Apart from acute psychotic states during military service, there has been a paucity of data available in the literature about the factors surrounding the onset of a schizophrenic psychosis, although this period of remarkably rapid and extensive change of behavior is of great practical and theoretical importance.

This is especially true if one includes as relevant data the examination of those others immediately playing significant roles in the patient's breakdown. These data are often neglected, or their significance is denied. For example, it was the reading of one of the early papers on the psychotherapy of schizophrenia by Laforgue (1936) that led one of us (DDJ) to become interested in the concept of family homeostasis. Laforgue mentioned that at a significant point in his female patient's therapy her sister (with whom she lived) became severely depressed. He attributed the sister's difficulty to a manifestation of the same unfortunate genetic structure that had caused his patient's schizophrenia. He did not note that the sister's depression was coincident with a sudden improvement in his patient.

Obviously, if schizophrenia is prejudged a hereditary disorder, the therapist's view of the data available to him, including precipitating factors, will be limited. Such a bias may be present when it is reported that an examination of the circumstances surrounding the onset of a schizophrenic psychosis demonstrates that there were no stressful factors operating and thus the disorder must have been psychologically (constitutionally) caused. It is our opinion that stress is a private matter and cannot be evaluated from a so-called normogenic viewpoint. That is to say, we hold that what is stressful to any individual depends on its meaning or significance in relation to his life history. It is well known, for example, that a success of some kind can play a crucial role in the onset of some depressions and in suicides, and is responsible for the onset of acute anxiety states in some neurotics. Particularly in the obscure matter of the precipitation of psychosis, we have a situation for empirical inquiry, not for a priori judgments from oversimplified assumptions. This need not mean that each case is unique and isolated; uniformities may be found at the level of personal significance. It is well to recall that even in the area of clearly organized disease, what seems "enough stress" depends on prior life experience, and, even more, upon the state of medical knowledge. Thus, microscopic organisms were once considered an insufficient etiological explanation of organic disease, whereas the notion of "bad humors" and "vapors" was widely accepted as sufficient, though these could not be observed at all.[3]

THEORETICAL VIEWPOINT ON FAMILY INTERACTION

Bateson, Jackson, Haley, and Weakland[4] postulated that part of the etiology of schizophrenia is a communication sequence they labeled "a double bind." A double-bind relationship, most simply, can be described as a hostile dependent involvement where one of the parties insists on a response to multiple orders of messages which are mutually contradictory, and the other (the schizophrenic patient-to-be) cannot comment on these contradictions or escape from the situation. Obviously, a double-bind relationship can exist only within a special family or group relationship, since, for example, a child could break out of a double-bind situation with his mother if his father were capable of handling such contradictory multi-leveled messages and thus setting an example and offering support to the child.

For purposes of description, we speak of the child's being in a double-bind relationship with the mother, and yet the mother is as much a victim caught up in a morass of her own maneuvers as the child is. In a real sense, she needs the child for her own mental economy. Evidence for this viewpoint can be found in observing what happens to the family interrelations when a schizophrenic patient makes a successful recovery while living within the family framework. Similarly, the siblings or spouse of the patient can be one factor in the double-bind situation and yet to the casual clinical observer may appear as the healthy one. The person who has culturally sanctioned motives and attitudes will have obvious advantages over the other partner. Such a person may be severely crippled, for example, by inflexible righteousness and morality, and yet never come near the confines of a psychiatrist's office. This whole question of "Who the kept and who the keeper?" which is central in the interview and discussion to follow, is a complex and important matter, which needs further study.

---

[3] For further discussion of this matter, see Jackson (1957a).
[4] For further discussion of this matter, see Jackson (1957b).

THE PATIENT AND HIS FAMILY SITUATION

X is in his middle 30's. He was born, one of several brothers, in Eastern Europe and was brought to the United States as a young child. His father died when he was an infant, and he was raised by his mother and an angry, violent stepfather, now also dead. The mother, who is a member of a reformist Orthodox sect, *X* describes as inordinately prideful, stingy, and retaining her old-country ways. *X* seems to have been somewhat solitary as a child, but there is no evidence he had any incapacitating difficulties, mental or physical. He completed high school successfully, and afterward, went into the Army. He had about two years of service in the United States and the Pacific areas as a laboratory technician. Two weeks before the end of the war, he had an especially good letter form his favorite brother, stating they should get closer together after the war. A few days later, *X* learned that his brother had been killed in action, and shortly after had a psychotic attack, of unstated nature. He was hospitalized, was returned to the United States, and three months later was discharged "in partial remission." *X* now appears to minimize this episode, saying he was not so much "crazy" as afraid he'd be killed like his brother and desirous of getting home.

After discharge he entered college, taking a pre-medical curriculum. However, in three years he had completed only two years' work, and in three more years he had done one year's work. He then left school and began to work at a variety of minor technical or clerical jobs, changing every year or so and repeatedly getting into difficulties with employers and other employees.

In 1950, he married a girl whose family came from a geographical and religious background similar to his own. Her mother had died when she was a young child, and at first she was reared by her father and his sister, but later was sent by her father to a Catholic school. Catholicism and her relationship to the nuns remain very important to her. Mrs. *X* has moderately severe epilepsy. At the time of the patient's second psychotic episode, which is discussed in the recorded interview, he and his wife and two small children lived in an apartment building owned by her suspicious, irascible, and aging father. His mother lived nearby and despite being a source of friction between the patient and his wife, was a frequent visitor in the home, partly because she was available as a babysitter. There were frequent arguments among the various family members over religion and finances. Finally, as described in the following interview, *X* again broke down and was hospitalized with a diagnosis of "acute schizophrenic reaction, paranoid type" and "schizo-affective psychosis."

INTERVIEW AND COMMENTS

This interview took place four months after the patient's break. He had then been seeing the therapist in 3 hourly interviews a week for 10 weeks. There had also been several joint interviews with the patient and his wife. All of these interviews were tape-recorded, with the knowledge of all parties. The first third of this transcribed interview, before discussion became focused on the circumstances of the break, is here excerpted and summarized to cover certain points importantly related to the later material or to our basic theory. The final two-thirds is given verbatim, with no editing except concealment of names. Our ideas and comments, developed subsequently, are interspersed in parentheses:

X: Could you help me get out of here? — I mean — within a month or so?

T: Well, I told your ward — I don't want to do anything to hinder you getting out of here.

X: Well, that isn't positive — I mean that's — didn't give me a push. I have to get a little help, to get out . . .

(X opens by asking for specific help. This is a realistic request in that the therapist might be able to influence an administrative decision, but X also shows his own feelings of helplessness, which appear more fully later on in the interview.)

Then X, in explanation of why the therapist should give him a push, starts to develop two themes of concern about staying in the hospital: 1. The present ward doctor, a woman, is about to leave, and whoever takes over might leave him in for months. 2. He is uncertain about going home and asks the therapist to take a stand.

X: I'd either stay here completely or go home completely — if you gather what I mean —

T: Why do you suppose you might have a feeling like that?

X: Well I don't know — why I might I mean it's the — as if it's the same question, in a small way it's as if why, uh, why did I have the nervous breakdown in the first place. It's just about the same question — and if I knew, I'm not saying I could do anything about it, but at least I could, at least I could — understand — what it was . . .

(X states he must either stay in or get out — a black-or-white viewpoint. This is almost immediately related to the psychotic break as "the same question" as that of why he broke down in the first place. X also deals with the question in terms of the "illusion of alternatives," a concept to be developed in the discussion.)

T: Has it got something, maybe, to do with changing what you're adjusting to — back and forth? That you sort of adjust to being home and then adjust to being here — or something like that?

X: It might be, that might be it. (pause) Well, I wonder if it really would do me good to to stay away from my mother more, like B. [his wife] seems to want — maybe it would help, uh — less uh, it would cause less conflicts; I'm not sure of it myself; but it might, might be part, it might be true; in other words it's a (pause)

T: This, again, is sort of around the topic — should you stay in one place, or can you live with more than one sort of thing at a time?

X: Well, in that case it seems as though B, B would be disturbed if I would see mother too much, or she more or less demands to know every single thing we say, and then she'd notice whether it was disturbing me or whether it would disturb her (pause)

(When the therapist essays a general statement about X's "this or that" problem, originally about home or hospital, X shifts to mention a similar conflict around "wife or mother," emphasizing his keeping away from mother more as possibly being helpful, though he lives with his wife, and the transactions immediately preceding his break mainly concern his wife. He is covertly asking how the therapist feels about his leaving or staying, and if there is a disagreement with the female administrator.)

X then shifts back to difficulties about getting out of the hospital — could his wife help? — and especially the change of doctors; maybe the new one will think differently about him than the old one. The therapist ties these several situations, and feelings of helplessness, together, then comments:

T: (It looks as if) you are afraid that one person will say one thing, and another person will say another thing, and you won't know what to do about it.

X: Well, that's right; in other words, all I can do is just, uh, take the general opinion. In other words, it's a — it's sort of a coming together of the minds. Like, well, in one respect if I should compare — uh — coming together of the mind of my mother and *B*, well, and if I compare that with, say, coming together in my mind of you and the [ward] doctor — if you and the doctor had the same opinion of each other as *B*. and my mother have of each other, well, they'd never be a coming of the mind together — there never would, but, thank God, there isn't that particular situation; there isn't an enmity between you and the doctor over me. See?

T: Um hmn.

X: Such as there is between my mother and *B*. So, of course, I imagine there is more hope of getting out — than, uh — than that.

(*X* now overtly connects the therapist and ward doctor with the mother and wife but does so by utilizing denial. It is not certain how much ground for fearing such a conflict he had in reality, though it can be said that if one existed, it would probably have been mainly covert, therefore all the more difficult for him. There may have been a repetition of his childhood situation, as covert or tangential maternal–paternal conflict seems common in the families of schizophrenics.

There is then some further discussion of *X*'s feelings of helplessness, which he contrasts with opening his mouth and saying how he feels. But if he does, his wife, for example, would get angry. She might even get a divorce. Why does he feel helpless? As *X* sees it, it is because if he should assert himself by voicing his feelings, he might be abandoned. But the situation is actually more complex than the mere alternative of keeping quiet or speaking up. It later becomes evident that also if he keeps quiet his wife is angry and implies he is only a "mother's boy" or a "weakling," which she does not want. Thus, the apparent alternative of keeping quiet or taking a stand does not offer a real choice — the two possibilities lead to the same outcome, the threat of abandonment. The question, then, becomes one of why he cannot see and comment on the fact that whatever he does he is blamed. This situation is the center of his helplessness.)

Then *X* says that sometimes he does try to get his way, and speaks of getting his wife to promise not to go out to church alone at night, because she once had an epileptic attack on the way; she told him about the fit, showed her bruises, but said, "Don't worry."

(X mentioned his wife's "spells" very briefly and obliquely in his previous remarks about having to avoid angering her. He seems to feel caught: If he is assertive, she might have a seizure — thus abandoning him, as well as increasing her "control by helplessness." If he is compliant, she goes out alone at night, and may have a seizure, too. He also allows himself to be trapped by the way she exhibits her epilepsy but then rejects his concern about it.

An earlier fear that his mother might be hurt by his violent stepfather, and he be helpless about it, expressed in other interviews, may underlie these current concerns. As a child, he learned there was a high value placed on his protective concern toward his mother.)

The therapist inquired about possibilities of argument or discussion between X and his wife.

X: Well, I'll say that these years we've been married, we've argued quite a bit —

T: Uh-huh.

X: and we — I guess she'd call them discussions; I call them arguments — over religion, over finances, over things she planned to do, and I've always tried to — well to me, to take the more cautious . . .

T: Uh huh.

X: Attitude, and as far as religion, well her, her religion is all, is all right, it's just the one and I try to — to show that, well in a way, I didn't quite agree with that, and, uh, I don't know. She seems to like to — I know she said she's had a lot of discussions about religions, and she defended Catholicism and nobody could beat her down on it, nobody could. She took pride in that, and I found out later that — even with my utmost reasoning and; uh, whatever I could do, I never could, uh — just like she'd say, I never could beat her down; she'd never agree. It's just like uh, she — an extreme case I was going to mention, she gave me her promise not to go to this church at night, and yet she went without telling me and then she said, "Well, that's not deception," because it's a good thing she was doing, and you only practice deception when you're doing an evil thing. Well, of course, what can — you see there's a definition that — how can you fight a person when they set their own definition? That isn't playing the ball.

(When he tries to discuss things, his wife defeats him by sticking to one extreme position, though one that also has strong cultural sanction. But if he does manage to seem in the right, despite his usual tentativeness, she shifts from one extreme to another, by redefining everything at a higher level of interpretation, which she controls. She deceives him about not going out to church, but because she is going to church, this deception isn't deception. X. is thus involved with a person who overtly gives him contradictory messages, and denies that this is so. It is our impression that pre-schizophrenics are particularly blind to changes of context as a controlling device by others. This difficulty in handling contradictions appears more fundamental than X's somewhat similar difficulty in handling opposing influences from two different persons.)

There is some more discussion of arguing. X reemphasizes with another example that if someone shifts definitions, you not only can't win; there's no getting together. He didn't think arguing was disturbing until he had this breakdown. People take advantage of others in arguments; but if you do, they may resent it and pay you back. (From here on is verbatim unbroken sequence.)

T: So that this sort of brings up some things we were talking about before. A couple of times you were on your way to getting your own way, and then you begin to feel sort of uneasy about it — even with B, a couple of times you were arguing with her about something, looked like she was giving in to you; you sort of then said: "Well, go do it your own way."

X: Well, I did that a couple of times, here, yeah. Only before, when I used to argue with her, I'd never do that; I — I, uh, I wouldn't give in that way. Uh, I imagine, uh, I'm getting back to where I could argue more now, but, uh — I'm thinking that the — maybe that isn't the best thing to argue, I know — all, the only — sort of a clue — that I have — it's, just before I had my nervous breakdown, I had an argument with my father-in-law, and I was kind of arguing with B in a way, although she didn't think it was much of an argument, but I got very disturbed over it. Only I know this was the week when I wasn't feeling well. And I even woke up — from a dream that was very uncomfortable, I couldn't, I don't know what the dream was, just sort of an uncertainty, just that's all I can describe it, an uncertainty, and, uh, when, uh — another thing — we stayed out a little late there. It was on account of B that I did that. I — I, that's why I'm kind of blaming her, for the occasion, and my father-in-law really raised the roof — and he seemed to despise us so much, and it hurt me; in other words, that attitude in his — it seemed to hurt me, and I could see that my mother was siding with my father-in-law, and that hurt me also. I tried to explain, but they wouldn't accept the explanation.

(X recalls having a horrible dream the week he got sick: He can only say it was about "uncertainty." But uncertainty is a main theme of the whole interview, and he goes on at once to mention one of the situations it is related to — being caught between two other people; the other being concealed or denied contradictory messages from one person. And he can't resolve the uncertainty, because no matter what he tries — argument or explanation — he is rejected. All these matters are mentioned in close connection with his psychotic break.)

T: What was this about?

X: Well, we went out to buy him some apples, and we, we stopped in at his apartment house and got some information for him, and B and I went shopping, and we spent quite a lot of time in the store, and where she likes to go. And we went out to change a wristwatch for her, and it was way on the other side of the city. And then she wanted to stop in at the convent — at the, the M ... High School, and she spent quite a little while there with the nun, and we were talking, and uh, fin — finally, I went home, but I phoned into the post office that, that I was ill, and, uh — I really wasn't too ill; I just couldn't make it on time. They, they have a ruling — if you don't make it on time they — especially for subs, like me, they could just send you home, see — without working.

T: Uh huh.

X: That's your punishment. And so I phoned in, and, that's, that's when my father-in-law got so disturbed, because he knew I'd missed the work — see, I missed the work; I said: "Well, it's not fatal; I haven't done anything wrong. They know I am not coming!" and uh, yet he, he just seemed so upset over it; and my mother told me: "He's been upset now for about three hours, waiting for you people to come home, you know — you — you've been gone all day."

(He was doing things for his wife and her father; this made him late, and he was blamed for it. Again, it probably appears to him that if he is "good," he may be accepted; but this is illusory. It seems that X is afraid to face openly even the possibility of a clear rejection — in this instance at the job — another uncertainty arising largely from an apparent "wife-or job" alternative — and has to deal with this evasively by saying he's sick and thereby lowering his self-esteem.)

T: What upset him so much about this?

X: Well, because we should have returned so much sooner, according to his mind, and what — what it, he thought we'd gone out here to Palo Alto to *B*, *B*'s aunt; that's what he thought, or else we took a trip somewhere. Uh, in other words, it just wasn't right for us to do that — that's what.

T: I find it a little difficult to understand what he was so disturbed about, particularly since just Wednesday afternoon *B* was talking about how lenient he was about her coming and going before she was married.

X: Well, uh, that's true, but this case of her — her aunt, see — she never, she never tells when she visits the aunt. He had a misunderstanding with her, and he doesn't like *B* to visit her, although now she says finally that he has agreed to that, to her visiting her aunt, but he still, he still doesn't want to have anything to do with that aunt, and, uh, I don't know — he didn't know that we went to the aunt — which, we didn't go, but he thought that we had taken a trip, and he was disturbed that — uh —

T: It looks like he thought — you might have?

X: Well, we might have, but that didn't seem to be the thing that was bothering him. The thing that bothered him was that I should've been to work on time; in other words, it's so important — to get to work on time and, and see — see the work is very important as far as he is concerned.

(*X*'s difficulties again force him to be caught in the middle. The father-in-law is probably angry with his daughter for deceiving him and for irresponsibly keeping her husband away from his work. However, he takes it out on the patient, who accepts the full blame; he can neither point out the father-in-law's contradictions about an agreement that wasn't agreement [as daughter's deception wasn't deception] nor get together with him to blame her jointly for being irresponsible. By his accepting being the scapegoat, perhaps *X* escapes, temporarily, from facing problems of contradictions, mixed feelings, and deception, with the father-in-law and with his wife.)

T: What importance does that — does it have to him?

X: Well, that I should have a good job, and keep the job, and not — not dillydally with it. Of course, I — I always — I know I said always — be punctual, and I always try to work good, and just — for my own, it's my own nature, and not just his. I know that.

T: Although what it strikes me, is that he certainly seems to take a very powerful concern.

X: Yes, it's a paternal attitude. Very, very interested in and — and, uh, in a way, I — I always wanted to cultivate his good will, like I told you all along; in this case I could see that, that we just had that argument and then, this happened, you see? It just sort of added fuel on the fire.

T: And, in this argument about you, uh — should have been there on time to go to work — your mother also got into this?

X: Oh, yes, she jumped in both feet and, "Where have you been?" and she didn't say too much to B; but she was really digging into me there, and, uh, well, I — I just told them: "Simmer down; simmer down," you know; "Everything is all right; there's nothing to get excited about."

T: Were you all together at this time?

X: Yeah; she was home looking at the kids.

T: Uh-huh.

X: When we got on a trip like this, I'd usually try to get my m — my mother to look after the children; it's one of the reasons I always like to have my mother in good terms with B so — just for that purpose.

T: So that really everybody — just before you had your break then, everybody was on good enough terms, so that

X: Oh yes.

T: You were all gathered together — in the house.

X: Yes, definitely, yes.

T: So that the great d — I mean regardless of some of these previous disagreements.

X: Yeah.

T: Uh.

X: Still . . .

T. The real thing didn't blow up until you got sick.

X: That's right. That's very true — yeah.

T: I mean, this in spite of . . .

X: Yes, in . . .

T: In spite of what I heard about before . . .

X: That's right. (overlapping)

T: About the time B was so upset — by hearing what your mother was saying and

X: Sure. That's right. In other words, this finally was enough of a — of an occasion to cause a permanent — or it looks like it's a permanent cleavage. In other words, he's when he's getting now to the point where you'd he calls my mother a snake — and he's so vicious against her, and B's threatening divorce, I want — well, you see this is, they're just playing it — pretty tough now.

(X accepts his father-in-law's control and interprets it as benevolent, a paternal attitude, to which he responds with an effort at "goodness" again; he aims "to cultivate his good will." Yet everyone is jumping on X; how does he himself invite this? Perhaps just by his "goodness." He fears that everything will fall apart and that he will be completely abandoned, left without anyone. A similar fear seems implicit in his statement that he wants his wife and mother to get along so that the children will be cared for. This fear seems extreme, but his childhood situation has given him real cause to be concerned about the solidarity of the home. It is perhaps also relevant to this abandonment theme that his first psychotic episode occurred shortly after the news that his favorite brother had been killed.)

T: Um hm.

X: That's it; that's all I could say.

T: But this, this situation when you got home then; it seems like you must have felt like everybody was jumping on you for something that wasn't even really your doing, and . . .

X: Well . . .

T: I mean, as you recounted it.

X: Well, I felt (overlapping)

T: It was mainly B was going from here to there, and taking a lot of time about it.

X: I felt that way because, whenever I go with B it takes so much, uh, time. In other words, I always — the time — try to hurry her up. "Hurry-hurry-hurry up" and, uh seems she isn't the hurrying type. And no doubt we, we stopped in, uh, a drive-in and had something to eat, and uh, all I know is that B wanted to go to this, un — convent; and I blew up, and I said: "No, you're not going; we're not going; we got to get home." See, I knew I had to get home; I thought I'd make it in time for work, and then, uh, I felt, then I had just this nagging. What it was — I — I know I wasn't feeling too well, and, I told her "Well, look, you're driving me nuts." Well, I really didn't blame her — I wasn't really blaming her for it. I said: I don't feel well; I can only do one thing at a time" — I know I said but this's actually the way I felt.

T: Um-hmm.

X: I couldn't seem to, to just be relaxed. I had to just keep my mind on one track and I said: "Well, if, if you'd like to go, to go to the convent, it's all right with me." So she said, "OK"

T: You mean you changed around —

X: Yeah, I changed, I changed around. I know I'd done that a couple of times before, but not too often, 'cause — maybe I felt sorry for her or somethin'. I knew this was an opportunity for her to see this nun she loves so much, and, uh, she always praised her so much and everything. She's just like a mother to her, and the one person in the world in whom she has complete faith, and all that sort of rot — well to me, you know, it's to me it's rot; maybe to her it isn't.

T: Why didn't she take care of going to see the nun? Instead of getting you to do it for her and miss your job?

X: Well, uh, in a way I guess she knew that I, I probably could call in, uh, late, and uh, so that's what happened — we

T: And what did *B* say when this argument developed when you got home?

X: She didn't have much to say about it. She was rather kind of quiet.

T: And she just left you to take it?

X: Well — she went in with the children, and I think she might have said a couple of things, uh, uh, but we did not mention the fact we stopped in at the, at the convent. I don't think I mentioned it — to my father-in-law.

(When the therapist puts some of the blame on the patient's wife, *X* rises to the occasion and agrees: He had told her: "You're driving me nuts," a comment on her communications. But he soon backs down again; as the interview goes on, in general he minimizes and excuses her part in the situation, and emphasizes difficulties with her father. This relative protection of her seems related to attitudes around "mother." Mrs. *X* went to the convent to see a nun who was "like a mother to her"; her leaving X to face the music later was excused by her going in to be a mother to their children, and so on. X also tends to minimize his own mother's part in the attack on him. X's emphasis on the father-in-law and minimization of any maternal part in his difficulties are similar to the situation we have observed in other families of schizophrenics: The father is rather like one of the children, and he collaborates with them — often by engaging in manifest, but unessential, conflicts — in screening the mother's activities from view.)

T: Why was that?

X: Well, I don't know. He, he may have thought that wasn't exactly a good excuse, you know? That if 't been a flat tire, or something wrong with the car, well, you see, that would've been a good excuse; but just going to the convent, I don't imagine that it would have been such a good excuse, and then my mother, I know she wouldn't agree with that.

T: Well, neither, neither one of them would have accepted this.

X: That excuse.

T: As any reason.

X: Yes, and I told them.

T   Even, even though your father-in-law was the one who put B in charge of the Catholic nuns in the first place.

X: Yes, that's right, and my mother had disagreed with him like that as though he had committed a crime. I know she, she'd mentioned it to him: "Why did you do that — why did you put your daughter, and make her a Catholic," and all that, uh. As far as she is concerned, see, she showed her intolerance to the Catholic Church right there, and many other times. So finally, you see, she's, she did work herself so that — that is why I don't blame myself — myself for anything that happened: I know I did open my mouth, in a few vital spots, such as to Father H., and

(It seems that only something practical and accidental would serve to excuse his lateness — something extraneous. Anything relevant, especially personal desires and feelings, would bring up all the old differences they seem unable really to resolve, such as that between X's father-in-law and wife over the convent and the aunt; X seems very eager to avoid such conflicts.)

T: Well, I still think about this particular time, which seems pretty important — and it looks like so you must have felt that you were sort of standing there all alone, everybody giving you hell for something that wasn't your fault.

X: Well, uh, I just took it.

T: Why should you take it?

X: Well, I don't know — that's a good question. I, I don't know; it's a good — maybe I, I should have blown up and let off steam; maybe that would have helped.

T: Why couldn't you just say: "*B* insisted on going to the convent"?

X: Well, you see, it's sort of a mixed-up affair, I, I'd say that, and then what, what would I get from *B*, see? You understand?

T: Well, didn't *B* insist on it?

X: Well, no, she didn't insist on it; that's just it — she, she asked; and then I blew up and told her "no."

T: Yeah.

X: And then I changed my mind and said: "Well, would you like to? All right? See?

T: So partly you, you went along with it.

X: See, I went along with it.

T: Well, then, we get back to the question: Why did you go along with it?

X: Well, that's a good question, too; like I said, I felt sorry for her and thought, well, she, if 't means so damn much to her, well let her have — uh, let her, let her have her way. I know she wanted to see her. She — I had a feeling if we wouldn't go, she'd be —

T: She'd make you suffer for it.

X: (overlapping): She'd be pouting down her nose, yes; she'd be pouting down on her nose.

T: O.K.; so in a way you feel she did make you go.

X: In a way, yes. It's in other words it's ah — I — I'd the experience before, and I sort of learned that. In other words, if I — if I'd agree to her wishes, you see, it'd be easier on me. She'd have a better attitude; she'd have a happier attitude. I don't know why that affected me so much when she had the — nasty attitude, and there'd sort of be of tension on me — for a long time; maybe it would last a day or two.

(Here *X* also shows again how he, too, can't settle on anything. Just as he is about to take a definite stand of his own, he backs down, again under the illusion that he can buy acceptance.)

T: Yeah, she would sort of hold a grudge on you.

X: Yeah, she'd hold a grudge and

T: Make you know it.

X: Yeah, and I thought: "Well what the hell! See 'em and, uh, and on the other hand, it turned out the other way. Those two were waiting for me with a — might say a loaded shotgun, I mean, that is emotionally; that's what it was — they just blasted into us and, uh, well, I thought, I didn't think much of it. Then, the next day, I didn't think anything untoward, I said, well, uh, I slept late, as is my custom, and, uh, went to work, and then after a couple of hours, I started to feel funny

T: Uh huh.

X: I, I didn't know why I, I, but first I thought the — the supervisor was watching me, and, sure enough, I kind of thought they were watching me, so, "Well, am I doing something wrong?" and, then, I, I had the feeling that there was tension in me, and, and if I could only last out until — well, until lunch time, or last out until, uh, a couple of hours, I'd be all right, it would pass.

T: Uh huh.

X: Well, seems though there was just a little too much tension just to pass that lightly; so, that's all I can say. It seemed to build up more.

T: Um hm.

X: And, uh, I got sort of befuddled state, where I couldn't seem to — my simple task was to separate long letters from short letters, see? It's very simple; I mean there's nothing simpler than that, and then I started getting confused.

T: Uh-huh.

X: I seemed to pay too much attention to the in-between letters. Couldn't decide whether they go with the long or the shorts.

(The problem of decision versus terrible uncertainty has been a theme throughout. It has appeared in relation to dealing with differences of opinion between two other people, and dealing with contradictory messages from one person. Here, as *X* nears his break, it reappears in a bare, almost diagrammatic form.[5] This instance is without manifest interpersonal context; however, it can certainly be related to the patient's own tendency to be an "in between," and his need to please and conciliate everyone, all the time, by "doing right.")

T: Uh huh.

X: So, well, I felt, I felt that was kind of funny: I talked a little to the guy who worked on the other side. And, then I, I couldn't seem to give the right answers; I was — I seemed to be too critical of myself. I don't know why. I thought the best thing would be to shut up, and yet I couldn't seem to shut up ...

T: Uh huh.

X: The best thing would be to just keep quiet; and if I could have kept quiet that would have been fine; but I, I didn't. I seemed to talk with the — uh — then I just get disturbed and wonder: "Am I saying the right thing?" Then I asked one of the guys, I said: "Well, I just don't feel right; what shall I do?" "If you don't feel right, why don't you go home?" I said: "Well that's a good thing. I mean, I don't, this would be the first time I'd have to go home in a year and a half." And I went up and asked — and, uh, well, later George told me, he said "Well, your face was white, just white"; so you see it really was evidently.

T: Uh huh.

X: The autonomic system, or something, wasn't working right. The blood was drained from my face, uh; something was wrong; so, when I went home, I took a jitney, and I just kept quiet all the way, just trying to think: "Well, how could I explain this to my father-in-law or to *B* or to mother?"

T: Uh huh. Sort of like things would be back where they were the night before?

X: Yeah, that's right.

T: Uh huh.

X: I thought well, well; then I started to get disturbed — sort of like in a trap or something.

T: Like there didn't seem to be any way out.

---

[5] *X*'s collapse over inability to discriminate between long and short letters sounds much like Pavlov's production of experimental neurosis in dogs by setting them a circle-ellipse discrimination problem, which was eventually made too difficult by changing the ellipse nearer and nearer to circular form.

X: There's no way out, that's right; and when I got in, I just started crying. Then when I was crying like I told you, I felt in a way: "This will punish the old bastard!" You know what I mean?

(*X* is more and more concerned with "rightness." "Am I doing right; am I talking right; am I even functioning right physically?" — but how can he find out? Desperate as he is, he feels it is also wrong to ask about it, or leave work; and if he goes home, it will be like the night before; so he's trapped. In our view of schizophrenia, the trap is real, and centers on the fact that the child must not bring it out if he does feel bad or upset, because this is an accusation to his mother that she is not a "good mother," and she cannot stand this. So the line of communication for possible correction of difficulties is blocked.)

T: Uh huh.
X: The old man. And this way, of course, I wouldn't talk with him or anything, and he just sat around for a while, then after th — minute you see, B managed to, take me to the, uh, hospital, but actually, you see, now that I look at it, nothing actually — st — uh — started, started me wrong — didn't happen, until I, I, in fact when I was in L. Hospital for a while, for a few hours, and they couldn't agree where to send me, or — I wanted to go home — see? I told B: "Well, let's go home; let's take a taxi and go home, or something." "No, let's wait a while," and then when they finally decided to, to take me to M. Hospital, I had the idea that this, uh, was one of the aides dressed up as a cab man.
T: Uh huh.
X: And I thought: "Well, they're just testing me out"; see, already I was imagining things.

(*X* has a delusion involving deception but explains it away, much as his wife explained away her deceiving him — "It's for a good purpose.")

T: Uh huh.
X: And then, uh, the funny thing is that that darned meter seemed to spin fast, you know, real fast — and then it slowed down; it almost stopped just — just — when, actually you know darn well that the meter just has one constant speed.
T: Uh huh.

255

X: So then that confused me; so I says: "Well, is the meter rigged?"; you know?

T: Uh huh.

X: For this — and then I was getting very upset. I, I was saying: "Well, you're going the wrong way"; I'd say: "Well, *B*, you should go this way"; then finally, after a while: "Well, you're going the right way; looks to me like I know part of the city" and uh, finally I mean I kept this up until the doctor at *M*. I don't remember the first night how I slept, but I sure got very upset for the next few days.

T: I wonder if we go back a minute again, to the night where the argument went on — uh — what did you do — while they were — while your father-in-law and your mother were telling you this was all so terrible?

X: Well, I know he was in no condition even to just talk to. He just s — stalked off, sullen, and I thought: "Well, I better let him cool off for a while."

T: He just sort of gave you hell and then walked away?

X: Yeah, and with her, I just tried to tell her, but she just, you know, mother was saying: "Well, you're wrong, you're wrong; you know you, you shouldn't have done that," uh

T: And you mean nobody even gave you a chance to talk back to them?

X: That's right. I couldn't reason with her; she's, uh, all in his favor, I mean, and so, I didn't say much to *B*; I know I was, but I don't know whether that was actually what caused it.

T: Well, I'm just trying to get a clearer picture of the circumstances.

X: That's what happened, though . . .

T: So you didn't really say much to anybody?

X: No. So, uh, well, it's hard to just keep, keep something in you in; just keep it in you, uh, and be to blame for it. I mean — that's

T: Sure.

X: Then I realized, you see, this was such a small item actually; this was a very small item. The thing that I really, I raised a fuss over, like I say, was when he accused me of not even paying the interest on the — this property, damn property, I — it's not worth over $10,000 or $12,000; he paid $17,000 for it, and uh, it is such an inconvenience after he bought it in, and then so many disadvantages.

T: How come you — when — after they all told you you were all in the wrong about this, you didn't say anything to *B* either?

X: Well, I felt that *B* knew the circumstance, and that she, she was with me all day, and, uh, (pause) I kind of felt that she sympathized with me in a way; you know what I mean? I mean, she didn't have much to say but I knew that she wasn't against me.

T: Was she there at all when they were giving you the devil?

X: Yes, she was right there.

T: Um. But she didn't speak up?

X: Well, I don't know, uh, whether she spoke up or not; if she did, I didn't pay much attention to it.

T: But, at any rate, you don't have any recollection of her saying anything about: "Well, I wanted to go to the convent," or anything of that sort?

X: No; no, she didn't. I don't think she (pause) Later, I think I told mother that we went to see this nun, and she says: "Oh, that's it"; you know, it's B's fault, you know. I think I told mother that — she jumped on B, as she usua — she usually does; she usually does blame B for everything, see? As far as mo — mother is concerned, everything is B's fault, and, uh, so, uh

T: "Later" when do you mean by "later on"? You mean that evening? Or

X: Yeah, she — that evening — yeah, I, I mentioned it to her. Then again; well, it's true, one thing mother knew a lot about our life, a lot of things. I, I'd tell her, uh, you know, in other words, uh, confidences, you might say. Uh, not about our very personal life but, you know, things like, like the — handling of the children, things like that. So, uh, now I feel calmed down to the extent that, uh, I feel like I could go back to work.

(X is again protecting his wife, by taking the blame instead of accusing her of making him late. However, this also enables him to interpret her silence as sympathy; if he doesn't take the blame, he fears losing this "sympathy." This is made clearer when he tentatively accuses her to his mother and mother totally takes his side, denying anything positive with his wife — "everything is B's fault." At this, X seems fearful that things have gone too far the other way, that his tie with B is being destroyed, perhaps because of the intensity of his own unresolved feelings that this arouses.)

T: You seem to have there some sort of a special feeling there about, uh, mentioning that your mother knows a lot about things — about your life with B.

X: Well, my feeling is this. See, B's, B was accusing me of being a mother's boy; that's one of her — things that she will not stand for, one of the reasons she didn't marry another person she met before she met me — how — to her it's despicable, and she got me to the extent where I admitted that I was a mother's boy; I mean she'd just badgered me

T: Made you.

X: "The hell with you. I am a mother's boy, then, if you ...

T: You just said this to get some peace, really?

X: Yeah, in a way, that's right, and, uh, finally, when she did grab that and then really started, I said: "Well, damn you; I am no mother's boy; if you think that — that I am," I said, "I am a human being, and I have my own opinions. I know I was raised by my mother, but what the hell am I supposed to be? Killed for that? Or what?" You know, "What can you hold against me for being raised by my mother? I didn't have a father"; so, uh, so I knew that I had, uh, that was when she was talking about getting a trustee for the children — which I don't know anything about. I mean, I don't know how that could be arranged.

T: It seems like you had a special

X: Yeah.

T: Kind of a — you had a feeling — I got an idea from the way you looked when you were telling me about — how your mother knew a good bit about the family, and I was just wondering what that feeling was — it seemed to mean something then.

X: Well, I don't know, uh — well, I don't know what that would be except I thought if Mother didn't know too much, she wouldn't have stuck her nose in so much that — she — to get it burned, so to speak, by *B*.

T: Uh-huh.

X: And her father.

T: Maybe some sort of.

X: She stuck her nose into (too?) personal affairs, such as, uh, oh, the way I do this and that, and, uh, and, uh, you see *B* knew it and, uh, and that's part of the reason why she — she's against her, because, uh ...

T: I was wondering if there was some feeling there that when you did bring up the matter of — it wasn't all your fault that you were late, that it had something to do with what *B* wanted, that, in a way, this made trouble, too. Like there, again, there wasn't any way out for you.

X: Well, uh ...

T: Like your mother seized on this not really to understand you or your situation, but, to stir things up between you and *B* again.

X: (pause) That's right; that's it; maybe I didn't realize it, but I know that; I knew she has been stirring things up between me and *B* for a long time, if you put it that way, you know? She'd, uh, pass these comments about how incapable she was, and, and this and that, so.

(If *X* turns to his mother, she uses what he says to attack his relationship with his wife. This increase of the conflict there obviously weakens him and makes him feel more dependent on mother. At the same time, his wife uses the fact that he goes to his mother, regardless of why or about what, to characterize him as a "mother's boy," although she is pushing him that way by putting so much off on him herself. It is a sort of double bind involving his relationship with two people, each focusing on only one level of his behavior, in the way least favorable to him, and rejecting his efforts to say there is something more to the situation, which they ignore.)

T: Well, it sure seems like (here *X.* interrupts).

X: With *B*, on the other hand, always saying: "We have to get closer together closer, and our love has to grow," and this and that. Well, I start getting confused; I don't see how I can meet those conditions unless — I couldn't see — in other words, she, lately she's been saying, that, that, that, uh, it depends on our love; it depends on — I don't mean intercourse; on other words, love, whatever it might, I can't even define the kind of love she means.

T: It's not really clear what she is really talking about.

X: Well.

T: When she says this.

X: That we have to understand each other, and love one another, and, uh, become two bodies in one soul; and, uh, well, you see that's kind of hard, uh, that, that's setting up a pretty rigid, uh, qualification.

T: (pause) Maybe you feel that has a little bit of flavor, that she wants you just to go along with her in everything.

X: Yes, and I imagine that's what I finally, finally concluded; I've been fighting it for years. I always wanted to have my own way, and that's why I always told her that if I decided to go to church, I might go to a Methodist church; I always wanted that out for myself, because I never, never would agree — completely; I said: "I might become a Catholic, but don't count on it. When mother dies; ya' know, they knew mother was against it. And so all — all that she's gotten, she's got from this, hate from my mother — I imagine I — without meaning to, I'd nurtured it, I'd given reason for that hate. In other words she thought if she could get mother out of the way, who knows, then I'd swing to her, actually I — I didn't think so; I felt the most important thing was to keep a job, make sure the children had enough to be brought up on, and, uh — ourselves, com — comfortable, you know?

(The wife emphasizes more and more that he must not be a "mother's boy" — she quit going with one before; so the threat of abandonment is there — while making it almost impossible to be otherwise: If he turns directly to mother, he is one, according to her, regardless of conditions. If he turns to her, since she says they should get closer, she has laid out all the specifications; she would be dominant, making him a mother's boy. He tries to be a man by working, but she keeps him away from the job; so everyone thinks him inadequate as a man there, too. All this time, she, as mentioned earlier, has various sources of support in relation — father, fine phrases, like "closeness," and so on, that are culturally acceptable, or that she can put over by skillful definition as "good," while all his needs are defined as "weakness" — so successfully that he increasingly accepts this; perhaps his illness may itself be seen as a resolution by accepting such accusations even more.)

T: Uh, well, as I, I think over what you tell me about — that night, it sure sounds like although you may have been involved in it to the extent of saying, "O.K., we'll stop at the convent, and you can talk to the nun," it sure does seem that once that was done, when you got home, everybody was — was giving you the devil and leaving you standing all alone, and the thing that you couldn't see any way out of at all.

X: Yes, but that really shouldn't have disturbed me; I mean, that's one thing I can't understand, because

T: Why shouldn't it?

X: Why should it? It's such a small item.

T: Your father-in-law gives you hell and walks off; your mother gives you hell and won't listen; your wife stand there and lets them give you hell and doesn't say: "I wanted to go to the convent, and that's why we're so late," and she walks off then.

X: Well, possibly.

T: I mean, you're getting hell from all sides and being left alone, to boot; it's a pretty rough situation.

X: Well, I didn't look at it; I mean I know I'd — I felt it strongly, I know that; in other words, you know, sort of, sort of a surprise, it happened so quickly; well, what the hell is going on, you know, and then (overlapping and indistinct here)

T: Yeah, must have been pretty confusing, to — having all this just sort of fall down on me.

X: It was a little confusing, but then I just thought: "Well, the hell with them!" That's what I thought; I just said: "Well, the hell with" — that's the way they feel — it shouldn't; I didn't think it'd bother me, but there is something deeper than that — uh, it's it seemed to — been a delayed reaction — in other words, I wasn't feeling good, even on that trip.

T: Uh huh . . .

X: In other words, I — I know I — I was having this feeling of confusion — so that was even before that argument.

T: Just this may have been added on to.

X: That's right.

T: Something else, but at least it gives us a — a picture of how you were in a difficulty with that, and we can talk some more then on what may have preceded it.

X: Yeah.

T: Well, I'm glad you were able to tell me about that today.

X: Well, I thought I told you this once before.

T: No, I never had anything like this clear a picture of it.

X: Well, I don't think it was — the — I — mean I wasn't sure — like I say, I didn't feel well before that even.

T: Well, we don't have to say this situation is the cause of anything, if this gives a picture of a difficulty you were in. O.K., X., I'll see you Monday. Hope you have a nice weekend.

X: Thank you.

COMMENT

We would like to review and emphasize several aspects of the material that seem to us to have particular relevance to the life situation in which X developed a psychosis, and to the therapeutic situation in which he reviews these matters.

Pattern of X's Life Situation

We have mentioned above our concept of the double bind as a situation (1) in which a person is faced with contradictory messages, (2) which are not readily visible as such because of concealment or denial or because the messages are on different levels, and (3) in which he can neither escape nor notice and effectively comment on the contradictions. We have tried to point out in our comments that X is repeatedly involved in such situations with the people most important to him. His father-in-law sends him out on errands and his wife delays him further, but when he is attacked by the old man for not behaving like a responsible person, X can only see the criticism as a "paternal" interest in his welfare. X's mother in this same context, and though she does not get along well with the father-in-law, berates X for upsetting his father-in-law; X attempts to handle the situation by saying it is unimportant. X's wife, after making him late, retires from the scene, leaving him to face the blame; he imagines she is "sympathetic" and had to leave in order to care for their children. In other examples, he appears caught in similar binds by the joint behavior of two persons — as between wife and mother on the "mother's boy" issue, or even by one person's blatant contradictions, as when his wife successfully insists that deception was not deception because it involved the church.

It is evident in the interview what strain and difficulty situations of this sort recurrently produced for X, even though he is still trying hard to minimize or deny this. Denial is his usual, though ineffective, technique for handling them.

However, as mentioned earlier, the double bind is not a simple one-way relationship but is an interaction in which both (or all) parties tend to be sharing important similarities of behavior, at least for relationships that persist over some time. This is rather clearly illustrated by the instance — not a unique example — in which X, when just succeeding in refusing his wife's unreasonable request to visit the nun, suddenly reverses and give in, pseudo-benevolently, if she "would like to." Clearly, X does not fully want to get free.

This poses the problem rather sharply, "Why did X and not his wife break down?" Since they were both caught up in a similar family situation, what visible difference in their handling of affairs might account for her continued social functioning and his failure and eventual psychotic break?

Who the Kept and Who the Keeper? Mrs. X's Transactions

It would be a simple matter to postulate that X is genetically more disposed to schizophrenia than his wife, and hence was the logical one to break down under the stress of an unhappy marriage. However, there are other considerations which might be offered as data relevant to Mrs. X's being in the more emotionally fortunate position.

1. She has fairly severe epilepsy and is "entitled" to the kind of consideration that the husband longs for. It is possible, additionally, that her disorder offers other psychological gains; e.g., it will be recalled that shock therapy for schizophrenia arose out of the observation that schizophrenia and epilepsy were relatively incompatible.

2. She was actively religious and able to use her religion as a strong lever to get "one-up" on her husband, who appeared to be a religious renegade but was not completely free. Her religious activities additionally provided certain positive figures both in reality and in fantasy for her emotional support.

3. Her inadequacies as a wife and mother could be justified from the standpoint of her illness and from the fact that her own mother was dead. That she exploited the latter fact is revealed in her attitude toward the patient's relations with his mother. He was criticized for being a "mother's boy"; yet her dependent relationship to her aunt and to the nuns was accepted, and indeed sanctioned, by the patient.

4. The cultural concept of "a mother" carried a good deal of weight for the patient and caused him, his wife, and his father-in-law to be acutely aware of his responsibilities toward her.[6] The "mother" concept further

---

[6] Perhaps it is relevant to note that statistics of hospital admissions for schizophrenia reveal that it is not until 40 years of age that the admission rate for women exceeds that of men. Additionally, prior to age 40, a sizable percentage of female admissions are unmarried or childless women. It is possible that more is involved in these statistics than the simple fact that the female schizophrenic-to-be does not marry, or, if she does, does not tend to bear children. Some such women may find a protective component, mental-health-wise, in being a mother of young children, either in the positive cultural sanctions and values accorded motherhood as such, or in the children's absorbing the most malignant aspects of the interpersonal difficulties.

provided a dilemma for the patient in that he was torn between his duty to his own mother and to the mother of his children.

Because of the conventional validity and unimpeachability of her rationalizations, and the similarity of her maneuvers to those of his own mother, the patient was almost totally unable to spot the contradictions in the wife's communications. Yet, of course, she was equally helpless to get much satisfaction from her relationship either with her husband or with her children; she was "successful" negatively rather than positively.

The concepts mentioned above are only a few related to observable features of the actual relationship that might be reviewed in reconsidering the problem of relative "ego strength" of the patient and of his wife. They suffer additionally from the fact that they are presented alone rather than in some stratified fashion, layered with the husband's and other relatives' own personality problems and interpersonal behavior. That is, in considering the nature of psychogenic stress and its relevance to the onset of a schizophrenic psychosis, it is necessary to review the type of perduring or predominant transactions that are occurring between the patient and the significant others in his immediate environment and their relation to the culture and to the patient's early past. Domination by weakness can be especially effective as a means of controlling the definition of the relationship if the person doing the defining is ill, female, or operates in a matriarchal environment. Thus, the patient's wife related to her father in such a manner as to appear submissive, like a good daughter; at the same time she was actively controlling him.[7] It is important also to note that the concept of a "good daughter" has a positive cultural evaluation, while the patient's being a "good boy" vis-à-vis his mother has a negative connotation. Although the wife's father made difficulties for her by his seclusiveness, irritability, and weak health, he was also busy catering to her needs and asked no more from her than the husband did. Who can say what might have eventuated if her father had died just prior to her marriage to the patient, and she

---

[7] A dramatic picture of the apparently submissive daughter who gets her own way, while placing responsibility for her behavior on the parental figures to whom she is "obedient," appears in Ann Whitefield, Shaw's heroine in "Man and Superman." It should be noted, though, that Ann is perhaps aware of her manipulations, and to that extent responsible, in contrast to Mrs. X's irresponsible unawareness and denial of control.

had been robbed of the prototype for her dealings with her husband, as well as losing an ally in her marital struggles?

The Illusion of Alternatives: X's Transactions

One aspect of being an American that receives attention from the public press is the freedom to do what one wants and to tell the other fellow to "go to hell." Americans, by reputation, are their own bosses and resent being told what to do. The stereotype is familiar, and in some ways resembles an attitude manifested by Patient X and by a number of schizophrenics we have studied. Overlooking the actual circumstances of concealed contradictory influences, the patient particularly feels as if he is the master of his fate, and hence holds himself responsible for making wrong specific choices or decisions and is haunted by obsessive doubts as to what choice to make. Actually, there is only an illusion of alternatives, since by the very nature of the double-bind situation, the patient will be "damned if he does and damned if he doesn't."

For example, one of the major points in the interaction described by X is his feeling that he must take the blame for his wife's making them late and that by doing so he minimizes the possibility of a fight between B and his mother. He states that B can't stand a mother's boy; yet by covering up for her, he becomes a "mother's boy." Additionally, she had told him that she had stopped going with a former suitor because she discovered he was a "mother's boy." She wants to get closer to X — in her words, "to become two bodies with one soul" — but this means to X a suffocating closeness in which she is the "one soul" and he is the "lost soul." He turns to his mother when he feels B taunt him. That he feels torn between B and his mother is exemplified in the statement: "I might become a Catholic when mother dies." His work makes him feel more like a man, but he accepts a situation that B sets up, in which he is forced to choose between her and his work. His defaulting in her favor increases his father-in-law's contempt for him, and so the possibility of the two men sticking together fades. It is not adequate to see that X has no satisfactory relationship within the family. Rather it is noteworthy how, for him, a troubled relationship begets further troubled relationships.

There is ample evidence that X sees himself as weak and helpless, and, on the other hand, as a good guy, who tries hard and who suffers from being "too nice." He would like some babying, but he marries a woman who despises weakness and utilizes helplessness to gain interpersonal power. He notes neither this contradiction in her nor its reciprocal in himself. Indeed, so long as X accepts denials and concealments he is offered and acts according to the illusion of alternatives as, of course, he is encouraged to do, the more the situation will tend to deteriorate. He tries to adapt to opposing manifest demands at different moments, instead of dealing with the over-all contradictions embodied. But as these varying apparent problems are at best merely tangential aspects of the real ones, X does not succeed in satisfying the others who make the demands, does not achieve acceptance and satisfaction, and is progressively more involved in fluctuating and contradictory behavior himself. This only reinforces the reciprocal double-bind involvements between them all.

We are primarily concerned here not with why X follows this unsatisfactory course and is unable to break out of it but, rather, with its nature and outcome. However, we may say, on the basis of additional interview material with X and with other patients, that we assume that X had countless experiences in his childhood, when his real dependency needs were great, that were prototypically related to the pattern described in this interview.[8] One such sequence from a nonpsychotic patient is described below because it was studied shortly after its inception and is probably more reliable than an adult patient's report of events in his childhood. The example appears as different only in degree from Patient X's experience.

A young adolescent who had a problem in not feeling like one of the boys, and who wanted to please his ineffectual father by becoming popular, returned home later than usual one day because he had been out with the gang. His enthusiasm for his new-found manliness was somewhat dampened when his mother greeted him with an underplayed "I was worried to death about you" approach. There was an unpleasant feeling in his stomach, and an old ghost reminded him that he was capable of worrying mother and that she would be free from worry if it were not for him. This feeling was a kind of unconscious heroin for him because, though sickening, it produced grandiosity and a special sense of preciousness. As a consequence of the incident with mother, he renounced the pleasure of roaming the streets with the fellows and came home promptly for the next few days; but then one night mother announced at the dinner table that there hadn't been as many phone calls for him lately. He resented her doing this in front of father, but the signal from

---

[8] Some consideration of the general etiology of such double-bind involvement is given by Bateson, Jackson, Haley, and Weakland (1956).

his stomach announced: "I am worrying her again." At this point he still attempted to solve the dilemma in terms of alternatives. These alternatives, stated roughly, were: "Should I spend more time at home or more time with the boys?"

Being still unsure, he returned home promptly the next day, only to find that mother had gone uptown and had left a note telling him so. Here was an opportunity to break the bind they were in, but it is in the nature of these reverberating cyclic sequences that he could not pull out. Instead, he stayed around the house and surprised mother when she returned by having started dinner. There was some mutual uneasiness about the "pansy" implications of his cooking dinner, but this was handled (as so many things had been in the past) by a covert agreement not to mention it to dad. And so the cycle was perpetuated.

The Psychotic Break

While we are unable to state at what precise point a psychosis eventuates in X or any other patient, it does seem to relate to the frequency, intensity, and timing of double-bind sequences. Constitutional factors, external stresses, and the experience of a previous psychosis are also possible contributory factors. We shall consider here the question of what sort of change in response pattern is X's development of psychosis, and what factors one can see that appear to have been temporarily related to it.

X's way of alternating conciliatory "good behavior" with occasional and abortive rebellious assertion does not gain him any control in his relationships, and indeed produces the opposite result. We can assume that his inability to deal with his wife's control through helplessness may have produced a covert competition with her that becomes manifest and explicit when he becomes psychotic. This is not to say that X deliberately becomes psychotic to get attention. Rather, viewing the matter in terms of communication, as X more desperately and unsuccessfully attempts to gain some control and satisfaction in his relationships, but fails with ordinary verbal means, his level of communication shifts. Thus, when he cannot separate the letters, he does not feel talking will help any, but he pales and a fellow worker notices he looks sick.[9]

---

[9] This shift may be compared with an example of culturally different levels of communication in social excuses pointed out by Margaret Mead: A Russian would not excuse himself from a party he did not wish to attend by reporting a non-existent headache, about

267

Yet X goes even further, into psychosis. Several factors may be significant for this ultimate development.

1. X escaped his job problem by illness but felt his family problems remained, just as they did after feigned illness the day before.

2. It seemed though, that some fortuitous, unplanned change at the level of physical objects, e.g., an auto breakdown, might alleviate the family struggle. Hallucination at least subjectively fits this specification.

3. He had already had an experience of a psychotic break; so this path was to some extent marked out for him.[10]

Becoming psychotic does put X at once in a position of maximum helplessness, because he is crazy and unable to do anything, while at another level it also gives him much more control. If he is more helpless than his wife and others, they X now take care of him. It is evident that as he becomes psychotic, the family members alter their behavior toward him, a change which he could not get them to make before.

Accompanying this alteration of relationships, and paralleling it in important respects, is a great alteration in X's perceptions and conceptions. This is the aspect of psychosis that has received the most attention from investigators. However, it is essential to see, as this interview illustrates, that X, in becoming psychotic, does not shift from perceiving correctly to "distorting reality." X's observations and communications are distorted before his break, and are differently distorted afterward.

Prior to his psychosis, X is maintaining a very special view of the world in his illusion of alternatives, an "either-or" way of regarding relationships. Particularly, he is distorting perceptions of his social world, the most fundamental "reality" for human beings. He is oriented to the material world and to limited transactions, but not to contradiction between levels or modes of

---

which he might then feel guilty. This is more characteristic of an American; a Russian would just have the headache!

[10] It is striking to notice that if X's retrospective account is accurate; his psychotic break involves at least three specific instances of idea and realization. He claims illness, then gets sick. He wishes for something wrong with the car, then sees the peculiar taxi meter. He tells his wife "You're driving me crazy," then breaks.

behavior. When he hopes for an accident to the car to provide him with an excuse for being late, he is on the slippery edge beyond which the material world gets distorted to provide hoped-for interpersonal gain.

When he becomes psychotic, he distorts material "reality," as with the taxi meter, and more limited social situations, as in his feeling watched at work. These distortions are more easily recognizable by the rest of us. Yet at the same time, he sees certain feelings and relationships more clearly than in his prepsychotic state. A patient who has felt guilty because he is not a good enough son and who, when he becomes psychotic, expresses concern over mother's suicide potential is not just expressing hostility but is acknowledging mother's depressive tendency.

Such insights are a mixed blessing, however. The patient can see and speak important truths because he is "sick" and out of the situation. But these perceptions are difficult to integrate because, since he is crazy, they do not count and others do not respond to his communications as messages to them. The so-called "social recovery" is the prime example of a person who manages to disregard a whole class of percepts by labeling them as his previously crazy self.

As mentioned earlier, it is not possible to establish with certainty the specific nature and circumstances of X's psychotic break. However, the available evidence suggests that after a long build-up of stress there was a fairly sudden and sharp break into overt psychosis. This seems to have occurred at a time when X's existing practice of denial and distortion of interpersonal realities was becoming inadequate to avoid choice and action, or, put with a different emphasis, when he was closer to being able to see his true situation, but not able to face it. Thus, on the day before his break, all of those most significant to him were attacking him in ways that must have made their contradictions especially blatant and hard to overlook, while simultaneously making it impossible to turn from one of them to another, as before, for even temporary support. Other available data also suggest that, despite his difficulties, X recently had been making some progress in his job. Just at this point, his wife attacks this by making him late. Was it becoming so clear that she did not want him to succeed that he could not, short of psychosis, fail to see this?

Then came the last straw, the matter of sorting the letters. This situation is an incredible parallel to X's dealing with interpersonal problems by the illusion of alternatives, as the problem with the letters is to make a correct choice between two polar alternatives. X does not see that his personal alternatives are not real ones, or that there are not really two distinct kinds of letters but only arbitrary definitions. With the letters, he must make a choice and cannot use the denial-and-avoidance techniques he employs with people. This appears to be that point at which he shifts from attempting to "solve his problems" to becoming "sick," whereby he is admitting he cannot solve them. He describes the sequence beautifully.

1. He felt they were watching him, as if waiting for him to make a mistake. (Later he produces something — paleness — and they do watch him.)

2. An apparently simple task, separating the long letters from the short ones, turned out to be impossible because of the in-betweens. In-betweens are not allowed.

3. He became increasingly critical of himself. This had worked to some extent in relating to people; it was ineffective with the letters.

4. The turning point was an involuntary behavior, which others noticed, and responded to. He became visibly ill and was told: "If you don't feel right, why don't you go home?"

5. Even the shift into the frame of illness was not enough, because all the way home he worried: "How can I explain this to them?"

6. Psychotic delusions allowed him to free himself of decision making. For example, the cab driver is a hospital attendant in disguise. There is no problem in "home" vs. "hospital"; it has been resolved.

The Interview Situation, and Psychotherapy

It is perhaps unexpectedly rewarding to raise the question: "Why did this interview centering on X's break take place just when it did?" — what were its circumstances? In no previous interview had he discussed this matter in any such detail, and in this one it was not brought up deliberately as a topic. Rather, the therapist merely followed up with some persistence the patient's early remark that his current difficulties about leaving the hospital are "just about the same question" as "why did I have the nervous breakdown in the first place?" The parallel situation in the present is his attempting to make a sharp choice between staying in the hospital or going home, while feeling helpless to do so. He fears that his fate really may be controlled by conflicts between others — the therapist and the ward doctor, and, beyond them, his wife and his mother again. He feels like a pawn in their games, but he now trusts the therapist enough to bring up his concern. Talking about his psychotic episode, although promoted by emotional and relational similarities, seems also to depend on at least three current differences from the old situation.

1. There is some real difference in the persons immediately involved and their behavior. The therapist and ward doctor at least present him with less concealed contradictions than his family members did.

2. Beyond this, also, the situation is less crucial for him; it is more limited and the persons involved less important.

3. He believes in doctors and accepts to a large extent that they are trying to help him. By talking about his hospital situation, he is working through an "artificial" psychosis, similar to the real one but more manageable. A parallel with the Freudian idea of "transference neurosis" is evident here; however, analytic thinking usually plays down the role of the actual therapeutic situation.

We feel that the similarity of circumstances between original significant events and their re-creation, review, and reworking in therapy is crucial, and is not confined to the session presented here. Especially, although detailed exposition and evidence must await later publications, we believe that something resembling the "double bind" must often be instituted on the patient by the therapist to obtain therapeutic change. This "therapeutic bind," however, must also differ in such a way as to require not the distortion, denial, or unawareness of the nature of vital interpersonal relationships of the patients but, rather, increased awareness of their true nature. Such awareness stands in contrast to both X's private distortions and Mrs. X's special manipulation of public stereotypes. It may not always be necessary. For example, in stable social contexts habitual patterns of behavior may serve to establish and regulate relationships in a reasonably satisfactory way. Thus, ordinary everyday relationships among "normal" people often do not involve much conscious awareness of their nature as such. But unsatisfactory relationships, with no mutually fitting behavior and views in important situations, may arise from social changes, cultural con-tacts, and individual idiosyncrasies. Then increased awareness may be an im-portant means of locating interpersonal dissatisfaction and making adaptive changes in relationships.

CONCLUSION

We present a transcribed interview in which Patient X, recovering from a schizophrenic episode, is describing the circumstances surrounding his psy-chotic break. We attempted to demonstrate that, despite the absence of any horrendous or earth-shaking occurrences, X, because of the circumstances of his rearing and current living, was under a very great stress. He was caught up in a series of self-perpetuating transactions, which we label "binds" because they inflexibly involve two people in a dissatisfying amalgam. X attempted to solve his interpersonal difficulties as though they were solvable if he could but make the right choice. This method, the illusion of alternatives, developed out of his inability to comment upon (notice) mutually contradictory multilevel communication sequences. His subsequent psychosis we see as restitutive, since his being "sick" encloses his attempts to form relationships within a new frame and allows him to view what he has been avoiding.

It is important to restate that we do not see X as having gotten "sick" (psychotic) in order to break the bind. The change is not voluntary, and the psychotic state and the being "sick" create a new set of problems as formidable in some ways as the previous ones. X starts the interview by indicating that all is not well with his hospitalized self. He fears the re-creation of the problems that drove him to the hospital in the first place. Fortunately, because of the therapeutic relationship, he can voice his doubts and fears and make some sense of them. The old ties are still operating, and X must also face another failure (his job and having to be hospitalized), so that he pays dearly for his new insights. He tells the therapist in effect: "What is a man profited, if he shall gain the whole world, and lose his own soul?"

References

Bateson, G., Jackson, D., Haley, J., & Weakland, J. (1956). Toward a theory of schizo-phrenia. *Behavioral Science, 1* (4); 251–264.

Block, J., Block, J., Patterson, V., & Jackson, D. A study of the parents of schizophrenic children, *Psychiatry*, to be published.

Jackson, D. (1957). The question of family homeostasis. *Psychiatric Quarterly* (Supp.) *31*; 79–90.

Jackson, D. (1957). A note on the importance of trauma in the genesis of schizophrenia. *Psychiatry, 20*; 181–184.

Kant, O. (1942). The problem of psychogenic precipitation in schizophrenia. *Psychiatric Quarterly, 16*; 341–350.

Laforgue, R. (1936). A contribution to the study of schizophrenia. *International Journal of Psycho-Analysis* 17: 147–162.

Pavlov, I. (1928). *Lectures on conditioned reflexes* (pp. 342, 359). Translated by W. Gantt, New York: International Publishers.

Stanton, A., & Schwartz, M. (1954). *The mental hospital: A study in institutional participation in psychiatric illness and treatment* (p. 342). New York: Basic Books.

Transactions of the third group process conference (1956), edited by B. Schaffner, University Seminar on Communications, Columbia University, New York, Josiah Macy, Jr. Foundation.

CHAPTER **20**

Introduction to
The Etiology of Schizophrenia[1]
(1960)

Just a little over one hundred years ago, Morel coined the term *dementia praecox* to describe certain cases of insanity. It seems fitting to celebrate this centennial by reviewing some of the ideas that have been held about this disorder and by making an attempt to relate them to current opinion in the field.

At present, schizophrenia is one of our major medical problems. This is not only because of its incidence (estimated at from one to three percent of the population) and its chronicity (keeping one quarter of the hospital beds in the country occupied), or because of the fact that its major incidence is during the most productive periods of life, roughly between the ages of 15 and 44. It is also because medicine has made progress against many other major disorders, thus allowing schizophrenia to loom larger by contrast. Perhaps also increasing acceptance of democratic ideas makes mental illness more an object of concern, especially in view of the fact that it often results in the individual's loss of his freedom. Still, public interest in mental illness is not widespread — a fact attested to by the considerable discrepancy in funds allotted for work on schizophrenia as compared with more attractive medical disorders. The public's reluctance to face mental illness places a special burden on investigators in this

---

[1] Reprinted with permission from D. Jackson (Ed.), *The etiology of schizophrenia*. New York: Basic Books, pp. 3–20.

field, and attempts to change prevailing attitudes, as in the open-door hospital idea, incur further public resistance. Thus it is likely that ideas held about schizophrenia — even by scientists — continue to reflect the old horror of mental illness as well as the feelings of despair aroused by the size of the problem.

Since 1940, roughly 500 papers have appeared in the medical literature on the etiology of schizophrenia. A much greater number has appeared on other aspects of the problem, such as therapy and problems of administration. These papers disagree widely with one another and reflect the fact that schizophrenia is a singularly difficult disorder to investigate. A comparison with papers published 30 years ago reveals less change than might be expected; although formerly the biochemical approach was stressed much more than the environmental, the range of viewpoints is wide both then and now.

Information theory, games theory, and the study of small group processes all present interesting possibilities for bridging the gap between "brain" and "mind" — yet most papers on the etiology of schizophrenia continue to dichotomize. Although the most ardent biochemist agrees that there are psychological consequences from the processes he describes and the most convinced psychologist is prepared to admit the biochemical nature of the intermediate processes involved, yet they are scarcely able to communicate their findings to one another, let alone relate them in any meaningful fashion.

So wide are the divergences that it is difficult and confusing to attempt to find any consistent patterns in research. From the organic point of view, one may say that the history of the study of schizophrenia mirrors very faithfully the major trends in general medicine during the past 50 years. When research into organic causes brought such spectacular results in other areas, it was very natural that it should be attempted in this one. The very labeling of schizophrenia as a "disease" makes an assumption that it is analogous to "diseases" and therefore amenable to a physiological explanation. Thus Mott's early findings of atrophy of sexual glands and his and Alzheimer's study of nerve cells of the cortex with supposed nuclear swelling, shrinkage of cell body, increased lipoid, and general gliosis (Motta, 1920) have continued to attract attention despite the careful work of Dunlap (1924) and others who conclude that schizophrenia is lacking in any fundamental or constant alteration of nerve cells and that such alterations as are found are reaction to various bodily conditions plus post-mortem and technical changes.

Interest in anatomy has also been reflected in the attempts to link schizophrenia with body type. The current view appears to be that thickness and thinness, tallness and shortness are all found in the schizophrenic population and that the more sophisticated methods of somatotyping are unwieldy from a statistical point of view. The linking of body type with that protean concept "schizoid personality" has not enjoyed much popularity in recent times.

Physiology has been represented in the study of schizophrenia most spectacularly by the work of Gjessing in his studies on periodic catatonia (Gjessing, 1938; Gammermever, & Gjessing, 1951). Other workers, however, have found a nitrogen phase exactly the reverse of that reported by Gjessing; and Hardwick and Stokes (1941) observed that swings in nitrogen balance were related to the state of general nutrition and could be avoided by improved nutrition without effect on the rhythm of mental illness. Indeed, some investigators report their difficulty in finding cases of periodic catatonia; and, except for Stokes and his coworkers, little has appeared recently on this fascinating concept. Selye's theories (1950) and renewed interest in the adrenal glands spurred ideas of physiological adaptation, stress, and schizophrenia, but this interest appears to have waned in the last few years. The unfolding secrets of the adrenocortex have no immediate application in psychiatry, as Cleghorn, Branch, Bliss, Holland, McDonald, and others have demonstrated. More recently, there has been much excitement and equally much controversy over such topics as serotonin, adrenochrome, ceruloplasmin, and taraxein.

It is interesting in view of the current murky condition of the etiology of schizophrenia to note hysteria's role in history (for we still have much to learn from some of the inglorious chapters of past psychiatric efforts). In the first place, hysteria has been like schizophrenia in being assigned multiple, shifting causes over the years, and these "causations" have had regional popularity. Secondly, the history of hysteria has been full of recommendations for therapy and reports of cures; and, as in schizophrenia, reports of cures have led to a reinforcement of the theory of causation, which led to further therapy, and so on. The unfortunate labeling of the syndrome (from the Greek "hysteron" meaning uterus) probably had its influence, and there is an analogous situation in the term "dementia praecox."

Perhaps the most important reason for noting the history of hysteria in relation to schizophrenia is that the disorder underwent a change in form and frequency once its essential cause was understood, and part of the reason for this remarkable change lay in the attitude of the medical profession. Nowhere more than in the works of Charcot (1881) is it apparent that many a hysteric was shaped by the institution he was housed in and the physician who treated him. Over and over again it has been necessary to learn the lesson that the observer influences the observed, and it is clear from papers comparing the effects of LSD with schizophrenia that the lesson will have to be learned once more. If LSD is viewed as an interesting chemical, perhaps closely linked to the etiologic agent of schizophrenia, patients are reported as confused, anxious, and hallucinating. If LSD is viewed as a vehicle for enriching the commonplace and touching one's untapped potential, the experience may be quite pleasant and nonhallucinatory. In some clinical laboratories, anxiety and somatic manifestations are emphasized; in some religious settings, the experience with LSD is described as uniformly pleasant. In the field of mental health, we have not only to reckon with the natural effect of the observers' own bias but we also have to deal with a second variable: the effect of this bias on the patient.

DISEASE OR DISORDER?

It has already been pointed out that the mere labeling of an entity can carry various implications as to modes of investigation and that the conception of schizophrenia as a "disease" has favored the physiological approach. This conceptualization arose quite naturally in Bleuler's time, when the psychiatrist had custodial care of the patient by day, and by night studied brain sections under the microscope and wrote up descriptions of his case.

Although Freud's discoveries might have influenced this situation, they had very little effect on ideas about schizophrenia, partly because Freud and his immediate followers were not much interested in psychoses, and partly because Kraepelin, the leading authority, had little use for psychoanalytical theories. As a matter of fact, he once stated, "As I am accustomed to walk on the sure foundation of direct experience, my philistine conscience of natural science stumbles at every step on objections, considerations, and doubts over which the lightly soaring power of Freud's disciples carries them without difficulty" (Keaffelin, 1918). Actually, there was no difference of opinion between Freud and Kraepelin about the etiology of schizophrenia even though Freud's theories set the stage for present-day psychological concepts. Although Zilboorg, Federn, and others contributed some psychoanalytic understanding of schizophrenic behavior during the 1920s, it was not until the 1940s that the problem received intense interest, sparked by Sullivan, Fromm-Reichmann, Fairbairn, and others.

At the time of the definition of "dementia praecox" in the late 1800s, medicine and European culture in general were intensely interested in theories of social degeneracy, based on notions of "protoplasmic inferiority." This is not surprising when one recalls that this society was one of rather rigid class structure, theoretically based on hereditary lines, and was at the peak of the illusion of the "innate superiority" of the "white races." The anthropometric studies of Lombroso were based on the theory that the more a man resembled an ape, the more he thought like one, and the less soul he had. Although his notions did not long survive in quite so crude a form, they were the proto-types of Kretschmer's and, later, Sheldon's work on body types and mental ill-ness. Both lines of thought are very old ones, based on the reasoning that there must be some correlation between outward form and inward nature. It is a region full of folklore and self-fulfilling prophecy — if redheaded people are not more hot-tempered to start with, they may soon become so if every-one treats them as if they were.

Concurrent with the study of dementia praecox, genetic and family stud-ies, especially in Germany, Italy, and England, established beyond the shadow of a doubt that criminality ran like a taint through some families. These inves-tigations and the study of mental deficiency, combined with fixed notions of genetic heredity that ignored social heredity, caused the whole subject to be-come of concern to the eugenicists. Naturally, the enactment of sterilization laws fortified beliefs about the organicity of dementia praecox, since obviously those who enacted these laws were convinced of the genetic basis.

The strides being made in the rest of medicine by Virchowian pathology stimulated psychiatrists to find the tissue basis of the "genetically induced degeneracy." Unfortunately, the schizophrenic's ability to develop tuberculosis and various other problems, many of them incidental to institutionalization, became a source of "proof" of protoplasmic inferiority. Some investigators found a death rate of nearly 80 percent from tuberculosis among schizophrenic patients. It took many years before this appalling correlation was related to epidemiological factors; however, at least one present-day geneticist still insists on a genetic linkage between tuberculosis and schizophrenia (Katz, Kunofsky, & Locke, 1957), although the evidence against this appears to be overwhelm-ing (Kety, 1960) and the rate may be as high among other chronic institution-alized patients, such as drug addicts.

The temptation to link the "phthisic constitution" (tall, lean, hollow-chested) with the leptosomic build attributed to the schizoid individual is ob-vious in the work of many early investigators and even some at present. In 1941, an apparently little noticed paper demonstrated that weight and schizophrenia were both matters of how many years residence in an asylum the patient had had.

One event that probably had a strong influence in supporting the idea of schizophrenia as a "disease" was the discovery that general paralysis of the insane was caused by the spirochete of syphilis, and that a specific therapy could be developed that was effective in treating this disorder. Paretics could be sorted out from the general mass of the "insane" and treated; and, naturally, such an event spurred efforts for similar discoveries in other types of mental illness. Although it was later demonstrated by several investigators that the form of the behavioral disorder in paresis related to the premorbid personality, the general stream of medical thought had swept by and on to attempts to discover the organic basis for other serious personality disorders. Attempts to discover spirochetes in schizophrenia continue to the present, despite repeated failures. There is also a "spread effect" noticeable in analogizing between paresis and schizophrenia in that papers attributing schizophrenia to various microorganisms appeared after the apparent stimulus of the discovery of the cause of paresis. The notion that syphilis in the parents could be passed on to the child as a predisposition to schizophrenia or other mental disorders was widely held, as is evident in Freud's writings. It represents a curious blend of genetics and microbiology and is held by several European investigators generally.

The idea of schizophrenia as a disease, especially as a degenerative cerebral process, has been considered questionable by some authorities for at least a hundred years. For example, the great English psychiatrist Maudsley stated:

There are commonly many partial causes of disease, some predisposing, some exciting, and the bodily derangements which so commonly exist in cases of insanity cannot always be regarded in the light of a cause; it often partakes much of the character of an effect. The physical acts on the mental and the mental back again on the physical and vice versa — cause and effect acting and reacting and mutually aggravating one another. The old rule "The cause having ceased, the effect ceases" is false as often as it is true; the effect often continues after a cause has ceased and thus abiding becomes in its turn a cause.

A contemporary of Maudsley, Clouston, stated: "It seems to me unphilosophical to say that 'mind' cannot rank as a causative factor; it seems contrary to plain clinical fact. To set aside the mental treatment of insanity would be to deprive ourselves of our chief therapeutic resource in many cases" (Lewis, 1951). One presumes he is talking of a treatment involving communicating a new and more rewarding attitude and behavioral pattern to the patient.

If we consider schizophrenia as a disease, it has several unique features. For one thing, the more florid the symptoms and signs, the better the prognosis. A number of genetic studies (quoted in chapter 3 of *The Etiology of Schizophrenia*) also show that the more heavily loaded the patient's genealogy is for schizophrenia, the more atypical the form and the better the patient's chances for recovery. This finding is compatible with theories of social heredity but does seem unusual compared to other medical diseases of hereditary origin. Again, the incidence of the disorder is unlike that of other hereditary diseases, which are of the order of 1:10,000.

Another peculiar feature, making schizophrenia unlike any other disease of which we have knowledge, is the effect of therapy. Improvement due to electroshock or insulin therapy may be permanent. For example, schizophrenics who have maintained their sanity five years after electroshock therapy are reported to have as good a chance as the ordinary population of staying out of a mental hospital. Is it likely that EST has remedied a metabolic defect? This would be very unlike the effects of using insulin for diabetes or adrenal extracts for Addison's Disease. Lauretta Bender (1955) followed her cases of hospitalized schizophrenic children through adolescence into adulthood; two thirds of them had improved. Although the author regards the disorder as organic and utilizes electroshock therapy, she does not make it clear how such progressive recoveries fit into the ordinary framework of disease.

The concept of schizophrenia as a disease also leads to unwarranted analogies with states brought about in sensory deprivation experiments, by toxic substances, and in model psychoses. Whereas these experiments can provide interesting comparisons with schizophrenia, they do not produce schizophrenia. The symptoms produced by these experiments are far more comparable to those produced by alcohol, anxiety, or various other factors in an individual — given the proper context. They show little in common with either the schizoid personality (basic to many theories of schizophrenia) or with that most chronic and progressive form of schizophrenia, the simple type.

Another puzzling feature of schizophrenia is that the chronic paranoid, who has nearly as bad a prognosis as the simplex patient, shows the least variation from the norm in physiological terms, weight, intactness of intelligence, dilapidation of habit patterns, and so forth. Thus, if one considers schizophrenia as a disease, it remains a paradox that the cases least amenable to treatment have the least resemblance to experimentally produced analogies and may demonstrate little in the way of toxic changes. Because most authorities agree that simple schizophrenia is not related to an onset caused by stress and because environmental factors appear to play no significant role, one would expect the constitutional factors to be higher in this form. Yet most genetic investigators (see Chapter 22) make no claims of a relationship between the amount of family history of schizophrenia and the form or severity of the illness of offspring.

DIAGNOSIS AND DATA

The concept of schizophrenia as a disease, rather than as a group of disorders or as an end state delimited by the capacity of the brain and the shaping of culture, has influenced the majority of investigators. Thus, because most medical diseases have a single etiological agent, this majority has approached schizophrenia in a reductionist frame of mind, looking for a rejecting mother or a specific toxin. The human being is relegated to the role of host — much as he is when his lungs harbor pneumonia — and all his supraorganic complexities are ignored. This reductionist, oversimplification tendency leads one to look for the "key to schizophrenia"; and premature claims that it has been found undoubtedly result in the abandonment of promising leads simply because they were not all-inclusive.

Anyone familiar with the biological and psychological literature on schizophrenia can recognize that the scattering of positive findings is frequent enough in both areas to make it unlikely that they are erroneous. Whether such experimental results are primary or secondary to the etiology (or etiologies) of schizophrenia is beside the point at this time. There is a crying need for descriptive data in the form of positive laboratory or clinical findings, even if such findings are the result and not the cause, and even if they encompass only a small percentage of the entire schizophrenic group.

The investigator of schizophrenia is very apt to have had medical training or to work under the direction of a physician. This fact also introduces certain biases, which have changed but little in the last thirty years. One such bias is the continued use of Kraepelin's categories despite repeated demonstrations that they have little practical utility and probably hamper our ability to conceptualize. Kraepelin's nosology presented a real advance 60 years ago, but present knowledge reveals that his categories of schizophrenia have no genetic or physiological basis and are inadequate as social descriptions. Yet thousands of residents in psychiatry are at this very moment filling out an uninspired initial history form and carefully endeavoring to place a round patient in a square diagnostic category.

Even granting the necessity of diagnostic categories for actuarial purposes and transmission of information, there is little reason for confidence in our present system. As Hock has pointed out (1957), Georgia is the only state that consistently diagnoses more manic-depressives than schizophrenics on first admissions, and discrepancies between various states may be as high as 30 to 60 percent. Furthermore, Penrose has demonstrated that the chances of being labeled schizophrenic increase in proportion to the length of hospital stay, regardless of initial diagnosis (1950). The term "schizophrenic" in medical circles carries almost as much of a ring of authenticity as "diabetic" or "tubercular." Yet it is actually nearly as much a fiction as that lovely legal appellation a "reasonable man." Even an objective, consistent observer is dealing with a subject who varies greatly from day to day and who, because of diet, exercise, and attitude, cannot easily be compared to the hypothetical "normal." As Kety (1960) revealed, most recent biochemical claims have been demonstrated to result from such artifacts — even including the amount of coffee drunk.

Diagnosis is no mere plaything of state hospital psychiatrists. Almost every paper describing an investigation into the etiology of schizophrenia starts out with "X number of schizophrenics," rarely described except for that loose and varying label. Even if patients are limited to one or another Kraepelinean category, there is little reason to assume that the comparability with another investigator's series has improved to a significant degree. It would appear from the few papers dealing with the reliability of diagnosis that variation between even experienced clinicians is so great that comparisons between groups used by different investigators are subject to large error. In one study, three psychiatrists agreed in only 20 percent of their cases and had a majority agreement in only 48 percent (Arnoff, 1954). Another study revealed that the widest disagreement occurred among the most experienced clinicians (Ash, 1949).

In view of this variation between judgments of schizophrenia versus psychoneurosis and between types of schizophrenia, it is difficult to justify or take seriously some of the precise statements that occur in the literature, especially the small percentage differences that are reported in the families of schizophrenics linking their blood tie with their chances of developing ("inheriting") schizophrenia. Either these are based on the investigator's own diagnosis (with the possibilities of creeping bias), or they are based on state hospital admissions with no attempt to compare the very varied criteria of diagnosis (Ash, 1949).

Hoskins has warned against "further pursuit of that will-o'-the-wisp, that semiprojective, synthetic artifact, the patient as a whole," in schizophrenia research (Hoskins, 1946). Still, it may be doubted whether this "will-o'-the-wisp" is much more arbitrary and artificial than abstracting aspects of a number of patients without regard to the context. When it is remembered that schizophrenia research may be divided between investigators with backgrounds in such varied fields as clinical symptomatology, psychodynamics, psychoanalysis, learning theory, personality theory, perception theory, group dynamics, sociology, cultural anthropology, and all of the biological sciences including biochemistry, genetics, neurophysiology, neuroanatomy, and psychological testing, the practical impossibility of any one investigator's having a wide enough background to "see the patient as a whole" provides the limitation.

Still another factor complicates research in schizophrenia: Patients do improve, and the investigator's medical orientation, his desire to cure his patients, may mislead him. Many a cycle of belief about schizophrenia has been characterized by the empirical use of an agent, response of the patient (usually 60 percent improved), and research into the mechanism of action of the agent. More than 50 etiological claims have been made in the course of such cycles, and many thousands of hours of patient research have followed. Among the more obvious examples are the introduction of thyroid by a Scottish psychiatrist and the study of this organ as an etiological factor or the empirical use of insulin shock therapy, followed by years of intensive research on the carbohydrate metabolism in schizophrenia. Perhaps one day we shall be able to isolate a specific percentage of improvement attributable merely to medical benevolence and the interest shown in the patient.

And then, investigators in this field, it must be admitted, show an all-too-human inclination to remain biased in favor of their own special theories. There are some who are unable to attribute sufficient power to interpersonal relations to be able to conceive even theoretically that some schizophrenia might have a psychological basis. There are also those who find it impossible to imagine a physiological base.

Obviously, if schizophrenia represents a group of disorders (and this would appear to be the most reasonable assumption on the information we have at present), then it is important that the investigator remember that theoretically many possible etiological agents exist and that it is quite possible in any given case there might be a complicated combination of such agents. Unfortunately most of us are not gifted with the broad view, and cultural factors appear to play a significant role in what views we have. A certain acquaintance with centers doing research in schizophrenia in many localities impressed me with the differences between European (and particularly Scandinavian) emphasis on organic factors and the psychological orientation of many American centers.

First, there are those who see schizophrenia as a strictly organic disease with its own periodicity. Causative factors include constitution, heredity, bacteria, parasites, glandular malfunctioning, and so forth.

Second, there are those who view schizophrenia as primarily an organic disorder which cripples the individual's attempt to deal with ordinary life stresses. In short, his biological vulnerability is too great to be compatible with life and the world.

Third, there are those who see the schizophrenics as individuals biologically incapable of coping with major environmental stresses. Major stresses may include such things as adolescence, marriage, parenthood, or it may be assumed that the schizophrenic encounters unusual stresses because of his particular environment.

Fourth, there is a group who view schizophrenia much like a psychosomatic disorder in which major stresses produce internal changes, which in turn bring about further changes, lower adaptive levels, and so on.

Fifth, there is a group of investigators who see the schizophrenic as a regressed individual who withdraws before an onslaught of severe psychic trauma inflicted at a very early age and revivified by developmental environmental factors.

Six, there are investigators who view schizophrenia as a subtly occurring maladaptation that in some sense is appropriate to the covert operations of the family group.

Seventh, there could be a group, but as far as I know it has no adherents, who would view schizophrenia as essentially a psychogenic disorder but who would see the various forms of its expression — catatonia, paranoia, etc. — as hereditarily determined.

POSSIBILITIES FOR THE FUTURE

The most pressing problem appears to be the development of new and more useful diagnostic categories and a conceptual scheme that will enable us to think of all the multiple factors involved, from social through psychological to biochemical, in a single framework that will accommodate all the factual findings and enable us to relate them to one another. It may well turn out that there is a continuum from normal to neurotic to schizophrenic, but that within this continuum are clusters of disorders, some of which can be labeled schizophrenic. These clusters, although part of a continuum, may be sufficiently distinct to be virtually qualitatively different from one another. It is my notion that when these clusters of disorders are viewed they will consist of an admixture of what might be called process features and reactive features as well as constitutional and psychogenic features. That is, biological and psychological factors operating over different time periods will produce different subgroups even if the factors are similar. To give a crude example, an individual with an IQ of 80 from birth is in quite a different position vis-à-vis himself and all those others than an individual whose I.Q. drops to 80 when he is 20 years of age — and this difference holds even if it were eventually established that IQ depends completely on the number of twists in the DNA molecule. Thus, there is not only the possibility of multiple causation in schizophrenia but also that a similar cause acting over a long or short period of time will produce a different schizophrenia.

If we can divorce ourselves from a Kraepelinean focus on symptoms, there are certain assumptions that appear to be worth considering and that seem to have scattered investigations to support them:

1. Schizophrenia consists of a number of etiological causes leading, according to the principle of equifinality, to a similar end state. The differences between these severally caused schizophrenias tend to be covered up and disguised by such factors as the ubiquitous biological adaptive functions in man and the human response to experiences such as institutionalization.

2. Some schizophrenics get well faster than others, and such cases often show more florid initial symptoms and have been subjected to more recent severe stress — either psychological or physiological — than the group with a poorer prognosis. There are, however, some apparently florid cases that deteriorate rapidly into an incurable state. Whether such cases are the result of a weak constitution or are individuals who have been struggling against overwhelming odds for years is not known.

3. In most investigations of a chronic hospital population, certain schizo-

phrenics will show marked physiological abnormalities. Whether these findings are cause or effect is unimportant compared to the fact that such cases are lost by averaging them in with other patients. The same is probably true of most other approaches, including psychological studies.

4. Social factors (age, race, religion, economic status, education, etc.) are so important in shaping the form and course of schizophrenia that no etiological study can ignore these variables, especially since they include the investigator's relation to the patient.

Assuming that the investigator accepts the presence of environmental factors in all cases (such as the reaction to being institutionalized), we are then left with two large variables: (1) time; (2) time acting on an X factor or factors. For purposes of this discussion, the experimenter can be left out since this will also fit into these two dimensions, as far as the effect on the patient goes, and his bias will exist whatever diagnostic scale is used. Also methodological procedures can be built into experiments to check on the investigator; for example, Maas, Varon, & Rosenthal (1951) have shown that the longer the investigator took to get a systolic reading the more favorable the results with the Mecholyl test.

The time factor can be construed as a continuum from progressive to reactive, and the X factor as a continuum from organic to purely psychological causation. These factors might represent a graph and clusters of patients compared with each other. It must be understood that this is a functional and not an etiological scheme, because the "organic" end of the scale can represent patients with changes secondary to their schizophrenia or patients who have a contributing dysfunction that is not strictly etiological, as M. Bleuler demonstrated in the relationship of goiter to the onset of schizophrenia.

A patient who fell in the AC quadrant would represent quite a different sort of schizophrenia than an individual in the BD quadrant. Examples of the ordering of data to place individuals on the graph would be:

Organic: History of schizophrenia in collateral or direct lines, abnormal EEG, leptosomic body build, endocrine disorders, lowered reactivity of central nervous system as measured by reaction to ACTII, glucose tolerance, resistance of insulin, lowered skin temperature, 17 ketosteroid excretion, delayed time sense, flicker fusion, increased protein in CSF, organic findings on Rorschach, and relatively low IQ.

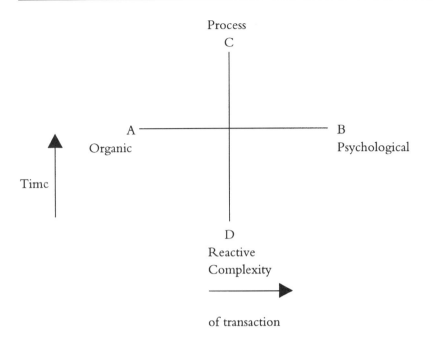

Psychological: No evidence of chronic or primary biological abnormalities, although some physiological disturbance may be expected on the basis of severe emotional disturbance. Evidence of precipitating factors, psychological disturbances in family, and history of childhood and adolescence compatible with development of "weak ego." Psychological tests including Rorschach reveal evidence of potentialities overcome by conflict. IQ apt to be normal to superior.

Reactive: Acute onset with florid psychotic symptoms, evidence of fear and anxiety and ability to bring family or authorities' attention to these difficulties. Rorschach would indicate increased color values and sometimes color shock, normal W and F+%, possibly a D approach and increased M. Factors such as upward mobility, recent shift in social status or in ecological niche or in range of experiences, such as sexual encounters would be expected to be common.

Process: No obvious precipitating factors, family (at least on the surface) appears relatively stable; or there is a long history of separation from significant family members. Chronically poor achievement in school and work. Patient comes to authorities' attention by a natural screening process, such as induction into the armed forces, social agencies, or wearing down of family members. Rorschach shows loose and confused sequence, confabulatory and contaminatory DW and lowered F+%.

Such a scheme, although it violates the current mind–body union emphasis, might have some usefulness in attempting to denote groups of schizophrenics. It deliberately cuts across the lines of the Kraepelinean categories of schizophrenia, which do not sufficiently take into account social and ethnic factors, the effects of institutionalization, and the shifts that occur with time from one nosological group to another.

There are current attempts to broaden the Kraepelinean categories; for example, the committee on nomenclature of the American Psychiatric Association lists in addition to the four classical types a chronic and acute undifferentiated form, a schizo-affective form, a childhood type, and schizophrenic reaction, residual type. These categories are deliberately loose, and attempts to define very specific forms have met with mixed reception. Included in these attempts would be the "acute periodic catatonia" of Gjessing, "Oneirophrenia" of Meduna and McCullough, "pseudoneurotic schizophrenia" of Hock and Polatin, and the ambulatory schizophrenia of Zilboorg. These nosological labels do not appear to be enjoying much popularity currently. However, the concept of reactive and process schizophrenia as described by Winder and Cantor, and the well-defined nosological category of "Paraphrenia," used extensively by English psychiatrists, seem to offer promise, although neither of these designations implies an etiology. Both of these concepts relate primarily to time. Paraphrenia, for example, is found in a group of older patients who gradually have become more socially isolated.

The problem of diagnosis obviously underlies the whole frustrating story of research in schizophrenia. Langfeldt, who has long concerned himself with prognosis in schizophrenia, attended an afternoon session of an American Psychiatric Association meeting in 1953 devoted to psychotherapy of schizophrenia. He remarked that the claims of improvement with psychotherapy he heard that afternoon, indicated that schizophrenia in Sweden and the United States were very different disorders.

But if we consider using a classificatory system involving time and a substratum on which time acts, then the symptoms presented by a given patient would not be the means of forming nosological classes. Instead, they would have to be related to the process-reactive, organic-psychological continua. There is reason to believe that psychological tests, perhaps especially psychophysiological measurements like flicker-fusion, offer promise in rating patients as to "fixedness" of reaction and as to prepsychotic potential (constitution?). However, there is a possibility of linking findings from learning and communication theories in such a fashion that the clinician can think about schizophrenic symptoms in a uniform way, whether he is studying them from social or biochemical viewpoints. The basic premise of such a system is that schizophrenics, whatever their basic pathology, are more human than otherwise and will communicate with the investigator if only by silence.

This type of diagnostic system we might label an "interactional diagnosis." For one thing, communication theory can be described in terms of neuronal circuits, synaptic facility and the like, and can also be thought of in terms of learning experience. An appropriate blend of information and learning theory would satisfy most of the present-day concepts about schizophrenia regardless of whether they are organic or psychogenic. Thus it is possible to imagine (like the computer model of the brain) that the manner in which information is utilized by the individual will depend on intactness and adaptability of his equipment, and that his output will be a combination of the kind of information fed him and the way his brain utilizes it. If Tom persistently calls a *cat* a *hat*, and also calls a *cow* a *how*, we suspect a defect in his speech mechanism somewhere along the line and investigate accordingly.

If, however, he calls a *cat* a *rat* and exhibits no other confusion between *c*'s and *r*'s, we assume he is confusing the objects of reference in the real world. This does not necessarily imply Tom has something wrong with his brain; he may have been trained to call cats *rats*. If we are able to win his confidence enough to induce him to change the labels, there may be no change in his perceptions whatsoever, but he is able to communicate his perceptions in an acceptable form.

It is quite possible that his perceptions are such that to him cats and rats are indistinguishable. If we give him a drug and he is able to relinquish his old "false" labeling system and substitute a more socially acceptable and discriminating one, we must discover whether the drug affected his perceptions, the circuits and synapses within his brain that enabled him to verbalize these perceptions, or whether his general attitude changed so that he no longer found satisfaction in a defiantly individual view of things and was more ready to conform to social norms.

If Tom does not mislabel a cat but reacts to it in a strikingly unusual fashion, such as trying to kill every cat he meets or running to the nearest bed and hiding under it, such reactions will soon cause him trouble in a world full of cat fanciers. Here again, it may be misperception: the cat is confused with an actually threatening or hostile figure. Or it may be simply another case of miseducation. That is, either the apparatus for perceiving the cat is out of order, or the cat has become a symbol in itself, standing for a wide variety of feared and hated figures in Tom's private world.

Modifications of the machine (substrati) and of the input are occupying the attention of an increasing number of investigators. It is possible to vary one with a substance like LSD, and the other by brainwashing techniques. The range from "observing the output with a nonintact computer" to "varying the input in an intact computer" corresponds to the "organic" and "psychological" dimensions in the diagnostic system suggested above. A communication framework encompasses neuroanatomical findings and the data of psychoneurology.

Thus, it would seem that detailed study of schizophrenics in terms of learning theories might have much to offer, whether one emphasizes taraxein or tension, adrenochrome or the folks at home. Sophisticated animal experiments in which learning experiences are related to breeding, hormone injections, and variable weaning times illustrate the possibilities of this framework; and because communication is learned, the two systems may be blended.

These overly simplified remarks are made not in the belief that they constitute more than the barest suggestion of a systematic approach but that they will indicate that anatomical, physiological, and learning experiences can be thought about within the same framework. Until such a system exists, all of us concerned with the tremendous problem that is schizophrenia must be aware of the research that is in progress.

References

Arnoff. (1954). Some factors influencing the unreliability of clinical judgments. *Journal of Clinical Psychology, 10;* 272.

Ash, P. (1949). The reliability of psychiatric diagnosis. *Journal of Abnormal & Social Psychology, 44;* 272.

Bender, L. (1955). The development of a schizophrenic child. In G. Caplan (Ed.), *Emotional problems of early childhood.* New York: Basic Books.

Charcot, J. M. (1881). *Clinical lectures on senile and chronic diseases.* London: Sydenham Society.

Dunlap, C. (1924). Dementia praecox: some preliminary observations on brains from carefully selected cases, & a consideration of certain sources of error. *American Journal of Psychiatry, 3*; 403.

Gammermever, J., & Gjessing, K. (1951). Fatal myocardial embolism in periodic catatonia with fatty liver. *Acta med. Scandinav, 139*; 358, 1951.

Gjessing, R. (1938). Disturbances of somatic function in catatonia with a periodic course and their compensation. *Journal of Afent. Sc, 84*; 608.

Haltowick, W., & Stokes, A. (1941). Metabolic investigations in periodic catatonia. *Proc. Roy. Soc. Med., 34*: 733.

Hock, P. (1957). The etiology of epidemiology of schizophrenia. *Am. J. Pub. Health, 47*: 1071.

Hoskins, R. (1946). *The biology of schizophrenia*. New York: W. W. Norton.

Kallmann, F. (1938). *Genetics of schizophrenia*. Locust Valley, NY: Augustin.

Katz, J., Kunofsky, S., & Locke, B. (1957). Tuberculosis in schizophrenia as compared with other types of mental disease. *Psychiatric Quarterly*, July.

Keaffelin, E. (1918). *Dementia praecox* (tr. Barclay, R. M.). London: Livingstone.

Kety, S. (1960). Recent biochemical theories of schizophrenia. In D. Jackson (Ed.), *The etiology of schizophrenia*. New York: Basic, pp. 120–145.

Lewis, A. (1951). Henry Maudsley; his work & influence. *Journal of Ment. Sc., 97*; 359.

Maas, H., Varon, E., & Rosenthal, D. (1951). A technique for studying the social behavior of schizophrenics. *Journal of Abnormal & Social Psychology, 46*; 119.

Mott, F. (1920). Studies in pathology & dementia praecox. *Proceedings of the Royal Society of Medicine, 13*: 25.

Penrose, L. (1950). Propagation of the unfit. *Lancet, 2*; 425.

Selye, H. (1950). Stress and general adaptation syndrome. *British Medical Journal, 1*; 1383.

Veith, I. (1956). On hysterical & hypochondriacal afflictions. *Bulletin of the History of Medicine, 30*; 233.

CHAPTER 21

Some Assumptions in the Recent Research of Schizophrenia[1]

Robert E. Kantor and Don D. Jackson[2]

(1962)

INTRODUCTION

When Harry Stack Sullivan asserted psychiatry to be an interpersonal science, he adopted a set of tacit premises about the social character of human conduct. To render these premises explicit and to spell out their research consequences is the object of this paper. The profit from doing so lies in the fact that Sullivan's assumptions have invisibly steered some of the present courses in research on schizophrenia. Laying open these latent influences may help to illuminate the paths of future leads.

At least three explicit propositions, each illustrated here by an operational hypothesis on which significant research has been performed, arise from Sullivan's fundamental position that man is a social creature who depends for his sanity, and indeed for his existence, upon the support and upon the continuous affirmation of his fellows:

---

[1] From *The Journal of Nervous and Mental Disease*, *135* (1), 1962. Reprinted with permission.

[2] Mental Research Institute, 555 Middlefield Road, Palo Alto, California.

1. The reciprocal adjustments of men to each other are primarily effected through channels of communication. Such learning starts early, and is transmitted to the child through a wide range of verbal and nonverbal messages from his parents. Research applications have focused on schizophrenia as a result of distortions in the vitally formative familial communications.

2. Human perception, another major modifier of behavior, is essentially a selective process which begins when the child takes the view of his "significant others" who teach him to pick out only certain events in his environment. Research here is based on the hypothesis that the level of the schizophrenic's perceptual organization can be a useful measure of the severity of his dysfunction, providing one knows something also of the context in which these perceptions occur.

3. Any human grouping consists of an enormous complex of expectations and comprehensions among its members that are continuously sustained and reinforced through acts of communication. The social world of the mental hospital, important for our purposes because schizophrenics are found here in large numbers, may be fruitfully studied as communication networks.

Corresponding to these three assumptions (and their research applications), the present paper, after setting the historical stage, will fall into three main sections, each indicating the kinds of studies now taking place, and something of their implications for an evolving definition of schizophrenia.

HISTORICAL BACKGROUND

A convenient date for the marriage between social theory and research on schizophrenia is 1929, when Professor W. I. Thomas pioneered the addition of a section of Sociology and Psychiatry to the program of the American Sociological Society. Presenting papers at the meeting (Eliot, 1955) were Trigant Burrow, Benjamin Karpman, Adolph Meyer, George E. Partridge and Harry Stack Sullivan. The next two annual meetings also provided space for this area of "social psychiatry," focusing on society's sins in the production of emotional turmoil. Sullivan, for example, discussed the effects of urban density on the emotional conflicts of children.

In 1932, the sociologist Robert Faris argued that if there really are cultural factors in psychosis, it ought to be possible to demonstrate them empirically through differences in rates of admission to various mental hospitals, depending upon the areas of origin of those admitted. Faris (1934b) found that a disproportionate number of schizophrenics came from "disorganized" ecological zones. He hypothesized that where social contacts are "adequate," and where social alienation is absent, schizophrenia is very infrequent (1934a). In his book with Dunham these theories were repeated (1939), inspiring several validating studies that in the main supported Faris and Dunham's original findings. Among these are the works of Hadley et al. (1944), Mowrer (1939), Queen (1940) and Schroeder (1942).

Fundamentally, the ecological position proposes that psychosis is a consequence of unfavorable social features. There are researches, for example, which inquire into the relationship between schizophrenia and neighborhood and occupational grouping (Clark, 1948; Tietze, Lemkau, & Cooper, 1941). Other work proposes that contemporary Western society, characterized as it is by high mobility both vertically and spatially, facilitates mental and emotional dysfunction of personality (Davis, 1938, Merton, 1949, Tietze, Lemkau, & Cooper, 1941). Still other studies stress the role of the "sick society" (Frank, 1936). Halliday's (1949) work on the rising incidence of emotional illness in Scotland was seen by him as the "medical approach to the study of the sick society." A frequent variation on this theme is the stress on intracultural contradictions as productive of mental breakdowns within individuals (Horney, 1937).

In its most recent version, the ecological frame of reference has led to investigations of the linkage between social class and mental disorder. Hollingshead and Redlich (1958), utilizing as their sample approximately 98 percent of those under psychiatric care at a certain time in the city of New Haven, reported that a disproportionate number of the patients came from the less privileged classes, and when the members of the more privileged classes did get into mental hospitals they tended to receive more active courses of treatment. Regarding this latter phenomenon, a late empirical article (Hardt & Feinhandler, 1959) presents data indicating that "the lower social class, the higher will be the percentage of male schizophrenics who are continuous long-term patients."

Intensively studying fifty patients and their families, Myers and Roberts (1959) concluded that the backgrounds of patients from different social levels differed markedly. The families, for instance, of those patients from less privileged levels were more likely to abandon the hospitalized person. Significant differences in class orientations towards the institutionalized psychotic were also discovered by another investigation (Cumming & Cumming, 1957).

Hollingshead (1961) has more recently proffered a rationale for this type of approach (called epidemiological by him, rather than ecological). He suggests that the focus on the social context of schizophrenia is a "descriptive phase" that should form the necessary underpinnings for a "determinative phase" that comes later and which contains explanatory powers. The position taken here by Hollingshead puts epidemiological data in a useful perspective and meets in part the objections of Blumer (1937) and by Zilboorg (1939) who stressed the limitations of the ecological hypothesis; both noted that most individuals living in conflictual or disorganized social groupings are not schizophrenic. What is needed, both implied, is an explanation of how and in what manner the social pressures are rendered into meaningful individual experience and conduct. In this same article, Blumer proposes the beginnings of such an explanation by noting that the symposium of psychiatrists and sociologists about which his paper was concerned presented a somewhat composite picture that conceptualized individual disorder as an end-product of unhappy experiences in childhood. What this really asserts, Blumer suggests, is the significance of the family group factor.

He thus clarified the fact that the psychiatrist's interest in environment is practically synonymous with the sociologist's interest in the totality of primary relationships in which the individual participates. Pollack (1952) noted a similar fact when he declared that what sociology can do for psychiatry "is to break down the concept of environment into its various components." One sociologist (Becker, 1959) pointed out that a child's "family of orientation" may include grandparents, uncles, aunts, cousins, or even boarders, who may be in continuous proximity to the growing child and thus may enter into significant interrelationships with him, and influence his growth processes nearly as much as do his parents.

Viewpoints such as these make it easier to conceive that families exist whose constellations are unusually hospitable to the formation of schizophrenia among their members. The influence of Sullivan (1947b) also comes into play here, especially his recommendation to investigate the schizophrenic's whole pattern of interpersonal relations before his breakdown, as well as his idiosyncratic language.

In general, the writers are trying to show in broad outline that these earlier approaches led up to contemporary studies (of family communications, of

Rorschach assessments, of hospital networks) that endeavor to get at the problems posed by the original theoretical statements.

STUDIES ON FAMILY COMMUNICATIONS

One insight implied by a sociological orientation might usefully be made plain: psychosis becomes understood as a situation within a primary group, rather than as the individual possession of one of the group's members. Jackson (1957a) utilized the idea, long circulated among psychoanalytic writings, when he noted that the trauma dealt to a schizophrenic is not necessarily a specific and transient hurt, but is rather a "condition operating in the patient's environment which has been non-discrete and continuing." As a logical corollary, he introduced the concept of "family homeostasis" (1957b), that schizophrenic conduct is a vital part of the precarious balance of the whole family. Once the idea is grasped that all the family personnel are interlocked in a pathological system of interaction, it becomes reasonable to study the communication channels among them. Bateson et al. (1956) noticed that the schizophrenic makes idiosyncratic and unshared interpretations of the information that he receives, which led to their "double-bind" hypothesis that the schizophrenic must have learned his communication procedures in a family atmosphere where the verbal and nonverbal levels of transmission clashed rather than meshed. This, in turn, resulted in the formation of a research project whose observations are focused on the actual exchanges inside the family on at least a triadic level (Haley, 1959; Jackson & Weakland, 1961; Weakland, 1960).

EMPIRICAL STUDIES ON PERCEPTUAL ORGANIZATION

Obviously the kind of data needed to corroborate such a hypothesis about the family etiology of schizophrenia are best found in longitudinal studies, but an implication, important for Rorschach research, has arisen in the course of theorizing. Jackson (1957a) highlighted the implication this way: "the reporting of the patient is more complicated than can be accounted for by repression or denial. There is truly a perceptual difficulty involved, which is partly a matter of what is paid attention to." Essentially, this is the more explicit version of Sullivan's general position that all human perception is a highly selective process that enables major modifications in conduct in accord with the shifting demands of living. "Selective inattention" is determined by security operations and acts to limit what a person can communicate to himself.

Employing the idea that perceptual phenomena could throw light on schizophrenia, Kantor, Wallner, and Winder (1953), using the visual productions (by Rorschach test) of 324 patients, demonstrated that "schizophrenic cases can be reliably differentiated into process and reactive groups," and offered some evidence that the former malignant type differed fundamentally from the latter benign type. Rabin and King (1958), in an extensive examination of the current contradictions in the literature on schizophrenia, noted that a great many of these contradictions disappear when the syndrome is understood as a set of plural states rather than as a unitary one, and declared that "the selection of a specific frame of reference in the determination of samples, such as ... reactive vs. process ... tends to be a most fruitful avenue of approach" (p. 278).

On the explicit assumption that the level of perceptual organization is somehow correlated with schizophrenia, Winder and Kantor (1958) applied "personality-age-level" ratings as an operational Rorschach device to differentiate successfully between the mothers of psychotic sons and the mothers of normal sons, using no other external information than their Rorschach responses. The device itself is of interest because it allowed further refinement in the clarification of the plural states of schizophrenia. Basically, "personality-age-level" scores are obtained by defining the protocol on a scale (five points in the cited study) whose points are determined by published normative data on the level of expected and average Rorschach performance at a given period of life, raging from very young childhood through adulthood. Process schizophrenics tend to get the age-level ratings of early life, whereas reactive schizophrenics score nearer the adult levels. Used in this manner, the Rorschach test yields a reliable score on the quantity of symptomatic severity, pointing to the possibility of being able to distinguish between groups of schizophrenic persons.

Neither one of the last two studies attempted to apply a dimensional approach to the problem, although an underlying dimension was inherent in the idea of genetic maturation of perceptual organization. Nor was personality theory attempted. The developmental interpersonal theory of Harry Stack Sullivan (1947a) seemed to offer an integrated set of concepts relevant to the next step in the widening of a theory on the multiple states of schizophrenia.

Sullivan's theory of personality development referred to the widely utilized idea that there are sequential steps in experience which all humans encounter in the course of maturation, and he added that each step in the maturational sequence contains a central problem that must be at least partially "integrated" (Sullivan's term) before a new organization of experience can occur successfully on the maturational continuum. At least five growth steps are discernible. Ranging from infancy to childhood, they are: the empathic, the prototaxic, the parataxic, the autistic and the syntaxic.

This idea of growth stages was not extended by Sullivan to cover a theory about the schizophrenias. Kantor and Winder (1959) proposed that it might be operationally fruitful to describe the schizophrenias as systematically distributed along the five-step continuum of social maturity, using the etiological notion, early proposed by Freud, that "incomplete integrations are antecedents of regressions, and that regressions and failures to progress developmentally are reflected in schizophrenia."

By using the Rorschach age-level score as an independent measure of regression or primitivization, then showing that it correlated significantly with case-history information as to the earliest developmental life-epoch in which the patient had encountered pathogenic situations, the authors, in an earlier paper (Kantor & Winder, 1961), demonstrated that the schizophrenias may be quantitatively depicted, assigning reliable measurements to describe that level of life to which the schizophrenic has returned. Basically, this study mathematically described a widely accepted concept: "The underlying psychological notion proposes that the earlier in developmental history that severe stress prevails, the more damaging will be the consequences on the subsequent course of interpersonal relationships." The data of that study support the hypothesis that malignant schizophrenias result from early and extreme life deprivations, while the benign schizophrenias are associated with later and milder conflicts. Incidentally it seems probable that the semantically dysfunctional schizogenic families described by Jackson, Bateson, Haley, Weakland and other workers are producing schizophrenics of the more benign varieties, rather than the malignant types whose language and thinking functions are usually primitivized to the point of almost complete incomprehensibility.

Perhaps the most promising aspect of this line of research (which classifies schizophrenics as a malign-benign continuum), is that it offered a reasonable way of explaining why earlier research announced sharp differences between different samples of patients on such tested performances as perceptions, thinking, learning, intelligence and physiology (Winder, 1960). Benign schizophrenics do appear to be consistent on these measures among themselves, as do malignant types.

Interesting research benefits might be expected from the explanatory advantages of the reactive-process viewpoint. Becker's study (1959), for example, used this concept of schizophrenia to reveal a worthwhile covariance between prognosis, case history and test measurements. King (1958) added the variable of physiological reactivity to these three by demonstrating the "predominantly reactive schizophrenics display a higher level of autonomic responsiveness after the injection of Mecholyl than predominantly process schizophrenics." Brackbill and Fine (1956) found that signs of brain damage were statistically greater among the process schizophrenics than among the reactive ones.

Such findings are of especial interest because of the consistent failures of past studies to relate biological to psychosocial variables with schizophrenic samples that were either undifferentiated or classified on the orthodox nosology (King, 1954). Since the process-reactive idea implies a potential for change in the seriousness of the schizophrenic dysfunction from one pole towards the other, it also implies that time-change studies can utilize the quantitative measurements introduced by Becker (1956), by Kantor and Winder (1959) and by future efforts to study the effects of environmental and chemical agents on the retardation and advancement of schizophrenia by measuring changes in the distress of the illness. Changes in the communicative context of the schizophrenic's world, for instance, could be evaluated by their effectiveness in pushing him toward either polarity of severity.

EMPIRICAL STUDIES OF THE MENTAL HOSPITAL

Several striking studies described the mental hospital as a communicative system, basing their working assumption on the viewpoint that a social group is a communicative transaction that guides the orientations of the patients.

As well as reviewing previous research on this subject, Stanton and Schwartz (1954) were able to show how psychotics' heightened unrest and loosening of reality ties related positively to staff indecision about handling of these patients' cases. When the same disagreements were worked through openly, the anxieties and dissociations of the patients tended to clear. Essentially, as Dunham and Weinberg emphasized, patients form social networks within the hospital that serve to convey information about ways to facilitate discharge (1960). Caudill, et al. (1952) noted that greater status accrues to those patients nearer to discharge from the hospital, and that therefore the social groupings function primarily as communication centers that dispense information related to the problem of accommodating to the staff in the optimal way to insure the speediest release. Patients, for example, exert pressure on each other to acknowledge their mental illness openly and not to mislead themselves with other rationalizations that may impede medical assistance. Similarly, Goffman (1959) observed that patients have to learn to picture themselves as mentally ill, and do so, in good part, because the other patients on the ward talk to them as if they were "sick."

Another form of combination in the mental institution is revealed in studies by Belkman (1956) and by Scheff (1961) whose interest focused on the "attendant system." Because the ward physician's duties are too numerous for effective ward supervision by him, the real control on the ward is exercised by the psychiatric attendant. What this means to the patient is that such essentials as access to the physician, ground privileges, and eligibility for discharge are all under the working sections of the attendant ideology; resentment on the part of the patient may be communicated to the hospital medical authorities as "disturbance" or "acute excitement," with the attendant thus achieving psychiatric authorization for the system.

It may be argued that both Belknap and Scheff were describing a state hospital model where the medical facilities tend to be minimal, and the tradition of psychotherapy relatively weak. However, their findings were confirmed by Goffman (1957a) who observed a large hospital with a comparatively vigorous medical culture. Focusing on the means by that the mental patient becomes incorporated into the social group of the hospital, Goffman comments that the "self is systematically, if often unintentionally, mortified," by an authority hierarchy that, in effect, creates a staff elite which may punish any member of the inmate class for offenses that are not classified as illegitimate outside the hospital walls. An oligarchy is thereby created, at least from the patient's viewpoint, which may decisively intervene in the vital matters of therapy and discharge.

Perhaps it is relevant to comment here that Goffman is particularly shrewd at discerning what is really operating for both patients and personnel in the mental hospital situation. He notes, for instance, that given the type of privilege system (1957a) the patient's most imperative need is not to cope with the internal pressures of mental dysfunction, but to survive emotionally under the unfamiliar vagaries of the hospital world. At another place (1957b) he offers the idea of the "ratifier's" role as important not only as society's agent in the incarceration of the psychotic patient, but also for lifting the onus of betrayal from the shoulders of the family of the patient in that he, the "ratifier," rather than the relatives, is the one who "enforces an estrangement which the next-of-relationships can enjoy yet feel no guilt of having created." Again, noting that society's actions implicitly define normality or abnormality, Goffman (1959) says, "the psychiatric view of a person becomes significant only insofar as this view itself alters his social fate — an alteration which seems to become fundamental when the person is put through the process of hospitalization."

CONCLUSION

Schizophrenia is undergoing a gradual redefining process as the research focus shifts toward the facts of life as they appear variously to sociologists, anthropologists, and social psychologists. In this regard, it is important that some studies on schizophrenia (regarded here as significant) have tacitly adopted a social-science viewpoint by defining combinations and perceptions, not merely as vehicles for the transferal of information, but as forms of conduct conducive to adjustment or maladjustment among interacting humans.

The present paper has proposed that flourishing lines of inquiry into the nature of schizophrenia (citing family, Rorschach, and mental hospital studies) have been nourished by the particular position of the social scientist — a position that adds new dimensions to the traditional psychiatric inquiries. The adoption of this particular position bypasses the study of the biology of schizophrenia but, of course, does not exclude or supersede it; in our present state of darkness, illumination from any direction seems equally beneficial.

References

Bateson, G., Jackson, D. D., Haley, J., & Weakland, J. (1956). Toward a theory of schizophrenia. *Behavioral Science, 1*; 251–264.

Becker, W. C. (1956). A genetic approach to the interpretation and evaluation of the process-reactive distinction in schizophrenia. *Journal of Abnormal Sociology and Psychology, 53*; 229–236.

Becker W. C. (1959). The process-reactive distinction: A key to the problem of schizophrenia? *Journal of Nervous and Mental Disorders, 129*: 442–449.

Belkman, L. (1956). *Human problems of a state mental hospital.* New York: McGraw-Hill.

Blumer, H. (1937). Social disorganization & individual disorganization. *American Journal of Sociology, 42*; 871–877.

Bossard, J. H. S. (1948). *The sociology of child development.* New York: Harper.

Brackbill, G. A., & Fine, H. G. (1956). Schizophrenia and central nervous system pathology. *Journal of Abnormal Sociology and Psychology, 52*: 310–313.

Caudill, W., Redlich, F. C., Gilmore, H. R., & Brody, E. B. (1952). Social structure & interaction processes on a psychiatric ward. *Amer. J. Orthospychiat.*, 22: 314–334.

Clark, R. E. (1948). The relation of schizophrenia to occupational income and occupational prestige. *American Sociological Review, 13*; 325–330.

Cumming, E., & Cumming, J. (1957). *Closed ranks: An experiment in mental health education.* Cambridge, MA: Harvard University Press.

Davis, K. (1938). Mental hygiene and the class structure. *Psychiatry, 1*; 55–56.

Dunham, H. W., & Weinberg, S. K. (1960). *The culture of the state mental hospital.* Detroit, MI: Wayne State University Press.

Eliot, T. D. (1955). Interactions of psychiatric and social theory prior to 1940. In A. M. Rose (Ed.), *Mental health and mental disorder* (pp. 18–41). New York: W. W. Norton.

Faris, R. E. L. (1934a). Cultural isolation and the schizophrenic personality. *American Journal of Sociology, 40*; 155–165.

Faris, R. E. L. (1934b). Insanity distribution by local areas. *Procedures of the American Statistical Association, 27*; 53–57.

Faris, R., & Dunham, H. (1939). *Mental disorder in urban areas.* Chicago: University of Chicago Press.

Frank, L. K. (1936). Society as the patient. *American Journal of Sociology, 42*; 335–344.

Goffman, E. (1957). The characteristics of total institutions. In *Symposium on preventive and social psychiatry* (pp. 43–84). Washington, DC: US Government Printing Office.

Goffman, E. (1957). On convergence of sociology and psychiatry. *Psychiatry, 20*; 199–203.

Goffman, E. (1959). The moral career of the mental patient. *Psychiatry, 22*; 123–142.

Hadley, E., et al. (1944). Military psychiatry: An ecological note. *Psychiatry, 7*; 379–407.

Haley, J. (1959). The family of the schizophrenic: A model system. *Journal of Nervous and Mental Disorders, 129*; 356–374.

Halliday, J. L. (1949). *Psychosocial medicine.* New York: W. W. Norton.

Hardt, R. H., & Feinhandler, S. J. (1959). Social class and mental hospitalization prognosis. *American Sociological Review, 24*; 815–821.

Hollingshead, A. (1961). Epidemiology of schizophrenia. *American Sociological Review, 26*; 5–14.

Hollingshead, A. D., & Redlich, R. C. (1958). *Social class and mental illness.* New York: Wiley.

Horney, K. (1937). *The neurotic personality of our time.* New York: W. W. Norton

Jackson, D. D. (1957). A note on the importance of trauma in the genesis of schizophrenia. *Psychiatry, 20,* 18110184.

Jackson, D. D. (1957). The question of family homeostasis. *Psychiatric Quarterly, 1*; 79–90.

Jackson, D. D., & Weakland, J. (1961). Conjoint family therapy. *Psychiatry, 24*; Suppl. to No. 2 (Chestnut Lodge 50th Anniversary Symposium), 30–45.

Kantor, R. E., Wallner, J. M., & Winder, C. L. (1953). Process & reactive schizophrenia. *Journal of Consulting Psychology, 17*; 157–162.

Kantor, R. E., & Winder, C. L. (1959). The process-reactive continuum: A theoretical proposal. *Journal of Nervous and Mental Disorders, 129*; 429–434.

Kantor, R. E., & Winder, C. L. (1961). Schizophrenia: Correlates of life history. *Journal of Nervous and Mental Disorders, 132*; 221–226.

King, G. F. (1954). Research with neuropsychiatric samples. *Journal of Psychology, 38*; 383–387.

King, G. F. (1958). Differential autonomic responsiveness in the process-reactive classification of schizophrenia. *Journal of Abnormal Social Psychology, 56*; 160–164.

Merton, R. K. (1949). Social structure and anomie. In L. Wilson, & W. L. Kolb (Eds.), *Sociological analysis* (pp. 771–780). New York: Harcourt, Brace.

Mowrer, E. (1939). A study of personality disorganization. *American Sociological Review, 4*; 475–487.

Myers, J., & Roberts, B. (1959). *Family and class dynamics in mental illness.* New York: Wiley.

Pollack, O. (1952). *Social science and psychotherapy for children.* New York: Russell Sage.

Queen, S. (1940). Ecological studies of mental disorder. *American Sociological Review, 5*; 201–209.

Rabin, A. E., & King, G. F. (1958). Psychological studies. In L. Bellak (Ed.), *Schizophrenia: A review of the syndrome* (pp. 216–278). New York: Logo Press.

Scheff, T. (1961). Control over policy by attendants in a state hospital. *Journal of Health and Human Behavior, 2*; 93–105.

Schroeder, C. W. (1942). Mental disorders in cities. *American Journal of Sociology, 47*; 40–47.

Stanton, A. H., & Schwartz, M. S. (1954). *The mental hospital.* New York: Basic Books.

Sullivan, H. S. (1947). *Conceptions of modern psychiatry.* William Alanson White Psychiatric Foundation, Washington, D.C.

Sullivan, H. S. (1947). The study of psychiatry. *Psychiatry, 10*; 355–371.

Tietze, C., Lemkau, P., & Cooper, M. (1942). Personality disorder and spatial mobility. *American Journal of Sociology, 48*; 29–39.

Tietze, C. Lemkau, P., & Cooper, M. (1941). Schizophrenia, manic-depressive psychosis and social-economic status. *American Journal of Sociology, 47*; 167–175.

Weakland, J. (1960). The "double-bind" hypothesis of schizophrenia and three-party interactions. In D. Jackson (Ed.), *The etiology of schizophrenia* (pp. 373–388). New York: Basic Books.

Winder, C. L. (1960). Some psychological studies of schizophrenics. In D. Jackson, (Ed.), *The etiology of schizophrenia* (pp. 191–247). New York: Basic Books.

Winder, C. L., & Kantor, R. E. (1958). Rorschach maturity scores of the mothers of schizophrenics. *Journal of Consulting Psychology, 22*; 438–440.

Zilboorg, G. (1939). Sociology and psychoanalytic method. *American Journal of Sociology, 45*; 341–355.

CHAPTER 22

A Method of Analysis of a
Family Interview[1]

Don D. Jackson, Jules Riskin, and Virginia Satir

(1961)

INTRODUCTION

During recent years, evidence has been accumulating that suggests that a significant relationship exists between family interaction and mental illness. However, hypotheses concerning this relationship have been derived primarily from experience in conjoint family therapy and attempts to validate them have been essentially retrospective. We are in the process of setting up a longitudinal predictive study of families in order to test predictively some of these clinical impressions. Currently, we are focusing on the development of methods that will enable us to identify more precisely different patterns of family interaction, and relate these patterns to various forms of mental illness. Specifically, this paper presents a brief theoretical framework followed by a detailed illustration of one such approach.[2] Also, we believe that this report offers (post-

[1] Reprinted with permission from the *Archives of General Psychiatry*, October 1961, Vol. 5, pp. 321–339, Copyright 1961, by American Medical Association.
[2] Submitted for publication April 10, 1961. This study was made possible by a grant from the Robert C. Wheeler Foundation. The conceptual notions have been developed in association with our research group, especially Gregory Bateson, John Weakland, and Jay Haley. Mental Research Institute founder and first Director, Mental Research Institute,

dictive) evidence in support of hypotheses relating family interaction to mental illness, or in more general terms, to personality development.

The article presents the analysis of the first 5 minutes of a "blind" tape. The tape was kindly supplied us by Dr. Lyman Wynn of the National Institute of Mental Health.[3] The only identifying data accompanying the tape was the notation that this was the 80th session of the family in which mother, father, and son (identified patient) were present. We were told that there was a younger son who was not present at the interview and that the identified patient did not participate until late in this particular session.[4] We therefore deliberately focused on the initial stages of the interview in order not to be influenced by the way the patient sounded.

Our immediate impression, after hearing only 2 or 3 minutes of the tape, was that this was not the family of a chronic schizophrenic with either insidious or acute onset. We also felt that it was not likely to be a family in which any of the children had had an acute schizophrenic episode. However, as it will be detailed below, we were much less sure of the second assumption than the first. The mother and father interact rather overtly with each other and there is open argument. Although each qualifies his statements (especially father) in a manner we have not yet encountered in an apparently healthy family, there is more open challenging criticism than we had experienced in families containing a chronic schizophrenic member. The parents of an acute schizophrenic with a good prognosis are somewhat less direct than this couple, although superficially, the argumentation may sound rather similar.[5]

In the present excerpt, the criticism is explicitly directed and explicitly responded to. In the family of the acute schizophrenic, it is our impression

---

Palo Alto, Calif. (Dr. Jackson); Assistant Director (Dr. Riskin); Director Training of Family Project (Mrs. Satir). *See References for discussion of theoretical base.

[3] Dr. Wynne's detailed comments on this analysis are included at the end of this paper. We wish to express our appreciation to him for his cooperation on this project.

[4] This was an error on our part. Actually, as Dr. Wynne pointed out in a later note, there were three sons, not two. Dr. Wynne also stated that although he appreciated that this first attempt at analysis be as "blind" as possible, in the future it would be important to know (a) more of the context of the session being analyzed, and (b) essential identifying data about the family.

[5] These comments apply primarily to middle-class families. Our experience with upper and lower class familieas in very limited.

that critical statements are more covert and/or the response is rendered tangential by laughing, changing the subject, etc.

The material presented below attempts to demonstrate two kinds of analyses of the data: (1) The patterns of communication between the parents are examined from the standpoint of communication theory as containing a primary message and the manner in which it is qualified. (2) In addition, inferences are made as to the kind of individual who would produce such a message in such a manner. Thus one method is to describe formal communication patterns between the parents and the other makes inferences about their motivations and the kind of life experiences that might have led to such behavior. It is obvious that these approaches are complementary rather than mutually exclusive.

Introduction to Communication Analysis

The system of annotations on communication patterns has been described at length elsewhere (Bateson, 1960; Bateson, Jackson, Haley, & Weakland, 1956; Haley, 1959; Jackson, 1958a, 1959); we summarize it here. Statements may be judged as "symmetrical" or "complementary." A symmetrical statement is a comment on the equality of some aspect of a relationship. The most commonplace example would be in the conversation of adolescent peers engaged in a competitive relationship. For example, A says "I can hit a ball better than you" and B replies, "I can hit farther than you." Equality may be expressed by the general notion, "I have the right to say this to you at this time," or it may be expressed in obvious form through content. A complementary statement is one that "asks" or "offers." Arbitrarily, we call "asking" the complementary one-down position and "offering" the complementary one-up position. Complementarity may have to be judged in terms of content and in terms of following statements. If one is presented merely with the statement, "I feel lousy," it may not be possible to judge whether this is merely a statement that refers to parasites, whether it is an asking for help or sympathy, or whether it means, "You are difficult to be around," unless the response and the response to the response are included. If the context is known — for example, if such a statement is uttered in a doctor's office and the vocalization is characteristic of a particular mood expressed in a particular tone in our culture — then one may feel reasonably sure as to whether it is a complementary one-down or one-up statement.

The justification for the use of "complementary" and "symmetrical" is described by Jackson (1958a). Briefly, the use of these terms is based on the assumption that the individual is constantly attempting to define and influence the nature of his relationships. It is conceivable, after making due allowance for context, that the patterning of complementary and symmetrical responses will give a rough and simple index to varying types of communications in families, and that these patterns in turn will be correlated with specific manifestations of mental illness.

Communications may also be analyzed from a somewhat different, yet related, point of view. Since all communications contain more than one message, one may qualify another in a contradictory fashion or the messages may be consistent. If there is a contradictory message, we label that message a "disqualification." If the disqualification occurs within a single communication, it may be either a "sequential" disqualification (verbal contradiction), or an "incongruent" disqualification. The latter may be either an affect-verbal discrepancy or a statement-context discrepancy. Thus, "go away closer" is a sequential disqualification, since one phrase "go away" is opposite to the following word, "closer." "Go away" uttered in a warm, loving tone is an incongruent message of the verbal-affect type, since there are opposite meanings conveyed in the verbal and tonal aspects of the statement. A wealthy man telling his wife he can't afford a new dress for her is an example of the statement-context type of incongruency.

One reason for making this distinction between sequential disqualification and incongruency between messages is that, in our experience, the more disturbed families utter a greater number of incongruent messages as compared to sequential disqualifications than do healthy families. A commonplace kind of sequential disqualification, for example, "yes" and then "no" is evidence of unsureness, doubt, and so on and may occur in any family particularly under stress. If it occurs frequently in a family without an appropriate context (for example, as being on the witness stand), it may be a sign of fairly severe family pathology. Incongruent messages may be labeled by the family as jokes, sarcasm, or special types of personal family humor, but if they occur in response to a message from another family member that requires an answer, and then the incongruency is not commented upon, it is usually a sign of pathology. "Pathology," in this sense, may refer to as simple a measure as the fact that incongruencies bring ordinary family business to a halt; for example, the wife doesn't know what her husband "really" would like for supper.

If disqualifications of any sort are frequent in a family's exchanges, the observer will be struck by the number of unresolved or "incomplete transactions." *A* will respond only to one of *B*'s messages, and *B* will respond to *A* with evidence the he, *B*, was not understood. The amount of unfinished business (incomplete transactions) with consequent dissatisfaction becomes very striking. To put it another way, the transaction is incomplete because *B* does not insist that *A* make himself clear and this lack will lead to further non-completions, since *B* will respond with only partial information about *A*'s meaning, and so on. For example, a wife says to her husband: "I think you ought to go on that fishing trip, since you will make it unpleasant for the family if you don't." If, in addition, this statement is uttered in a biting, cold tone, then there are several messages at different levels to which the husband might respond. Our analysis of his relationship to his wife would be based on which aspect of her statement he responds to and how he qualifies his own communications. There is quite a difference between his stating, "You just put me in a bind. If I go, you will be angry; and if I don't go, you'll be angry because you'll be expecting me to make trouble"; and his stating in an explosive manner, "Dammit why can't I ever do what I want to. Okay, I'll stay home, but I don't think you're being very fair."[6]

The type of family just described, we have labeled elsewhere (Bateson et al., 1956) as "unstable, unsatisfactory," for issues are always being raised but never concluded. In this type of family, an event that calls into question "who has what rights in the relationship" will provoke discord without solution. The cardinal principle in this kind of family (unstable, unsatisfactory) is that neither husband nor wife will be able to deal with the issue of who has the right to determine the nature of their relationship and under what kinds of circumstances. Hence, children, sex, relatives, recreation, and other areas that call for collaboration or at least cooperation immediately bring up the question of "who will decide what," which leads almost invariably to discord.

Another kind of response to the wife's statement given above would be casual and quiet, and on the surface it would appear that the husband and wife got along very well. An example of such a response would be the husband's stating, "Oh dear, I can't go this weekend anyway. My boss will be coming to

---

[6] This latter response is characteristic of the husband in the family being presented in this paper. The husband gets angry, creates tension in the family, but obeys his wife's command, thus making his show of strength a sham and forcing on her a responsibility she hasn't asked for.

town." This change of context avoids the issue of "do you have the right" and "under what conditions — to tell me what to do." The cardinal principle in this kind of family (stable, unsatisfactory) is that the question "who will decide what" is never raised. It might be followed by the wife's asking about the boss's plans and concluding with the statement, " I wish you had let me know sooner. I want to get the house cleaned up." The husband could then respond, "Now, now, dear, you're a good housekeeper — it's just that you have so much to do." This kind of exchange, apparently friendly and superficially agreeable, is characteristic of some of the sicker, middle-class families we have seen. Since the complexities of modern living demand that each spouse have certain areas in which he or she must make decisions that affect their relationship, avoiding this issue or failing to resolve it makes for an increasing complexity. As a consequence, behavior by the family members becomes apparently inappropriate and unpredictable. Symptoms are the outcome. They are related to shifts in the levels of communication, which, in turn, are the results of attempting to respond with multileveled statements to disqualifications in messages among the members.

Introduction to Interactional Dynamics

In this section we describe how each individual's expectations are revealed through family interaction in the interview situation. We focus on the individual's perception of the self (how I see me), the perception of the other (how I see you), and the perception of the other in relation to the self (how I see you seeing me).

Given these perceptions, we are then able to make further inferences in relation to motives. In particular, we are interested in those attitudes such as: "am I lovable?" "am I acceptable?" "do I have self-worth?" We are also concerned with how an individual responds in the interview situation when his expectations and needs are frustrated. In other words, we are looking for what a person is implicitly trying to say in terms of his relationship with other family members. This can obviously be considered from many points of view, but we are focusing on how one individual tries to influence the other to respond to him in terms of his perceptions and expectations.

Another dimension of the analysis of the interactional dynamics involves making re-constructions (postdictions) of the early life experiences based on our observation of the current interaction. This is based on the assumption that earlier experiences with the parental figures affect the ways that one later perceives one's self and others, and that early patterns become "ruts," so that every problem tends to become a replica of the original problem.

Further, given an assessment of the interacting parental dynamics, we want to indicate how the children are integrated into the parental relationship. For example, such questions as: Do the children fill an emotional void in one or both parents resulting from a lack of gratification in the marital relationship; are the children essentially outside the relationship; are the children seen as narcissistic extensions of one of the marital partners; are the children seen as essential communication links between the parents since direct channels are blocked; does the child who becomes a "cross-monitor" help block more direct communication (Jackson, 1958a).

Interactional Dynamics Analysis Transcript	Interactional Dynamics Analysis	Communication Analysis
1. *Husband* Well, last time we were together Mrs. B. gave a very ... well a rather (Pause) dissertation, and one of the things I got out of it was she said that uh if I seem to make up my mind sometime and go ahead and do something I want to do and have the courage to do it, or something of that sort (evidently turns to wife) you remember that? (hedging — slightly whining)	1. Husband reminds therapist that last week wife said "I should do what I wanted to do." (Husband is saying "last week wife gave me permission to please myself and indicated by so doing I would please her ...")^Ψ (Does this complaining tone mean wife doesn't keep promises?) (*I am a little boy who must ask permission from mother.*)	1. (CD)* The message "I should be more assertive" is framed by: (a) My wife told me to, and (b) you therapists are responsible — isn't that right? Thus, the interview begins with the husband's difficulty in making a symmetrical statement because it would raise the question with his wife, "Who has what rights in our relationship." Anything that is further stated must be viewed in the framework of "she told me to" and "you said it was all right."

Ψ Statements ranging from those being of low inference (having no parentheses), through those of medium inference (having parentheses), to those being highly inferential (having parentheses and italicized).

---

* CD — Complementary one down comment.

2. *Therapist*
Uh-huh.

3. *Husband*
Well so when I tried a little sample of that Saturday, she just raised hell. (mimics, with raising voice) (he laughs) (evidently turns to wife) Your reaction was interesting. I just said that I was going to play ... this was Friday, wasn't it? (tries to sound factual)

4. *Therapist*
You were what?

5. *Husband*
This was Friday (sounds factual) I'd been away on this trip. Didn't have any vacation Friday.

---

2. Therapist makes affirming response indicating husband should continue.

3. Husband tells therapist he tried to please himself but wife objected. ("Wife doesn't mean what she says. She gives permission but takes it away, and this is what I expected. As usual, I can't please her.") (Husband's comments are indirect criticism of wife and at the same time a plea for understanding from her.) (You must never make women angry. Women don't like grown-up men. I resent this.)

4. Therapist asks for more information.

5. Husband says "after working hard, I wanted to enjoy myself." ("I had justification for enjoying myself but

---

2. Therapist makes a neutral comment which in this context means go ahead.

3. (Sym$^\Xi$ to CD) Husband starts again with a symmetrical statement "My wife is like this." He almost immediately disqualifies himself by "little sample" and by using an exaggerated tone, for example on the word "raised," thus criticizing her without risking being overt about it. He does not state "I am critical of my wife." Instead, by mimicking her, he implies "this is what she sounds like."

4. Therapist asks for more information.

5. (Sym to CD) Again he starts out with a symmetrical statement but again disqualifies himself in 2 ways: (a)

$^\Xi$ Sym — Symmetrical comment

Thought I was going to play golf, (pause) and so made this statement, I was going to play golf, and she started in (apparently mimics her complaining tone) well, Dick wanted some kids to go swimming and one thing and another. And she had to do some shopping because Pete was coming over, bringing his friends over. And immediately got angry about this. (someone coughs) At one point, it involved things about (mimicking) I was selfish and I wasn't thinking about anybody else and all this sort of thing. (back to reportorial tone) Meanwhile I had arrived at the suggestion that part of this was because Pete had to have the car over here. That, I imagine Pete had nothing to do Friday morning and he could solve this whole thing extremely simply by just coming home and taking his mother shopping. (sounds

my wife says children's needs come first. Wife criticizes me for not dropping my needs and meeting children's needs, but I saw a reasonable way that both my needs and theirs could be met.") ("Wife refused to accept this way, but continued to favor the kids. My wife is unreasonable. You, wife, lie when you say you want me to do what I want to do") ("If I want to do what I want I have to defy you, wife. Doing what I want to do can only be an act of rebellion.") (*You always have to defy mothers to get what you want. If you rebel you make them angry, but if you don't rebel they think you are weak and you remain a little boy.*)

He gives up his reportorial tone and factual reporting and then mimics his wife again, implying that she is unreasonable and she will not let him determine what goes on in the house; (b) he then adopts a suffering, complaining tone during which he apparently turns to his wife and addresses her directly in a challenging way. In addition, he seems to be indicating to the therapist what he has to put up with.

heroic) And I would call him up and ask him to do this. At which point (mimics) don't you dare — all that sort of thing. (suffering, complaining) I mean everything here was pinning this whole business on what Dick wanted to do with his little children, what Pete might be just inconvenienced one way, slightly one way or another. And you were just going to see by God if you could not keep me from, if you could keep me from playing golf, I *do believe*. (pause) But I did. . . .

6. *Wife*	6. Wife denies	6. (Sym) The wife's
(Overlaps husband's statement) The way you take it. (quietly determined)	husband's accusation. ("I am not bad, you are. You are misunderstanding me.") (Wife feels that men are really just little boys, they are to be humored, not to be taken seriously.) (*Father was ineffectual and treated by mother as a little boy.*)	statement, "the way you take it" is said in a quietly determined voice, indicating all too clearly "you are unreasonable and I have to put up with you." The measured tone is an appropriate qualification of the content.

7. *Husband*
And I call up your son and he was glad to come over and help you and all this and that. So this was your reaction to me deciding I wanted to do something and meaning it. (more tentatively) wasn't it?

7. Husband says ("I proved to you that I had a reasonable idea but you won't accept proof. You just want to deprive me. You are unreasonable.") (*Mothers lie when they say they want to be accepting. They are always depriving. Men have no way of influencing women.*) (You want the children on your side and are against me. You make me feel that my children and I are rivals: When I try to be the father, I am left out. You don't really want a man." ("Isn't it true that you are unreasonable? If you can admit to being unreasonable, then we both can feel equal. How I feel depends on how you feel.")

7. (Sym to CD) Husband ignores the challenge, apparently, and resorts again to an attempt at a symmetrical statement. Again he backs down by ending on a question "Wasn't it?" This is an invitation to being cut down. (Note that so far there have been no completed transactions.)

8. *Wife*
(With a sigh -icy) That's the way you like to take it. You must remember when you left (deadly, bitter) you said (mimics) that you may not be here.

8. Wife says, "I am justified in criticizing you because you are so unreasonable." (You can't count on men.)

8. (Sym to CD) Wife repeats her statement with greater emphasis, for example the sigh implying his unreasonableness. Although the statement is uttered generally in a deadly bitter, icy tone and she

315

continues in a symmetrical position, she disqualifies it slightly by mimicking him in the words, "May not be here." She ends in a one-down position as she appeals to the therapist, "Listen how unreasonable he sounds."

9. *Husband*
(Filling in her last statement) Thursday. And you know my custom is I would let you know. (injured innocence) (Wife murmurs) so what's the difference? (loudly)

9. (Husband says "You are unreasonable for labeling me as unreasonable.") (Men can't please women.)

9. (Sym to CD) Husband again resorts to making a symmetrical maneuver by simply reporting the facts, but ends again on a question "What is the difference?" which obviously calls for a response from her, thus putting him in a complementary one down position.

10. *Wife*
What's the difference? (exaggeratedly factual) Because Pete had called up very nicely and asked if you were back yet or if I knew and I

10. (Wife says "How can I help but criticize you when you are so unreasonable; you are just a blustery boy.") (*Men cannot be counted upon. Men are*

10. (CU[φ] to CD) Wife responds to his one-down position by taking the complementary one-up position, stating by her tone and her factual

---

φ CU — complementary one-up comment.

said — No, I didn't. So he said he'd like, he'd bring the car back but I couldn't as I explained to you, (slightly faltering) get the car and drive Pete back to the hospital because he had booked up the evening, because that was the night that Dick had a baseball game which you simply accepted. And I, I uh, (exaggeratedly factual) we had made our plans because we hadn't heard you'd come back or not. Dick invited some boys over there and when you came back and you were sore at me. It wasn't that . . . (mimics) you just came out and said (mimicking — slightly faltering) by God, I'm home, by golly I'm going to have the car by golly, I'm going . . . the hell with — (Wife gets increasingly louder) (factual tone — mimicking attitude)

unreasonable. Father was an unreliable, unpredictable, unreasonable man who couldn't be counted on either.) (Wife has a need for a husband who will confirm her expectation that men are unreliable, but on the other hand desperately hopes they won't turn out that way.)

content "I am reasonable; you are unreasonable." She then weakens her position when she uses his technique of mimicking again, again asking for his support.

317

11. *Husband* (Interrupting) (sounds very defensive) I wasn't saying anything like that. (loud) I just said I was going to play golf.

11. Husband rejects wife's accusation. By defending himself husband automatically denies wife's plea for a strong man who will understand her. (He comments instead — "I didn't mean to hurt you, I just wanted to do something for myself.")

11. (Sym to CD) Husband responds to first part of wife's message by attacking. He becomes literal "I just said I was going to play golf" rather than dealing explicitly with her message that he is unreasonable. He thus invites a reiteration from her. His defensive tone (hurt?) is perhaps a comment on her using the one-up position to criticize him.

12. *Wife* (Mock horror) Oh-h-h you just when I said —

12. (Wife attacks him for being a little boy.)

12. (Not determined) Her exaggerated mock horror is a comment on his being a child, but she is utilizing a child-like technique and it is thus not a strong ploy. She does not continue to usurp the one-up position, perhaps because she recognizes that she has gone too far in criticizing him. This pattern would suggest that apparently they have an inflexible set of rules as to how far they can go in devastating each other. Wife attacks husband

for being a little boy, which makes her seem like an evil mother because husband cannot better tolerate her criticism. She is hurt by his being hurt. And this circularity seems to serve as a governor on the extent of their relatedness.

13. *Husband* (Sharply interrupting) It was not until you started (she interrupts, some overlapping) (fast, sharp interaction, each being exaggeratedly factual), not until you started.

13a. *Wife* I said . . .

13b. *Husband* . . . yelping about it. This seems almost petty of me to bring a thing like this in here but it goes back to this point that you were saying (mimicking) by golly you would like to see me make up my mind some time or other what I wanted to do and do it.

13. (Husband says "I am not a bad little boy, you are the unreasonable one.") (If this interaction continued, their mutual hurt would show. In order to avoid this, husband joins in setting the automatic governor in motion and returns to opening gambit saying — "I don't want to hurt you, I am only trying to do what you want me to do. Damn you. Please let me!")

13. (Sym to CD) The governor now in effect, husband returns to the starting statement. Even the content of his statement says clearly "You went too far and now let's start over." He is back to his original position.

319

14. *Wife*
What did you learn that week end, John? (quietly determined, matronizing)

14. Wife changes subject ostensibly. (Wife implies she is speaking to a little boy who is bad — she therefore acts ostensibly like a solicitous mother. Wife is wanting to give by being mothering to husband even though critical. The tone is softer — making a bid for closeness — conciliation to husband.) (Wife, if denied gratification of her needs to be given to further denies them by defensively taking the role of mother.)

14. (CU to Sym) In the absence of an intervention by the therapist, wife responds to husband by asking a therapist-like question, thus switching the context from their private circular interaction. Wife's attempt to get out of the rut misfires because she frames it with a superior tone, thus baiting him; so he must reattack instead of responding helpfully.

15. *Husband*
Hm?

15. (Since this mothering is seen by husband as defensive, as a disguise to the lack of gratification of her needs, it is not possible for him to fully respond to it. Husband seems taken aback and behaves as though he doesn't hear.) (Mothering probably feels phony to him.)

15. Husband is unclear which message to respond to, therefore he stalls.

16. *Wife*
What did you learn
(pause) after all that
snorting around? (more
critical and with slight
edge)

16. Wife initially
repeats mothering tone,
but changes to critical
one in tone and word
after being denied any
response to her offering.
(*Wife feels confirmation of
her expectation that men
will not accept any giving
from women, therefore
women are useless in the
eyes of men.*) (Wife
denies being put in this
position by accusing
husband of being
incapable of giving or
receiving.)

16. (CU to Sym) Wife
interprets husband's
stalling as a lack of
response to the helpful
aspect of her statement
and reinforces the
superior aspect in order
to punish him. This is
not being a "good
therapist" and invites
attack from husband by
her failure.

17. *Husband*
I learned that you just
do a lot of yelping no
matter what (sharply
critical) Another thing
is yesterday was another
example. (Wife —
"Um hum") Uh, you
wanted to go
swimming. (gentle,
definitive, teaching
quality) And because
Dick —

17. Husband denies
wife's accusation ("I am
not ungiving; your
demands are insatia-
ble.") (*Your needs, like
those of all women are so
great they are incapable of
satiation.*) (Wife says
apprehensively — "Go
ahead. I know you are
going to blame me but
you are not going to
get away with it.")
(Husband continues . . .
"You say you want to
do something for
yourself, but you let the
kids interfere just as
they interfere with my

17. (Sym to CU)
Husband responds with
the expected attack,
using "yelping" instead
of "snorting." As soon
as he is critical, he
attempts conciliation by
being solicitous in the
manner of a therapist.
However this effort on
husband's part to
become a therapist,
although conciliatory,
labels her a patient and
will bring forth a
rebuttal, which will lead
to a symmetrical
relationship such as
these two have.

pleasures. You blame me for not pleasing you when you really won't let yourself be pleased.")

18. *Wife* (Interrupts) I didn't say I wanted to go swimming. I said I may go swimming. But didn't want to rush. (edgy, exasperated) (tersely) And we were going out at 4 o'clock. (Defensively starts to get legalistic)

18. (Wife denies she desires pleasures. "My concern is for you and the children. My pleasures are only secondary to yours and the children'.") (*Women dare not expect pleasure or gratification. Wife's mother was a martyr, thus she expects it is woman's role to suffer.*)

18. (Sym to CD) The expected rebuttal occurs but with a revealing edge to it. By denying husband's implication that she is entitled to want for herself, she indicates that their relationship is one in which wanting is bad. However, her defensive tone disqualifies this definition and invites the husband to pursue his attack. They have now reversed roles. He is telling her she should be more assertive, and she is denying it as he was doing earlier. It is as if each had told the other: "If you would get more for yourself, I could too." Although husband has her on the defensive, it is the same old issue, there has been no progress toward clarification.

19. *Husband*
(Interrupting) But you hinged all this around Dick, not liking to do something or other. (Patient, Patronizing — trying to be factual.)

19. (Husband says, "you, wife, can't openly ask to have pleasure though you really want to. You can only attain it under the guise of doing it for the children.") (*Husband's mother would have used him against his father as wife uses Dick against him.*) (Husband feels competitive with son and at the same time critical of wife for using Dick.) (It could additionally be that husband suspects women can ask for what they want, but they consciously deny this. Husband is attempting to get wife to acknowledge this.)

19. (Sym) This again is a symmetrical statement in which he accuses her of taking second place to the children. At the same time in this context he removes himself from the charge of being a spoiled child since he, too, is put in second position.

20. *Wife*
Well, I didn't want to go swimming by myself. (defensive) (faster) You were (quite fast, almost stumbling) I was half planning on doing something like that and I (defensively)

20. (Wife denies that she can't ask for pleasures. "It appears that I can't because you desert me and I have to turn to Dick. It really is your fault since you don't give to me. I'd really want to receive.")

20. (Attempts CU but settles for CD) She again switches context by ignoring the "Dick" charge. This may have been partly caused by his ignoring her statement "and we were going to go out at 4 o'clock." Her content is disqualified, however, by her fast, defensive

vocalization. She again uses a similar type of message to his — an apparently factual statement disqualified by hurt defensiveness and inviting further movement from the spouse. Wife has ignored husband's implication that when she puts children first, he suffers.

21. *Husband*
(Interrupting) Then you couldn't. (indignantly) You had to rush back to cook him his supper and the other night you cooked him his supper and he didn't even eat it. (pause) I mean all this stuff starts hinging around what do these little rascals want to do (mimicking) all the time (pause) and are they absolutely first?

21. (Husband says "I don't believe you want to give me anything. You don't give me anything. The children get more than I do and they are not as appreciative as I would be." (*Husband feels unloved and that his mother was depriving in a manner that prevented overt labeling by him. Thus it is important that he get his wife to openly acknowledge her deprivation of him.*)

21. (Sym to CD) Here he nearly reaches his finest hour. "You sacrifice me for the kids and it doesn't pay off." But on the threshold of becoming one-up, he backs down and asks: "Is it necessary?" which is an invitation for wife to take a CU.

22. *Wife*
Well I always (quieter-regaining her composure)

22. Wife is taken aback by the extent of husband's accusation that children come first, especially since wife

22. (Sym) She doesn't immediately respond to his invitation to take the one-up position, perhaps because she is

324

views him as one of the children. She views his accusation of partiality as a comment on her being a bad mother. (Her need to maintain a good-mother image might also relate to her not perceiving illness in Pete until external factors force it to her attention.)

still caught by the first part of his message.

23. *Husband* (Interrupting) — interfere with you and interfere with me and interfere with everything else. (Indignant and angry)

23. In order to avoid a direct frontal attack on wife for not caring about him, husband points to the children as the reason for his being left out, inferring that wife would care for him very much if she were able to, that is, the children prevent her from doing this. It would be dangerous openly to accuse wife of not caring lest he receive concrete evidence of her not caring, that is, his own unworthiness. (*His mother's preferential treatment of him, much like his wife's treatment of Pete, resulted in feelings of privilege,*

23. (CU to Sym) Her refusal to accept his message that "we are both losing out to the kids" leads to further attack, in which he overgeneralizes and thus leaves himself open.

*and, at the same time an
inadequacy to live up to
them. He repeats this
pattern with his wife.)*
(Husband's preferential
position with his
mother makes him a
hopeless competitor
with his father and
denies him an identi-
fication which would
enable him to carry out
his fathering role. *Thus
fathers can't help their sons
because they are rivals.
They can only look out for
themselves.*)

24. *Wife*
I always knew you
were jealous of your
children.
(contemptuous, cold,
critical, definite, sounds
almost triumphant)

24. (Wife says "I know
you always felt like a
rival with your chil-
dren. Which means that
you make me a mother
instead of a wife. Thus
I am deprived of a
husband.") (Her cutting
tone indicates the
attitude, "You aren't a
man.") (*Since wife
married such a "man,"
she has no expectations of
being treated as a wife.)
(Her mother did not
openly label her father as
"no good" but implied
men are ungiving and
women must be the*

24. (Strong Sym) Again
as in sequence 14, she
nails him with a
"therapeutic"
interpretation, which
fails for the same reason
(Cf. 14).

responsive ones. Wife's father cooperated in this attitude by being dead tired, too busy. Thus she was denied an opportunity of being a Daddy's girl and thus was not prepared to be given to by a husband.)

25. *Husband*
I (only mildly defensive) am not jealous of them.

25a. *Wife*
Yes you are (as he says)

25b. *Husband*
I just expect equal rights. (long pause) You do all this self-sacrificing all the time and what does it get you? (righteously indignant)

25. Husband denies rivalry with children. ("It's your fault that I am not a man. It is not the children but your preferential treatment of the children that makes me feel deprived. Why do you treat yourself this way? I could help you if you would let me.") (This man needs the evidence of external validation from wife to give him feelings of self-esteem.)

25. (Sym to CD) He attempts to escape damning charge by restating his message, "Don't put them in front of us." As usual, however, his bid is double-edged and difficult to respond to. His major message is, "Why can't we get together?" but it is disqualified by his angry tone and the label, "You are bad" attached to being self-sacrificing.

26. *Wife*
I am not self-sacrificing, John. (pause) (soft) You think so . . . (mimicking through phony toughness) you want me, it's like the last time, you want me to treat your children

26. (Wife says "I almost believe you would like to be a man, which means I could be a wife, but I know really you want me to be a mother to you. I can't even be a mother to you because your picture of a mother is

26. (Starts Sym and ends CU) She responds to his implicit charge rather than to his attempts to get together. Again she out-maneuvers him by switching the context to "You loved your mother and she was

327

the way your mother treated you. (bitter contempt) She ran her little roost over there and this thing was done this way. You liked it. (biting)

unacceptable to me and I can see what your mother did to you. I deny that she and I have anything in common. Your attitude prevents me from having anything to offer.") (Thus wife expects external validation is necessary for her own feeling of worth as a wife or mother.)

wrong so I won't be like her." This is a double-leveled message that is difficult to respond to. If he accepts the "you like it," he accepts a damning charge as well. If he agrees mother was wrong, he is ignoring the charge "you loved her" and may step into further difficulties, namely, "You don't love me any more than you loved your mother." If he could rise to a new level, namely, "I care for you as much as I did my mother," he could handle her message.

TRANSCRIPT WITH INTERACTIONAL DYNAMICS AND COMMUNICATION ANALYSIS

There are several generalizations that might orient the reader toward following the parental interaction in the transcript to be presented:

1. The parents make no attempt to include the identified patient (their son) and they speak of him and his brother (who is not present) in much the same manner.

2. The parents are defensive and righteous and each is insecure in regard to his role. Thus, they cannot aid one another and must resort to blaming each other.

3. The mother appears to achieve an edge in the power struggle between them but as mentioned below, this position is not maintained. She is able to use the children against the father and he is unable to avoid falling into this trap because he is defensive about his attitude toward his sons. Apparently he competes with his sons for his wife in a fashion that makes him feel like one of the children, thus lowering his own self-esteem and elevating the relative position of his wife. This makes the husband defensive and he attacks the wife for being a bad mother. The wife then becomes anxious and feels deserted over the husband's abdication of his role, which is seen by her as neglect. She then reinstitutes the struggle by attacking him for his neglect of her. This pattern between the parents produces an oscillatory interaction, which is apparent even in this brief excerpt.

4. Although we state that the fighting between the parents is more overt and explicit than the family of the acute or chronic schizophrenic, it should be pointed out that this couple is unable to resolve anything by their struggle and this is an indication of significant pathology. They play what Berne (unpublished manuscript) has labeled "the Game of Uproar."

5. Because the therapist makes no attempt to break up the parental struggles, we can assume that he has been through this before. Since there is more impotence than destructiveness in the argumentation, the therapist is not alarmed by any untoward effects. This hypothesis is supported by the cyclical nature of the parents' encounters. One or the other backs off before things get out of hand and reenters the area and a new fight starts. Without the therapist's intervention, the couple behaves as if a psychological governor were limiting the range of their oscillation. One can, therefore, imagine this couple going through life not agreeing but not disagreeing to the extent of separation.

CONCLUSIONS

On the basis of the analysis of the above portion of the tape, we make the following conclusions about this family:

A. We view these parents as upwardly mobile, middle-class individuals.

1. Wife expects men to be unpredictable, weak, withholding, and unnur-
    turing, as seen in her expectations of her husband. Because of men's
    weakness, wife feels that women must, of necessity, step in and be the
    strong ones as her mother probably did. Women cannot hope to be pro-
    tected, cared for, and understood by men because men prevent it by
    being weak. This is a comment on her feminine identification. These ex-
    pectations blind her to any evidence to the contrary.

    Her hopes on the other hand are that men be predictable, strong,
    giving, and nurturing; thus her frequent verbalizations "Be a man, don't
    be a man." "Be aggressive, don't be aggressive." The former aspect rep-
    resents her hopes and the latter, her expectations, which she succeeds in
    evoking, because wife expects that men are weak and helpless. This
    would seem to be a clue to wife's relationship to her mother, who was
    likely withholding. In relation to women, wife probably sees herself as
    undesirable, inadequate, and basically a child.

2. Husband expects women to be overwhelming, the mainstay of the fami-
    ly, partial, depreciating, unpleasable, infantilizing, as seen by his ex-
    pectations of his wife. "Women do not like grown-up men. They only
    say they do." Husband hopes that women will permit him to have a
    position of equality with them, will relate to him as though he were
    strong, important, grown-up. On the other hand, he expects this not to
    happen. We see that he ignores efforts on the part of his wife to treat
    him this way. He behaves according to his expectations of women's ex-
    pectations and depreciates his own hopes. Therefore by necessity, he
    must communicate in multilevel messages. In relation to men, husband
    probably feels unable to compete and be esteemed.

3. All of this results in a lack of mutually satisfying communication between
    husband and wife — "no closeness," about which the couple openly
    complain. They feel inadequate, undesirable, unloved, incapable of loving
    or being loved. This is spelled out in terms of criticism of each other.
    The communication is carried on at the level of their defenses against
    their mutually felt but unverbalized low feelings of self-esteem. Each is
    trying to force the other to increase his feelings of self-worth, which,
    because of the other's low expectations and his own low feelings cannot
    be supplied. On the other hand, despite the long history of deprivation,

each still is actively trying to increase his feelings of self-esteem and be giving to the other, unsuccessful as these efforts turn out. This pattern is in contrast to families that seem sicker to us, where there seems to be only futility and despair.

B. From our knowledge of the present interaction between the husband and wife, we may make further inferences in relation to their own respective families of origin. It would seem that the expectations of each spouse, as revealed, for example, by their criticisms or demands on each other, would enable us to speculate as to what kinds of relationships their own parents might have had in order to provide the matrix for the development of these expectations. We therefore make the following reconstructions on the families of origin:

1. Husband had a father whom we would consider withholding, restrictive, punitive, an average provider but basically ineffective. Husband's mother was probably a "giving," strong, (iron-hand-silk-glove) orderly, demanding woman. We would see her as depressed and unhappy, with husband feeling ineffective in being able to please her. Husband's mother was the openly accepted, undisputed authority with father being covertly rebellious, particularly with money, but openly accepting her authority. Husband's mother was a precise, aggressive woman, socially adept. His father was also a socially correct, but passive businessman who was probably closely tied to his business.

2. Wife had a fairly materially successful father. Mother of wife was an overly demanding woman who expressed this covertly. We would expect that wife saw her father as literally absent or remote, ineffectual, and unable to provide emotionally. Wife's mother was the boss in the family, but this could not be explicitly spelled out. Wife's father covertly acted out against mother's covert authority in some self-punishing way so that it turned out that mother was a martyr and father was an unfortunate man. Wife could not comment on the relationship between her parents.

The chances are, in our experience, that in a family characterized by a symmetrical relationship such as in this one, the first child brings up the question of "Who is in charge of what?" In such a family, first child also may be made a bearer of parental ambitions, as well as a repository for

331

the uneasiness and self-doubt. In this family, then, we would expect that the first child, Pete, would be used by the parents to facilitate communication between them. (We would predict that if something were to occur to prevent their using Pete, they would use the second child in the same way.) The second son, Dick, might have an easier time of it. In view of this mother's overprotectiveness and the father's helpless competitiveness, Dick is apt to be the spoiled child with some ability to manipulate other people and some actingout behavior.

C. The identified patient, Pete, might manifest some of the following symptoms because of his focal position in the parental struggle.

1. He must be responsible and succeed; yet success would increase father's competitiveness and reveal the shallowness of mother's attachment to Pete. Therefore, Pete must also fail. These mechanisms occur against the backdrop of the parents' mutually depriving interaction. The parental interaction heightens Pete's success-failure conflict, and in turn this conflict highlights the parents frustrating struggles with each other.

2. Pete must fail in such a way that neither parent can view the failure as a comment on their relationship with their son. His failure is apt to provoke comments from each in blaming the other. At the same time, since he perceives himself as outside their relationship and feels hopeless about breaking into it, he would be fearful that both might turn on him. His failure, therefore, would be of the "quiet type" such as increasingly poor grades, decreasing socialization, etc. Failure of this sort would lead to evanescent concern and interest as well as criticism on the part of his parents, but there would be no follow-through until he becomes so overtly symptomatic that they seek medical help. It is postulated that there has been a long delay in seeing difficulties as "symptoms," since each parent would label some aspect of Pete's behavior as an extension of faults in the other person, therefore "bad" rather than "sick." They would each procrastinate, blaming the other for the "bad" behavior in Pete, for which they hold the other responsible.

3. Withdrawal would keynote Pete's defensive operations because it allows him to feel he leaves the relationship rather than being left out of the

parents' interaction. In addition, withdrawal will dull the hurt of experiencing their bitter clashes. This family is intact enough so that Pete could not withdraw in an obvious fashion, such as becoming a vagabond or hiding in his room, but he might withdraw by preoccupation, especially if his parents' strivings link this to intellectualism, "the absent-minded professor" (and if his fantasies take the form of non-comments on his relationship to his parents, for example, rather than what he would like to do either with or to his parents). Pete's comment is "I am not separated from you; I am just involved with myself." As long as the parents accept this thesis, Pete is forced to acknowledge that he is alone, and this will lead to depression that will be noticed by them. The parents are then forced to view him as sick. If they delay in this recognition, the next step might be suicidal comments and possibly a suicidal attempt. Although we have no direct data on this, we would not be surprised if he had actually threatened to make a suicide attempt.

4.   Pete's model from both parents is a longing hunger that one must not reveal lest he become vulnerable. Therefore, blame and alibi play an important part in accounting for why things are not at they should be. While there is no evidence from the tape directly, one might infer that Pete used physical illness, procrastination, and "I don't feel like it" as part of his avoidance mechanisms.

5.   There is a family fiction that Pete and Dick both must go along with. This includes:

   a.   Father is stereotyped as trying hard, but he shouldn't put the family last as he does. He is also depicted as a dictator who invokes fear.

   b.   Mother is more loving and reliable and puts the children first. Actually, it seems to us that father identifies with his sons and is more forgiving than mother represents him as being, even though he is competitive and temperamental. He is not much of a dictator and his wife indicates he is more of a windbag than a strong force. He supports her view by being unable to make symmetrical comments without framing them as "This is the way you told me I should be." Such a comment frames the whole session. Mother is such a deprived person that much of her apparent giving to the children is actually using them against father to point up his deprivation of her and to replace him via the sons. This retaliatory gesture states "Since you won't give to me, I have to use my sons." Pete's understandable failure to fill father's shoes, would decrease his self-esteem, and produce sexual problems. While there is no direct data, the problem would take the form of concern over masturbation (Jackson, 1958a), and doubts about his masculinity. Such problems would increase the parents' anxiety and render them incapable of aiding Pete.

Rather than being discrepant as being presented in the family fiction, both parents are evenly matched. They are in a constant struggle for love from each other and only tangentially relate to their children. They are mirror images and use much more similar communication devices than any set of parents we have so far analyzed. The extent of their involvement with each other leaves little involvement with the children except as the child: (1) reminds each parent of some aspect of himself; (2) can be used to replace deficiencies in the relationship of the one spouse with the other; (3) can be used as a weapon by one spouse against the other. Pete, then, serves as a repository for the faults they see in the other, and simultaneously disguises these faults in them, thus resulting in labeling Pete the sick one. Dick, on the other hand, might be the child who represents the more carefree wish of each, and any problem he might show would be interpreted as "cute" or childlike.

SUMMARY

In this paper we have presented an analysis of the first 5 minutes of a family therapy interview. The analysis has been from 2 points of view: (1) in terms of communication theory, which is concerned with the formal aspects of the interaction; (2) in terms of the interacting dynamics of the spouses, with emphasis on how each one's needs and defenses are affected by the affect of the other spouse. We have tried to reconstruct (post dict) the possible bases for their interaction in terms of their early life experiences. From their patterns of interaction we have attempted to predict the psychiatric symptoms of their oldest son, and also some character traits of his younger brother. Our immediate purpose in this analysis has been to illustrate a method of analyzing family interaction, with the ultimate intention of applying this method to a longitudinal predictive study that would test hypotheses relating family interaction to mental illness.

References

Bateson, G. (1960). Minimal requirement for a theory of schizophrenia. *AMA Archives of General Psychiatry. 1*; 477–491.

Bateson, G., Jackson, D. D., Haley, J., & Weakland, J. (1956). Toward a theory of schizophrenia. *Behavioral Science, 1*; 251–264.

Berne, E. Unpublished manuscript.

Haley, J. (1959). The family of a schizophrenic: A model system. *Journal of Nervous & Mental Disorders, 129*; 357–374.

Jackson, D. D. (1958). Guilt & the control of pleasure in the schizoid personality. *British Journal of Medical Psychology, 31*;124–130.

Jackson, D. (1959). Family interaction, family homeostasis and some implications for conjoint family psychotherapy. In J. Masserman (Ed.), *Individual and family dynamics*. New York: Grune & Stratton.

Jackson, D. (1959). *Analysis of schizophrenic families*. Read before GAP, November.

CHAPTER 23

Family Research on the Problem of Ulcerative Colitis[1]

Don D. Jackson and Irvin Yalom

(1966)

Chronic ulcerative colitis is an enigma today, despite many years of study and voluminous publications by persons of diverse interests and backgrounds. As Lepore (1965) stated: "its etiology remains unknown and its treatment unscientific." Since Murray's paper (1930), which noted the connection between emotional factors and both mucus colitis and ulcerative colitis, there have been many inquiries into the psychological functioning of ulcerative colitis patients. In general, there has been agreement that ulcerative colitis patients usually suffer from serious psychological illness. Descriptions of personality organization in such patients, based on psychological testing or therapy observations, include the whole panoply of our nosological types. Frequently mentioned characteristics are: obsessive-compulsive character traits, narcissism, a marked pseudo-mature veneer covering a deeper petulant infantilism, rigidity, and guarded affectivity, underlying depressive trends, and psychosexual immaturity. Patients often exercise marked denial and have difficulty in effectively expressing aggression. The psychological aspects of the precipitating stress have been

---

[1] From the *Archives of General Psychiatry*, October 1966, Vol. 15, pp. 410–418. Reprinted with permission.

studied by several investigators with some consensus about the psychological vulnerability of the ulcerative colitis patient to separation, or the threat of separation, from a significant other.

Developmental studies and speculations have, in the main, been limited to descriptions of the pathological relationship in the ulcerative colitis patient and his mother. There has been little mention of other members of the family and to our knowledge, and according to Finch (personal communication, 1965) there have been no descriptions of conjoint family interaction in ulcerative colitis. Such data, of course, has not been easy to obtain. Students of psychosomatic illness have become increasingly dissatisfied with attempts to reconstruct the family atmosphere from histories obtained from patients. Wenar (1963), among others, has demonstrated the unreliability of histories received from mothers about such important events in the life of their offspring as hospitalization and major illness; consequently, the recall of any effectively tinged material is suspect. This difficulty is at least partially overcome in the utilization of the conjoint family interview, which does not depend on retrospective history-taking. In the conjoint family interview, current interaction of the family is observed behind a one-way glass screen, and audio and visual material is available for lengthy study following the interview. There are, of course, drawbacks to this technique. The family's behavior is observed in an unusual and artificial situation, and cannot definitely be considered typical of their everyday life. It is conceivable, for example, that parents in this study might be burdened with guilt over their child's ulcerative colitis, and might withhold "incriminating evidence" from the interviewer. The recent work of Rosenthal (1963) has demonstrated, in striking fashion, the influence of the interviewer, and although this has not been shown to occur in family interviews, we assume such bias to be present. We consequently present our observations on ulcerative colitis families as tentative, incomplete, and lacking in scientific rigor. However, other investigators may profit from a chance to agree or disagree with our findings, and their interest may lead to further studies.

In the past decade, information derived from the study of families through the device of conjoint family therapy (Jackson, 1959) has provided considerable information about the characteristics of certain types of families, especially those containing a schizophrenic or delinquent member. The interactional profile of abnormal families has been shown to vary when measured by a variety of methodological tools. It is not unrealistic to suppose that a typology of families might eventually be derived. The purpose of the present study was to explore whether or not psychosomatic families have a characteristic interactional profile. For this reason a severe psychosomatic disorder, namely ulcerative colitis, was chosen. Although it is unlikely, in our opinion, that ulcerative colitis is the specific etiological result of certain family interactional patterns, this does remain a possibility. It seems more likely that it is a disorder produced under stress where certain genetic factors already exist. It is also important not to overlook the possibility that a chronically ill child is the source of the stress, rather than one of its products. For this reason we are currently undertaking a larger study in which families with a child with ulcerated colitis will be compared with families in which a child has a chronic illness not related to psychological factors.

Our sample of eight families is small, but they displayed a strikingly high degree of similarity in certain interactional patterns and the data seemed worth reporting. The families attended 4 to 20 conjoint 90-minute sessions that were labeled as investigatory interviews. The interviews were tape-recorded and generally witnessed by observers. The identified patients were all children (six boys and two girls), ranging in age from 7 to 17 years. In all cases the original parents were living with their biological children; the families were white and middle class; and they were not in the midst of current financial or other crises that would tend to obscure the effect of the chronically ill child upon them.

THE IRON FAMILY

As a typical family in our group, the "Iron" family serves as an introduction to the characteristics we encountered.

The first thing one notices about all five members of the Iron family is their extreme quietness; one observer characterized them as the "most deadly quiet" family he had ever seen. All the interviews were characterized by embarrassment, soft voices, silence. The circumstances of their life are also quiet. The father, in his 60s works for Civil Service, where his wife is also employed. He denies ever having had any specific ambitions except to work on a farm, which he did for several years. Shortly after his marriage, however, he took a job in a hardware store, and stayed there for 20 years before changing to his present job. The family now lives on a farm outside of the small town where both the parents grew up. They seldom go out, except to visit relatives. They do not travel. The eldest daughter, Anita, 21, remarked that she had to "push them out the door" on their anniversary. The parents explain that they used to go out but stopped when the mother started working — although this was ten years ago. They add that rather than spend $20 on a restaurant dinner they prefer to spend the money on their children.

They are a very child-oriented family.

Besides Anita, there are two children: Susan, 17 (the identified patient), and Ken, 15. They confirm their parents' claim of family closeness, and indeed the family seems to "stick together." On several occasions in the family interviews, it appeared that this effort extended to the attempt to suppress any evidence of dissension within the family. They seemed afraid to express themselves, and any personal expression that occurred was quickly covered up by another family member's action. The eldest daughter mentioned that she had raised sheep when she was a teen-ager and added that although her father approved of this her mother had been against it. There was a sudden tension in the room. Anita then said that this was the only time her parents had ever disagreed, and the topic was changed.

There were other instances of this apparent concealment. In one of the interviews it was learned that there had been some kind of "unpleasant episode" the previous Saturday morning. With persistent inquiry the therapist was able to find out that Ken, who was always polite, laconic, and virtually expressionless — had expected to be picked up by two other boys in his class at 7 A.M. and had arisen early and waited for them. At 10 A.M. he was still waiting and the father then suggested that he telephone the home of one of the boys and find out what had happened to him. Upon doing so, he learned that he had been "stood up." In the presence of the therapist, the father complimented his son on his not being upset by the incident, or at least not being "really" upset. When the therapist suggested to the boy that he had waited three hours before telephoning because he perhaps did not want to find out that he had been stood up and chose to hope that maybe at any moment the other boys might arrive, the boy showed some feeling, appearing to be at the point of tears. The father was mildly annoyed with the therapist and felt there was "no use making a big deal out of it." The family rallied, changed the topic, and the door was closed on this episode.

On another occasion it was revealed that there had been some dissension in the family over what television show to watch in the evening. Although it was apparent that this was a current issue, the mother said that it had only happened when the children were very young. The father, disqualifying the issue further, suggested that it was not much of a problem since the television was supposed to be turned off at 7 P.M. each night. It was never clear what rules, if any, were enforced.

The family was equally reticent about their physical disorders. At first they denied that these existed; later it was learned that aside from Susan's ulcerative colitis, there had been gastrointestinal trouble for the mother and father. The mother complained of some bowel trouble ("trouble down there," as she called it) which she said was very similar to Susan's problem. The father has had three severe ulcer attacks, the most recent one requiring hospitalization and blood transfusions.

The hesitation in the family became — as might be expected — a major subject of the interview sessions. Each time we mentioned their reluctance to answer they suggested that they simply could think of nothing to say. Finally, we advanced the question of whether they had really had nothing to say or whether they felt they were not permitted to say things within the family. At this, Anita blurted out a memory: she was younger, she would want to talk, and would come into the room, but everyone would tell her to be quiet because they were watching television. The mother and father quickly denied that this had happened; a few minutes later the girl herself denied she had ever mentioned such a thing.

OBSERVATIONAL DATA FROM THE FAMILIES

The style of behavior we discovered in the Iron family was characteristic of the other families as well. To describe it, we came to use two essential terms: "restricted family" and "restrictiveness." By a "restricted family" we mean a family whose members have a marked inability to engage in, or even to recognize, contingency possibilities, that is, opportunities for kinds of behavior outside the pattern of their immediate lives. White, middle-class individuals normally have all kinds of opportunities to engage in a wide variety of activities, endeavors, and styles of living. If there are no obvious physical or cultural reasons for the individual's not making use of a considerable number of these contingency possibilities, it would then appear that he has learned some prohibition against doing so. This seemed to be true in the restricted families we studied, and the learning process itself proved to be at least partially observable in the interview sessions. The ulcerative colitis families in our study seemed to back each other up on their acceptance of limited behavior, and to discourage such behavior as humor, novelty, creative response, and so forth. For this process we used the term "restrictiveness."

Our overall assessment of what was demonstrated by the conjoint family interviews follows.

1. Restricted families have observable rules and transactions that confine the members to few and limited interactions within the family group. There are rules as to who can say what to whom, with negative sanctions used against the individual who says more than he "should." Family members seem to hold each other in check by placating, nullifying, and subduing each other. Voice tone is often quiet and expressionless. Arguments and emotional comments, anger, and affective responses, are in most instances avoided. There appears to be a conscious awareness of pain, disharmony, and unhappiness in the family and yet an agreement that this will not be mentioned in front of other family members. Usually it was possible to obtain some statement of the unhappiness in the family by interviewing individual family members alone. In a few cases, after a number of interviews, some mention of family problems occurred but this situation was the exception rather than the rule. Furthermore, there is a lack of tender, affectionate interaction between the parents.

We also noted that within the family system an individual often behaves in such a way that he invites sanctions from others and responds to feedback from them as if it were a command. Thus someone may act reluctant to depart and his spouse may say, "don't go." The reluctant spouse may then reply, "O.K., if that's the way you want it." An individual may utilize restricting techniques or behaviors on other family members and in the process also restrict himself. This is usually done in one of two ways: 1. His relationship to the one that he is restricting in turn restricts himself: For example, the husband of the phobic wife is restricted in turn by her anxieties and fears and yet he continues to reinforce her phobias by failing to provide her with exposure to novel contingencies. 2. The individual may influence others to join him in a restricted shared pattern, as is obvious in the case of a paranoid two-against-the-world union.

(Tables 1, 2, 3 follow. Text continues on page 350.)

Table 1. *Families with Ulcerated Colitis*

FAMILY RULES

Family	Response to "How did you meet"	Restrictiveness (Activities, Range of Behavior, etc.)	Scapegoating Of Parent	Parental Roles	Marital Relationship
1.	Fate. Met in bowling alley.	Mo restricts because of phobias. Neatness & dietary demands.	Mother[1]	Fa described as a "softie." Mo does the disciplining.	Mo bored by Fa's account of war exploits. Unfriendly to his fine description of his first impression of her. Parents rarely spend time together except for occasional bridge games.
2.	Mothers forced meeting.	Parents never go out together. Maintain	Father	Fa not in charge. Gains ascendancy in family through violent outbursts of impotent rage.	Fa beats Mo. Says Mo has never shown him affection. Mo says she is unable to. Many attempts at separation; never final. Times

[1] "Mo" is mother; "Fa" is father; "I.P." is identified patient.

342

#						
3.	Fate. Met through job. No positive reaction to each other.	Parents do not leave I.P. for vacations. Have gone out six times in two years in spite of opportunities for free movies.	Father	Mo immersed in mothering role. Fa feels helpless, ignored & indecisive. Goes into ineffectual rages.	parents spend alone together end in some kind of explosiveness. No one in family talks about caring for anyone.	Fa is self-effacing.
4.	Fate. Met at church. Were "only two single people there."	Everyone protects everyone else's feelings. Parents out together only twice in 5 years	Mother	Both immersed entirely in parenting. Fa ostensibly protects Mo.	No feelings expressed by either partner. Fa complains Mo does not care about him. Mo says he is impossible to please.	Fa. Self-effacing.

despite urgings to the contrary by children. Only concerns are: first, safety; next achievement.

5.	Fate. Met through the Grange. Lived in same town.	Feelings not discussed or expressed. Parents rarely go out together.	Conspiracy of silence.	Much time spent with family.	No expression of positive feelings. Mo complains of Fa's un-demonstrativeness. Fa very withdrawn.
6.	Fate. Mo entertained servicemen & met Fa while he was in Air Corps.	Parents never go out together. Never hire baby-sitters.	Mother	Fa sees Mo as inconsistent with the children. Fa retreats & fails to back her up.	No expression of positive feelings. Fa immersed in work, spends little time in home. Previous separation.
7.	Fate. Met because of war.	Mother is only one to express over anger. Extreme re-strictiveness of feelings otherwise. I.P. fearful.	Conspiracy of silence.	Fa somewhat childlike, disorganized, unrealistic. I.P. often assumes adult role.	No overt feelings of any kind expressed, but Mo subtly undermines Fa.

Fate. Same town & school. Families knew each other.

parents go out together once a month. Everyone nice to everyone else. Very guarded family.

Conspiracy of silence.

...deprecatory.

Table 2.

HEALTH OF PARENTS / EXTRAFAMILIAL RELATIONSHIPS

Family	Health of Parents	Health of Siblings	Father's Job Picture	Peer Relationships	Grandparents
1.	Mo was hospitalized for gyn disorder, which is discussed openly & at length. Mo is phobic. Had "nervous breakdown" when I.P. was 2 1/2 yr. old. Also had bowel trouble. Fa preoccupied with own physical injuries.	Sister has fainting spells, is sullen & withdrawn during sessions.	Passive. Ineffectual at work & sessions. Lack of affect. Admits reluctantly that his problems have to do with lack of drive & ambition.	I.P. had few peer relationships when young.	No known difficulties.
2.	Mo has had double hernia, D & C, deviated	All siblings are emotionally disturbed.	Sees himself as a failure.	I.P. has few peer relationships. Fa has few.	Mo's father was a philanderer.

345

	nasal septum, hysterectomy, thyroid difficulty. Mo had "nervous breakdown" prior to marriage to Fa, after losing boyfriend.				Fa's parents separated when he was 7 yr. old; he felt fatherless.
3.	Fa in good physical health. Mo has gastric ulcer & also many phobias.	Sibling age 4 yr.	No ambition toward job advancement in spite of finanical worries.	Mo has few peer relationships. Asks Fa's permission to go to luncheon.	Mo's father rarely home when she was small, due to job. Fa's father died when Fa 2 yr. old. Had weak stepfather.
4.	Mo had multiple surgical procedures. Somewhat phobic and emotionally unstable.	Disturbed. One sibling has trichotillomania & hysterical deafness. The other is depressed.	Fa self-deprecating and underachieving.	I.P. & mother have few peer relationships.	Mo's father died in psychiatric hospital. Fa's parent killed in auto accident with Fa driving.
5.	Mo had acne & mucous colitis. Fa has recurrent bleeding peptic ulcer.	One sibling withdrawn, depressed, has acne. 21-yr-old sister has acne, does not date, is attached to sheep.	Extremely low job satisfaction. Tends to overlook anything unpleasant.	Parents have no peer relationships.	Mo's father paralyzed.

6.	Mo hospitalized 11 times in 17 years for "back trouble." Complains about pain but does nothing about it. Mo has tics & is extremely phobic.	Siblings tense. I.P. is calmest. One sibling has tics & temper tantrums.	Unhappy & frustrated at work. Uninvolved & noncommunicative.	Parents and I.P. have no close friends.	Mo's father became ill before I.P. was born, was ill for 12 yr. until death. Fa's father was depressed, alcoholic, committed suicide.
7.	Mo often depressed. Fa is unrealistic, disorganized, somewhat paranoid.	Insufficient information.	Spends long hours at work, but little job satisfaction. Many business failures.	I.P. has no friends. Blames this on his ulcerated colitis.	Mo's mother paralyzed with multiple sclerosis. Fa's parents separated; saw own father rarely. His mother was extremely religious. Unstable life.
8.	Mo had gyn surgery; also history of depression & "sleeping sickness" from mumps, back trouble.	Insufficient information.	Many business changes & failures.	Parents have few friends.	Fa's parents were divorced when Fa was 15 yr. old. Fa's father was alcoholic.

Table 3.

IDENTIFIED PATIENT I.P.

Family	Sex and Age of Onset of Ulcerated Colitis	Onset of Ulcerated Colitis in Relation to Family Events	Mother-Identified Patient Relationship	Father-Identified Patient Relationship
1.	Male, age of onset of ulcerated colitis unknown	1 to 2 months following Mo's hospitalization for gyn disorder.	Very close, dependent relationship. I.P. can talk with mother.	No closeness, though I.P. expects father to discipline him.
2.	Male, 12 yr.	Parental separation preceded onset of abdominal pains. Colitis followed Mo's hospitalization for hysterectomy. Flareups related to arguments between parents.	Coalition between I.P. and mother.	Intense, complex feelings between I.P. & father. Fa jealous of Mo's relationship to I.P.
3.	Male, 6 yr.	Related to time of marital difficulties between parents when Fa was fire captain.	Mo focuses of I.P. to the exclusion of Fa & sibling. Passes phobia on to I.P.	Fa has no investment in I.P.'s health because of Fa's jealousy of him.
4.	Male, 12 yr.	Colitis associated in time with birth of the youngest sibling	"ESP" type of communication.	No communication. Fa knew I.P. was sick only because of

348

		(continued)		weight loss. I.P. cannot talk with father.
		& with Fa's molestation of a schoolgirl. Later aggravated by Mo's gallbladder surgery.		
5.	Female, 16 yr.	Colitis associated with gradual breakup with boyfriend.	Strong identification of Mo with I.P.	Fa favors I.P. At times may scapegoat her.
6.	Male, 10 yr.	Mo's father died one month prior to onset. Mo was very upset.	I.P. tuned in on Mo's back pain; sounds like her. Mo talks for I.P., "reads children's minds."	No communication.
7.	Male, 10 yr.	Colitis began after father deserted family.	Unclear.	Peer-type relationship.
8.	Female, 15 yr.	Associated with financial difficulties & moves in family. Coincided with some difficulties with school.	I.P. assumes maternal role, while Mo becomes inactive.	Unclear.

Restrictions on family interaction appear to lead to restrictions on behavior in the world at large. There seems to be a curtailment of geographical movements by these families, and a lack of participation in new contingency possibilities outside the family system.[2] It was difficult to imagine what they had done in pretelevision days. The parents remain aloof from the social community, they have few or no peer relationships, and are engaged for the most part in work or child-oriented activities. Most of the families have rarely, if ever, used baby-sitters. Many of the families seem to have little or no social life except for their relatives or in-laws. While this may be have been a cultural phenomenon that was the result of a biased sample, it appeared through discussions held with the family members, that the extended family was used not only for solidarity purposes, but in some cases, because the parents in families suffering from ulcerative colitis were afraid not to visit their relatives. One exception to this "extended family ties" situation was more apparent than real. The parents had left the East and fled to California to get away from their mutual families, but they were still preoccupied with their relatives, quarreled over them with each other, and accused their parents of forcing them together in an unsatisfactory marriage.

The whole family seemed to behave as if reducing varieties of behavior would reduce the possibility of one's behavior being taken as a relationship message by another family member. Thus, if an individual engages in outside activities, in addition to those prescribed by law or custom (for example, school, and church) such behavior could be taken as an avoidance of the family or of some particular member within the family or of being interested in some other family more than in one's own. A corollary of this is that the family that restricts behavior in order to avoid negative relationship messages

---

[2] A supplementary concept to the idea of "restrictiveness" is "recursive arborization." The word "recursive" refers to the fact that the same basic set of rules are the building blocks for the rules generated in any situation, and "arborization" refers to the fact that there is a branching out of these sets of rules to meet new situations even though the same basic set of rules are simply recurring over and over again. Under the process of recursive arborization, novel situations will have to be treated similarly in order for the same basic rules to apply for all situations. One way to do this is for an individual to ignore new contingency possibilities or distort them so that the percepts will fit the sample rule in which system he operates. The term "recursive arborization" is borrowed in part from computer language.

must also teach its members not to notice this restriction or it would lead to mutual blame, rebellion, and more. Evidence for this finding occurs in the fact that although none of the parents in these ulcerative colitis families used baby-sitters as often as twice a year, and some had not been out together in many years of marriage, they chose to think that this was typical for others in their socioeconomic group. The parents wittingly or unwittingly supported the fiction of a close, loving family.

Another form of restrictiveness was an excessive concern with medical matters and physical health. In some of the families, there was not only the apparent over concern with health conditions, but the mothers had had multiple surgical procedures and frequent hospitalizations. In addition, the mothers were frequently phobic, and their hypochondria and phobias caused further social and geographical restrictiveness.

In none of the families did the father feel satisfied with his job, nor was there evidence of any ambition. Thus, there were no work-oriented social activities to speak of and no chance for the family to extend its knowledge of new situations through the father's job contacts or through job travel. It seemed to us to be an unusual finding that in all eight cases the father's lack of ambition and low self-esteem were obvious, as was his resignation to the task of merely being a breadwinner. The father's low titer of self-esteem was a clearly visible part of the family tradition. Although the family rules permitted no one else to comment on this, most of the fathers openly discussed their dissatisfaction and resignation. For example, Mr. H commented that he wanted his daughters to get a good education in order to get "a better husband than their mother did." Mr. A and Mr. C held themselves up as bad examples for their sons. (See Table 2 for details of fathers' work history.)

2. Communication in these families was exceedingly indirect and seemed, on occasions, to be deliberately so. Thus, data would be given in a rather loose, tentative fashion so that it could easily be altered if another family member complained or questioned it or disagreed. Mr. D, for example, commented that when he returned from another state he got a job and the family moved into their present neighborhood. Later on in the same interview, the mother commented on the same material but stated that it took him a considerable period of time to find a job. When Mrs. D was describing her "sleeping sickness" she said it took her several months to get over it. In the same interview, when her husband described her

"illness," he commented that it took her "years" to get over it and there appeared to be some implication that she was still "nervous." The investigators were never quite sure what the illness was. One of the inviolable family rules was that there were to be no relationship comments made overtly and the children in these families were instructed in the rule both implicitly and explicitly. Thus, when Mrs. D stated that she had been "jumpy" as a result of the "sleeping sickness" and the identified patient remarked that his mother was still jumpy, the father immediately denied this. Then the identified patient said that all he meant was that if you said something to Mother when she was not expecting you to, she had a startle reaction. Father responded, stating that he (the patient) also had a startle reaction, so did he and so did everyone. The Iron family, as has been seen, repeatedly disqualified data to the point of denial. In C family, the father expressed some emotion by weeping when talking about his younger sister. Characteristically, he would not pursue the topic and it was never learned what was behind the tears. Mr. O explained that he cannot get involved or excited about family matters because he had been through so much in World War II and had seen things that were really emotional and everything subsequently paled in comparison.

3.   The observers were impressed with the amount of apparent mental pathology in the siblings. It was not uncommon for the parents to comment that they would be surprised if nerves had anything to do with ulcerative colitis because the identified patient was frequently the least nervous and most stable of the children. Outwardly, this appeared to be true. In the O Family, the sibling, an older sister, had had several syncopal episodes, severe menstrual disorders, and was surly and withdrawn. In the Iron family, all the siblings had very severe acne, the younger brother appeared markedly depressed, the oldest girl, 21, had no heterosexual experimentation. She felt inferior to her boyfriend, and unable to talk to him, so to remedy this she took the inappropriate step of enrolling in a night course in basic English. The two siblings in the H family were severely disturbed, one, age 15, continually pulled out her hair and ate it, the other, age 18, was very depressed, dependent, and had had no dating experience. Both the male siblings in the R family appeared socially retarded, neither having any peer relations. One, age 16, had multiple tics and many phobias, refusing, for example, to drive or date. All of the C

children appeared to be quite disturbed, had many rebellious episodes with various authorities, had run away from home, and one of them appeared to the observers to be actively psychotic during at least one of the family sessions.

4. The communication of restrictiveness from generation to generation is apparent in all of these families. The parents do not push the children out of the family circle and although they may comment on the child's lack of socialization, little or nothing is done about it. In most cases, the fact that a child has ulcerative colitis appears to be an excuse for the restricted family, but the accuracy of this observation will need to be verified by studying other families with chronically ill children. It appears that in subtle ways, the parents deliver a message to the child that branching out and leaving home is fraught with danger. Mrs. C, although she seemed unhappy in the fact that her 6-year-old boy was not riding his bicycle or leaving the house, repeatedly warned him not to walk with his hands in his pockets because he would have no way to protect himself when he fell. The H family actively restricted their daughter's dating, commenting on the frequency with which people get robbed, raped, or knifed. The O family were cautioned by Mother on the danger of germs and the family nourished the myth that "Mother would crack up at the slightest injury to any of us." It was also stated on another occasion, "She wants us in a straightjacket so we won't get hurt." The parents set an example for the children, as has been seen, by being severely restricted themselves in their social activities. In some cases this was unbelievably rationalized. The C family went out occasionally but said that they were afraid that the children might burn the house down and so were reluctant to go out very often. The A family, who had not been out together in years, attributed this to the husband's long working hours, and said they did not take trips as a family because "it was too much of a chore to be constantly preoccupied with looking for rest room signs." Mrs. O asked for help from Mr. O in taking over the socialization of the little boy, but forbade them to go hunting or fishing (Mr. O's sports) because she did not like the idea of "animals getting gored."

It appeared also that restrictiveness was enforced through physical posture; almost invariably members of both observations held themselves in rigid, wooden attitudes.

5.   In nearly every family the father of one, or more frequently of both spouses, had died when the child was young, or was an alcoholic or deserter, or had committed suicide (Table). As in the previous items, this could be a simple chance finding, but it also could be a source of the family's restrictive behavior. One wife remarked that she did not say as much to her husband as she would like to because his father had committed suicide and she was afraid she might push him in that direction. The lack of a model of a father provided difficulty for these parents in relating to their own children.

SUMMARY AND CONCLUSIONS

From a study of eight families in which the identified patient had ulcerative colitis, from observation of several other such families, and from discussions with families, and from discussions with family therapists, who had treated such families, we were struck by the similarity of behavior among these families when interacting in conjoint family therapy. All the families appeared to be severely socially restricted and actively restricted each other in the range of permissible behavior. Data collected on individual family members as to their "outside the family" behavior corroborated the impression that they existed in a narrow band of social participation when compared to the group of "ordinary" families under study at the Mental Research Institute. The limitation in the range of interaction, the careful dealing with each other, the handling of a variety of situations in a similar fashion, suggest at one and the same time a feeling of despair and yet a feeling of family sameness that almost seemed like solidarity. Wynne's term "pseudomutuality" best describes the apparently false solidarity of these families.

Our sample was a white, middle-class one and we have no data to control for the effect of a chronically ill child on family interaction. It is obvious that the study needs to be broadened, both in the size and range of the sample, and a control instituted for the effect of a chronic illness by utilizing disorders that have no known emotional etiology, such as cystic fibrosis and muscular dystrophy. We would like to check on the social habits of the ulcerative colitis families by comparing them on a variety of measurements with a normal sample, as well as the above-mentioned chronically ill child sample. Three terms: "restrictiveness," "restricted family," and "recursive arborization"

354

are introduced as possible conceptual aids in the study of family interactional patterns.[3]

References

Jackson, D. (1959). Family homeostasis, family interaction, and some implication for family therapy. In J. Masserman (Ed.), *Science and psychoanalysis volume IV.* New York: Grune & Stratton.

Lepore, M. J. (1965). The importance of emotional disturbances in chronic ulcerative colitis. *JAMA, 191*; 819, March 8.

Murray, C. (1930). Psychogenic factors in the etiology of ulcerative colitis and bloody diarrhea. *American Journal of Medical Science 180*; 239, Aug.

Rosenthal, R. (1963). Three experiments in experimental bias. *Psychological Reports*, 12; 491–511.

Wenar, C. (1963). The reliability of developmental histories. *Psychosomatic Medicine, 25*; 505–509.

[3] This study was supported in part by National Institute of Mental Health grants No. MH-08720 and No. MH-11362-01, the Louis and Maud Hill Family Foundation, and the Wheeler Foundation.

Index

Ackerman, Nathan, xv, xxi, 160, 162, 173
acting out
    in children, 63
    psychotherapy of women with hysterical symptoms, 72
Alexander, F., 12
ambulatory schizophrenia, 288
analog communication, 187–188, 194–198
"Analysis Terminable and Interminable" (Freud), 157
Andersen, Tom, xx, xxi
Anderson, H., xxi
anger, expressing, 198–199
anorexia nervosa, family homeostasis and, 108
Arieti, S., 154, 155n1
assault, 77. *See also* trauma
auditory hallucinations, masturbation of schizophrenic and, 92

Bateson, Gregory, x, xvii, xxiii, 3, 93, 111n2
    on communication, 202, 206–207

Communication — The Social Matrix of Psychiatry (Bateson & Ruesch), 167
    on learning, 211
"A Note on the Double Bind" (Bateson, Jackson, Haley, & Weakland), 96, 145–152
    on schizophrenia, 79, 237, 296
"Social Factors and Disorders of Communication: Some Varieties of Organization" (Bateson & Jackson), 96, 185–200
"Toward a Theory of Schizophrenia" (Bateson, Jackson, Haley, & Weakland), 95–96, 111–134, 146
Beavin-Bavelas, Janet, xvii, xix, 201
Pragmatics of Human Communication (Watzlawick, Beavin-Bavelas, & Jackson), xix, xx, 135n1
Becker, W. C., 299
behavior, communication and, 146–148
Belkman, L., 300
Bender, Lauretta, 280
Bergman, Joel, xxi